Pentecost Island
Books 1-3

Pippa
Eliza
Nell

PENTECOST ISLAND 1-3

Also available in print
Pentecost Island
Books 4-6
Tamsin
Evie
Cherry

Also available in print
Pentecost Island
Books 7-10
Odessa
Sienna
Tess
Isla

This book or any portion thereof may not be reproduced or used in any manner whatsoever without the express written permission of the publisher except for the use of brief quotations in a book review.

This is a work of fiction. Names, characters, businesses, places, events, locales, and incidents are either the products of the author's imagination or used in a fictitious manner. Any resemblance to actual persons, living or dead, or actual events is purely coincidental.

Cover Design: Annie Seaton
Editing: Susanne Bellamy and R.L. Aiken
Copyright © 2020
Annie Seaton
All rights reserved

ANNIE SEATON

DEDICATION

To girlfriends all over the world.

PENTECOST ISLAND 1-3

ANNIE SEATON

Pippa

Pentecost Island 1

PENTECOST ISLAND 1-3

Chapter 1

Pippa

'Babe, can you pay the electricity bill today in your lunch hour?' Darren shook my shoulder as I snuggled into the pillow.

I lifted my aching head as I came out of the realms of sleep. I tried to blink, but my eyes watered from the strong-smelling gel he insisted on using.

'Shit, what time is it?' I put my hand to my eyes as I sat up. My head throbbed, and my nose was blocked.

'Eight-fifteen. You'd better hurry up.'

'Why didn't you wake me up? You know I was supposed to go in early today.' My throat hurt so much that the words came out croaky. We'd got home late last night, and I blamed my scratchy throat on too many drinks and Darren smoking beside me all night.

'Oh, sorry. I forgot you've got that big thing to do today.'

'Yes, the presentation to the new advertising firm.'

He nodded with a smile before he moved to the mirror and combed his hair. 'And that's going to mean another big pay rise for you?'

'I hope so.' A ripple of dissatisfaction niggled through me. All he seemed to worry about lately was how much my next pay rise was going to be. To be honest, I was getting a bit sick of it, but in my usual way, I didn't want to rock the boat, so I didn't say anything. I'd picked up the bar tab last night, too.

Darren was always chasing deals. He was a freelance finance consultant, and the next big deal was always around the corner. Trouble was, it hadn't arrived yet.

I was starting to realise that what Darren said and what actually happened were two very different things.

I frowned as he picked up the can of gel and sprayed his hair again. He might be good-looking, but he worked hard at creating the image of a man around town—as well as spending what I earned to keep that image going. I had to get this pay rise; things had been getting a bit tight lately, with him rarely contributing to our joint bills account. Tam and Nell both disliked Darren, and that meant I'd seen a bit less of them over the past twelve months.

'A user,' Tam said.

Nell shook her head. 'And a loser.'

I loved my friends and I was sad that we had drifted apart lately. We were all busy in our various careers. Tam was a chef at one of the posh restaurants on the coast, and Nell was an accountant, and even though we lived close by, there hadn't been much socialising lately. Not with them, anyway. Darren and I were out every night of the week.

But I knew if we met up with the girls for coffee or drinks, I'd be tempted to dump my relationship dissatisfaction on them, and that would be disloyal to Darren.

'Where are you going today?' I swallowed, and my throat felt like razor blades were lodged in there.

'A couple of meetings and then a business lunch.' He turned to look at me. 'You look like shit, babe.'

'Thanks. I don't feel very well. Can you grab me a glass of water and a couple of Panadols, please?'

A couple of minutes later, he was back and handed me a glass of water and two tablets.

'Thanks.' I swallowed them and drank the whole glass of water. 'I thought you were paying the bills yesterday. What about the car rego?'

'I was a bit short. I picked up the tab for the lunch with the guys from the car dealership.'

'How much was that?' I'd handed over five hundred dollars in cash yesterday morning for the bills. 'What about your business credit card?'

'I maxed it out, and I needed cash for the balance at the restaurant.' He had the grace to look sheepish.

'The balance? Bloody hell, Darren. How much was lunch?' I took a deep breath, and my chest hurt.

'Don't stress, babe. This deal should be signed off tomorrow. I'll pay you back once I get my card paid off. Jazz and I are working on this new project, and we need a little bit more cash for the advertising campaign.' He leaned down and brushed his lips across my forehead. 'Have you got any cash?'

Advertising campaign? A boozy lunch?

He must have seen the look on my face, and he put his hands up. 'It's okay. I just need some petrol. No more business lunches this week. I promise.'

'This week?' I shook my head, and even that hurt. 'There's two fifties in my purse. Take them.' I sank back into the pillow. 'I'll let the Panadol kick in, and then I'll grab a shower and get out of here.'

'Put lots of makeup on. You really do look like shit.'

'I love you, too.' I held his gaze, not able to stop the sarcasm in my voice, but he looked away. The way I felt this morning, I didn't care about much at all.

'Honesty. You always say it's important,' he replied as I got another brief kiss on the top of my head. 'But I do love ya, babe. You know that.'

'I do.' Although I wondered about that, too, lately. There hadn't been much happening in the intimacy department, and even before I'd got crook, the occasional kiss or hug had been more brotherly than lover-like.

I snuggled back down beneath the doona with a sigh.

PENTECOST ISLAND 1-3

Ever since I'd lost my parents and gone to live with Mum's Aunty Vi on Pentecost Island, I'd yearned for a love like my parents had. Living with Aunty Vi had been interesting . . . and different, but she'd loved me unconditionally. I survived high school on the mainland, staying with one of her friends at Cannonvale through the week and coming back to the island each weekend.

One thing Aunty Vi had tried to teach me was to be independent and not rely on others so much. She was better than the counsellor I saw at high school, but I don't think they had much success together. The counsellor had always called it an acute lack of self-confidence.

Tam and Nell said I had abandonment issues; good friends always tell it how it is, don't they? I knew they were probably closer to the mark. Luckily, there had been enough money in Mum and Dad's estate for me to support myself through uni. My two besties had stayed in touch by email in the seven years I'd lived with Aunty Vi, and I guess because it was easier to pour my heart out in emails than it would have been in person; our friendship had never missed a beat, and we picked up where we'd left off when we met up at uni after high school.

Those uni years had been the best years of my life—so far. We pretty much drank our way through the first two years, but the three of us picked up great jobs when we graduated. And as well as my great job in marketing, I picked up Darren.

Although, I guess you could say he picked me up. He swept me off my feet at the *Piccolo* bar in the Valley one night just over a year ago and I finally thought I'd found love. I turned my head into the pillow, ignoring the hot tears that seeped from the corner of my eyes.

I don't have time to feel sorry for myself.

Five more minutes. Then, a hot shower and a handful of cold and flu tablets. I had to go to work. My—our—whole future depended on today's presentation. Darren seemed to have no hesitation in treating my income—and bank account—as his. When we moved in together six months ago, we'd started a new joint bank account for bills and stuff like that and were supposed to be putting in five hundred dollars a month each.

With a sniff, I closed my eyes as the painkillers kicked in.

##

The loud music of my phone ringtone woke me. I opened my eyes to bright light streaming through the window and the sound of heavy traffic outside.

I grabbed the phone. 'Hello?' I tried to say, but no sound came out.

Clearing my throat—it still hurt like hell—I tried again. 'Hello?'

'Pippa, where the fuck are you?' Eric's voice was loud.

'I've got the flu.' I coughed, not to make myself sound genuine but because I could barely breathe.

'You'd better be close by because Clarissa has just got coffee for the advertising guys to stall them. How far away are you?'

I sat up and swung my feet over the side of the bed. I knew I wouldn't be going anywhere when the room spun, and my head thudded. I reached for a tissue on the bedside table and wiped my streaming nose before I answered him.

'I'm still at home. I just woke up.'

'What the fuck? You have to get here, Pip! You've got ten minutes max. Do it.'

'I'm dying. I can't even stand up.' The room was spinning like a merry-go-round, and a Ferris wheel rolled into one. 'I'm sorry, Eric, I was coming in, but I went back to sleep.'

'Such dedication. Fucking hell, you know what this means to us?'

'I know. Don't stress. I've done all the work. It's in my

PowerPoint.' As much as I hated to say it, I closed my eyes and took a deep breath. 'The presentation is in the shared drive on the network, but it's password protected.'

'Right, Clarissa can do it then. She's blonde, and she's got boobs. That might make up for her lack of smarts.'

I gritted my teeth.

Why did I surround myself with sexist men?

'What's the password?' he snapped out.

Even though I had a temperature, more heat ran up my neck as I gripped the phone. 'Darren for me. Darren with a capital D, underscore, the number four and then me.'

'Jesus,' he said. I could almost see the eye roll.

'Tell Clarissa she'll be fine. Just tell her to stick to the slides, and you can answer any questions.' Saying those words was one of the hardest things I've done in my life. I wasn't going to beg, but I wanted to remind Eric that this presentation was the culmination of two months of bloody hard work and lots of research, and I had done it singlehandedly. 'And Eric, just remember, no matter how good she puts it across, it's *my* work.'

'I know that. But Pippa? *You* remember, if we don't get this contract, you're out of a job. The blame will be squarely at your feet.'

Chapter 2

Pippa

Blasted flu.

If I had to get sick, I couldn't have picked a worse day if I tried. My typical bad luck, and surprisingly, there was not a hint of pink in sight.

Some people have problems with black cats and walking under ladders. Aunty Vi had a phobia about spilling salt, and God forbid, if you ever put shoes on the table in front of my mum, life was not worth living.

My bad luck omen is pink. Not Alecia Beth Moore—the rock star—but pink, the colour. Although, if I'm honest, I must admit the time that Tam and Nell wanted me to go to the Gold Coast to see Pink, I was a bit reluctant, but in the end, I agreed, and it was a great concert.

No accidents and no dramas.

That was back in the days before Darren.

Pink—the colour and Darren have been life changers for me.

It all started at the swimming carnival the year I was in Grade Five. If there was one thing I hated then, and I still do almost twenty years later, it's diving head first into water. That's how I became the school backstroke champion in Grade 4. You start the backstroke race already in the pool, and you don't have to dive into the unknown.

I wonder what a psychologist would have to say about that?

PENTECOST ISLAND 1-3

The Fairlands State School swimming carnival was always held on the last Friday in January when the new school year began after the long and lazy summer holidays.

I was one of those nerdy kids who loved school. I guess the time I spent learning new things—and I had a huge thirst for knowledge—made up for the parts of my life that were lacking. Although in my pre-teen years, I didn't realise anything *was* lacking. I didn't know any better until I went to live on the island with Aunty Vi.

I loved that first week of school so much: empty exercise books ready to be filled with sums and stories and neatly covered with crisp brown paper, new pens and pencils, and a brand-new lunchbox. Everything was new and glitzy before chaos took over again.

The only thing that ruined that week for me was those coloured pencils. I always began the school year with a big flat tin of coloured pencils. God knows where Mum got them. Everyone else had textas, but Pippa Carmichael had to have the Derwent coloured pencils from Mum's stash from God knows way back when. *No one* had tins of pencils in 1999. No one else had even *heard* of them.

My mum had been a hoarder. She was different from my friends' mums, and she was the person who began my run of 'pink' bad luck.

God rest her soul.

As a child, I often wondered if Dad would still be alive if I hadn't worn pink to the airport that day. That year, he'd gone away on Boxing Day and was due back at the end of the first week of the new school year.

I was determined to beat Jill Hurley in the fifty-metre backstroke. Until the year before, Jill had won *every* race *every* year; her parents managed the local swimming pool, and all she ever did was swim laps up and down Yeronga pool. They even made her train before school. I used to feel sorry for her with her chlorine-green hair that looked like clumps of straw by recess every day; she copped a bit of bullying about her hair, but it didn't seem to bother Jill because she was the school champion.

In Grade 4, I beat her in the backstroke event, which led to my entry into the friendship group that still includes me today—well, before Darren, anyway.

Tam and Nell came up to me after the race and high-fived me as I clutched the blue first-place ribbon to my flat chest.

'Way to go, Phillipa,' Nell had said with a wide smile.

'It's Pippa,' I said shyly. 'Or Pip.'

'Well done, Pippa,' Tam pointed across the pool. 'Do you want to come and sit with us?'

I'd followed them to the grassy corner at the end of the grandstand, and a friendship was born that day. I'd only been at the school for a year and a half, and up until then, I'd been quite happy to sit and read in my lunch hour while the other girls played softball.

I was used to being alone and didn't mind it. Fairlands State School had been the third one I attended in my first four years at school. Mum had always been a bit of a gypsy, and I knew she hated the big two-storey house that we'd moved to in the flash suburb of Fairlands. Dad had bought it for her when I was nine, and I was too shy to try to make friends with the kids who played in the street after school. I preferred to have my nose in a book.

The other problem was Dad and Mum weren't married, and that set me apart at that swish suburban school in Brisbane. Most of the mothers on our street were lawyers or had some sort of high-powered job—and had husbands, house cleaners, and gardeners — and the kids had nannies. It wasn't the right sort of street for us. I had a Mum—a stay-at-home Mum, and a Dad. When he was there.

Don't get me wrong. Dad was my *real* dad. It's just that

my parents hadn't ever got married. Dad didn't care either way, although I think he would have liked Mum to have been Mrs Brody but she didn't believe in marriage. Once I came along—and you have to laugh at this—I think she decided she didn't believe in kids either. But for some reason, she'd insisted that I took her surname when I was born. I've never figured out why, and Aunty Vi had just shrugged when I asked her.

It sounds like I didn't have much respect for my Mum, but for the twelve short years of my life, I had a mother; I adored her. We spent a lot of time home alone because Dad worked down on the oil rigs in Bass Strait; he was one of the first fly-in-fly-out workers before it became commonplace.

Blue collar worker, and not married," I heard Tabitha Stevenson's mother say one day with a sniff when I was in Year Four. I could never figure that out, because as far as I could see, Dad didn't own one shirt with a blue collar.

But one thing I figured out very early. Mum loved him more than she loved me. But I could cope with that because Dad loved me too, but when he died in an accident on the oil rig Mum's heart broke, and I wasn't enough to fill the gaping hole in her life.

I had a gaping hole in mine too, but I had to cope, especially when that hole exploded a few months later.

But I was telling you about the swimming carnival.

Because Dad worked on the rigs, he was away for a month at a time—thirty days on and thirty days off—so it was pretty special when he came home.

Mum would get herself all glammed up. And I'd always get a new dress to wear to the airport.

The last time Dad came home to us was at the end of January 1999, when I was eleven years old.

When I looked at the calendar on the fridge and saw the big *pink* heart that always indicated the day of Dad's return, my stomach sank. He was coming home on the Friday of the swimming carnival.

Going to the airport to meet Dad was important, but so was keeping my status as Fairlands State School's senior backstroke champion. I'd trained all holidays and didn't want to miss out on it. Tam, Nell, and I had spent the summer holidays at the local pool. They were starting to look at boys, but I was focused on my backstroke.

I walked out onto the front porch, where Mum was reading a letter. She looked up at me with a smile and held it up. 'Aunty Vi has invited us up for a holiday.'

'Who's Aunty Vi?'

'My great aunt. She lives on an island up in Queensland.'

For a moment, I forgot the swimming carnival. 'Are we going to go?'

'We'll see.'

I was used to that. That meant no, it wouldn't happen. Ever.

'She says to tell you how proud she is of you.'

'Me?' I screwed up my nose. 'She doesn't even know me.'

'But I write and tell her all about you. She knows how hard you work at your school work and how clever you are.'

I shrugged. What an old lady in another state thought about me didn't impact on my life.

'Mum?'

She looked at me over her half-glasses, and as always, I was struck by how beautiful my mother was. No wonder Dad loved her so much; she could have been a movie star. The only thing I got from Mum was her hair colour. Not red, but a sort of pale ginger. She had fair skin like Snow White, but I'd inherited Dad's olive skin and green eyes. It wasn't until I was older that I realised what a strange combination that was.

'Yes, Pippa?'

'What time does Dad's flight arrive?'

'Five o'clock. We'll go after school. I don't want you

PENTECOST ISLAND 1-3

missing a day of school.'

Yes! Relief ran through me. I was determined to keep the blue ribbon for backstroke. I hadn't even mentioned it to Mum. She didn't come to the school, and she didn't ever do tuckshop. And I don't think she'd even noticed the ribbon stuck to the side of the dressing table mirror for the past year. If she had, she'd never have said anything.

Like I said, she loved me—I think—but she wasn't one of those school mums that those things were important to.

The week before Dad came home every second month, there was always a mad flurry in the house. The rooms all smelled like furniture polish, and baby violets filled tiny little vases on every space. The kitchen benches were covered with fresh-baked bikkies and cakes cooling on wire racks.

I loved that week because the rest of the time, we lived in chaos and made do with bought biscuits and takeaway food.

A bit like Darren and I do now.

I guess I did get more from Mum than the ginger hair.

The morning of the 1999 Fairlands State School swimming carnival dawned clear and sunny. The air was still and sultry, a typical Brisbane summer's day. Anticipation curled in my tummy as I packed my black togs and towel into my school port.

When I looked out my bedroom window, my only wish, apart from winning the race, was that the afternoon storms would stay away until Dad's plane landed safely. When I headed down to the kitchen, there was no sign of Mum.

I was sitting with my nose in my book, eating my WeetBix, when Mum called me from the bathroom down the hall.

'Pip, come here, sweetie.'

'Coming,' I called as I wolfed down the last spoonful and put my book aside.

When I walked into the bathroom, Mum pulled out a packet of bobby pins. I was the only girl in my class who knew what they were.

'You washed your hair last night, didn't you?' She opened the packet.

'Yes, Mum.' I looked at the bobby pins as worry curled in my stomach.

No, please God, no. Not today.

She picked up a water bottle. 'Come over here.'

'What for?' I scowled and then quickly got rid of it. I would do what Mum wanted.

I always did.

I knew it wouldn't take much for her to stop loving me, so I was a model child no matter what rebellion festered inside.

I guess that set up the adult I grew to be. I hated confrontation, and I turned a blind eye to some of the things that Darren did that really bothered me.

The counsellor that Aunty Vi sent me to on the mainland told me I craved love and didn't want to risk losing it. He was talking about Mum, but I guess the pattern had continued with Darren.

'Seeing you washed your hair last night, I'll only have to dampen it with the spray.'

I looked down at the bobby pins she'd tipped into the pretty pink-flowered bowl on the side of the vanity. 'Why?'

'I found you the prettiest pink dress to meet Dad tonight, and I want your hair in curls.'

Found? I knew what that meant. In one of the trunks in the shed.

'I have to go to school soon.'

'It's okay. I've got a matching pink scarf to cover the bobby pins,' she said. 'You'll have to wear the dress to school because I'll pick you up before the bell goes, and we can go straight to the airport. Now lean forward. I'm going to try something new.'

PENTECOST ISLAND 1-3

Long story short; it was the worst day of my life until the day Dad died.

My togs and towel stayed at home, and I avoided everyone—even Nell and Tam—and sat up in the back corner of the grandstand in the second back row, in the bloody stiff pink shiny dress, and I watched Jill Hurley race home to take first place in the senior backstroke race.

'Fancy sending a child to school like that,' one of the mothers sitting behind me said in a loud voice. I sat still and straight.

The pink scarf Mum had wound around the forty or so bobby pins that were creating ginger kiss curls over my head didn't stop the hot sun from burning into my scalp where the scarf didn't quite meet.

'Disgraceful, but what else would you expect? The mother's not quite right in the head.' I wasn't surprised to hear Mrs Stevenson chime in.

I buried my head in my book as embarrassment made me feel like vomiting.

The plane was late, and the thunderstorms were rolling in when my long and lanky Dad walked into the arrival hall at Kingsford Smith Airport. He swept Mum into a hug and kissed her just like they did in the movies.

'Pip, you look gorgeous,' Dad said as he turned to me and lifted me high, even though I was eleven and too big for that. The stiff fabric of the dress crackled as he kissed my cheek. 'Don't worry, darling. I know Mum dressed you up, but you look beautiful. When you get home, how about you get your togs, and we'll go for a swim down the pool?' He lowered his voice and whispered in my ear. 'After I eat all the yummy things, I'm sure Mum's been cooking all week.'

He knew my mother so well. And they loved each other so

much. My heart broke when Dad was killed, and then when Mum died six months later, and I went to live with Great-Aunty Vi, I didn't think I'd ever be happy again.

It took a long time.

'I missed you, Daddy.' My voice was quiet, but he'd already turned back to Mum.

Okay, so my hair might have been in pretty curls when we met my father that night and the shiny stiff pink dress that Mum said was made out of something called taffeta might have looked okay, but I was devastated.

I had another year to wait until I could try for the race again.

But twelve months later, I was at school in another state and didn't care about winning a stupid race.

I didn't care about anything.

But worse than not being in that race that day, I knew, somehow, as I traipsed along behind them, that even though I was in their presence, I wasn't as important to my parents as they were to each other.

I've never worn pink again.

Chapter 3

Pippa

As I eased my aching body into the hot bath water, steam tickled my blocked nose, and for a brief second, I was able to inhale before it clogged again. Agitation filled me, and I clenched my hands as I thought of the presentation that Clarissa, my assistant, would be in the middle of giving.

The presentation that would give me a good chance of promotion. As the lavender-scented water covered my shoulders I reached for the face washer and the bottle of eucalyptus oil and dabbed a few drops on the cloth before I put it over my sore nose.

A measure of calm descended as the pungent smell cleared my sinuses, and I could breathe through my nose again. I laid my head back and tried not to worry. There was nothing I could do, and I knew that the presentation I'd prepared was top-quality.

The water was warm and soothing, and the second lot of painkillers I'd swallowed while the bath was filling began to take effect. Maybe I could go into the office this afternoon and remind Eric again that it was my work they were using to woo the advertising company. No, my work that they would win the contract with.

Be positive.

That was an affirmation that Aunty Vi had taught me.

The two Ps. Positivity, Pip, she'd say. Over and over again.

Enough times that I'd taken it on board and turned a corner a couple of years after I'd moved to Pentecost Island.

Aunty Vi had been good for me. I closed my eyes as I imagined what she'd say about Darren. She wouldn't be impressed. Maybe I was going to have to rethink that part of my life.

Later. I'd sit down with him when I felt better and tell him that the money train was about to stop. I could do it, and if he didn't like it, he could leave.

It would mean that he didn't love me, and if I really thought about it, I wondered if I did love him. Certainly, I wouldn't say I liked our lifestyle. We had to be out every night being seen, although how that was going to help his business, I was yet to find you. I'd sit him down for a talk after the new contract at work was in place.

I lay there in the hot water, going through the data slide by slide, and hoped that Clarissa was going slowly enough for Eric to add his bit.

I blinked when I heard the front door of the apartment open. Darren was supposed to be in meetings all morning. He wouldn't expect me to be home, and I opened my mouth to call out to him to let him know I was in the bathroom. I quickly shut it when his deep laugh followed a high-pitched giggle. I tipped my head to the side, confused, and listened.

Maybe he'd turned the TV on. Another giggle, but this time, it was from the hall outside the bathroom.

'No, really, I need to have a shower first, Daz.' The female voice was unfamiliar. 'I'm all sweaty.'

'You'll be even more sweaty soon. Come on, babe, the bedroom's this way.'

'No, I'm having a shower. You can join me.' The high-pitched voice made me nauseous.

'Okay, we'll start in the shower. There's some really sexy oil in there. I can't wait, babe.'

The impatient tone was one I knew very well. And *my* expensive body oil had been a birthday present from Tam.

Babe!

I sank down into the bath and let the bubbles cover my

shoulders and breasts as disbelief filled me.

What the hell?

The bathroom door opened, but Darren was too intent on the skinny woman in the hot pink underwear to even notice I was in the bath. His lips were attached to hers, and his eyes were closed, but his hands were having no trouble undoing her bra.

My vision was filled with pink underwear.

Bloody pink, of course.

I closed my eyes, opened them and blinked again. This time to a red haze of anger.

You lowlife bastard.

I stared at Darren's hands as they dropped lower, and he pulled her pink G-string down. It was like watching a movie.

But this scene taking place in the bathroom of my apartment was reality, and I wasn't going to watch for another second. She was undoing the buttons of his shirt, and I wondered if I was in some flu-induced hallucination. But the cloying smell of Giorgio perfume wafted over as her G-string hit the tiles. So strong, the horrid smell even got through my blocked sinuses. Darren threw his shirt to the floor and turned around to open the shower screen.

I wished I'd had my phone with me. When he saw me lying in the bath, my modesty kept intact by the bubbles; the look on his face was priceless. His mouth opened, and his skin went that red, mottled colour it did when he played squash. Or had sex.

'Jesus, babe. What are you doing at home?' His mouth opened and shut, and the bimbo turned around and squealed. She reached over and grabbed a towel from the rail beside the vanity.

My towel.

'Don't worry, sweetheart.' I was so proud of my calm voice as I lifted a casual hand and pointed to the bimbo's bare boobs. 'I've seen it all before. But maybe not so saggy.'

'Bitch,' she said as she reached down and picked up her

pink bra and G-string from the floor—my floor—because I paid the rent on this place.

She opened the door, and it slammed behind her. Then, she disappeared into the hall.

'Better go kiss your girlfriend better, *Daz*,' I said in as cold a voice as I could muster with a sore throat and a blocked nose. 'I've obviously upset her.'

'Babe, it's not what you think.'

'So what was it? And what do I think it was?' My laugh was almost hysterical. 'You were about to screw that bimbo in our bed? No, wait, it's my bed because I paid for that too.'

'Calm down, Pip. I'm sorry. I made a mistake, you've been so busy lately and all tied up with your fucking presentation. It's the first time, I swear.'

'Is it?' I said, remembering an earring I found in the kitchen a few weeks ago. I'd put it in my bag and tried to give it to Nell and Tam, but neither of them had recognised it.

'Get out, Darren. Pack your gear and leave. I'll give you half an hour, and then I'm coming out. If you're not gone, I'll . . .' My lip quivered, and I swallowed as my mobile phone rang in the bedroom. 'Get my phone for me on your way out.'

He had the decency to look down as he picked up his shirt and put it on.

'And take Miss Pink with you.' It's a wonder the ice in my voice didn't freeze the bath water.

##

There was no point ringing Eric; I had to see him face-to-face. Half an hour later, I was dressed and striding down the footpath beside the Gold Coast Motorway. The traffic was loud, and the wind coming off the sea was cold. At least it cleared my head a bit; I didn't feel too bad now, but I'm sure it was the adrenalin charging through my blood that had got me this far. I hadn't worried about dressing in office clothes.

PENTECOST ISLAND 1-3

As soon as I read Eric's text message, I climbed out of the bath, dried myself—with a clean towel—and grabbed a pair of jeans and T-shirt. I didn't even brush my hair. My hands were shaking too much—I wasn't sure if it was the flu or bloody rage. Darren was still in the bedroom, but there was no sign of the bimbo.

'Babe . . .' he said, reaching out to me with one hand. 'I'm—'

'Fuck off, Darren. And fast.'

I shoved my phone and keys into my pocket and left the apartment. Slamming the door didn't make me feel any better.

I was not going to be fired by a text message.

If Eric had something to say, he could say it to my face. As I crossed the driveway of the apartments, the postman dropped some letters into the back of the mailbox. I pulled out my key and tried to insert it into the lock, but I was shaking so much that it took two attempts. I pulled out two letters, shoved them in my back pocket, and took off for the office.

Clarissa was stepping out of the lift when I entered the foyer of the office building. Joe, the security guard, was sitting in his usual chair, and his eyes widened when he looked at me.

I stared back and didn't smile. So yeah, my hair wasn't brushed, my T-shirt was wrinkled, and I looked like shit. I didn't care. I felt like shit, but anger was keeping me energised.

I stabbed at the elevator button and ignored Clarissa, who had waited by the lift panel.

'Philippa—' She was crying.

'Not now.' I stepped into the lift and pushed the button for the fifth floor. The doors slid closed to Clarissa's sobs.

Too late now, sweetheart. She'd obviously stuffed up.

Joe must have rung Eric because my boss was waiting for me in the corridor outside the lift bank. Suddenly, my energy depleted, and my breath caught. I put my hand out and steadied myself on the wall as Eric stared at me.

'You cannot fire me by text message.' My voice was ragged, and my legs were trembling. Reaction to the situation and the one-kilometre fast walk had set in.

'I can, and I did. You lost us that contract.'

'I am sick, Eric. And I did no such thing. I did all the groundwork, and if they didn't want us—the company—it wasn't my fault. Maybe you need to look further than blaming me.'

For the past few months, I hadn't been one hundred percent content at E and J Marketing. Eric's focus was different from mine, and I didn't agree with his vision for the company. But it hadn't been my place to say. It was his company, and he paid my salary. A damn good salary.

'Wait here,' he said tersely. Eric turned and disappeared into the office, and I leaned against the wall. Within a minute or so, he came back out carrying a small cardboard box. 'Clarissa packed up your drawer and desk cupboard after she did hers. Your termination pay is in your account.'

'And a reference?' I drew myself away from the wall and stared him down.

'If you insist. I'll email one.'

'And what do you mean before Clarissa packed up her desk? Are you blaming her too?'

'No. I can't afford to keep her on.' His voice was bitter. 'I'll be lucky to keep the company.' He glared at me.

What was it with men that nothing was their fault?

I took the box and turned my back on him as I waited for the lift.

I was out of a job.

I had no boyfriend, and I felt like I was dying.

I walked home slowly, and when I pushed open the apartment door, I was relieved to see that Darren had gone. I put the box of my work stuff on the kitchen bench and took the two letters out of my pocket. The first letter informed me that the apartment owner had decided to move back in, and I was being given a month's notice.

At least that was the third thing; surely nothing else could go wrong today.

As I glanced at the sender of the second letter, a strange feeling replaced the anger that had consumed me since Darren had shown his true colours with Miss Pink.

Positivity, Pip. I could hear Aunty Vi's voice as I slit the envelope open.

##

'We're coming over. With chicken soup.' Tam's tone brooked no argument, but I shook my head as I held the phone to my ear.

'No. There's no point. I won't be here. Meet me at the top bar of *Solaris* in an hour,' I said.

'You sound like—'

'Shit. I know,' I finished for her. 'And until I get changed and put some makeup on, I look like it too. Darren told me that when I chucked him out.'

'You what?' Tam squealed, and Nell was obviously in the room because I could hear the glee in Tam's voice as she turned away from the phone. 'She's chucked Darren out.'

'Best news ever!' I heard Nell's voice in the background.

I might not have a job, a boyfriend, or an apartment, but I did have loyal friends.

'I have news, and I have a request, so meet me at *Solaris* in an hour and bring an open mind.'

I was about to celebrate with the last two hundred dollars that lowlife Darren had left in my account. Luckily, my termination pay hadn't hit the bank before he'd cleaned out what was in there. But you know what? I didn't give a rats.

The letter I held in my other hand was the fourth life

changer for the day.

Chapter 4

Tam

'Do you think Pippa's having a breakdown?' Nell frowned as she outlined her lips with her signature red lipstick. 'I've been worried about her for a while.'

'I hope not. But I know what you mean. She'd slipped back a bit.'

'She's been pretty fragile ever since that lowlife moved in.'

Tam shook her head; she'd thought the same thing but didn't want to say it. 'I always think about her mum when she gets down.'

'Well, she sure didn't sound fragile on the phone. I think she's finally woken up to him. I mean, she sounded crook, but there was some life in her voice for a change.' Nell grabbed her purse off the table. 'I'm ready.'

It didn't take Tam long to get ready. Pippa's actions were way out of character, and she was worried about her. She never talked about her mother and what had happened when they were in primary school, but Tam still remembered the day as though it was yesterday. Mr Zagami, the headmaster, had come to the door of the classroom himself, and Pippa had been called out.

Tam's mother had told her that she was too young to go to a funeral, and all Tam could think of was Pippa being there by herself. She and Nell got to see her for a few minutes when her aunt brought Pip back to pack up her things in the house.

It had been an awful few months, but as soon as Pip was settled on the island with her aunt, she and Nell wrote to her every week. Her aunt—or great-aunt, they found out later—had given her address to Tam's mum. It had taken a few months before they got a reply, but Pippa eventually wrote back to them.

'Are you almost ready, Tamsin?' Nell's call interrupted her thoughts.

'Coming.'

She quickly changed into a dress; if they were going to *Solaris,* she'd go vintage.

'Oh, nice,' Nell said when Tam went into the living room. 'Where did you get that?'

'When I went up to Brisbane last week.'

'Looks great.'

Nell had moved in with Tam as a temporary measure between jobs two weeks ago. She'd moved to the Gold Coast from her last position with a well-known accountancy firm in Brisbane and was taking a break from work until she got herself settled on the coast.

'Come on, let's get going. You know, Pippa. If we're late, she won't hang around.'

Solaris, the "in" bar in Surfers Paradise, was within walking distance of Tam's apartment. Located on the top floor of a twenty-six-floor apartment block near the main shopping centre, with a rooftop pool and gymnasium, it had become the hangout for the beautiful people of the coast over the past year. Nell and Tam had been there one Friday night when it had first opened; Pippa wouldn't go because Darren was tired or some other excuse he'd come up with. The two drinks had cost them a fortune, and they'd soon moved on to their favourite hotel.

Nell rolled her eyes as they walked along Cavill Avenue. 'Remember the first time we met Darren?'

'How could I forget it? He was so obviously trying hard to impress us.' Tam pushed the button at the pedestrian crossing as the late afternoon peak hour traffic sped by. Her mind was elsewhere. She had enough problems of her own, but she hadn't told Nell yet.

'I've never been wrong when I meet someone.'

'Your instincts are always right. You need to give Pippa lessons. She's had a couple of doozies.'

Eventually, the walk light turned green, and they hurried across the road.

'No matter how hard I tried, I couldn't convince her he was a loser.' Nell shook her head. 'It was so obvious.'

'It was because he showed her a bit of love and attention— a few bunches of red roses, a couple of nights out on the town— and she thought she was in love. Poor Pippa can be so needy.'

'We'll look after her. I wonder what he did for her to chuck him out. And I wonder why she wants to meet us at *Solaris* of all places.'

Tam shrugged. 'I don't know. I've got no idea why she picked there, but I'll tell you one thing. I'll only be having one drink. I'll tell you why now, but don't mention it to Pip. She sounded low enough on the phone.'

'Tell me what?'

'I lost my job this afternoon. I think I'm going to have to move back to Brissie.'

'Oh no. Not when I've just come down to the coast. What happened?'

Tam worked in an exclusive jewellery outlet in the Pacific Fair shopping centre. 'The Werners have decided to retire. They don't want to sell the business. They're closing up shop instead.'

'Oh no. When?

'Three weeks. But they've been good about it. They said they'd give me a couple of months pay. And I'm forever grateful to them for taking me on with no experience.'

Nell nodded. 'Yeah, it was a big shift from head chef at Pepper's to selling jewellery.'

'But a necessary one.' They exchanged a glance. Nell was the only one who knew why Tam had quit her job in the hospitality trade.

The doorman at *Solaris* nodded at them as they walked through the revolving door and headed for the lift. Tam chewed on her lip, wondering what sort of state Pippa was in and again wondering why the hell she wanted to meet here. Her stomach dropped as the lift gained the top floor in less than five seconds, and she let out the breath she'd been holding when they reached the top.

The coconut-scented air was cool on her skin and she smiled. Even though it was expensive, it was a quirky bar. Retro design, with bright colours that relaxed you as soon as you walked in.

The bar staff wore Hawaiian shirts in reds and blues, and Malibu boards were suspended from the high ceiling. Surfer music provided a catchy background tune.

'I wonder how they get that coconut smell to pump though the air con,' Nell said as she looked around. 'It's just like being on the beach and walking past someone lathering up.'

Tam had to lean closer to reply. The surfie music got louder as they walked towards the bar. 'I don't know, but I love it. Makes me want to go lie on a beach somewhere. Maybe they put reef oil in the filters.'

Nell laughed. 'We live on the most famous beach strip in the country and how often do we get to lie on a beach?'

'Not often enough.'

It was still a bit early for the after-work crowd, and there were only a few people sitting on the high stools at the bar.

'Looks like we've beaten Pippa,' Nell said looking around.

'Unless she got here first and didn't wait.'

'Nah, she would have texted.'

Tam walked along to the end of the bar. A floor-to-ceiling glass wall provided an amazing view over the ocean. The water was the deep blue of late autumn, and the white surf curled in crisp waves that broke close to the shore. A lone surfer waited for a wave, but the sand was crowded with tourists catching the last of the afternoon sun.

Tam took a deep breath. She'd have plenty of time for walks soon. And to lie on the beach. The last thing she wanted to do was go back into hospitality. She pushed back the frustration that niggled in her chest. She'd enjoyed being a chef—cooking was her first love—but the long and late hours had played havoc with her health. Not to mention the emotional mess she'd got into with Chad. She'd not told Pippa about it; she and Nell had made a pact to keep negativity away from her.

'Hey, Pip.' Nell called out and Tam looked across to the left of the glass window where a row of soft brightly-coloured sofas lined the wall. Pippa was sitting on a red one and Tam smiled.

They had been friends since primary school, and Pip could still surprise them. She was a stunning looking woman who wore her beauty unconsciously; she didn't have a vain bone in her body. Her hair was a pale ginger, and her skin was olive. Green almond-shaped eyes and lush lips set in a heart-shaped face, and a tall fine build set her apart in any crowd.

Not to mention her fabulous sense of fashion. The outfits she put together worked for Pippa, and Tam knew if she were to try to wear the same clothes, she'd look ridiculous with her dumpy figure and curly blonde hair. That's why she wore dresses and kept her hair up.

Pippa spotted them and jumped up. Her retro short culotte set looked like something from the 1940s and her hair was twisted into an old-fashioned French roll, but as Tam got closer, the pink nose and the tired eyes stood out like beacons.

'You look like you need a rum, aspirin and lemons, sweets,' Tam said. 'I'll go get you a Bundy.'

'No. I've already ordered a bottle.' Pippa gestured to the

table where a bottle of champagne and three glasses sat on a tray.

'Wow,' Nell exclaimed. 'Moet! Are we celebrating the demise of Darren?'

Pip pulled a face as she flopped back onto the sofa.

'That's one of the things to celebrate. I should have listened to you two when you told me he was a loser.'

Tam shook her head. 'You had to find it out for yourself. Not worth risking our friendship over.'

'It wouldn't have come to that.' Pippa lifted the bottle and poured the first glass, bubbles cascading over the side. 'You gals always come first with me, you know that.'

'And Darren didn't like that,' Nell said.

'Here, let me do it.' Tam held her hand out for the bottle. 'It's too good to waste.' She looked quizzically at Pippa when she passed the icy bottle over. 'How much did that set you back?'

'Okay, it's bribery. I know how much you pair love your bubbles.' Pippa sat back and folded her arms. 'That bottle, my dear friends, cost me my last two hundred dollars.'

'You're mad.' Tam knew her eyes were wide as she poured the second glass. 'All the more reason not to spill a drop though.'

'What do you mean your last two hundred dollars?' Nell looked at Pip as she took the glass from Tam.

'Darren cleaned our bank account out. And the lowlife must have guessed my password because he transferred money from *my* account too before he withdrew it all.'

'Jesus, Pip.' Tam was indignant. 'What are you going to do about it? See the bank?'

Pippa waved her hand. 'He can have it. It wasn't that much. Most of my money is in a term deposit. It's worth it to get rid of him. At least he withdrew it before my termination pay went in. I've changed my banking password, so he can't get his hands on that.'

'What termination pay?' Tam stared at Pippa.

PENTECOST ISLAND 1-3

Pip's eyes were hard and glittering, as she dug a tissue out of her bra and wiped her nose.

'Are you on any meds for that flu? Should you be drinking?' Tam couldn't help herself.

'Stop being mother. I'm a big girl, Tam. And no, just paracetamol. A good night's sleep will fix me up.'

'What termination pay?' Nell repeated Tam's question in a gentle voice.

Pippa leaned back in the sofa and picked up the third glass of bubbles. 'It's been a very interesting day. Where shall I begin?'

'At the beginning, please.'

Pip closed her eyes as she sipped.

Tam lifted her glass and wrinkled her nose when the Moet bubbles tickled.

'First thing was, I woke up with the flu. I went back to sleep when Darren left and when I woke up, I was late for work for my presentation.'

'That big one? The one that was going to set you on a skyrocket trajectory in marketing?' Nell's usually soft voice rose.

'That's the one. I was as crook as, and I overslept, and then Eric rang absolutely peed off. Clarissa did the presentation instead of me. But it did have one good outcome. It meant I was there when Darren brought his bimbo home for a lunchtime romp in my bed.'

'Oh, Jeez, Pip. I'd like to say I'm sorry, but I'm not.'

'It's all good. As he was leaving, I got a text message from Eric telling me I was out.'

'Out what?' Tam took a swig of her champagne.

'Out of a job. Sacked, fired, *finito*.'

'Bloody men,' Tam said. 'But you've got company, sweets. She looked across at Nell. 'Until Nell picks up a job, that makes the three of us unemployed.'

A smile broke over Pip's face. 'Really. You've lost your

36

job too? That's fantastic!'

Tam pulled a face. 'That's not quite the word I'd use.'

'Oh, I got notice to leave my apartment too. But . . . ta da . . . Pippa reached over and pulled out a letter from her small bag. 'There was one more thing that happened today and it means if you two are prepared to be flexible, I can offer you both a job.'

'A job? What sort of job?' Tam said.

'What do you mean flexible?' from Nell.

Pippa sat back and folded her arms. 'If you could do any job you wanted, anywhere in the world, what would you choose?''

'Trick question?' Tam asked with a frown. Pippa was not usually spontaneous. A decision could often take her a few weeks of deep consideration before it was made.

'No, I want a truthful answer from both of you. Nell?'

'If I could go anywhere? Hmm . . .' Nell tapped her lip. 'It would be somewhere warm. No winter, lots of blue skies, and near the ocean.'

'And the job?' Pippa asked.

'Number crunching, of course. I'd like to be in charge of a business.'

'Tam, your turn.'

'Easy,' she replied as she stared at Pippa. *What was she up to?* 'I'd have my own restaurant. Same as Nell, no winter, blue skies, and near the water.'

Pippa leaned forward and lifted the bottle, before she topped up the three glasses and bubbles overflowed down the sides of the fine crystal glasses.

'Pip, don't waste it,' Nell cried.

Pippa grinned back at her and then put her glass down before she sneezed. She blew her nose and her voice was croaky as she picked up her glass again.

'I want to propose a toast, but I won't do it unless you both say yes. If I was able to offer you both a job, the perfect jobs that you've both just described, what would you say?'

Tam looked at Nell, and Nell stared back at her before they both turned to Pippa.

Tam was the first to lift her glass. Nothing ventured, nothing gained, even though she didn't have a clue about what Pippa was on about. Nell followed suit.

'Yes,' they said together.

'I am proposing a toast to our new business venture. We have an accountant, a marketing expert, and a top-class chef. Here's to us.' She waited for the others to clink their glass on hers, and then chuckled. 'Okay, now I'll tell all.' She lifted the letter. 'This is our ticket to freedom and achieving our dreams.'

'Come on, Pip, the suspense is killing me.' Tam sat forward.

'Ta da.' Pippa pulled the letter from the envelope and began to read.

'Dear Ms Carmichael, I apologise for the time it has taken to finalise the estate of your great aunt, Violet Daphne Carmichael, but as there is another resident on the island, the ownership of the property had to be carefully established. The surveying has been completed and I am pleased to advise that there are no encumbrances on your property on Pentecost Island, and the deeds are in the process of being transferred to your name, as sole beneficiary of Miss Carmichael's estate.

The estate consists of her house and the western half of the island. The island has been divided evenly, between your portion and the other owner.

I would be grateful if you could call me to organise a suitable time to attend my office in Mackay, and I will take you through the process of finalising the legal documentation.

Your sincerely.

Charles Morton

Morton and Morton, Mackay.'

'Bloody hell.' Tam stared at Pippa. Her face was flushed, and her eyes had lost their hardness.

'Pentecost Island? Where we spent that holiday with you in Grade Ten? Where you lived with your Aunty Vi?'

Pippa nodded. 'The very same. And the island where we are going to start up our own resort. I have a chef and an accountant. How long before you can pack up and come with me?'

Tam and Nell looked at each other.

'Can we have some time to think about it?' Nell, always the sensible one asked.

'Why? You both told me what you want.'

'But what about the money?' Tam put her glass down on the table. 'Setting up a resort won't be cheap. And if I remember your aunt's house, it wasn't in a very good condition fifteen years ago. What's it like now? And what are we going to live on?' She shook her head. 'Fish and yams? Pip, you've always been a dreamer. Have you really thought this through?'

Pippa nodded. 'I have. And to make your decision easier, I want you both to know that I desperately want both of you to come with me. I *need* you gals with me.' She grinned. 'Who knows, there might be a Darren up there and I'll stuff up again without you to watch out for me.'

Tam shook her head, but she smiled as her interest fired. 'That's emotional blackmail, Pippa Carmichael.'

Pip sneezed again and wiped her nose. 'I rang Mr Charles Morton this afternoon. Not only did I inherit half the island, but Aunty Vi left me a significant amount of money. I'm going to do this properly. You'll both be on a salary while we go up and start work. Planning, renovating and building, and working for ourselves while we create the best resort in the Whitsunday Islands. If you don't want to, I'll hire another accountant, and another chef. And I have to fill a lot more positions eventually anyway.'

Nell was the first to hold up her hand for a high-five. 'I'm in.'

'And me.' Tam followed suit and held her hand up. 'Don't think the pair of you are leaving me here by myself.'

They all linked hands.

'What do we say?' Pippa said with a wide grin.

'All for one, and one for all,' they chanted together, and burst into peals of laughter, ignoring the curious looks of the other customers and the barmen.

Chapter 5

A month later

Pippa

Everything went like clockwork. I packed up the apartment, and Tam had no trouble getting out of her lease. Rental accommodation was short on the coast, and the owner was ready to move in as the removalist loaded my furniture in the truck. I'd sold my bed to them; that was one thing I didn't want to take to Aunty Vi's house.

Not that I had much furniture, but between the three of us, we had filled a truck and rented a storage shed at Airlie Beach until we sussed out the state of the house and worked out what we'd need to take over to the island. How to get it there was a problem we'd sort out later. It was going to be hard enough getting us over there; the weekly launch that had taken me to the mainland and returned me to the island when I was at boarding school had stopped running two years ago.

The last time I visited the island was just before that. I sat beside her on the wide front porch that looked down over the bay, and she'd told me she was thinking about moving to the mainland.

'I'll miss that view,' she said. 'It's been a part of my life for over sixty-five years.'

I'd blinked back tears. 'I'll bring you out here for visits if you move.'

'No, once I go, it's for good. If I came back, I wouldn't want to leave. Getting old is a bastard, Pip. I can't see well enough to read any more, and my hips are just about worn out.'

'For eighty-five, I think you're pretty damn good,' I'd

retorted so I didn't cry.

'I'm not complaining. I've had a marvellous life, and girl, I want you to promise me that you will too. Take life by the horns and go for it.'

I swallowed as I remembered that conversation. Aunty Vi certainly wouldn't have approved of Darren. I didn't ever see her again. She died the weekend Darren and I moved in together, and I'd told myself it was a bad time to go up.

Besides, she's dead, babe,' Darren had said. 'She wouldn't know if you were there or not.'

No, Aunty Vi certainly wouldn't have liked Darren.

Or Brett or Rob before him. At least I hadn't moved in with them.

'I'm going to stay here until I have to move. If I have to, I'll sell it eventually,' she'd said on my last visit. There's been a few developers after it over the years.' She shook her head. 'But lately, so many of our island resorts have closed, and the bloody Chinese are buying the islands. I'd love to see my place turned into a resort, but it won't happen in my lifetime.'

It had only been a few months later that she called me and told me that she had moved to the mainland. Aunty Vi had no close family, and the whole time I'd lived with her, no one had been to visit. Darren and my job had taken all of my focus in those months, and I guess I'd just assumed that when she moved away, Aunty Vi had sold up, so when I received the letter from Mr Morton about my inheritance, it had been a shock.

So, my new life—taking it by the horns—was about to begin. And I was going to follow Aunty Vi's dream. It was the least I could do to make amends.

I was meeting Tam and Nell at the Gold Coast Airport at three o'clock. I had one final look around the apartment, left my keys in an envelope on the kitchen bench and closed the door behind me for the last time. The taxi I'd booked was waiting in the car park at the back of the apartment block, and the driver jumped out and grabbed my two bags. He was a good-looking guy, about thirty.

'Going on a holiday, gorgeous?' He gestured to the straw hat I was clutching.

I nodded, ignoring the come-on. 'Yeah.'

I climbed into the back seat, and he talked all the way down the motorway. I did my best to ignore him, but he was kind of cute.

By the time we got to the airport, I found out he was studying law at Bond University, had just broken up with his girlfriend, and was looking for a good time.

He asked for my phone number when I paid the bill, but I shook my head. 'No point, I'm not coming back.'

I learned two things from that taxi ride, and I didn't like the first one.

I was still a sucker for any good-looking guy who put the hard word on me. Just as well, Tam and Nell were coming north with me. Despite my age, I still had some growing up to do.

The second thing I realised made me smile. I *wasn't* coming back.

Tam and Nell were at the coffee shop at the northern end, where we always met when we were travelling together. Nell was in shorts and a T-shirt, wearing a baseball cap, and holding her ratty backpack.

Tam was in the usual retro dress, and the bright colour made me smile. The red background had huge yellow poppies printed on it, and the poppies matched her patent leather shoes and matching shiny box handbag. Her blonde curls were held up in a clip. Poor Tam had a thing about her body image. She was curvy and always looked stunning, but she translated that to *fat*. Or chubby. Or dumpy. Whatever her current word was.

After hugging both of them, I shook my head. 'Tam, you

do realise that there are no vintage stores where we're going, don't you?'

'I know there are no stores on the island.' She grinned. 'But there are planes that will take me back to the city when I need to shop.'

'Girlfriend, you won't have time to shop,' I said with an answering grin. For the past four weeks, we'd pored over business plans and dreamed and laughed. A lightness had taken over my usual serious nature, and the intense motivation that had driven me to succeed in my marketing career had transferred to this new project.

But this one was all mine, and whether it was successful or an abject failure would be on my head. Too many doubts about whether this idea of taking life by its horns and going into a new business were starting to fill my head at night.

We flew into Hamilton Island after dark and headed for the hotel where we'd booked three beachside bures. To their credit, both my friends had insisted on paying for their accommodation, and I smiled as I reluctantly agreed. Even though I had a significant amount of money invested to use for the development of the resort, I was being cautious. Until I saw the house on the island, I had no idea what it was going to cost to realise Aunty Vi's dream. We were going to spend a couple of days on the island and check out the local contractors. I'd made some early enquiries while I packed up.

'The repairs from the cyclone a couple of years ago are mostly finished on the island resorts, and on the mainland, so I'm hoping that it won't be too hard to get tradesmen to come out to Pentecost,' I said to Nell and Tam as we walked across the foyer after we checked in.

'We're not on the payroll yet,' Tam said. 'This is a little holiday before we start work.'

'And we have to suss the island out before you decide to go ahead, for sure,' Nell, ever the voice of wisdom, added. 'Maybe it will all be too hard, and we'll have a holiday and go back to the Gold Coast.'

'So, until then, we treat it as a holiday, and we pay our share.' Tam nodded.

'Have I told you recently that I love you both?' I said.

Tam shoulder-bumped me as we headed outside, keys in hand. 'That doesn't mean much because you said you loved Dazza too for a while there.'

I bumped her back and grinned. 'But you two have endured longer than anyone. Remember that time in Grade 5 when we all sat on that swing at the gate of the school, and we made a vow?'

'Oh God, I'd forgotten all about that.' Nell swung her backpack off and carried it.

Tam nodded. 'Me too. You've got such a good memory, Pip.'

I didn't want to spoil the mood by saying that it was only good because most of my happiness was set in memories. I swallowed and shook away the maudlin thought.

'Yep. We vowed no matter where we were and what we were doing, we were going to get together somewhere exotic on our thirtieth birthdays.'

Nell giggled. 'And we thought thirty was old.'

'I thought twenty was old when I was a kid,' Tam said. Her eyes lit up as she looked at us both, and the huts came into view. 'And hey, we're all going to turn thirty in a few months.'

I spread my hands as we stood looking at the gorgeous grass huts we were about to sleep in. 'Maybe it was a premonition. We have the exotic location at our fingertips. We're already here, gals.
'

Chapter 6

Tam

'This is absolutely incredible. I'd forgotten how beautiful it is up here.' Tam stood on the beach in front of the bures. Sapphire blue water dotted with the white sails of boats moving through the channel between Hamilton Island and the big island to the north had been a constant feature of the landscape since she'd walked outside with her first coffee of the morning, and Pippa and Nell had joined her.

'I thought we needed to get a feel for island life tourist-version before we head over to Pentecost and start work,' Pippa said.

Tam had noticed Pippa was on edge when they arrived last night, and she couldn't put her finger on what was wrong. She knew better than to delve too deeply when Pippa went quiet.

Maybe it was the thought of going to the island and knowing that Pip was a shocker at picking partners; this was the third guy who'd let her down. No matter how much Pippa said she was over Darren, Tam knew she was still hurting. Not from breaking up but from the betrayal.

Then again, maybe it was the thought of the big step they were all taking. It was good that they'd all have their own space in the three huts for a few days; they were going to be living in close proximity on an isolated island for a long time.

Nerves coiled in Tam's stomach as she wondered if she and Nell had agreed too readily. The prospect of what they were going to do was exciting, but the planning and organisation were the parts she was worried Pip hadn't given enough thought to.

'Good idea.' Nell's words interrupted her musing. 'Pippa,

while I think of it, what's the phone service like on the island? Will we even have service? My mum wanted to know when I called her last night to let her know we were here safely.'

Pippa shrugged. 'I'm not sure. When I lived out there with Aunty Vi, it was before we all had mobile phones. When I last visited, I didn't turn my phone on.' She put a finger to her lips and frowned. 'She had some sort of radio thing in the small room off the kitchen. Do you remember that when you visited?'

Nell shook her head. 'All I remember is exploring the island. It was a long time ago. What about you, Tam?'

'I remember it raining for most of the week we were there, but we spent most of the time outside. I remember the water and the house. But Aunty Vi did let our parents know we were there, so there must have been some form of communication.'

'We'll make some enquiries tomorrow. I think we need to sit down and make a list of things that we can't do without before we head over on Saturday. The first thing I have to do is find out the best way to get over there. We might have to charter a boat. One big enough to take our stuff over.'

'The ferry doesn't run anymore?" Nell asked.

'No. But once we get to the island, I know there's an old launch that Aunty Vi had. Or there was, and the solicitor did mention it as being part of the estate.'

'Can you drive a boat?' Tam was beginning to wonder if they had gone in too deep, too fast.

'I could when I lived there, but she was an old tub even back then.' Pippa turned away and put her hand up to her eyes. 'Finish your coffee and come for a walk. I saw a track heading along the back of the beach to some more huts when I went for a walk earlier.' She pointed to the east. 'If we walk to that rocky outcrop, we should be able to see Pentecost Island.'

As they walked, Pippa was quiet, and Tam glanced at Nell, who nodded slightly.

PENTECOST ISLAND 1-3

'Let's get this list sorted while we walk,' Tam said cheerfully. 'Nell, what can't you do without?'

Nell smiled. 'Apart from the givens of food and water'—

Pippa finally smiled. 'And bubbles.'

'And bubbles,' Nell agreed. 'I guess it's my laptop and internet access. I've got my dongle, but that relies on phone service.'

'Until we get there, I'm not even sure if we have electricity. There were a couple of generators there when I was a kid, but it's all an unknown.'

'What about you, Tam?'

'My cooking tools. Do you think we should go over for a day trip, check it out, and then come back? I know it's going to be pretty basic—' Tam looked up as Pippa spoke over her.

'No. We'll need to have a few days there, and then once we do that, there's no point in coming back to stay here. We'll get sorted and then come back over in the launch and get whatever we need. When we're ready, we'll have to get our stuff out of the storage shed and get it over somehow.'

They came to the end of the track. 'Are you up for a bit of bush walking?' Pippa asked.

Nell looked hesitant, but Tam nodded. 'Why not? We're going to have to get used to doing it rough, I think. At least after our walk, we can go to the breakfast room and be waited on. I'll bring a pen and my notebook, and we'll make a comprehensive list.'

'And then after breakfast, I'll go down to the marina and suss out some charters to get us out there.' Pip's face had brightened a bit, and relief filled Tam. Whatever had been on her mind, it seemed she'd let it go.

'Come on, girls,' she said. 'Let's go exploring.'

They followed a narrow track away from the beach. Lush forest surrounded them, and the light was dim as they crossed a small creek of crystal-clear water that ran from the top of the hill behind them to the sea. Brightly coloured parrots hung from the trees, and then suddenly, they all flew off, squawking in a wave of colour.

'It's pretty,' Nell said. 'And I remember the parrots on your island, Pip.'

Pippa stopped walking. 'Pentecost *was* beautiful, but I want you both to be prepared to see it how it might be now. There's been a cyclone through a couple of years back, and there could be damage, but Mr Morton did say the house is intact.'

'How does he know so much about the place? Did he come and have a look?' Tam linked her arm with Pippa's, and they started walking again. The track widened, and a glimpse of blue appeared ahead through the lush foliage.

'I'm not sure,' Pippa said slowly. 'Maybe he got a local to come over?'

'Whatever we find, it's a fabulous adventure and a challenge, and no matter what we find, we will make it work. I'm already brimming with ideas for an outdoor restaurant on a jetty and new menus.'

She reached down and squeezed Pippa's hand. 'Pip. Thanks so much for including Nell and me in this. It's a wonderful opportunity. And I know it's going to be a lot of hard work, but hey, what a place to do it.'

'Yes. It is going to be hard work, and we're all going to learn new skills.' Nell moved to Pippa's other side as they approached the water. 'But when any of us get down and wonder what we're doing, we'll bring each other up. I'm excited now, but I think we'll probably have some doubtful days.'

The track ended, and Pippa ran ahead to the rocks, leaving Tam and Nell behind.

'Is she okay, do you think?' Nell asked as she watched Pippa climb the rocks. 'She's been very quiet today.'

49

PENTECOST ISLAND 1-3

Tam nodded. 'She's come out of it a bit. It's just Pippa processing things her own way. As well as our friendship, remember, we've both got families to fall back on. Pip's only got us.'

'It's not going to be easy, but we will have to be there for her too. But I'm really looking forward to starting work.'

'Me too,' Tam said. 'Come on, let's go see if we can find this island.'

They stepped out of the forest into brilliant sunshine. Pippa was way ahead of them, standing on the edge of the rocky headland and looking to the south. Her hand was shading her eyes, but when she turned around as Tam and Nell approached, her lips were wide in a happy grin. She lifted her other hand and pointed to the volcanic plug rearing from the deep blue water in front of them.

'There she is, my lovelies. Pentecost Island.'

Chapter 7

Pippa

We had a quick lunch in a coffee shop near the marina. Tam and Nell were going for a walk along the shopping precinct— all research, they assured me—and I was going down to the marina to make some enquiries. Since I'd seen Pentecost Island across the water, I was itching to get there, but we needed to be prepared first.

Over lunch, I told the girls what Mr Morton had said. 'I'm not too worried about it, but he reckons we're going to meet some opposition with my plans for the island.'

'Planning stuff, I assume, but that's where we'll do our homework once we get over there. Who knows, we might be remembering an idyllic location that only lived in our memories,' Nell said.

Tam gestured to the view across from the coffee shop. 'Even with the crowds here and the little motorised cart things and all the noise, this is still pretty idyllic. Look at the colour of that water.'

'And the palm trees with those hammocks. I think we definitely need to consider hammocks between palm trees,' Nell butted in.

'We have lots to do before hammocks,' I said with a smile. 'But listen, don't mention to anyone that we're heading over to Pentecost Island. I'd like to keep it quiet for a while in case there is any opposition.'

'It's not part of a National Park, is it?' Tam asked.

I shook my head. 'It never used to be, but while you're out and about, can you see if you can pick up maps? And look for some with walking tracks and stuff too.'

PENTECOST ISLAND 1-3

##

We needed to purchase the basics, food, and plenty of bottled water—in case the tank was dry at the house—but first, I was on a mission, so I set off for the marina. Back in my high school days, I'd made friends with a guy on the ferry that had done the run out to Pentecost Island three times a week. In those days, there had been hikers and birdwatchers who'd camped on the beach, and it was that client base that I had in mind for our resort.

Eco-resort was the term that Tam had come up with as we'd had a coffee before we'd got on the plane at the Gold Coast.

I liked it. And I could already see the advertising possibilities. Not a low market backpacker type of establishment, but high end with decent facilities rather than basic huts and shared facilities. These days, it seemed that there was a higher call for luxury—or maybe that was just me. Research would inform our final decision.

'I'll meet you back at the hotel in a couple of hours,' I said as we left the coffee shop.

The chances of my friend Jiminy—yes, that was his real name—still being around were pretty slim. The whole dynamic of tourism, and subsequently tourism around the islands, appeared to have changed, according to the brochures I'd read in the compendium in the hut.

As well as reading them, I took some photos of the shopping precinct and the views as I walked slowly down to the marina.

The marina was busy with a variety of vessels coming and going. A small tinnie holding a couple of fishermen motored along the break wall, and a couple of larger rubber ducky tenders came in from catamarans anchored in the bay. A massive superyacht with a US flag on the top sat at the end of one wharf. Tourists milled around eating ice creams and taking photos. A couple of teenagers sat at the end of the first wharf, fishing lines dangling in the water.

The island had a happy, peaceful feel to it, less frantic and cosmopolitan than the busy Gold Coast where I'd spent the last ten years.

An unfamiliar relaxation settled in my bones, and the usual shaky tingling in my fingers had eased since we'd arrived. Up until I'd lost my job, as soon as one project had ended, there had always been another one ahead, with the pressure to perform and make money for the company. My level of stress had impacted on me physically, and if I was honest, it hadn't been good for my mental health either. Pressure had come from home, too.

Over the last year, when I'd get home, stressed and tired, Darren always wanted to go out and hit the high spots.

'I have to be seen, babe,' he'd say.

Wanker.

Now, the only pressure on me would be that of my own making. I had loved my job with Eric, but with the new project, it was all mine and I held control. We'd spend the first few days on the island doing a feasibility study; if it wasn't going to work, well then, there was nothing to worry about. I'd convert Aunty Vi's old house into some sort of comfortable accommodation, and if I didn't go down the eco-tourist resort track, I'd live there while I considered my future.

But I was determined to make it work.

I walked along the main wharf until I came to the end, where the ferries had moored over ten years ago. The big barge that brought goods across from the mainland had just departed, and two men were loading boxes onto a truck.

To my delight, I recognised Jiminy. I waited until he'd loaded a crate onto the back of the truck before I walked across and called out. 'Jiminy! Jim!'

He turned and stared for a moment before a grin crossed his face. Dropping the rope in his hand, Jiminy strode across the wharf to where I was waiting.

'Well, look what the tide's washed up! Phillipa Carmichael!' He held his arms wide, and I stepped in for a hug.

'I didn't expect to see you still working here,' I said, kissing his cheek.

'The island is my home. Always will be.' He stepped back and looked at me. Jiminy and I had been great mates back in our school days. He was a few years older than me and had left school to work on the boats when he was in Year 11, not long after I'd started my first year at Prossie High. I'd got to know him when we'd caught the ferry over to the mainland at the end of each weekend for the school week, and he'd been kind to a nervous first-year high school student. After he'd left school, he'd worked on the ferry on the Pentecost Island run, and we'd become good mates. But our friendship went the way of many, and we'd lost contact when I left the island and headed south.

'Wow, look at you, girl! All grown up. Last time I saw you, you were heading off to your last day at Prossie High School.'

'That was well over ten years ago, Jim. I went to uni and got a job, and when Aunty Vi moved to the mainland, I had no reason to come out here to the island.'

The other man started the truck, and Jim gave him a wave. 'I'll meet you up at the store, Bill,' he yelled across the wharf. The driver nodded, and we stepped to one side of the narrow concrete wharf as the truck moved slowly past us.

'I'll walk up with you, and we can have a catch-up. How long are you on Hamo for? A holiday?'

I shook my head. 'Sort of. Just a short one. I came down here to find out how I can get out to Pentecost Island these days. I know the ferry doesn't run now, so I guess it'll have to be a private charter?'

Jiminy walked along beside me. He'd grown into a tall man and was obviously fit. His shoulders were broad, his skin was tanned, and his face already had that weathered look of the boaties who spent their lives on the sun and water. I guess he'd be heading for his late thirties now.

'You won't be able to go out there, sorry, Phillipa.'

'I go by Pippa—or Pip—these days.' I turned to him with a frown. 'And what do you mean? I know the ferry doesn't go out there now, but has something changed since Cyclone Debbie? Is it too hard to get into the bay now?'

'No, the new owner has made it a private island. No day trippers allowed.'

'New owner? Private? What do you mean private?'

Jiminy scratched his head. 'I guess because he lives there, and he's discouraged visitors. I don't know that he can say no, but none of the charter boats go out there now.'

I stopped walking and crossed my arms as disbelief hit me. 'Well, I'll be going out there. Have you still got a boat, Jim?'

He nodded. I started walking again, and I caught him up.

'You remember Aunty Vi? Where I lived when I was in my teens?'

'Yes, of course I do. She was great friends with my nan when they were in the aged care home at Prossie. I used to see her a fair bit when I went to visit. My nan died last year. Your Aunty Vi was a sweetie.'

'She was. She was also a very private person and didn't want to have a funeral or any fuss or bother, but I do feel guilty that I didn't even come up when she passed away.'

Or before, I thought, I didn't say it because the guilt was too raw.

'Life intrudes.'

'It does, but I should have come.'

Jiminy shrugged. 'Maybe. Maybe not. She was gone, so would it really have made a difference?'

'I guess not.' What he said made sense, but I should have come up to visit Aunty Vi when she was in care. I used to call her each week until Darren arrived on the scene. she'd said that she didn't want me to visit, and I knew that she'd meant it. There was no beating around the bush with her, and she was sharp as a tack until her body let her down. I was sad, but Jiminy talked sense. I stopped and put my hand on his arm. 'Tell me about this person who says they own the island.'

The look he shot me was curious. 'I don't know for sure that he owns the island, but he owns a fair chunk of it and he's built a big flash house up on the point. You know, just above that lovely beach with the coral heads at each side of the bay?'

'I know it well. I used to call it Swan Bay. I saw some swans there once when I was first at Aunty Vi's. They reminded me of that story—' I cut off. Telling Jiminy about a fairy tale that had fascinated me ever since I was a child was irrelevant. 'Bottom line, Jim, Aunty Vi has left me her house and at least half of Pentecost Island, so he can't own *all* of the island. But please keep that to yourself. I need to find out what's going on.'

'No problem. And that's great news to know that it's yours.'

'I'm considering doing some development out there, so I'm very interested to hear what you know about them.'

'Just a him, he's English. He lives on the island alone and is supposed to be a bit of a recluse. And you know what the islands' gossip grapevine is like. All sorts of rumours abound. He's supposed to be a movie star one day and then a billionaire investor the next. Last I heard, he was a famous author, but I've never seen his name anywhere.'

'What is his name?' I asked.

'Rafe Rendell.'

I shrugged. 'Never heard the name either.' But I noted it so I could Google him when I got back to the hotel.

'Since he arrived in the islands a couple of years ago, he's not been receptive to anyone going on the island. All the birdwatching and the climbing have stopped now. I haven't seen a boat there for a long time. I mean, you still see the private charters go down that way, but it's not a good place to moor the way the weather blows in from both the south and north, so most sailors keep going down to Shaw Island.'

'So . . . if I want to go out there—' I shook my head — 'I mean when I go out there. We've only booked on Hamo for a couple of days to get some provisions together.' We'd started walking again and reached the edge of the marina, and the road was above us; a couple of the electric buggies that tourists used to get around the island whirred past.

'How many of you?'

I shook my head. 'Three of us, and we need to get out to Aunty Vi's. Do you still have a boat?'

Jiminy chuckled. 'Is the Pope a Catholic?'

'Okay, smartie, let me clarify that. Do you have a boat that I can hire for you to take us out to the island on Sunday?'

'Of course, I have. But none of this hiring business. I'll take you out as a friend. Sara and I were talking about taking the kids out this weekend.'

'Sara? Kids?'

Jiminy positively beamed. 'My wife and two kids, Lola and Baden.'

'Congratulations.'

'Life's been good to me. How about you, Pippa? It's a long time since you left. You said we? Married? Kids?'

I shook my head. 'No, I've been a career woman through and through. It was time to take a break. When Aunty Vi's estate came through, and she left me the house, I decided to move up here for a while.'

'The rumour was that Rendell bought old Ma Carmichael's place, as the locals call it. It was an affectionate term.'

'I remember. So you can take us out there?

'I can.'

'That would be fantastic.'

Jiminy pulled the gate to the marina shut behind him, and the loud clang startled a flock of parrots in the tree above us. 'Do you remember where I used to live with Mum and Dad?'

'No, I don't know where you lived. I only ever knew you on the ferry on the way to school and when you worked on the ferry that took me out to the island.'

'We live up on the hill past *Qualia*. Next door to where I grew up.' He grinned. 'I'm afraid I've led a boring life. I've never left the islands.'

'I don't think that's boring. It's the most beautiful place in the world.'

'We're happy here. *Qualia* is a flash resort. We're about a hundred metres past it. Why don't you and your friends come up tomorrow? It's well signposted. You can meet Sara and the kids, and we'll work out the best time to go on Sunday. I'll check the tides.'

'That sounds perfect.'

'Say late afternoon tomorrow? Come for sundowners.' Jiminy stopped at the end of the road that led to a small car park where the loaded truck was parked.

'We'll see you then.'

'Good to have you home, Pippa.' Jiminy waved and headed off towards the truck.

I nodded slowly as they drove off. It was good to be back in the islands, but I wouldn't be home until we set foot on Pentecost Island the day after tomorrow.

If all went to plan, I was going to be home for a long time.

Chapter 8

Pippa

Hearing what Jiminy had to say about the new resident on the island had got me thinking. I wasn't worried about the local gossip because no matter what was said or believed to be true, the bottom line was I was the legal owner of at least half of the island and Aunty Vi's sprawling house on the eastern point.

No. It wasn't Aunty Vi's house. It was *my* house, *my* land, and half *my* island.

And all my future.

But there was a new consideration to take into account. What happened with the island and the house and what I could do with it might depend on the person who owned the other half. Wondering how I could find out more about this guy, I knew that unless I wanted to get a rehash of the gossip, I couldn't just wander around Hamilton Island asking questions.

Maybe I could ring Mr Morton at the solicitor's office?

I glanced at my watch, but it was almost five and, being Friday afternoon, I doubted whether I'd be able to get onto him. I bit my lip and stared at the whitewashed wall of the hotel as I approached. If I left the call too long, and there was no phone service on the island, I wouldn't be able to find out anything about this mystery guy who had come from nowhere to be a half-owner of Aunty Vi's island.

My island.

I was still wondering what to do when I spotted Tam and Nell on the balcony of the outdoor bar. They were each holding a fancy cocktail glass filled with a bright green frothy concoction.

'You've started early.' I climbed the steps, pulled up a stool and leaned back with a contented sigh.

'Mocktails. Pineapple and lime. We were hot after our walk,' Nell said. 'And shopping.'

Tam nudged me. 'Hep, Pip. Check out the cute barman. He was checking out Nellie here, and they had a very long conversation about the one that she'd like best.'

Nell flushed beetroot red. 'Tamsin, stop it! He was only asking what my favourite fruit was.'

Tam winked at me as she kept teasing Nell. 'Trust me. He was chatting you up, girlfriend.'

'He was not.' Nell's voice was indignant, and the blush spread to her neck. When we went out, Nell was always the quiet one, and any time a guy came near her, her confidence instantly disappeared. I'd often wondered what made her that way, but she'd never shared. Tam said something had happened at uni, but Nell had never told us any details. But we had both noticed how she retreated into herself as soon as a guy showed any interest in her.

'A mocktail sounds good to me. I've had a long walk, and I have news.' The barman was at my side before I could even think about a drink—he *was* cute but not my type. In fact, after Darren, I had decided that no man was my type. I might do an Aunty Vi and live on the family island until I was old. I couldn't help grinning at the barman as I ordered my drink. 'One of those, please.'

'Certainly, madame.' With a wide smile and an exaggerated half-bow, for God's sake, he headed back to the bar.

I loosened my shoulders and focused on relaxing. 'How did you go?'

Nell leaned forward, her face almost back to its usual colour. 'Great. The general provision store has got everything we need.'

'You're exaggerating, Nell.' Tam laughed. 'It's got the basics, so don't go expecting gourmet meals straight up.'

I shook my head with a smile. 'We sure don't expect that

yet. I don't even know if we'll have a stove. Or power. So long as we've got bread and cold meat, and fruit, and an esky with some ice, we'll survive the first few days, so let's just see how we go. Your job is to keep us fed while we sort out a boat and communication. We're going to be working our butts off for the first few days, I think.'

'Do you know how much I'm looking forward to this?' Nell spread her hands and gestured to the lush foliage hanging above the balcony and then out to the calm blue sea. 'No way is this going to be hard work. No traffic, no car fumes, no crowds, and just a gorgeous view to look at.'

'It's been fun wandering around the island today, getting that atmosphere and thinking that we're going to create something like this. On a smaller scale, of course,' Tam added.

'It's going to take a while,' I said. 'But yes, hopefully we are. I think—I hope— we can make a go of it.'

Tam leaned back and lifted her green drink. 'Time will tell. And if it doesn't work out, well, we'll have given it our best shot.'

As I looked at my two best friends, the warm and fuzzies hit me. They were good people and had remained loyal to me through my ups and downs. Now, they were going to take a chance and had moved up here to help me establish the resort that Aunty Vi had dreamed of.

How lucky was I to have picked these two women as friends all those years ago?

'After this drink, it's time for some bubbles to celebrate being here. And then I think we should go out somewhere nice for dinner to suss out the restaurants.'

Tam laughed. 'Any excuse for bubbles with you, Pippa.'

'Okay, maybe you're right, but we do have some celebrating to do. And I want you two to know how much I love you both and how grateful I am that you've come to the islands with me.'

'Such an awful place to be,' Tam said with a smile.

'Thank you.' I said as the barman put my drink on the table.

Nell looked down.

'In a few minutes, could we please have a bottle of champagne and three glasses?' I asked.

'Sure. I'll be right back.' He tried to catch Nell's eye, but she wasn't having a bar of it. Tam and I exchanged a look.

'There's an Italian restaurant at the end of the street here, and I sussed out the menu,' Tam said after a moment. 'It looked divine.'

'As you do.' I closed my eyes as I sipped the fruit drink. It was sweet and bitter at the same time. 'Sounds good. Do you think we should book?'

'I'll ask the barman when he brings the bubbles. Unless you want to, Nell?'

'I am immune to your teasing, Tamsin.' Nell pulled a face. 'I'm used to it.'

The bubbles were delivered and poured into crystal flutes, and when Nell, with a defiant glare at Tam, asked the barman about the need to book at the Italian restaurant, he offered to ring and book a table for us.

'Thank you,' Nell said quietly. When he'd gone back to the bar, she lifted her glass. 'To us. And to . . . I think we need a name for the resort, Pippa.'

I lifted my glass. 'To us. To friendship. We'll think of a name at dinner.'

'And to success,' added Tam as we clinked glasses. 'I think we should make a night of it and all get glammed up. It might be a while before we go out again.'

'Can't I go like this?' Nell didn't look impressed.

'You can't wear shorts and a T-shirt out for dinner, Nell.'

'Okay. Long pants and a T-shirt then. I didn't bring any

good clothes. They're all in storage.'

Tam lifted her glass again 'Not a problem. There is a perfectly good resort wear shop opposite reception. We'll go shopping after our bubbles.'

'I agree. They won't take shorts and T-shirts at that restaurant. It looked pretty upmarket,' I added.

'All right. There might be one dress in my suitcase.' Nell pulled a face.

'Oh my God, Nell brought a dress?' Tam put her hand to her chest in mock surprise.

Nell pulled a face. 'Just as well I'm not the sensitive type. I don't know how I'll put up with you pair on a deserted island for too long.'

'Not so deserted, apparently,' I said with a frown. 'But I'll tell you all about that over dinner.'

Polishing off a bottle of bubbles didn't take long with three of us, and it was only an hour later that we were all glammed up and walking along the street to the restaurant that Nell's barman had booked for us.

'You look gorgeous, Nell. You should wear dresses more often,' I said.

Nell shook her head. 'Nope, I'm happier in my shorts and tees. My red lipstick dresses me up.'

Tam and I giggled. We were all happy and talkative as we walked along, and I linked my arms with my friends. 'I haven't felt this relaxed since—'

'Since before you met the dazzling Dazza,' Tam said drily.

'Yep, I'd agree with that,' Nell said. 'It's good to have the old Pippa back.'

'Not so old,' I protested.

'We are,' Tam said. 'We'll have our big thirtieths on the island.'

I chuckled. 'And we'll probably be too tired to celebrate.'

It was early but the restaurant was already half-full as we waited at the door. The maître d' came over and greeted us.

'A table for three, *bellas*?'

'We've booked. But I'm not sure what name it was booked under, 'I said.

He ran his finger down the reservations list. 'A ha. I have found it. A booking that says three beautiful ladies." He looked at us with a smile. 'I presume that is you, unless you are being joined by more?'

'No, we are three,' I said.

He led us across the restaurant, and we were tucked into a corner alcove but beside a large window that gave us a view of the water

'I hope when you build our little restaurant—' Tam began.

'Hey, enough of this little, 'I said. 'It might be small, but it will be exclusive.'

Nell rolled her eyes. 'Did you find out how we can get over to the island, before we start making these grandiose plans?' She leaned back as the waiter picked up the linen napkin and flicked it open onto her lap.

'You won't believe it, but I came across one of my old friends who used to be a deckie on the ferry when I was at high school. Jiminy's going to take us out to the island on Sunday, in his boat. He's invited us up to meet his family tomorrow, and to organise what we need to do.'

'Jiminy?' Tam grinned. 'As in Jiminy Cricket in the cartoons?'

'No, it wasn't cartoons,' Nell interrupted. 'It was Pinocchio. We used to watch it when we were kids. Remember, Tam?'

'Jiminy is his real name, and he's a great guy,' I said. 'He used to look out for me when I started at the new school when I left Brisbane.'

The drink waiter hovered beside the table and waited for us to stop speaking. 'Here is the drinks menu, ladies. I'll go and get some water, and I'll be back to take your orders for drinks in a moment.'

Deciding against another bottle of bubbles, we each ordered a glass of wine. 'Might be more expensive, but it will save us a headache in the morning,' I said. I'd managed to let go of *most* of my worries now that I'd found a way to get to Pentecost Island, but I wanted to have a clear head.

Tam and Nell were talking about the order they were going to place at the store tomorrow, and I let my thoughts roam. The anticipation of getting out to the island where I had spent my formative teen years was building.

I frowned. Damn, in the rush to get ready, I'd forgotten to Google that guy on the island. I was tempted to pull my phone out, but I resisted. When Tam and Nell drew breath, I jumped in.

'I have more news, too. Apparently, we have a neighbour on the island.'

'A neighbour? I didn't know there were other houses there?' Tam said.

I shook my head. 'There didn't used to be. Jiminy said this guy's built a house at the other end of the bay and is a bit of a recluse.'

'Will it affect your plans to open a resort?' asked the ever-sensible Nell.

I shrugged. 'I guess that's what we have to find out. Actually, that's part of your brief, Nell. If you don't mind, if you're happy to, I'd be really pleased if you could chase up permits and all that sort of stuff. I wouldn't have a clue where to start. I've been thinking about all of our strengths and what we need to assign to each of us.'

Tam put her hand up with a giggle. 'I bags cooking.'

PENTECOST ISLAND 1-3

'That's a given. But I guess until we get out there, we don't know what we'll have to do first up.'

'I was joking. You know I'll help with anything that needs doing. I won't be cooking for a good while. Let's just focus on relaxing tonight,' Tam said. 'Once we get to the island, we'll be able to divvy up our responsibilities.'

We all agreed, and an hour later—and another glass of wine each— our giggles became louder and more frequent as we talked about our plans.

'Maybe we could hold celebrity weddings on the island,' Tam said.

'Maybe we could offer it for that Survivor TV show,' Nell added. She'd relaxed and managed a pretty smile for the waiter as he brought our bowls of chilli crab linguini to the table.

I let out a satisfied sigh and sat back as Tam dissected her meal and tried to work out the recipe.

'Definitely one for our restaurant,' Nell said as she wiped the sauce from her plate with a piece of garlic bread. 'And come on, you gals, we have to think of a name for the resort and the restaurant too.'

I nodded, but my attention wandered when my gaze settled on the couple sitting at the table across from us. They were having an intense conversation, and their voices carried across to me as there was a lull in the background music. The woman's back was to me, and her white-blonde hair was done up in an elegant French roll held by a diamond clip.

I could tell a real diamond at thirty paces.

Jewellery was my weakness, but one that Darren had never picked up on, even with many hints from me over the time we were together. The woman sat stiffly, and her shoulders were so straight and still the tension between them almost twanged in the air.

I let my gaze move to the guy across from her, and my

breath caught.

My God. What a beautiful face. Even with the frown that marred his forehead. He was so good-looking he could have been a movie star. My mouth dried as I stared at him. Jet-black hair hung over eyes set wide above chiselled cheekbones. His olive skin had twin patches of pink high on his cheeks, and full lips and a five o'clock shadow gave him a rakish look. When he lifted his head to look at his partner, his eyes were a brilliant blue.

I had never seen such a gorgeous face in real life. On the movie screen maybe, but not in the flesh. It was hard to look away, but as he wasn't looking in my direction, I kept watching. His attention was totally focused on the woman across from him.

He was gorgeous, maybe, but definitely not happy with the set of those lips.

I felt like a voyeur as his gaze flicked over to meet mine. He must have sensed my interest. I was stunned by the intensity of his stare, and I couldn't look away. His eyes were almost challenging me.

To do what? Look embarrassed? Look away?

I did neither and simply let my eyes hold his. The strange feeling in the pit of my stomach was one I had never felt before.

Finally, he broke that connection as he turned back to the woman. I felt sorry for her. They were obviously having an argument about something, and I felt as though I had intruded on a private moment. An angry moment.

How sad to come to a beautiful place like this for a holiday and be unhappy.

I shrugged and turned my attention back to my friends.

'The Happy Life Island Resort,' I said.

Tam and Nell stared at me, and both shook their heads.

'Ugh, yuk. No.' Tam pretended to put a finger down her throat.

I smiled and tried not to look back at the guy across from

PENTECOST ISLAND 1-3

me. 'Okay. Hit me with some names.'

Chapter 9

Rafe

I forced my eyes away from the woman who held my gaze.

Jenny reached out and took my hand, but her eyes were hard. 'Rafe, it's been two years, and you haven't taken on board what we said. You have to listen, and you have to get over what happened.'

'Get over it?' The words burst from my mouth just as there was a lull in the conversations in the noisy restaurant, and a few heads turned.

'With the advance you've accepted, you're going to have to give us something,' she said. 'Something without the cynical viewpoint and such stereotypical females.'

'Straight to the point, I see. A phone call would have done it.' I stared at her. 'Jenny, if that's the only reason you came all this way, you've had a wasted trip. You can go back to London and tell Bryant I don't give a flying fu . . .fig if it takes me twenty years to write this book. If that doesn't suit, I'll give you the advance back. I'm not ready yet. How many times do I have to tell you that?' I was angry—as I was too often these days—but I kept my voice low. 'I don't even know that I can deliver what you want anymore.'

The candle in the middle of the table flickered as a gust of wind blew in from the water. As the restaurant filled, the waiter opened a concertina glass door, and we now had an uninterrupted view of the water and the setting sun. The colour of the sky was beautiful, but I didn't care. Once, I would have been storing words in my head or pulling out the notebook I had always carried with me.

PENTECOST ISLAND 1-3

Jenny's fingers tightened on my wrist. 'We don't want the advance back. You must write this book. If you don't, it is a criminal waste of your talent.'

My laugh was cynical. 'A waste of my talent? Or a waste of the money that Little Hampton would make when they publish it? Don't talk shit to me, Jenny. I've always had an honest relationship with you and Bryant, so don't let me down now.'

She held my gaze, but her gaze wavered a fraction. She'd been sent to do a job, and I knew Bryant had hoped that I would give in because I cared about Jenny. Jenny and Bryant knew me too well. They were the owners of Little Hampton Publishing, which published my first three books, and we had become friends over the past five years.

I knew I could make a life without another book. I was making a lot of adjustments lately—for the past seven hundred and one days if I was counting—and I didn't need any more pressure on me, so I took refuge in sarcasm.

'Really, Jenny? You tell me it will be a loss to the world? A criminal waste, you say?' I laughed. 'How sad that you and Bryant won't make all that lovely money if I don't write it. Isn't it all about having another bestseller? Isn't that what publishing is all about? You take my creative work, and you turn it into a book. You give it an enticing cover, check I haven't made any mistakes, and then you send it out to the world. You want me to follow it around from town to town, to country to country, and then you guys make ten times the money I do.'

My sigh was long and low when Jenny's eyes glinted with tears in the flickering candlelight.

'I know you don't mean any of that. I can see through you, Rafe. It's a cover for how you're feeling. If it makes you feel better to lash out at me, go ahead. I can take it. I just want you to stop beating *yourself* up. *It. Wasn't. Your. Fault.*'

A glimmer of regret spiked through me, and I pulled my

hand away. I looked down at the red and white checked tablecloth. 'I'm sorry, Jenny. I know I'm being a proper bastard but that's the way I am these days. I'm better off away from people, and then I can't lash out.'

Her voice was soft. 'You haven't always been this way, Rafe. I know you've buried yourself away on this tropical island. How much longer are you going to cut yourself off from civilisation? When are you coming home?'

'I am home, Jen.' I reached out and took her hand again and tried to soften my words with a gentle touch. 'And this is all the civilisation I want. This is where I'm going to stay.'

'Rafe, please. You have to listen to me. You know we love you like one of our family. It's not the publication we're worried about. All right, it is a small part of it,' she conceded. 'But we worry about *you*. On this island by yourself. What if you had an accident? Who do you talk to each day? Who would even know if you needed help?'

'No one, and quite frankly, Jenny, it suits me like that.'

'That makes me sad.'

'You think *you* know sad?' My words tumbled out, and I couldn't hold them back. 'You try it for a while. See what it's like to lose the person you loved. It's destroyed my faith and, with that, my ability to trust. And if that's impacting on my writing, I'm sorry, that's the way it is.' My voice was harsh. 'I don't want to get over it. It was a very good lesson in life.'

'I think you're doing yourself a disservice, Rafe. Do you think you need professional help to work through these feelings?'

My laugh was bitter. 'So I can write this next blockbuster for you guys?'

'What are you trying to achieve living over here? What do you do with your day?' Jenny's voice trembled. 'I'm going to be hard on you here.'

'Okay, hit me with it.'

PENTECOST ISLAND 1-3

'Just remember we love you. We *do*. I thought we had a friendship. What we don't want is to see you wallowing in self-pity for the rest of your life. As hard as it is to say, Rafe, you were let down by Rebecca. It happens every day to lots of people, but you've taken it too personally. Burying yourself away over here has just built the hurt up in your eyes, and, when you analyse it, was it really that bad?'

'So you're a psychologist, now too, Jenny?'

'Maybe. Please promise me that you'll think about it. Forget the book, but please, please try to get over it. Seek some help. Talk to someone.'

I dropped my gaze to the table. I was not too fond of that look in her eyes. It made me feel like a right bastard. 'I know you both just want the right thing for me, but Jen, I'm not ready to write. I'm sorry, I don't know how I'm ever going to be ready again.'

She opened her mouth to answer, but the waiter interrupted before she could speak. Neither of us had noticed him standing there, and he looked embarrassed as he handed us each a menu. 'I'll give you a few minutes to decide.' He gestured to a board that was propped against the empty table beside us. 'They are the specials of the day. I can highly recommend the crab. It is caught fresh each day.'

In one of my books, I questioned the meaningless things that make up each day of our lives. What did it matter what we ate? What music we listened to? Where we went? I must have had a premonition. One that my life ahead was going to be this vacuum that I had lived in for the past two years.

As much as I hated to admit it to myself—or Jenny—her words had touched me. I knew I was a selfish bastard, but I told myself if I lived my life in isolation, I wouldn't impact on anyone else.

'It's called depression, Rafe,' she said quietly.

As we sat there in silence, a peal of laughter caught my attention. The woman who had looked at me before was sitting with two others I hadn't noticed previously. As always, I took note of what was around me; it was a habit I'd had all of my life. I'd been interested in people, and that was what drove my storytelling once.

The woman who'd held my gaze was stunning; her hair was the colour of a pale apricot, her skin was flawless, her eyes beautiful, but her eyes held an empty sadness that I recognised. The other two women were laughing as they spoke; the one with short dark hair had expressive hands that she used nonstop with gestures that accompanied her words, and the other—a well-endowed blonde with messy curls sat back and watched, but the woman I focused on laughed as she listened to them. The three women were all dressed in bright colours, and they filled the restaurant with vibrancy and life.

Even the one with the sad eyes.

What would it feel like to be happy again? To have the joy of life within, and when there was nothing more important than sharing a meal and happy times with friends? For the first time in a long time, interest rippled through me, and I wondered what they were laughing about.

At the ripe age of thirty-five, I had turned into a bitter man. I knew I needed to pull myself out of this morass of pity I lived in every day, and I knew that if I was to survive emotionally, I was going to have to make some changes in my life.

I jumped when Jenny spoke. I must have voiced my thoughts aloud.

'Yes, Rafe. That's what you have to do. Why don't you come back to the UK with me? Bryant found this really good retreat in the Cotswolds. I'm sure it would help you.'

'A rehab centre for the terminally pissed off? Maybe I could write a book about that while I was there?'

PENTECOST ISLAND 1-3

I felt bad when Jenny's eyes welled with tears again.

'I'm sorry, that was my version of a joke.'

She didn't reply.

'All right. I'll try to get something to you in the next few months. Is that enough of a promise?'

'That's a start. If we haven't got anything from you by the end of the year, we'll have to reconsider the contract. If it was just Bryant and I, it wouldn't matter, but we have shareholders that we have to answer to, Rafe.'

'I understand totally,' I said in my business voice.

We sat in silence until the water came back to take our order. The laughter from the table near the window was infectious. One of the women had a giggle that made me want to smile. I saw Jenny glance over at them.

'Good to see happy people having a good time,' I said to lighten the atmosphere.

She nodded.

The waiter returned and placed a bowl of breadsticks on the table.

'Are you ready to order?' His pen was poised over the notepad.

Jenny looked at me, and I shrugged.

'We'll both have the crab you recommended.' She passed the menus to him.

When he'd gone, Jenny looked at me. 'You've lost a lot of weight, Rafe.'

'I don't need to eat much. I expend very little energy sitting at a desk looking at a blank screen all day.'

The heavy silence descended again. As we sat there, the woman with the apricot hair rose and walked across the restaurant past our table. Her eyes were downcast, and I got the impression she was trying to avoid making eye contact.

My gaze stayed on her back as she passed the table. Her

hair hung to her waist like a rippling fall of water. She turned her head as one of the other women called out to her.

'Pippa! Ask for the dessert menu on your way back.'

Pippa. The name suited her. If I'd been creating a character with that name, she would have looked exactly like the woman now standing at the bar. As I stared, our eyes connected. She lifted her chin and didn't look away until the barman came to take her order. For a moment, I frowned; I'd heard that name before, but I couldn't remember where.

But for some unknown reason, I had felt myself come alive a fraction, and it hurt like hell.

Chapter 10

Pippa

I always woke up with the sun, and on Sunday morning, I was packed and ready to go two hours before we were due to meet Jiminy at the marina. Tam, Nell and I each had a suitcase and a backpack. Jiminy had organised to have our provisions delivered straight to the marina at nine o'clock this morning, so there was little to take with us apart from our luggage.

The afternoon before had been pleasant. Jiminy's wife, Sara, was shy, but their two children had made up for her quietness, talking nineteen to the dozen and wanting to know all about the island we were going to live on.

'Will there be pirates?' Baden had asked. 'And buried treasure?'

'Can we come and visit?' his sister interrupted.

'It would be way cool to have visitors,' I'd said. 'You make sure you get your dad to bring you out to see us.'

Baden had a lunchtime birthday party to attend today, so Jiminy was running us out by himself and then heading straight back to Hamo.

Their house was set high on a hill and looked out over the Whitsunday Passage. I'd never get tired of looking at the incredible blue water, no matter how long I lived there.

Seeing Jiminy and his tight-knit little family had made me a little bit sad, and this morning, that emotion was mixed with the anticipation of going out to the island. It was times like that when I felt lonely, and knowing that I had no family—unless you counted Aunty Vi's sons, my two distant second cousins in England—always had me searching for someone to love.

No more, I chastised myself sternly. Remember Darren.

I glanced at my phone. It wasn't even seven yet, and I was showered and packed. I unzipped my suitcase and pulled out my joggers and a pair of socks. I'd go for a walk and be back in time to have breakfast with Tam and Nell before we went down to meet Jiminy at the marina.

I pulled my hair into a high ponytail, slipped my socks and joggers on, and then closed the door of the hut behind me. There was no sign of life from the two other huts where Tam and Nell were sleeping. I set off for the hill that led up from Whitsunday Boulevard to a lookout called One Tree Hill. I breathed deeply as I walked, and the slight unhappiness that had dogged me all night was soon replaced with serenity. I strode up the hill and was puffing with exertion by the time I reached the lookout, but the effort had been worth it. A spreading poinciana tree, massed with brilliant red flowers, caught my breath. The lush green grass was covered with petals, and the bench seat in the middle of the lawn beckoned, but I straightened and looked across the water. A series of bays indented the shore of the island.

This lookout faced to the north, so I couldn't see the volcanic peak of *my* island rising from the sea to the southeast. As I stood there drinking in the vista below me, footsteps broke the silence as another early morning jogger took on the challenge of One Tree Hill.

I made my way to the edge of the small cleared area and turned away from the road. I wasn't in the mood to talk to anyone. I wanted to appreciate this view and get my thoughts in order.

I waited until the footsteps faded again, and then I turned around to head back down to the resort. To my surprise, someone was sitting on the bench seat beneath the tree, and I put my head down as I walked past.

'Good morning.' The voice was deep and held a cultured English accent.

PENTECOST ISLAND 1-3

I lifted my head, prepared to nod and kept walking, but was taken aback to see the same man who'd locked eyes with me last night in the Italian restaurant.

My steps slowed as he looked at me, and again, I felt that strange pull into his eyes.

'Good morning,' I replied as heat filled my face.

I put my head down and hurried towards the road down the hill, relieved when he didn't speak again.

Despite the walk back being downhill, my heart was still pounding hard when I reached the resort and went back to my beachside hut. I was still hot, so after I took my shoes and socks off and put my canvas sneakers on, I washed my face with cool water. I stared at myself in the mirror, wondering why one person and such a brief encounter could have had such an impact on me.

It must be because he was such a fine-looking man.

##

I met Tam and Nell in the breakfast room of the resort. On the way I checked out of my hut, leaving my suitcase and backpack at reception. The girls were buzzing with excitement. Keeping in the nautical mood, Tam had shed her usual dress and was wearing a pair of 1940s high waisted shorts and a *pink* T-shirt patterned with white sailing boats. Her curls were held back by a pink bandana. She looked gorgeous, but . . .

'Did you have to wear pink today, Tamsin?' I said.

'A new start for all of us, Pip dear.' she said with her arms folded. 'You—we—are leaving the past behind us. I found the T-shirt at one of the stores in the shopping street, and I couldn't resist. It's loose enough not to cling to any wobbly bits.'

'Oh, for goodness sake,' I said crossly, forgetting about the pink. 'You look great. I'll forget about pink if you accept that you are *not* fat.'

Tam bobbed her head, and the two high pigtails jiggled, and she looked about eighteen. 'All right, I will. And pink will be fine anyway.'

'Hope so,' I muttered as I picked up the coffee pot and poured a straight black before I sat down.

'Excited, Pippa?' Nell was dressed in her usual khaki shorts and T-shirt.

'A bit. I couldn't sleep,' I replied after the first slug of coffee hit my bloodstream. 'I was up at the crack of dawn and went for a walk. To be honest, I've been worrying about what we're going to find there.'

'Better to be realistic and not be disappointed,' Tam said.

Nell stood and went over to the breakfast bar and came back with a plate loaded with fresh fruit. 'For sharing.'

'Thanks, Nellie,' I said.

'Have I got time to have a hot brekky?' Tam asked. 'The menu looks interesting, and I want to see how they present it.'

I pulled out my phone and checked the time. 'We have thirty-five minutes to eat and get to the marina, so you'll have to be quick.'

'We'll need the energy.' Tam jumped up and went over to the waitress to place her order.

I picked up a small piece of watermelon and nibbled on it. 'I don't think I can eat anything much.'

'You okay, sweets?' Nell asked. 'You look a bit pale on it.'

'Yeah. Just nervous. I wonder if I've made a huge mistake. Maybe I should have stayed away and just put Aunty Vi's house on the market. If this doesn't work out, it's going to be twice as hard to leave the island again.'

Nell shook her head. 'What happened to the two Ps? Positivity, Pip!'

I chuckled. 'I guess Darren and losing my job happened. You're right, Nell. I've been in a strange mood since dinner last night. I need to pull myself up. It will be fine, and if it's not, we'll make sure it is.'

'That's better.' Nell nodded and smiled.

Twenty minutes later, Tam had demolished the strangest-looking—green—eggs I had ever seen— and Nell and I had cleared the fruit plate. I stood and gestured to the door.

'Come on, you pair, the first day of the rest of our lives is about to begin.' I giggled. 'Tam, you've got egg yolk all the way down the front of your fancy pink T-shirt. You'll have to get changed, love.'

I couldn't help my smirk.

'Can't take you anywhere.' Nell nudged Tam and giggled with me.

'I'll go and sponge it in the ladies.' Tam flounced off, and Nell's infectious giggle made me smile.

Tam was quick. We loaded our bags into one of the electric buggies at reception and were down at the marina in no time.

'Hey, Pippa! Over here.' Jiminy called from a boat halfway along the first wharf, and we wheeled our suitcases down the ramp and along the wharf. Even though it was coming into winter, the sun was warm. The water glistened as the seabirds swooped overhead. My mood kept improving with each step I took.

'Morning, gals. It's a great day to be on the water.'

'Nice boat, Jim,' I said.

'She is, and even better, she's all mine.'

An engine roared on the other side of the wharf, and a huge black speedboat took off into the channel, leaving a wake of white foam behind.

'But a man can dream,' Jiminy said, gesturing towards the black boat that was quickly disappearing. 'One day, I might have something like that. If I win Lotto, that is.'

I gestured to the rows of luxury boats opposite where his boat was berthed. 'There seems to be more expensive boats here than when I caught the ferry to school.'

He nodded. 'There's a lot on international boaties make the

marina their home base, and they sail and motor around the islands in the winter.'

'Did you hear that, Tam? If we could set up some sort of mooring, there's an instant clientele for the restaurant.'

'Big plans, Pippa?' Jiminy said.

We hadn't gone into much detail when we'd visited his place yesterday.

'Some plans, but we have to suss out the island first. It's a while since I've been there.'

'Be prepared,' he said. 'Years of tropical growth, a cyclone and a couple of big blows might have done some damage to the old house.'

'Only one way to find out. Are we ready to go?'

'Yep. Your provisions were delivered half an hour ago, and they're stored below.'

'Thank you.' I turned to Jiminy. 'Let's go!'

The deck vibrated beneath my feet as he started the motors. I found a spot near the helm and stared ahead, waiting for that first magnificent view of Pentecost Island to appear as we rounded the point. Centuries of volcanic debris had fused into solid rock, and the way that my island—*yes, my island*—rose from the depths of the Coral Sea was nothing short of spectacular. The first time I saw it as a lonely eleven-year-old, it made a tremendous impression that stayed with me over the years.

Magical was the word I'd used back in those early days with Aunty Vi.

It had been magical. I had healed on that island, and I had learned to be strong and independent.

It was time to do it again.

Jiminy steered us out into the passage and headed south, following in the wake of the black boat. He put his hands to his eyes as he looked ahead. 'I thought it might have been.'

'Might have been what?' I asked.

'Your neighbour on the island. He has a boat like that, but it's unusual to see him out and about. You never know, you might be lucky enough to meet him on your first day.'

I shook my head. 'No, my first day is going to be spent having a look at the place. Is there phone service this far out, Jim?'

'Yes, there's service all the way down to the Shaw group of islands these days.' He turned the boat in a wide arc to miss the rocky peninsula as we neared the southern point of Hamilton Island.

'There she is,' I exclaimed excitedly as my impressive island came into view. She rose almost two hundred metres above the sea at her highest point, and it wasn't until you got close that you could see the wide and flat parts of the island around the base of the mountain. Aunty Vi's house was tucked into the side of the hill overlooking a bay on the north side of the volcanic peak. According to Jiminy, the new neighbour's house would be far away enough not to bother us. At a pinch, we might see his lights at night, but I could live with that.

I just hoped that he could too.

The information that he was a recluse didn't reassure me. I wondered how he'd feel about a resort development on the island.

Anyway, we'd been here first. The house and island had been in the Carmichael family since the 1930s when the islands had first been settled. Hopefully, he wouldn't spend a lot of time here if he was some rich dude.

I leaned back with a contented sigh as Jiminy turned the boat towards Pentecost Island.

I was on my way home.

Chapter 11

Rafe

Jenny's flight to Cairns, the first leg of her flight home, left early, and I made a quick trip to the general provisions store on the island. I placed a large order for meat, fresh fruit, and vegetables and arranged to have them delivered to my boat immediately. The pantry in the house had enough dry goods to see me out a few more months. It cost me an extra fifty dollars on top of what I'd paid for the groceries to get it down there straight away, but it was worth every cent. I was anxious to get back to my island.

On the way to the marina, I called into the bottle shop and picked up a bottle of Glenfiddich whisky. I resisted the temptation to get half a dozen. I'd made Jenny a promise that I would start work and take comfort in no more than two whiskies each night, which would help me keep my promise.

Somehow, talking with Jenny opened up something in me. When I woke up in the hotel room this morning, the heavy feeling that pressed on my chest as soon as I became aware each day had lightened a little. I'm not sure where it came from, but I embraced that unfamiliar lightness.

Jenny had hugged me tight as I'd waited in the departure hall with her.

'You take care of yourself, Rafe. Bryant and I worry about you all the time. You are a dear friend, you know'—she held my gaze intently—'and we worry about you.'

I nodded tersely, quickly returned her hug, and stepped back. I was a typical Englishman, and I showed little emotion to the world. Maybe that was half of the problem as to why I was having trouble moving on with life.

PENTECOST ISLAND 1-3

An hour later, as I stood in my boat heading towards my island refuge, I realised that I felt better than I had in a long time.

It was a brilliant June day, and I drew in a deep breath and filled my lungs with clean, salt-laden air. The manor house in the Cotswolds she had suggested for "recovery" was not one bit tempting despite the wonderful location and cooler weather. For the first time, a smile tugged at my lips. I would seek my own healing here.

Jenny and Bryant were good friends; they were probably the only people in the world who knew where to find me and the only ones who cared.

I had no other friends left, and I had no wife.

I took a deep breath and inhaled the salty air to banish the anger that came knocking with that thought.

'I am in paradise,' I said beneath my breath. 'I own a beautiful house on a tropical island. Money is not a problem, and I have a book to finish. I promised Jenny, and I'll do my best to get something done.' Saying the words aloud made them real.

Maybe I should talk to myself more.

I glanced behind and eased back on the throttle as I approached Pentecost Island. When I'd seen the portion of the island advertised for sale, the name of the island had caught my attention.

I had flown down from Cairns to see the property, and the island had instantly hooked me. I'd wanted to isolate myself, and here was the perfect place to build the house I had always wanted. I made an offer to Vi Carmichael the same day. I had offered her triple what she was asking so I could buy the whole island, but she refused.

'Half or nothing. No point trying to make me budge, boy because I won't.'

She'd been an interesting woman, and once I accepted her terms, we sealed the deal with a handshake and a whisky. The plans for the house were already in my head, so I had them drawn up, signed a builder, and the house was finished within four months. Amazing how money talks.

I'd known—or hoped— that I could be happy in a beautiful setting like this.

The island is dramatic in the way it rises from the sea. Cloaked in forests of eucalypts and pine, with shadowy gullies of rainforest as you climb around the mountain, there are many places you can walk. Rocky granite outcrops amongst the forest add to the desolate geology of the island. On each end of the island is a swathe of verdant green grass. My home sat above one such clearing, and the other grassy flat is near the old abandoned house on the north end of my bay.

As I turned, I spotted two sailing catamarans heading south towards Shaw Island. Behind them was a motor launch, which, as I watched, turned to the portside and headed towards the island.

Since the cyclone that had hit the region in the first month after my arrival, the bay on the north-western side was impassable. There was only one entry into the bay on the eastern side beneath my house on the cliff now, and to my knowledge, it was not widely known. I had watched a few catamarans come to grief at low tide on the exposed reef where the previous entrance to the channel on the northern point had once let boats enter. Ma Carmichael had told me that over the years, it had been a popular place for an overnight mooring, and she had called it Happy Bay.

'I made lots of friends from all over the world on those years,' she'd told me one night as we sat on my veranda overlooking the mooring. 'But when my niece came to live with me, I didn't think it was the right thing to do. Partying down on the sand each night with folk who were looking for good times in happy company. Over the years when Pippa was here, fewer boats came to moor in my bay each winter.' She'd lifted the tumbler to her lips and sighed. 'When Pippa left for university, I figured I was

PENTECOST ISLAND 1-3

too old for that party scene these days.'

Pippa! I knew I'd heard that name before when the woman in the restaurant had called out last night.

Surely that beautiful woman wasn't the same Pippa that Ma had talked about? It would be too much of a coincidence.

As I eased my craft through the passage between the coral heads, I stared at the launch that was stopped at the outer edge of the bay. The skipper was pointing across the bay to where the old house was hidden behind the forest. I cut the engine, and I waited and watched. The old house at that end was a solid structure and had survived the recent cyclone. It had been empty since Ma had left, and the only life there now was the wild goats I occasionally saw. The last time I had walked over there, the trees had grown over the house like a canopy, increasingly encroaching on the dwelling.

A couple of times, the skipper ventured close to the reef, but he obviously knew what he was doing because he pulled up each time he came close to the coral that would be exposed at low tide.

To my dismay, on his third attempt, he somehow crossed the coral, and the boat made its way to the shore.

What the hell did he think he was doing?

There were others on the boat with him, and I stared, waiting to see what they were going to do. Technically, they had every right to be there as my property boundary extended only halfway along the bay, but on the few occasions that boats had managed to moor at my end of the island over the past months, they'd listened to me and had soon left when I told them it was private land. I watched as he climbed over and untied the rope of the tender and motored into the shore. He tied the rope around a lone palm tree on the beach and then got back into the tender and headed back to the launch. As I watched, a woman on board passed him two white boxes. The same ones that the provisions came in from the general store.

This wasn't looking good.

Once he'd put them down, a second woman passed him a couple of crates, and then a third woman appeared and passed some more boxes over.

Once they were loaded, he pulled the rope above the tender that was now secured to the launch, and that way, he was able to pull the boat right up onto the beach. He unloaded the boxes and crates and then pulled his way back to the launch.

Bloody hell.

This time there were suitcases, swags and backpacks offloaded.

What did they think they were doing?

I started the motor and eased into the small wharf that I had built at the base of the cliff. I quickly unloaded my provisions, placed the bottle of whisky into my backpack and carried them up the steep path to the house.

When I reached the top, I turned around. The sound of the launch starting, drifted up to me.

The vessel was leaving the bay, and, to my dismay, three women stood waving to the skipper. My stomach sank as I recognised them.

It *was* Ma Carmichael's Pippa.

##

Pippa

Jiminy was full of apologies that he didn't have time to come to the house with us.

'I've only got another half hour to get Baden to Daydream Island,' he said apologetically. 'Who'd ever have thought that a kids' party would be held at a resort!'

'It's fine,' I said. 'I really appreciate you bringing us over today. I wish you'd let me pay you for your time.'

He shook his head emphatically. 'A favour for a friend, Pippa. I just wish I had time to help you up to the house, and more important, check it's habitable.'

I waved my hand dismissively. 'It will be fine. Now that I know there's phone service out here'—Tam had kept a check on it the whole boat trip across— 'I'll give you a call in a day or so.'

'And if there's any problem settling in today, you call me this afternoon. Okay?'

'I promise. Now go. You don't want to be late getting your son to the party!'

Jimmy turned back to the boat and paused. 'Ah, I forgot. Did you think of buying diesel for the generator?'

'Um, no.' I shook my head.

He pulled himself along to the boat and disappeared below deck. A moment later, he reappeared, holding up a plastic fuel container. 'Take this. I doubt there will be any at the house. This should keep you going for a few days.'

'Thank you. That was the one thing I didn't even consider. I'll pay you for that.'

'Next time,' Jiminy flashed a grin, and within a minute, the boat was pulling away between the coral heads.

When the shingly sand on the beach crunched beneath my bare feet, I knew I was home. All my doubts faded, and happiness filled me. Although a little bit of sadness tugged, knowing that Aunty Vi wasn't up in the house waiting for me, in the time that had passed since her death, I had adjusted. At least she'd not spent a long time in the aged care home. Even though she'd tried to tell me she enjoyed living there, I'd heard the sadness in her voice when she'd talked about the island. But being away from here, it had been easy to forget and cope with grieving. This was where she had lived for most of her life. Aunty Vi had been a caring woman, and she had taught me so much when I turned up at her doorstep. She'd taught me to believe in myself, and she taught me to trust myself. I was angry that I'd let Darren— and Eric in his own way—take that away from me over the past couple of years.

'Promise you'll go back there one day, Pippa,' she'd said the last time I'd spoken to her.

'I promise.' But never had I imagined it would be so soon.

I was here now, and life was going to be good. I had a goal, and I knew Aunty Vi would have approved.

'How about we call it Aunty Vi's place?' I turned to see Tam and Nell watching me. I looked around and then down at the suitcases and boxes.

Tam shook her head. 'And you call yourself a marketer? Doesn't appeal to me. No one would know who Aunty Vi was.'

Nell pointed to the boxes. 'We'd better get the food out of the sun.'

'How about we just carry everything up and put it under the trees there in the shade? It's not too hot yet, and then we'll go and check out the house.' Tam's smile was as wide as mine.

It took three trips to carry our luggage and the boxes from where Jiminy had placed them near the edge of the water up to the shade at the edge of the forest.

'Do you remember how to get to the house?' Tam asked quietly.

'Of course I do. I lived here for eight years, remember? I was almost nineteen when I left.'

'That's over ten years ago,' Nell said.

'What's with the age thing? Please stop reminding us that we are heading for thirty.'

'Well, thirty doesn't bother me,' said Tam. 'I'll wear it like a badge of honour.'

'I'll remember that and give you a big three O badge next May,' I joked as I turned towards the gap in the trees where the path to the house began. I stood where the butterflies used to come out of the dark forest, and when I saw the path, my pace quickened as anticipation kicked in.

Home.

I could hear Tam and Nell behind me as my feet took me towards the house. They seemed to know where to go without any conscious thought. Although the path was overgrown, it was still easy to see where it had led for almost a hundred years.

Tree branches met in a beautiful lacy green arch above my head, and I just had to keep an eye out for the occasional log that had fallen across the path. When I came to the small clearing where the path intersected with the track that led up to the mountain, both paths were blocked with fallen trees. It didn't bode well for the site of the house. I'd heard that it had been a ripper of a cyclone that had pummelled the islands for almost thirty-six hours. I stood with my hands on my hips and looked around for the best way to get through. On the mountainside, there was a narrow gap between the fallen trees.

'Are there snakes on the island?" Nell's voice was hesitant as she caught me up. 'Will there be any under those dead trees?'

'No snakes, just death adders.'

'What!'

'And just some tree snakes and the odd brown snake and. They won't hurt you unless you stand on one.'

'Gee, thanks, Pip. You've filled me with confidence.'

'It's okay. I never saw one snake the whole time I lived here.'

Tam caught up, and Nell stayed close as we squeezed through the narrow gap on the right of the fallen trees. Lizards and unseen creatures scuttled in the forest on either side, and birds sang above us. It was almost as though they were greeting me.

The house was only a couple of hundred metres from the shore, but it was well hidden, tucked into the side of a small hill that protected it from the prevailing winds. Until you reached the grassy glade where the house was, you never would have guessed there was a building in the forest.

I pushed aside the foliage of the large, broad-leaved bottle tree that had been there for many years. I'd spent a lot of time up that tree pretending I was in the Enid Blyton Magic Faraway tree when I was a child.

The book had probably been too young for the twelve-year-old I had been, but Aunty Vi had introduced me to fantasy books. I would climb that tree when I felt sad. As the years passed, the memory of my Mum and Dad had faded and the time that I spent up there lessened.

I stepped into the glade and drew a deep breath.

Taking a step towards the house I jumped as a bird squawked and flew off protesting as his peace was disturbed. Tam and Nell stepped out of the forest behind me.

'Oh wow, it looks the same as I remember,' Nell exclaimed.

Apart from the encroaching vegetation, the house itself didn't look any different, and I bit my lip as my heart filled with emotion. Aunty Vi wouldn't be stepping out to greet me like she always had when I came home from school. A couple of fallen trees blocked the path and I stepped around them and walked slowly across to the steps.

'I'd forgotten what a big house it was,' Tam said. 'I guess I thought it seemed big because I was a kid at the time I came to visit you, but it is huge. Look at the verandah. It goes all the way around.'

'And look at those trees. I remember when we came to visit, you took us up a hill and made us climb a tree behind you so we could see all the islands from the top,' Nell said. 'I remember how scared I was.'

'And your Aunty Vi told us how, whenever she couldn't

PENTECOST ISLAND 1-3

find you, you were guaranteed to be up a tree somewhere.'

'It wasn't that often,' I protested, reaching out and touching the handrail. It was in good condition—surprisingly, all the outside timber seemed to be. I put my head back and looked up. The roof looked okay, too; I couldn't see anything loose or broken. How had it escaped the ferocity of that cyclone?

'Do you have a key?' Tam asked.

I patted the small bag that was on my hip. 'I do. Mr Morton gave it to me when I went to Mackay.' I grinned. 'Just as well, Darren was gone before I heard about my inheritance.'

Tam nodded. 'The smartest thing you ever did was chuck him out. Otherwise, he might have been here with you today and not us.'

'Maybe,' I said as I climbed the steps, the key clenched in my hand.

I'd been so focused on my own issues I hadn't thought to ask the solicitor what was at the house. I knew so little about what Aunty Vi had done when she left.

Guilt lay heavily on me, and I lifted my chin as I stepped onto the verandah. It was covered with leaves and animal droppings, and the furniture that had once been here was gone.

I wondered whether it had been taken away or whether it had blown away in the cyclone. Aunty Vi had been on the mainland by then, and I'd called to check she was okay.

God, I'd been slack. It was as though I had totally shut out memories of my life up here.

And my life before I'd moved north to live with Aunty Vi.

Even when I'd talked to the therapist I'd seen for a few months after Aunty Vi had died, I hadn't ever mentioned that her death was the catalyst for my mood swings.

The front door was closed and locked, and the curtains were closed on the windows that faced the verandah.

A cloud passed over the sun, and a shiver ran down my

back. The air was still and quiet, as though the natural world was holding its breath like I was. I jumped as Tam and Nell came up close behind me.

'Come on, Pip. Let's get inside. We need to check it out and get the food up here to the house.'

I turned around. 'Now that we know the house is intact, do you want to go and start bringing it here while I check out the inside.' I needed to be alone, but that wasn't going to happen.

Tam shook her head. 'No way. We want to see it too.'

'Okay.' I put the key in the lock and turned it. In all the time I'd lived here, the door was never closed, let alone locked.

The heavy wooden door opened with a creak. Tam and Nell were close behind me as I stepped inside. There was a small room inside the front entry, where I'd left my shoes, school bag and raincoat when I'd come off the boat every Friday.

The room was empty. No hats or rain gear hanging on the large hooks. I pushed open the door that led into the lounge room.

My eyes widened as they adjusted to the dim interior. The room was bare. A fine layer of dust covered the floorboards, but that's all that was in the room. Faded squares on the cream-painted walls were all that remained of the paintings that had once hung there.

I walked across the room slowly, and my sandals made little noise on the dusty floor. 'This goes through to the kitchen,' I said. 'Brace yourselves, ladies. This is going to let us know how much we're going to have to rough it for a while.'

I breathed a sigh of relief as I walked into the kitchen. The scrubbed pine table and the eight chairs were still in the middle of the old-fashioned kitchen, and a variety of pots and pans hung over the gas stove that was set back into an alcove.

'Hmmm. I didn't think of gas either, 'I said. 'I've gone soft. Too used to electric light switches and microwaves at my fingertips.'

PENTECOST ISLAND 1-3

Tam walked past me and opened some of the cupboards. 'There's still dishes and things in here, but they're going to need a good wash.'

Nell crossed to the sink and turned the tap on. There was a grinding noise and then a splutter as brown-stained water spat out of the tap into the sink. She let it run, and it gradually cleared. 'We have water,' she said triumphantly. 'Come on, Tam, we'll go back and start bringing the gear back. Pip, while you look around, see if you can find a broom, and I'll sweep through the kitchen before we put everything in here until we get sorted.'

'Thank you. I really appreciate you both being here with me. I'll check out the rest of the house, and then I'll come and help.'

I was getting used to being here, and Aunty Vi's absence wasn't hurting as much. Tam and Nell headed back outside, and I walked up the hallway that led to the bedrooms and to the large room at the back that Aunty Vi had called her studio. She'd dabbled in painting when I was a teenager, and it had been her space. You only ever went in there if you were invited. I poked my head into the rooms along the hall as I made my way to the back of the house, and they were all the same as the lounge room. Dust-covered wooden floors and bare walls. The windows were shut tight, and the curtains were closed to keep the light out.

The studio was the same when I opened the door. I had my own space—you couldn't really call it a bedroom—on the verandah on the opposite side of the house. It had timber shutters that rolled down from the ceiling, and I used to shut them to keep the weather—and the insects—out. Some nights, I'd leave them open while I got sleepy, and I'd lie there and look up at the stars.

Aunty Vi had always told me that my Mum and Dad's spirits were up there in the stars, and some nights, I had looked so hard that my eyes would ache and water.

I walked through the bathroom and smiled at the pink

shower curtain that I had forgotten about. The door to the verandah was closed, and I turned the handle and stepped into the room that had been mine.

My breath caught as I stared around. I blinked, and my hand went automatically to the cord that I had used to pull to turn the light on, but of course, there was no power.

The room was as I had left it when I went off to university. The bed still had a green chenille coverlet on it, and the bookshelf at the head of my bed was still full of my books. I walked to the end of the verandah and pulled open the curtains that covered the small window near the door that led out to the open verandah.

I shook my head. It was as though I had never left. My posters were still on the walls, and the teenage possessions I had left behind were still on the cupboard. Aunty Vi had believed me when I'd promised I'd come back one day. She must have instructed that my room remained untouched.

My legs trembled as I walked back to the bed, sat down, and picked up the dog-eared copy of the *Magic Faraway Tree.*

Chapter 12

Tam

Tam looked across at Pippa. When they'd come back with the last load of boxes, Pippa's eyes had been red; she'd obviously had a weep but had pulled herself together before the girls returned.

'Thanks for carrying it all in. I feel slack. Sit down for a while, and I'll dig us out a cold drink.' Pippa went over to the eskies.

The three of them pitched in, and by late afternoon, the house had been swept out, swags had been set up, and now they were in the living room lit by half a dozen candles sitting on plates on an upturned box that had held some of the provisions. The eskies were in the kitchen, and the dry food had been stowed securely in a cupboard.

'Shame it's just the three of us sitting here tonight. It's quite romantic, isn't it, girls?' Tam said as she looked around. Pippa and Nell both looked tired, and Pippa had a smudge of dirt on her nose.

Pippa snorted. 'I don't know about romantic; all I know is I'm tired.'

Nell held up her phone. 'It might be romantic, but the only thing I'm worried about is how to charge my phone and laptop.'

'Don't worry now. I'll get the generator going tomorrow. I've just got to put the diesel in and do something.' Pippa giggled.

'Do something?' Tam shook her head and chuckled. 'You've always been such a hands-on person, Pip.'

Pippa pulled a face at Tam. 'When I look at the generator tomorrow, I'm sure I'll remember what we used to do. If not, I'll get someone over from the mainland to show us.'

'Or I can Google it,' Nell offered.

Tam gestured to the eskies in the kitchen. 'We've got enough ice to last us for a couple of days and a swag each, and we are on the island. What more could we ask for?'

Pippa raised her eyebrows. 'Electricity, real beds, and a plan.' She hesitated. 'And about a million other things I could think of if I wasn't so tired.'

'Well. I don't think we need to rush these things, do we, Nell?' Tam looked across the room. 'It's all about mindfulness. Living in the moment. And hey, what a real moment. On a tropical island with my two best friends and an exciting future to plan.'

Tam had shared her concern about Pippa with Nell earlier when they'd carried the boxes up from the beach. Pippa had been sweeping the house out, and Tam had voiced her concerns. They'd both promised to help keep her spirits up.

'I think it's a great idea and such a windfall for Pip, but I don't know whether she's put enough thought into it. I know her heart's in creating a resort here, and that's what we have to trust and back her up.'

'It came too soon on top of Darren doing the dirty and losing her job,' Nell said. 'I worry that she's grasping at straws and letting her memories sway her.'

'Maybe.' Tam had nodded. 'Just look at it this way. She owns the house and half of this island. I think if we can help her settle emotionally and give her as much help as we can, she'll be fine.' They linked fingers and made a pact before they came back to the house.

Tam looked across at Pippa now. Her face was shadowed in the flickering candlelight, but she looked calm. 'What do you girls fancy for dinner?' Tam pushed herself to her feet. 'What gourmet meal would you like me to whip up?'

Pippa waved a lazy hand. 'Surprise us.'

PENTECOST ISLAND 1-3

'Does anyone want a wine while I cook?' Tam asked, crossing to the esky.

Pippa shook her head. 'Not for me. As soon as we eat, I'm going to crash. We've got a big day tomorrow. Cleaning up and lots of plans to make.'

'And don't forget you have to get the generator going,' Nell interjected

'Yes, getting the power going is a priority.' Pippa nodded and yawned at the same time. 'I shouldn't have got up so early this morning and gone for that run up to the lookout.'

Tam ferreted around in the kitchen and made them each a baguette with potato salad, pastrami, and a dab of dressing from the special bottle she'd slipped into her luggage. She was looking forward to thinking about food again, and that gave her motivation to get in and help Pippa get the house cleaned up and ready to start planning. Tam yawned and pushed her plate aside. 'I'd kill for a coffee.'

'Unless you feel like going out and lighting a fire, you're going to have to do without your coffee tonight, love,' Pippa said as she stood. 'We've got plenty of water, although I suppose we do need to conserve it until we can find out what we've got here.' She collected Tam and Nell's plates and turned to the kitchen in the dim light. 'Once I get the power going, I'd like the three of us to sit down tomorrow and make a list of what we need to do first to make this place liveable, and then we'll start a feasibility study of whether the old place is worth doing up.'

Tam and Nell exchanged a worried glance as Pippa's voice trembled.

'Let's all call it a night. Pip, we'll have this place shipshape and up and running before we can blink. Not the resort; I mean, just for us to live here while we plan. Leave those plates. We'll clean up in the morning when we can see what we're doing.' Tam stood and yawned again. ' All this fresh air is killing me. Oh,

98

Pippa, I forgot to tell you.'

'Tell me what?'

Tam slapped a hand lightly against her forehead. 'How could I have forgotten? When we were at the shops at Hamilton Island on Friday, you'll never guess who I bumped into.'

'Chris Hemsworth,' Pip said with a grin.

Tam shook her head. 'I wish. No, it was Evie Bannister.'

'Evie from uni?'

'That's the one.'

'On holidays on Hamo?'

'No,' Tam's voice was excited. 'Would you believe she works there? She told me to tell you if you're ever looking for anyone to help with the landscaping, she's available for contract work.'

'You told her about what we were planning here?' Pippa frowned.

'No. I mean, I didn't tell her that it was your resort. I said we were coming back here to do up your aunt's place, and she said if you were looking for a landscape gardener, she could help out. It could be useful in a while.'

Pippa nodded. 'I always liked Evie. I've still got her number on my phone. I'll give her a call and see if she'd like to come out and have a look around in a week or two. It's one thing that we can get started without much cost. Just getting the tracks clear and planning where we can have our walks will be a good start to the outside and activities that we might plan.'

Tam was pleased when Pippa's shoulders straightened, and the spark came back into her eyes.

'So, tell me before we call it a night. What's your gut feeling? How you feel now that you're on the island? Do you still want to go ahead with this crazy plan of yours?'

'Crazy? Don't tell me you don't want to stay?'

Tam shook her head with a smile. 'I'm keen, but I think we

should take a couple of weeks and have a bit of a break and let you settle.'

'What do you mean settle?'

'You've seemed a bit anxious, I guess. Just over the last few weeks, and a bit more before, when we came back with the boxes.'

Nell nodded. 'But if this is what you want, Tam and I are both happy to help and stay here with you.'

Pippa walked over and stood beside her two friends. 'I love that you care about me enough to be worried, girls, but I've never been so sure of anything in my life.' She reached over and looped her arms around Tam and Nell's shoulders. 'Look at this place. Look at the potential, and more than that, for me, it's home. I'm really happy to be here. I just got a bit teary when I went back to my old room, and Aunty Vi had everything left there the way it used to be. I guess she always knew I'd come back one day.

'I want to do her proud and build up the best resort we can. No two weeks of thinking about it. I've made my mind up. Are you in?'

There was no hesitation as Tam and Nell looked at each other and nodded before completing a circle with their arms.

'We're in.'

Chapter 13

Pippa

I woke up at dawn the next morning. I'd opted to leave my swag, and I came into my old room, swept it out, opened the blinds, and pulled down the flyscreens. I grabbed the light blanket out of my suitcase and put it on the bed.

Waking up in my childhood bed was a strange feeling but a good one. I lay there for a few minutes, watching the sunlight play on the wall. The leaves of the tree outside my room formed lacy patterns on the wall as the first breeze of the day puffed in. The winter season was ahead, and the prevailing winds were always from the southeast. A small gecko scurried across the ceiling as I watched, and I smiled, wondering what other wildlife was in the house.

If there was one thing Nell hated, it was critters of any sort. Spiders, snakes, cockroaches, bugs; I wondered how she'd cope in the tropics where they were all bigger and there were more of them. Before she'd climbed into her swag last night, she had shone her flashlight in all the dark corners of the living room and then scurried in, quickly zipping herself in.

'I feel quite safe in here,' she said. 'I might sleep in my swag even when we get the place sorted.' Tam and I had looked at each other and burst out laughing.

'I'm serious,' came the response from within the zipped-up swag.

'We can do mosquito nets,' I said.

'I'll think about it,' was the muffled response.

I'd blown the candles out and used the flashlight app on my phone; there was just enough light to make my way to the door. I slipped out onto the verandah and sat on the steps for a while before I'd headed to my bed. The sky was ablaze with stars and the only sound was the gentle wash of the water on the beach below us. It was as though the Gold Coast and my life down there had never happened.

I was so grateful to Nell and Tamsin for coming to the island. They had put their trust in me, and that was another reason to work hard and get this place up and running. The pressure that had been on me had dissipated. I hadn't missed Darren one bit and I realised what a lucky escape I'd had. I'd made some poor choices but the energy and passion I had put into my career down there was now going to be redirected, and it was up to me to make this venture succeed.

I smiled as I made my way along the verandah to my bed, excited about what the next weeks would bring.

I'd slept deeply and without dreaming, and when I woke, I felt renewed, full of life and energy and ready to face what the day would bring.

I climbed out of bed and pulled on a light cotton jumper and a pair of loose pants. My sneakers were by the door where I had left them, and I slipped into them and then pulled my hair back into a ponytail.

There was no sign of life in the living room from the two swags, just a light occasional snuffle from Tam's swag.

I opened the door quietly and stepped out into the morning.

The air was clean and pure, and silence surrounded me. No sound of traffic roaring up the Gold Coast Highway, and no garbage trucks clanging and banging as they emptied bins.

With a smile I picked up a long stick and set off up the track. Now don't get me wrong, I wasn't going to attempt the mountain this morning, but there was a hill to the east overlooking the valley that also gave a spectacular view of the water.

I also had an ulterior motive. From the first hill I'd get a clear view of the new house that I'd seen across the bay when we came in on the boat yesterday. You couldn't see the house once you reached the sand, and I was curious about the other inhabitant of the island and how having a neighbour was going to pan out.

He might be a recluse, and he might not like what I was going to do, but there was nothing he could do to stop us.

At least I didn't think there was. I'd go over this afternoon and introduce myself.

It would be much better to introduce myself and start up an amicable relationship and have him happy with what we were planning on doing.

'Pollyanna,' I muttered to myself. 'And pigs might fly.' If what Jiminy had heard was correct we were in for a battle.

I grinned. And if there was one thing I had thrived on in the workplace and done very well in, it was developing strategies to get what I wanted.

I came to the place where the path to the mountain and Red Wave Wall crossed the beach track, and I began to climb. Half an hour later I'd shed my cotton jumper and was down to my T-shirt and long pants. I reached the flat ledge halfway up the hill where I knew I'd get the first decent view of my neighbour's house.

I drew in a deep breath and my fingertips tingled with excitement as I turned to survey the vista in front of me.

It was too early for much water traffic out on the Whitsunday Passage, but in the distance, I could see a couple of catamarans heading south, their headsails white and billowing in the wind.

Another brilliant day beckoned as the sky and the sea melded together in a deep turquoise. A couple of fluffy clouds drifted in from the east, but they soon dissipated. I was surprised at how clear the track was. It had been more heavily vegetated when I'd lived here ten years ago; I wouldn't be surprised to find that our neighbour was using it. Either that or there'd been a lot of hikers or

PENTECOST ISLAND 1-3

birdwatchers, but Jiminy had said very few came to the island now. I frowned as I remembered that there had been quite a few climbers attempting the peak and Red Wave Wall when I'd lived with Aunty Vi. Another market for our resort. Rock climbers, birdwatchers, and those who simply wanted to chill. I was even considering a spa idea; I had some great marketing ideas for a pamper package, and I knew there was a market there for that service.

Excitement sizzled through me as I thought of the different services our resort could offer.

I always thought of the project in terms of *our* resort; it was going to be a group venture—Tam and Nell were as big a part of it as I was.

I turned slowly to look at the house on the hill opposite. For a moment I couldn't see it and then I nodded slowly.

Very clever.

The house had been built to blend into the environment. In fact, if you didn't know it was there you would probably glance around and not notice it nestled into the hillside. The timber work was a natural colour, and the roof was green. As I looked, I could see the shape of the building. The morning sunlight reflected off one window in a bright flash. There was no sign of life, but it was early, and most people wouldn't be up and about yet. I wondered if anyone lived there with him.

I sat on the wide rock ledge and drew my knees up to my chin. I wasn't going to worry about anything.

Worrying about a problem wouldn't change it, or make it go away. Aunty Vi had taught me that. She had made me confront my fears and talk about the things that mattered to me. And she'd taught me what was important. I think she would have been a bit disappointed in me over the past few years. I'd made some poor choices: Darren and the job I'd put all of my energy into.

Then again, she'd been astute, and we'd spoken regularly

until she'd passed away. I knew she would have had a reason for leaving me half the island. And I wasn't going to let her down.

I let the beauty of the island seep into my soul and whispered under my breath 'Aunty Vi, I promise you that I'm going to make this a place you would have been so proud of.'

The sun climbed higher as I sat there, and finally it was the grumbling of my stomach that pushed me to move. I stood, ready to go back to the house and start work.

One last look at the beautiful view for the morning. I turned my head and scanned the water from south to north. A sea eagle swooped above me and then down to the water; my gaze followed it to a motor launch making its way past the island. As I stared out over the water the sound of stones rolling down the hill brought me out of my reverie.

I turned as the noise got louder, and I tensed, wondering if I was about to be confronted by one of the wild goats that had been on the island since being introduced, and then abandoned back in the 1930s.

There hadn't been many of them left when I'd lived here but we used to see the occasional one in the drier months as they foraged closer to the house for food. I stood back and waited, hoping it wasn't a buck because they could get quite nasty. My stomach gurgled again, but this time it was from nerves rather than hunger.

I frowned as the noise got closer. They weren't goat footsteps; there was somebody up the track and walking down the hill towards where I was standing. I glanced down to the beach, but there was no boat or tender pulled up onto the sand. I wondered whether there were hikers or birdwatchers who had come onto the island from the bay around the other side.

A man appeared around the bend in the track.

He pulled up short when he saw me, and my mouth dropped at the same instant that his eyes widened. A strange feeling rippled through me.

His voice was quiet as he came down the last small incline and stood beside me. 'Hello, so we meet again.' He didn't seem the slightest bit surprised that the woman he'd met on One Tree Hill yesterday morning was now on a hill on an island a few kilometres away from Hamilton Island.

The same man who had stared at me in the restaurant two nights ago.

'What are you doing on my island?' I asked, determined to take the upper hand. And if I was honest, I wanted to take control of the conversation because looking at him made me feel strange. 'Are you following me? And where's your boat?'

But it was as though I hadn't spoken.

'Can I ask you something?' he said. His eyes hadn't left mine, and heat ran into my face.

I wasn't scared of him. Somehow, I knew he represented no danger to me, but I still wanted to know what he was doing here. A suspicion half-formed in my mind as I looked back down at the bay and confirmed that there was no boat moored there. Only the black boat owned by my neighbour. 'After you answer my question. What are you doing here? It's a private island and really not available for casual day-trippers.'

'I know I could ask you the same question.' His eyes were still intent on mine. 'What were you laughing about in the restaurant the other night. You and your friends?'

What was it with this guy? Had he thought we were laughing at him? Why did he want to know? Bizarre.

Without thinking the words tumbled from my lips. 'We were trying to think of a name for our—' I broke off. If he was who I thought he was, I wasn't going to tell him anything.

'For your . . .' he prompted.

'For my house.'

'Which house?'

'You are very curious, Mr—?'

He held out his hand and I took it reluctantly. My arm tingled as his fingers held mine.

'Rendell. Rafe Rendell. That is my house.' He gestured across the bay. 'And you are Pippa?'

I frowned and spoke slowly. 'Yes, Pippa Carmichael. How do you know who I am?'

'You're at Ma Carmichael's house?'

'I am.' I lifted my chin. 'Ma Carmichael? You knew my aunt?'

'I did. I met her before she moved away. She was a kind woman.' His eyes were distant now as though he was remembering Aunty Vi. 'I used to visit with her when my house was being built.' His voice faded and his eyes narrowed. 'She mentioned that she had a niece called Pippa who had lived here with her for a while.'

'Well that would be me.' I kept my eyes on him.

'I heard your friends call you the other night in the restaurant.'

'Well, Mr Rendell, she never once mentioned you, or the fact that you built a house on my island.'

His expression tightened. 'Your island?'

'Yes. My aunt has passed away, and I've inherited the island.'

'Not the island.' He shook his head. 'You may have had full access before. Maybe you're not aware of the fact that the island is now half mine. I don't want to share it with anyone, so I'm prepared to make you a very generous offer for the remainder.'

The remainder? Anger took root in my chest. He had totally dismissed the loss of Aunty Vi and wanted my island.

He could go take a flying leap.

The wind was picking up and even though we were in the tropics, it could be cold blowing off the water until the sun reached

PENTECOST ISLAND 1-3

its zenith in the winter, and I crossed my arms.

'Oh, are you now?' I said.

Anyone who knew me well would have recognised the tone in my voice. That was the one thing that Darren had taken notice of. He knew when my voice lowered to that level, it was time to take a hike and let me have my say.

'Yes, I am,' he said. 'Very generous.'

I held his gaze for a moment or two and he didn't look away.

I turned my back and walked down the hill without another word, but I was conscious of his eyes on me the whole way. It was a relief when the path turned into the shaded forest.

So much for starting off in an amicable relationship, Pollyanna.

But my temper didn't cool at all.

So, he would make me a very generous offer, would he?

Pah! Mr Rafe Rendell could try, but if anyone left the island it wasn't going to be me.

Chapter 14

Pippa

'Now you have to loosen the bleed screw a couple of turns,' Nell read from the generator manual that we'd found in the shed behind the house.

Tam leaned forward and she was so close to me her hair brushed against my cheek.

'Tam, move back. You're blocking my light,' I said as she peered over my shoulder. 'Okay. Got that. What now, Nell?'

'Pump the primer pump until diesel fuel comes out of the loose bleed screw,' Nell said slowly. 'Sheesh, Pip. This might as well be written in Chinese. It means nothing to me.'

I pressed the soft rubber button in and out a few times and smiled as diesel trickled onto my fingers. 'It's okay. I remember now. Aunty Vi let the generator run out of fuel a couple of times and this is what she did.' I sat back and rocked on my heels. 'It'll start now, so stand back, gals.'

I pressed the start button and the sound of the motor purring was like music to my ears, and it even made up for the stink of the diesel that pervaded the air and covered my fingers.

I turned to look at Tam.

Her grin was as wide as mine and she high-fived me. 'You rock, girlfriend.'

Nell took off as soon as the generator fired. 'Ew, it stinks.'

I picked up a rag and wiped the fuel off my fingers. I hated the smell of diesel. As soon as I'd walked into the small shed, I'd wrinkled my nose at the pungent smell. But with that smell came good memories, and now we had a generator humming along, and with it, power to the house.

I gestured to the door and Tam followed me out into the fresh air. Nell was standing beside the clothes line.

'Now what?' she asked.

'Now we have electricity that means lights and power points.'

'And that means I can charge my phone!' Nell hurried towards the house.

By the time Tam and I reached the back steps, Nell was inside.

'And that means we can have a hot breakfast. If there is power, I can use that skillet pan that I saw in the pantry to cook us an omelette. What do you think?' Tam asked.

'Sounds good to me. First thing I'm going to do is have a wash.'

When I'd got back from my walk up the hill, Tam and Nell had been up and dressed. The first thing I'd wanted to do was try to get the power going so we'd headed straight out to the shed.

I didn't tell them about my meeting with Mr Rafe Rendell straight up, as Nell was intent on telling me about the lizard that had been in the hallway when she'd headed to the bathroom.

'They're harmless, just skinks.' I said. 'You'll get used to them. And I'm sorry, it was my fault. I opened the blinds when I went to bed so I could see the stars. It would have come in that way.'

Getting the generator going had restored my confidence. I honestly thought that we'd have to get someone over to help us but doing it myself gave me a huge boost. Having power would make such a difference, but I had to remember to get enough diesel to keep it running. It would mean a trip over to Hamilton Island, or even a phone call to see if we could get a delivery. It was the sort of thing I'd taken for granted when I'd lived here. Aunty Vi had just kept things running, and I'd been oblivious to how it all came together. I didn't even recall her going to Hamilton Island or the mainland, and I guess she got stuff delivered back in those days.

Keeping my mind on those day-to-day problems we would face meant that I wasn't thinking about meeting my neighbour on the hill. He'd really pissed me off with his attitude and his plummy voice. He obviously thought he was something special.

I curled my fingers into fists and frowned as my nails cut into my skin. The bloody hide of him. So, he wasn't prepared to share my island with me. He would buy it off me so he could have it all. Who the hell did he think he was?

Typical man. What was it about men these days? They were so bloody selfish. It was all about what *they* wanted.

What Jiminy had said about Rendell being rich must be true, because how many people would have enough money to offer to buy an island?

I pulled the bathroom door shut a little harder than I should, and it closed with a bang. I strode down the hallway and Nell looked up from where she was sitting on the floor in front of a double power point. Her laptop and her phone were already plugged in, and I could see the charging lights glowing.

'What are you looking so cross about?' she asked with a frown. 'Is the power still on?' She leaned forward and looked at the phone.

'Power's fine,' I said. 'I was thinking about bloody men and how they always think they are so entitled.'

Her eyebrows shot up. 'Men? What men?'

'I met our neighbour when I went for my walk.'

Tam came in from the kitchen wiping her hands on a tea towel.

'The mysterious neighbour?'

I nodded. 'Yep, we only have the one. Thank God.'

'Did you go over there?' Tam turned back towards the kitchen door. 'Come in here and tell me about it, I've got butter melting in the pan. I just came to tell you both that I've boiled the

PENTECOST ISLAND 1-3

jug and we have coffee.'

Nell stood and we both followed Tam into the kitchen. The smell of chopped onion and herbs filled the kitchen with an enticing aroma and my mouth watered.

'Sit.' Tam pointed to the kitchen table.

We both did as directed, and I smiled as Tam slipped a cup of coffee across to me.

'Now, tell us about this guy.'

'I was on the hill when I heard footsteps. He was out walking on the hill too, and he came past where I was standing checking out his house.'

'Embarrassing.'

'No, not at all. I have a right to go wherever I want on my side of the island.'

'So what's he like?' Tam asked as she cracked eggs into the pan.

'I guess the old maxim would fit. Tall, dark and handsome.'

'Interesting,' Nell said.

I shook my head. 'No, he's arrogant. I didn't like him.' I cupped my hands around the coffee mug and inhaled. 'And he thinks he's going to buy my half of the island.'

'Really! What did you say?' Tam lifted the wooden spoon and looked across at me.

'Nothing. I gave him a very cold look, bid him a good day, and headed back here.'

'Hmm, a good neighbourly start,' Nell said.

'I'm not sorry. He started it. And he said he'd met Aunty Vi too.'

'So he's been here a while then?' Tam narrowed her eyes as she flipped the omelette.

'Apparently.'

Nell picked up her mug. 'I suppose you have to look at it

from his viewpoint. He's paid a fortune to buy his own island—'

'Uh uh.' I shook my head. 'Nell, It's not *his*. It's been in my Mum's family for almost a hundred years. He's bought a bit of it and built a house. I can't believe Aunty Vi sold off a portion of the island and didn't tell me.'

'Who wants toast?' Tam lifted the pan from the stove. 'I found the toaster in the pantry. Pippa, did you ever consider she might have done it to fund her move to the aged care facility? It meant she didn't have to sell the house and was able to keep that for your family and at least half the island. I'm sorry, chicky, but I think you're going to have to get used to having him here.'

I sipped my coffee. 'I'm going to go to see him and sort it out this afternoon. The sooner he knows that we're here to stay, the better. He might decide to go.'

'Did you find out his name?' Nell pushed her chair back. 'I'll get my laptop and Google him. If he's rich enough to buy half a tropical island there should be some mention of him somewhere.'

I waited until she came back to the table. 'Rafe Rendell.'

'Sexy name,' Tam said. 'How old is he?'

'You've already seen him. He was in the Italian restaurant the other night with a blonde woman. The one with the real diamond clip in her hair.'

Tam and Nell both looked at me blankly as Nell opened her laptop.

'Nope, didn't take much notice of who was in there. We were having fun deciding names for the resort,' Tam said. 'So how old?'

I shrugged. 'Maybe this side of forty.'

'And he has a wife here too?'

'I've got no idea. Whoever she was, I did notice they seemed to be fighting over dinner.'

'Ooh,' Tam said as she slid three loaded plates onto the table. 'More and more interesting.'

'I can't believe that neither of you noticed him.'

They both looked at me.

'You obviously did,' Nell said.

'I like observing others.' Heat ran up into my face.

'Especially good-looking others,' Tam said with a giggle. 'I'm quite looking forward to meeting our neighbour.'

'Can't find him.' Nell clicked on her keyboard with one hand and picked up her fork with the other. 'I'll have to try a deeper search strategy.'

Nell was our IT guru. If there was anything to be found on Rafe Rendell, she wouldn't give up until she'd discovered it.

'Jiminy said there was talk he was a movie star, didn't he?' Tam joined us at the table. I smiled. She'd found a tablecloth in the pantry and had put a sprig of wild parsley in a jar in the centre of the table.

'That was gossip, I think,' I said.

Nell nodded as she forked omelette from her plate. 'Yep, all gossip. I've found him. I think.' She turned the screen so I could see it. 'This is a Rafe Rendell from England. He's got dark hair and he's a chartered accountant from Oxford. Is that your Rafe?'

I burred up. 'He's not *my Rafe.*'

'You know what I mean,' Nell said. 'Is that him?'

I peered at the screen. 'I think it is, but he looks way younger there.'

Tam leaned over. 'Show me.'

When Nell obliged, Tam nodded. 'Wow. He is a good looker. Movie star looks.'

'That photo was taken fifteen years ago. It was in staff photo files of a company. Now that I've found an image and you *think* that could be him, I can run a reverse image search, and it should pull up any other photos without his name in the text. If there's any more to be found, that is.' Nell put her fork down and her fingers clicked on the keyboard.

'That's all Chinese to me,' I parroted Nell's words when she had read the generator manual.

'We each have our skills.' She flashed a grin my way. 'You got the power going. I can find our neighbour on the internet. Give me ten minutes.'

All was quiet as we ate, and Nell focused on her laptop.

'That was yum, thank you, Tam.' I pushed my plate away and sat back. 'Okay, now that we've seen the place, I'd like to make a list of what we need to do and allocate some jobs to each of us. Are you cool with that?'

Tam nodded. 'As long as I can fit a swim in somewhere. That reminds me. There's no sign of any boat here.'

'I know. I thought of that when I was going to sleep last night. It's the one thing I must sort quickly. We can't be isolated here.'

Tam leaned back in her seat. 'Speaking of skills, what part of the house do you want to start with, Pip? Have you got any ideas about the general layout of the resort?'

'I have.' I'd been thinking about that before my encounter on the hill earlier. I reached over and pulled over the notebook that I'd put on the table earlier and opened to a blank page. Picking up a pencil I quickly sketched the shape of the bay where we'd got off Jiminy's boat yesterday, and then put a square where the house was.

I grinned as I sketched. Having those new pencils each school year of my childhood had developed an ability to draw. Although maybe it had been there all the time, and my mum had known that.

I put the tip of the lead pencil on the curve of the bay. 'I was thinking about starting small and exclusive. Maybe half a dozen huts similar to the ones we stayed in at Hamilton Island. You know, like Lord Howe Island. A maximum number of guests.'

PENTECOST ISLAND 1-3

Nell looked up; she'd been listening as she searched. 'Will that be feasible financially? Every accommodation company I've done the books for over the years, says it's bums in beds that counts.'

Tam giggled. 'And if you only have a small number of beds, that's not many bums in beds.'

'True. Maybe, I'd better rethink the small, because we're going to have to hire staff.'

'What about the house? Are you going to make that part of the resort?' Tam asked.

'I've got two ideas. First one is to develop the kitchen and living room here into the restaurant. You'll need to tell me what you'll need. It'll mean that we'd have to live at the back of the house, and that could be a problem as we get more staff.'

'Maybe. What's the other option?'

'An entirely separate guest area down on the bay. I know if I'm on holidays I like to be able to see the water, so I was thinking about the kitchen adjacent to the huts with a big outdoor restaurant. You know, like the huts on a bigger scale? Flag stones on the floor, and no walls.'

'Have you thought that out? What about the furniture being exposed to the weather? And the bar? You'd have to be able to lock it up.'

'There used to be a resort over on Long Island like that when I was in my teens,' I said. 'I went over there for a sixteenth birthday party once and it stuck in my mind. We called it Gilligan's. There were little wallabies hopping around and birds wandering through. It was like an outside barbeque area, but I think we could do it in an upmarket way.' I had sketched what I was imagining as I described it and Tam leaned closer and nodded.

'I like the idea and it would be great from a marketing point of view. But I'm sure you've already got a handle on that.' Her blonde curls bounced as she nodded. 'This is going to be so much fun.'

'And a lot of hard work,' I said.

'Jackpot,' Nell interrupted, and we turned to her. 'More than three hundred images of him, but not one with the name Rafe Rendell on it.'

'Three hundred? Why would someone have three hundred photos online?' I said.

'Someone famous?' Tam ventured.

'Do you think it's the same guy?' I asked.

'Come around and have a look, and you tell me. You're the one who's seen him in the flesh.'

Tam and I both stood and walked around the table to look at Nell's laptop screen.

The screen was filled with photos of the man I'd encountered on the hill an hour ago. The same dark hair falling over his eyes. Eyes with that same intense blue-eyed stare looked out from the large photo in the centre. It captured his face perfectly.

'That's him. Exactly. It could have been taken this morning.' I swallowed. 'So, he is famous?'

I really hoped he wasn't, but my confidence in that being the case had plummeted. Famous usually meant rich. And rich would mean that he would have the resources to fight the resort being developed on the island.

Nell shook her head and zoomed out. 'Well, if it's the same guy he has a different name. That's a photo of Jack Smith on the back cover of his book that came out two years ago.'

'Jack Smith, the author?'

'Yes.' Tam nodded. 'It's *the* Jack Smith who wrote that book that was made into a movie last year. The one like a James Bond movie, but different. The hero was softer.'

'*The Legacy*,' I said. 'I saw it at the movies with Darren.' As much as I hated to admit it, *The Legacy* was one of the best movies I had seen in recent years, and I'd bought the DVD when it came out.

'Yes, that's the name of this book. The photo is on the book jacket. So, you think it's him?'

'It has to be unless he has a twin.' I leaned closer and a shiver ran down my spine. 'Jiminy said one of the gossip thingies was that he was an author. I guess he was right.'

'Maybe this is where he writes and why he's so focused on privacy?'

'He introduced himself as Rafe Rendell, so maybe he has a doppelganger? But whoever he is, I have no idea what he does here. We barely spoke.'

'He certainly is a looker.' Tam said. 'If you had a name like that why on earth would you write a book under the name, Jack Smith?

'I have no idea.' I shrugged.

'Do you want me to open some of the articles about him, so you can read them, Pip?' Nell looked across at me, but I shook my head.

'No. I don't care what he does or what he calls himself. I'm not selling my half of the island to Rafe Rendell or Jack Smith, whoever he is.'

'Maybe if you find out more about him, you'll know what you're up against.' Nell was always smart.

'No. I know what media spin is. Whatever is written about him will be purely to sell his books or feed the gossip machine.' I tapped my finger against my lips as I thought. 'I'll see him later today. But first, my lovelies, we have some work to do.'

Chapter 15

Rafe

I spent the morning staring at a blank page, but despite the screen remaining empty of words, for the first time in months thoughts swirled around and ideas came in thick and fast. At the same time, along with the plot lines that were fighting to come to the fore, was the image of the woman I'd now encountered three times. If I put those encounters in a book, Jenny—my editor—would say that it was an unlikely coincidence. The seeing her three times, I mean.

But no matter what Jenny would have said about that is a story, I would have kept it there. I'd learned to follow my heart with my stories, and my readers were loyal.

Those readers I was letting down by not producing the next decent book.

Jenny had stopped forwarding the reader emails, in a bid to let me "find myself". That was what she'd called it when I'd first moved to the island.

I looked down at my hands and slowly flexed my fingers. It was a process to get the thoughts from my head onto a keyboard and into a semblance of a story on the screen. Once, it had been easy and I hadn't appreciated the ease with which I'd done it.

When I had moved to the island, I had hoped that ability would return, but I had spent more than two years wasting time and feeling sorry for myself. Words had come easily, but when they formed a story, they had been bitter, and somehow, whatever I wrote had been tainted by the hurt and emptiness inside me. And now, just when the positive ideas were coming back, my solitude had been interrupted. I didn't dare think that there was a connection between the beautiful niece of my elderly friend, and the surge of positivity that was making my fingers tingle.

I wondered how long Pippa Carmichael— who seemed to be stuck in my thoughts—was going to stay here. I'd seen two others get off the boat yesterday—obviously her companions at the restaurant the other night— and I knew they had to be staying in the old house although it had stayed in darkness last night. The occasional flicker across the bay had told me that they were relying on candlelight.

Hopefully that would mean that they wouldn't stay long, and I could go back to my peaceful existence. She'd been rude and the fact that she said she'd inherited half of the island didn't sit comfortably with me. Even though I was sorry that Ma had passed on, I wasn't happy about sharing the island with anybody.

No matter how beautiful she was.

Life had taught me that women were not to be trusted. Behind the most beautiful façade and loving exteriors, there was always a self-centred shrew who wanted her own way. I had to keep that to the forefront of my mind.

Jenny had told me to wake up to myself, but she didn't know anything about my life before I had begun to write. I wasn't going to dwell on that either.

I pushed the beautiful ginger-haired owner of the other half of the island out of my thoughts and focused on the ideas that were vying for my attention. My fingers began to click on the keyboard, and I let myself become lost in an imaginary world. An imaginary world where the bitterness had left, and there was hope for the future

A long time later, the growling of my stomach brought me back to the present. I glanced at the time on the bottom right of the computer screen and was surprised to see it was late afternoon. I glanced to the left of the screen and was even more surprised to see that I'd written six thousand words.

A reluctant smile tugged at my mouth as I stood and stretched. It might be a crap story, but at least I'd made a decent start and the relief that brought was indescribable.

I made my way to the kitchen and made a sandwich and ate it as I stared out over the water. Already the next chapter was nagging at me, but I needed to get some fresh air, and I needed to stretch my muscles. I grabbed a bottle of water from the fridge and headed outside. The clouds had blown in from the south east, and there was a smell of rain in the air.

I tried not to be concerned about the occupants of the house across the bay, but I couldn't help my gaze lingering as I headed for the track.

Apart from my boat, the bay was deserted and there was no sign of life. I hoped that as I'd worked, a boat had come in and whisked away the unwanted visitors. A slight pang of regret settled in my chest. I had sort of enjoyed talking to Ma Carmichael's niece.

Even though her reaction to my offer to buy the rest of the island had not gone down well.

I looked up and was surprised to see the woman in my thoughts walking on the path towards me.

It was almost magical, as though I had conjured her up, and I blinked to clear my vision.

She stopped walking and stared at me.

'I thought you'd gone,' I said. I knew I sounded rude this time, even though I hadn't meant to.

Her hands went to the hips and her chin lifted. 'And where would I be going to?'

I stared, letting my eyes roam over her features. Her face was beautiful, even as her brow wrinkled in a frown.

'I assumed you wouldn't be staying long,' I said.

'Well, you assumed wrong, and really, is how long I stay

PENTECOST ISLAND 1-3

any of your business?'

I bristled. 'Perhaps not my business, but I would like to know what's going on, on my island.'

Her eyes flared with temper, and I could see her fighting to control it. 'I believe we had this discussion this morning.'

'Perhaps we did, but that doesn't counter the fact that you are trespassing.'

The hold on her temper failed. 'Trespassing?' she spluttered.

'Yes, this track is on my land.'

She looked around. 'I see no boundary, and I find it hard to believe that my aunt would have sold the land with access to Red Wave Wall and the mountain.'

'This is my land. I own down to the glade where the two paths join. So technically you are trespassing.'

'So, if I want to climb the mountain, I can't?' Her eyes narrowed as she challenged me.

'That's correct. Unless you asked politely, and I granted permission to you to walk on the part of the track that is on my land.' I was beginning to enjoy myself. Her olive skin now had a tinge of red on her cheeks, and when she wasn't talking, her lips were set in a straight line.

'Well, I'm going to have to request that you hand that bit of land back to me, as I will need access to the mountain.'

'There are other walks on the island,' I said to be difficult. It didn't bother me to have her use the track, but it was interesting pushing her buttons and getting a reaction.

'My guests will want to climb the mountain.'

'You're being joined by more people?'

'Eventually,' she said with a narrow smile. 'I was actually on my way over to your house to talk to you about that.'

'Eventually? You have more friends joining you?' I repeated dully as the prospect of my peaceful solitude was

122

shattered. 'How long do you intend to holiday on the island?'

'Oh, it's no holiday, Mr Rendell. I've moved back home, and I'm here to stay. I'll need access to this land for my guests.'

'Guests?' A suspicion was beginning to form in my mind. 'When you say guests, I am getting the impression you're not talking about friends who might come to stay.'

'Oh, you are very astute. I am talking about *paying* guests. Guests who will be staying at my *resort* on Pentecost Island.'

'What!'

'I would like to have a conversation, and come to an agreement. Perhaps we could go to your house?'

'The only agreement I'm interested in is buying the island from you.' I stared at her for a long moment. She held her chin high and didn't break eye contact.

This time, it was me who turned away. I didn't care if she thought I was rude. The only thing I cared about was the fact that my idyllic life here was at risk.

Idyllic? a voice nagged at me. Far from idyllic if the truth be known.

No way was there going to be a resort on *my* island. Boatloads of people disturbing my peace, walking on my tracks and interrupting my solitary existence. Stickybeaks peering at my house; it wouldn't be long before they realised who I was. I'd had enough of the hordes peering at my little cottage back home in England before I'd headed to the tropics.

I would fight any move she made. I didn't care what it cost.

Her voice followed me as I headed down the track. 'When you regain your temper, Mr Rendell, come over to the house. I'd like to talk some more.' The wind caught her words, but I'd heard enough. I ignored her and kept walking. I was sure I heard a laugh follow me into *my* rainforest.

Chapter 16

Pippa

'That's so good of you, Jiminy. Are you sure you have time to take me over?'

I was at the marina on Hamilton Island. We'd been on Pentecost Island for five days and had started to run out of supplies, and diesel for the generator was getting low so I'd called Jiminy. He'd collected the three of us from the island early this morning and brought us across the passage. Tam and Nell had headed off to the general provisions store to stock up on food.

The good news was that Jiminy had located Aunty Vi's launch in storage on one of the back wharves of the working marina.

'Old Ma—I mean your aunt— obviously paid to have it maintained, Pip,' he said as we walked past the workshops on our way over to the back wharf. 'The launch might be old but she's in tip top condition.'

'Excellent. We won't need to trouble you to take us back.'

'It's no trouble. You're sure you're right to take her across to Pentecost already?'

I looked up at the sky. There was barely any wind and the forecast that I'd seen on the board as we'd walked off the tourist wharves was for a still and fine day. 'I'll be fine. I used to take her out when I lived here, with no trouble and in seas rougher than this. I'll get you to come on board with me while I make sure I remember everything, and then we'll be fine.' I turned to him with a frown. 'I did notice it took you three attempts to get into the bay at the island the other day though. That's my only worry.'

'Maybe you could get your neighbour's permission to take

it into this jetty?'

'Hmm. Maybe.' I shrugged. 'I guess the worst he can do is say no after I go in there. We'll unload and then I'll take her around to Back Bay and put her on a mooring if he says no.'

'Sounds like you've got it all sorted then.'

I nodded. Even though we'd only been on the island five days, we'd achieved a lot. Nell had been online every day, as well as making many calls. She knew exactly what approvals we needed before we opened the resort, and she already had the paperwork underway.

Tam and I had chuckled when Nell had removed the small portable printer and scanner from her suitcase, but it had been worth its weight in gold this week. Nell had printed out the forms, I'd signed them, and they'd been scanned and sent off to the various relevant bodies.

We'd already had an email reply from the local Tourism Board who'd been excited to hear of our proposal.

Let us know when you're up and running and we'll do a feature.

Woo hoo! That had been a bottle of bubbles night.

We were all tired and pleased to have a day away from the house. Tam and I had scrubbed the house from top to bottom and I planned to get our furniture out of storage, and have it sent over as soon as we could organise delivery. We'd cleared the path from the steps to the track, and I'd mown the grass at the back of the house with the ancient mower I'd used as a teenager. I could feel a little bit of the happiness growing in me, and the person I'd been at the Gold Coast seemed to be fading more every day.

So far we'd had a dream run, and were moving a lot faster than I'd thought was possible.

The only fly in the ointment was our neighbour.

I was so deep in thought I almost bumped into Jiminy when he stopped in the middle of a finger wharf.

'There she is, Pippa.' He pointed to the boat rocking gently in the wash from a boat that was going past.

Nostalgia flooded though me as I looked at the classic lines of the old launch. If I closed my eyes, I could imagine Aunty Vi at the helm in her faded green hat and her fishing shirt. She'd been such a character and I had loved her so much. Again, regret spiked though me; I had walked away from that life.

'I should have come back to see her,' I said quietly. 'Aunty Vi, I mean.'

Jiminy looked at me and I could see he understood. 'It's called life, Pip. It often gets in the way of what we should do. You're back now, and I know that's what she would have wanted.'

I nodded. 'It is. And I am going to work my butt off to build a successful resort on the island.' I put my hands on my hips and turned to him. 'And I don't care if it's a bad marketing move. I'm going to call our resort Ma Carmichael's.'

'Good on you, and I like it. Ma Carmichael's has a ring to it.' Jiminy's teeth flashed in a wide grin. 'Come on, let's get you on board and see if you can really remember how to steer a boat.'

My hands stayed on my hips as I accepted the challenge. 'Bring it on, Jimmy.'

By the time Tam messaged me to see where to get the groceries sent to, I was easing the launch into the wharf near Jiminy's boat. I'd convinced him that I knew what I was doing. I'd taken the launch out of the marina, done a couple of quick circuits of the bay, and a longer trip over to Dent Island.

'Not bad for a landlubber,' he said as I eased the launch up to the concrete wharf and he dropped the fenders.

'Hey, I'm an old salt from way back,' I protested with a grin.

As Jiminy jumped off, Tam and Nell appeared carrying four bags of groceries each.

'You should have waited for me. They look heavy,' I said.

'There's a few more. You can come on the next trip.'

'No prob,' I said. 'I still have to get a drum of diesel too.'

'Having a boat is going to make life a lot easier. You'll have to teach Nell and me how to drive it,' Tam said as she held the bags out to me. 'This will make it a bit easier.'

'Absolutely,' I replied, pleased that Tam had offered.

'See you later,' Jiminy called as he headed over to his boat. 'You call me if you need anything.'

'Thanks, mate.' I waved back and he disappeared below deck on his boat.

Nell reached into one of the bags and passed over a couple of envelopes. 'A couple of replies already,' she said.

'Thanks for getting it, Nell,' I said. We'd organised for our forwarded and any new mail to be left at the post office on Hamilton Island, but I was surprised to see that there was some after only five days. I glanced down at the two envelopes. One was from the local council, but the other was from Morton and Morton, Aunty Vi's solicitor.

As Tam and Nell came aboard, I slit the envelopes open. The one from the council was an acknowledgement of our application to develop the resort.

'Four weeks, the council says,' I grinned. 'Until we have a go-ahead.'

'Fantastic.' Nell's smile was as wide as mine.

'Thanks to you, Nell. I'd still be trying to find out what to do. Appreciate it.' I opened the second envelope.

My mouth opened in disbelief as I quickly scanned the contents, and my stomach clenched as anger kicked in.

'Bloody hell. Who does he think he is!'

Nell was standing beside me. 'Who? The solicitor?'

'No, our neighbour. He's already made an offer on the house and my half of the island.'

'That was fast. A good one?' Tam frowned as she came

across to stand next to Nell.

'I have no idea,' I spluttered. 'He wants to meet and talk. I don't care if he offers me a million dollars, it's not for sale.'

'We've only been there a few days,' Tam said as she read over my shoulder.

'And we've left him in peace. If anyone's leaving the island, he can go.' My hands trembled as I read the brief letter. 'It looks like he wants to make this very hard. Last time I spoke to him, he walked away from me.'

'Looks like he doesn't want to play fair,' Tam said.

'Or share. Looks like he wants the whole island,' Nell added.

'He might be famous, he might be rich, and he might want my island, but he's a jerk,' I said stuffing the letter into my bag. 'And you know what? I'm not going to let him bother me.'

'Good girl,' Nell said quietly.

'Come on, let's go finish and go home.'

##

It was only a thirty-minute trip across the water from Hamilton Island to home. It was closer to Lindeman Island but that was another resort that had closed down over the past few years. I'd been encouraged by the letter from the Tourism board; they had expressed their pleasure at the proposal.

"Since the cyclone and the recent shark attacks, the media has focused on our region, and tourism has dropped off," the manager had written. *"If you need any assistance at all, please contact me. There are a number of grant initiatives available for application this winter."*

I'd been thinking about the focus of our development, and I was keen to get over to the mainland and meet with the manager.

'What do you think about a trip to Airlie Beach tomorrow?' I turned to Nell and Tam as we came around the northern point of the island. 'We could get our gear booked onto the barge and get the place organised.'

Neither of them answered. Tam was out of earshot, and Nell was engrossed on her phone screen. I didn't bother asking again as my eyes moved to the bay ahead. I'd watched Jiminy bring his boat in the other day, but that had been at high tide. The tide was ebbing now, and the water was swirling in eddies around the coral heads. If I tried to go in close to our place, there was a good chance I'd hit the coral and then we would be in trouble.

There was no choice. I looked ahead to the jetty on the other side of the bay and headed into the enemy's territory.

Uh oh . . .

Said enemy happened to be sitting at the edge of the wharf. He stood as the launch approached and I swallowed back the hope that tried to wheedle its way in. He looked like a normal guy; his stance was relaxed and casual. Cut-off ragged denim shorts, a loose white long-sleeved shirt that gave him a rakish air.

'Oh my God. He's even better looking than he was in the photos. Look at those legs,' Tam breathed out in a hushed voice.

I couldn't help it. I looked at Nell and we both giggled.

'Down, girl,' I said. 'Remember the last guy whose legs you salivated over?' Tam had met Tyrone on a dating app, and that date hadn't had a good ending. He'd taken her to watch his wife in a triathlon—the wife she hadn't known about.

Poor Tam. She was always looking for happiness. She needed to learn—like I had—that there were other ways to find happiness.

'Don't even think about it, Tam,' I warned as the launch approached his jetty.

I may as well have not spoken. As we got closer, she picked up the rope and my neighbour had no choice but to catch it.

'Thanks.' Tam's voice was cheery as she slid over the side of the launch onto the jetty. As I concentrated on easing the vessel up against the jetty, I was aware of her chatting away to him. Once

I turned the motor off, I walked along to the bow and jumped onto the jetty. Nell was also standing with them by the time I got off the boat.

Glittering eyes locked with mine over Tam's head.

'Afternoon,' I said in the friendliest tone I could muster. 'We've come in on the wrong tide and I was hoping you'll let us unload here for a few minutes and then I'll take the boat around to Back Bay.'

Rafe—or Jack, whatever moniker he went by—walked across to where I was standing, and I couldn't believe it when he actually smiled at me. With a wave of elegant fingers at the boat, he nodded.

'Leave it there until the tide's up. Or for as long as you need to. There's plenty of room for two boats.'

I stared at him, but he kept smiling. Was this the same man I'd had two difficult conversations with? I narrowed my eyes; maybe he was trying the "be nice" approach. After all his letter to my solicitor was in the boat behind me.

Yes, that's what it was. I knew exactly what he was up to.

Tam walked across. 'I've just invited Rafe over for dinner.'

I tried to keep my mouth shut but I failed. 'What?'

And?

He must have been a mind reader. 'I'd be delighted to join you and get to know my neighbours.'

Suspicion vied with determination as I looked at him. He could be as co-operative and friendly as he liked, but there was no way he was getting his greedy hands on my half of the island.

'I got your letter,' I said tersely. 'The answer is no. So, there's no need to waste your time coming over for dinner.'

'Pippa!' Nell's keep-the-peace voice at any cost was horrified.

'It won't be a waste of time.' His voice was smooth. If he thought his sexy voice and perfect looks—and his money— were going to sway me, he was way off track.

I shrugged and mumbled under my breath. 'Whatever. Your time to waste.'

The three of them continued to talk as I climbed back on board and collected the first of the grocery bags.

And the mail.

The drum of diesel would have to stay until I figured out how we'd get it up to the house.

But that was the least of my problems.

'So, Pippa. It looks like you're going to be staying a while.' The suave voice of my biggest problem followed me as I lugged the grocery bags along the wharf.

'Very perceptive,' I said tersely.

'Here let me,' he said.

I stopped and looked at him. 'What exactly are you doing?'

Satisfaction rippled through me as his expression changed when he turned away from Nell and Tam.

'Being a gentleman.' Despite Rafe's friendly tone, his eyes were hard and cold. 'I was going to carry the bags for you.'

'No need. We're—I'm—fine.'

Nell rolled her eyes at me as she held her hand out for one of the bags. I shook my head and put them down at the end of the wharf. It only took me a couple of minutes to secure the launch and I ignored the conversation that continued at the other end of the jetty.

And the occasional laughter. Honestly, Tam and Nell were supposed to be on my side. I gave the last rope an extra hard tug, picked up more grocery bags and headed up the beach to the track.

Nothing was more satisfying than being a martyr.

Again, I was conscious of his gaze boring into my back—and my bare legs—as I walked away. Why was it that I was always walking away from this guy knowing he was staring after me? Why couldn't he just leave me in peace and let me get on with getting my life back on track on my island?

I struggled along the track with the heavy bags.

What the heck had the girls bought?

Eventually, the sound of hurrying footsteps reached me from the track behind, and I paused. Tam came up behind me.

'Here, stupid, give me one of those bags. Honestly, Pip, you can be so precious sometimes.'

'Precious!' I wheeled around to face her. 'What the hell do you mean by that?'

'Forget it,' Tam said, but I was on a roll now and I was ready to have a go. It felt good to let my simmering temper out.

'What the hell are you thinking inviting *him* for dinner tonight?'

'You don't get it, do you, Pip? Honestly, no wonder—' She broke off and looked at me as we trudged along the overgrown track to the house.

'Keep going,' I said coldly. 'No wonder what? You said, "Honestly". So be honest. Spit it all out.'

'Okay, I was going to say no wonder you had all that drama with Darren, and he let you down. No wonder Eric shafted you. You don't listen and you don't think. You don't read people.'

'I'm reading *you* loud and clear now,' I spat out.

'Okay. So listen to me. What's the best way to find out what Rafe is doing?'

'So it's Rafe now, is it?' I widened my eyes at her and fluttered my eyelashes.

'Jeez, Pip, listen to yourself.'

'Why did you invite him over? He's the enemy.'

'You don't think you are being overly dramatic?'

I shook my head and then stopped. 'Maybe a bit.'

'I invited him so you two can sit down and have an honest conversation about the situation. The worst that can happen is that he will go away and still want to buy the island. The best thing that can happen is that he might see your point of view.'

'Or I might see his? Is that what you're saying? You told me to wait a couple of weeks when we got here. Have you changed your mind about staying, because if you have, just go. That's fine by me.'

'No, that's not what I meant at all. I know what this place means to you, and I'm on board with the project one hundred percent. That's why you—with our help—have to sort the situation out now. It will be much better doing it face to face rather than through lawyer's letters.'

I looked at her and didn't comment.

'Pip?' Tam put the bag down and held out one hand.

'Probably,' I conceded.

'After all, the island has been in your family for many years. How long?'

I shrugged. 'Since about the 1930s.'

'And that's a bloody long time,' Tam said. 'I'm totally with you. You need to keep it in your family and do what you want to do with the resort, but, girlfriend, you need to learn how to go about things.'

I sighed and squeezed her hand. 'I'm sorry for snapping, Tam. And yes, I know what you mean. I make poor choices, I'm lousy at reading people.'

She shoulder-bumped me and reached down to pick up the bag. 'But you're pretty damn good at picking friends.'

'I am,' I said with a smile. 'This is so important to me, so tell me why I should be nice to the guy?'

Tam shook her head as Nell came up behind us.

'Are you pair fighting?'

We both shook our heads this time.

'No, we're not fighting,' I said. 'Tam's just giving me a lesson on being sensible.'

'About time.'

'Thanks, Nell.' I rolled my eyes so she could see it.

'I think it was a great idea for Tam to invite him for dinner. He seems like a nice guy and he said to tell you to leave the boat there.'

'What?'

'He said to tell you there's no need to move it. He really doesn't mind if you leave it at his wharf.'

Shock filled me. 'Did he say that?'

Nell nodded. 'Yeah, he seems like a really nice guy. A real gentleman.'

If I was honest, I had to admit that he had mostly been polite when I was talking to him. It was just that blasted letter that had got beneath my skin. And the way he'd turned his back at me. But to be fair, I'd done exactly the same thing to him.

Nell held her hand out for the third grocery bag and Tam chuckled as we made our way towards the house.

'My God, how about that sexy English accent?' she said. 'I almost swooned. He's a Colin Firth voice double!'

I smiled. 'You're hopeless, Tam. Don't go having a romance with our neighbour.' My smile widened as I turned to her. 'Then again, if it's the only way to keep the island it might be worth a shot.'

'Nope, I'm happy to look and listen. He's way too cultured for me.'

Even though we all laughed as we walked back to the house, I was still smarting inside from Tam's words.

##

Tam and I had been prone to arguments since our primary school days, and Nell had always been the peacekeeper, but there was no need for her to intervene this afternoon. Tam and I had made our peace, but I knew it was still fragile. Had I made a mistake inviting them to come with me?

I stuck my head into the kitchen as the smell of garlic

tickled my nose.

'I'm going out to the back garden for a while. I want to get the herb garden ready so I can buy some plants when we go over to the mainland.'

'Make sure you're here for dinner.' Tam put the saucepan she'd been lifting down onto the sink. 'Pip?'

'Yes?'

'Are we good?'

I nodded slowly. 'You were hard on me, but I guess I deserved it. And yes, we're good.' I headed out the back door to the garden.

I knew Tam would be upset if she knew my intention *was* to be absent when our neighbour arrived. I'd avoid that stand-around, have-a-drink, social chit-chat before we sat at the table. I'd come in for dinner, and then as soon as we'd finished eating, I would find an excuse to go to my room. I wanted to make some calls anyway. That would be a good excuse. No one had asked me whether it suited me to be neighbourly tonight.

I'd endure the meal, and try to keep my temper, but I didn't have to spend the whole evening in his company. I would ring Evie and see if she had some time to come across and talk about expanding the walking tracks on my side of the island.

Yes, I had it all sorted. What was it they said about the best-laid plans? Would I ever learn?

Chapter 17

Pippa

My plan backfired spectacularly. The light was fading fast but I'd spent a good two hours digging, clearing, and laying garden beds edged with some old timber lengths that I'd found behind the shed. I turned them all over carefully before I dragged them over. Despite what I'd said to Nell, the last thing I wanted was to come across a snake hibernating for the winter.

Even though the breeze drifting up the gully was cool, perspiration was running down my neck and my legs. I reached into my pocket and found a hair elastic and twisted my now damp hair up into a high ponytail, and let the breeze cool my neck as I turned the last end of the garden bed.

I heard footsteps behind me as I leaned down on the shovel to turn a particularly hard piece of ground. 'Is Mr Sexy Voice here already?' I called out.

There was no answer and I paused. I'd put my foot in it. Resting the shovel against the shed wall I turned slowly just in time to see the glimmer of a smile before his expression went bland.

'Are you expecting more guests for dinner? Or should I be flattered?' My neighbour's voice held a tinge of amusement.

'Oops.' I shrugged and picked up the shovel again. I wasn't terribly concerned about what he thought of me. 'Flattered maybe, but the tag wasn't my creation.'

'No, I didn't for one moment think it would be. Your description would be more "Mr Pain in the Arse", I would imagine.'

Just as well Tam wasn't here to hear him say that because

he even made the word "arse" sound sexy. I lifted my gaze from the hard ground and caught a wide smile on his face. So, he did have a sense of humour after all.

'You pick the name, you take it.' This time the corners of my lips lifted in a brief smile.

There was an awkward silence for a couple of minutes.

'Is dinner ready?' I finally said as I picked up the shovel and put my work boot on it and pressed hard, pleased when the hard soil turned over.

'No, I came out here to have a chat to you. I distinctly got the impression that the dinner invitation was not unanimous.'

I shrugged. I seemed to be doing that a lot lately. 'No skin off my nose. Tam's a great chef, and she was happy to cook a meal for you.'

'If you would prefer me to leave, just say so.'

I went to shrug again, and then forced my shoulders to stay still. I carefully placed the shovel against the wall and folded my arms. 'I'd prefer you to leave, but you're here now, so we might as well have it out.'

He folded his arms. I had to stop thinking of him as "he".

'Okay, what do I call you? Rafe or Jack?"

One eyebrow lifted, and damn if it wasn't as sexy as the voice. It was one of those sardonic lifts that I would love to be able to do. When I lifted my eyebrows for effect, I usually got a laugh from Tam and Nell, and a comment about Groucho Marx eyebrows.

'You know who I am?' The voice was a bit cooler now, as though somehow, we had breached his privacy.

I suppose we had in one way, but hey, if you were famous, you wore it.

'Yes, we've done our research, and we know who you are or to make it easier for us, we know the *two* people you are. So which one are you?'

PENTECOST ISLAND 1-3

To his credit, he looked ill at ease. Maybe embarrassed. He was different to what I had expected from the few brief encounters we'd had.

'Call me Rafe . . . please. . . that is my name.'

'Very well.'

He lifted his hand and pushed back the lock of dark hair that gave him that rakish look. 'And may I call you Pippa?'

'That's my name.'

'I know. Your aunt told me about you.'

My head flew up. This time it was *my* privacy that had been breached. 'Oh? Told you what?'

'She told me she had a niece called Pippa, and that she hoped you'd come back here one day. When the house stayed empty, I wondered if she'd changed her mind about leaving it to you.'

'You seem to know everything then.'

'May we sit down?' He gestured to the small table and chairs that I'd retrieved from the garden shed when I'd mowed the lawn the other day. I was quite proud of how the garden was looking, and I knew this would be a pleasant outdoor area for guests to have breakfast. A pretty native vine with small yellow flowers spilled over the pergola that joined the shed to the back of the house, and the original uneven flagstones edged the lawn. Aunty Vi's birdfeeder hung crookedly from the corner and I made a note to fix it later as we walked across to the table. It was a pretty spot, and I'd spent the last two afternoons out here thinking. I could sense that I was changing; the longer we were on the island, the calmer and more confident I was. I wasn't as anxious as I'd been before, and those constant worries that had dogged me—work and Darren, and the fear that I wasn't good enough—were slowly receding.

Rafe stood until I sat down on the wrought iron chair, and then he sat. I wasn't used to good manners.

Heat filled my cheeks when he put his hands on the table and looked at me. His fingers were pale. Long and elegant. Honestly, with his dark hair and that English skin, he looked like he should be in some period drama, not sitting with me on a tropical island.

I was conscious of my messy hair, stained clothes and dirty hands. I probably smelled too, because I'd found a sealed bag of Dynamic Lifter in the shed and had dug it into the garden.

In contrast, Rafe sat there, spotless in his loose white shirt, and a woody fragrance drifted across from him.

I pulled a face and scratched at my neck when a bug landed on it. 'I guess you want to chat about the letter you sent to my solicitor? Maybe it would have been better to make the direct approach than write?'

'I hadn't met you when I wrote it. I'd posted it before you arrived on the island. Yes, I agree, a direct approach is more appropriate now that you are here—and much more polite. That is what I would like to discuss now.' His gaze swept the small garden when he finished talking, and I sensed his approval.

'What? Being polite?' I couldn't help myself. I sat straight and spread my hands flat on the table.

'No. Discussing the situation.'

'There is no situation,' I said.

He looked at me now, and I held his gaze. A small frisson of something fired, and my fingers felt funny. I moved my hands down onto my lap. I wasn't going to get angry or emotional; being able to control my response was an indication of how I'd calmed since we'd arrived.

'You need to accept that I'm not prepared to sell.'

'What if I increased the amount I'm prepared to offer?'

I shook my head. 'The island is *not* for sale. Not at any price.'

He dropped his head, and I noticed his fingers tense on the

PENTECOST ISLAND 1-3

table. A glimmer of sympathy ran through me.

I wasn't prepared for the bleak look in his eyes when he finally lifted his head. 'What can I do to get you to understand my reluctance to lose the island?'

'Lose it?'

He waved those elegant fingers again. 'Lose my privacy. That was the reason I came here. Your aunt understood that I needed it.'

'And why does it have to be here?' I was not going to give an inch. 'Surely there are many other places you can have this privacy.'

'Perhaps there are, but I've been here two years now, and I've made myself a home.'

My eyes narrowed. 'Yourself? I wondered if that was your partner you were with the other night?'

His gaze was steely. 'No, that was a business dinner. Not that that is any of your business.'

Ha! The gloves were off.

I smiled and kept it sweet. 'You're right. It's not my business. Equally so, what I intend to do with *my* island is not yours. As far as I can see, the only thing we have to discuss is you handing back the access to Red Wave Wall. In fact, I'd like to see the document that defines the boundary of your land. I can't believe that Aunty Vi would have handed over the access.'

'It's my land, and I'm happy to show you the proof of that.' He gestured around with one hand, and for the life of me I couldn't take my eyes off his fingers. 'Look around you. Do you really want strangers traipsing over this island?'

I held his gaze. His blue eyes were fringed with lashes as dark as his hair.

'You don't have the right to tell me what I can do on this island. Pentecost Island has been accessible to birdwatchers and rock climbers for almost a hundred years, and we are going to build a resort that allows them to stay here in comfort while they explore the island.' I kept my voice hard but even. I was not going to get emotional.

'And what will that mean for my privacy? Privacy on my land that I bought in good faith, believing that this island would remain the sanctuary that it is,' he said.

'Sanctuary for who? You? Don't you think that's a bit selfish? A whole island just for one.'

'In a word?' His voice was as hard as his eyes. 'No.'

'Well then, like I said before, you are going to be very disappointed. Because this resort is going ahead. For the life of me, I can't understand why my aunt sold it to you in the first place.'

'I can tell you why. She had no choice. It was either sell to me or the consortium that was going to buy the whole island. If that had happened, we wouldn't have this argument here. You would have gotten your inheritance in cold, hard cash, and you could have started a resort wherever you wanted. I was the only buyer prepared to take half. I did you a favour.'

'Well, it doesn't look like that from where I'm sitting. Are you always used to getting your own way?' I stood, and the chair scraped noisily over the flagstones.

'When I am dealing with reasonable people? Yes.' He stood slowly, and his chair made no noise as he pushed it beneath the table. 'But I should have anticipated that dealing with a woman would be a waste of time.'

'You dealt with a woman when you bought the place. But I guess that was different because you got your own way then.' I leaned forward at the same time he did, and our noses were almost touching as we glared at each other. The anger coming off him was palpable. His shoulders were stiff, and his mouth was set in a straight line.

'It will be a waste of time this time because, Mr Rafe Rendell, you will not get your own way. And it has nothing to do with me being a woman. I own this land, and there will be a resort here sooner than you think. If you don't want your precious privacy disturbed, go and buy another island. *You* are the one who's going to have to leave.'

'Well, then I guess. . .' He moved back, and I sensed his capitulation was close.

'You guess you accept that there is going to be a resort here?' Triumph ran through me, but his next words were like a bucketful of cold water.

'No, I guess you are going to have to give this project of yours some more consideration. Because I will do everything I can to block your plans.'

By the time I had processed his words, he was heading back towards the house—my house.

And my dining room table.

And now I was expected to sit and be civil across a meal?

His threat had been very real, and I had no doubt he meant every word. And I guessed he had the money to back it. I had the inheritance from Aunty Vi, but I imagined it was nowhere near the amount of money he'd have to fight me.

No way could I sit at dinner and pretend everything was hunky dory now that we'd both said our piece. I picked up the shovel and pushed it into the ground, satisfied when the hard earth yielded at my first push. I muttered beneath my breath as I finished turning the soil in the last garden bed. I was looking forward to getting some plants in and watching the garden regenerate.

I was looking forward to seeing the house renovated and the resort huts and restaurant go up along the foreshore.

I was going to regenerate here, too. I was not going to let Rafe Rendell get beneath my skin. I needed to get my head and heart in sync. I was not going back to dinner because he would be in my house, being waited on and mooned over by my two supposed friends.

I pulled my phone out. Stuff staying here. I'd take the launch over to Hamilton Island and catch up with Evie. Tam and Nell could entertain our famous neighbour to their heart's content.

Evie picked up on the first ring.

'Evie, It's Pippa Carmichael.'

'Hey, Pip. I was going to call you tomorrow. I've got some spare time, and I was going to sail over and visit you.'

'I was hoping to come over to Hamo and see you tonight. Do you have plans?'

'Damn, not tonight. I'm over on the mainland. I don't come back across the Passage until tomorrow. But I was going to come straight to Pentecost Island if it suited you and catch up with the three of you. It's been ages since we were all together. I found a photo on my phone the other day after I bumped into Tam and Nell. The four of us sitting on a beach when we were on a uni break. They were good times.'

'That was a great holiday. Look, Evie, come over tomorrow. I've got some work coming up I'd like to discuss with you.'

'Sounds great. I'll leave here early, so I'll be there mid-morning.'

'Sailing across, you said?'

'Yep, I've fallen in love with this place, and I bought myself a boat. She's rough but good enough to live on and get me across to Airlie Beach, where I've been getting most of my work. I've had a three-month contract over there working on the new foreshore development, but I finished up this week.'

'Perfect timing then,' I said. 'Can't wait to catch up tomorrow.'

Chapter 18

Tam

'Thank you for inviting me, anyway.'

Stunned, Tam stared at Nell as Rafe closed the door behind him quietly. He'd made his apologies and said he wouldn't be staying for dinner after all. He'd been polite, but his words had been clipped and brief, and his body language screamed stress.

Big time.

'What the heck did she say now?' Nell spluttered. 'I thought you said Pip had mellowed a bit towards him?'

Tam shook her head. 'She wasn't happy about him coming over, but she was going to talk to him.'

'Well, she obviously has. Did you see how upset he looked? I feel sorry for the poor man.'

Tam crossed to the gas stove and lowered the flame beneath the stir fry that she was keeping warm. 'Yeah, me too. But there's something there that doesn't jell for me.' She reached for the rice packet. 'We might as well eat now. I wonder where Pip is.'

'What do you mean by doesn't jell?' Nell stood by the table as Tam poured rice into the saucepan of boiling water.

'You found him on the internet. He's from England. He's obviously rich and famous, so why is he holed up here on a small island off the east coast of Australia, protecting his privacy at all costs? There must be a story behind it. Something's not right.'

Nell looked thoughtful. 'Maybe. There were no recent articles about him, and it's been a couple of years since his last book came out.'

'And he's here by himself. My curiosity is at "Danger, Will Robinson level."'

'You could be right. But Pip still needs to tone down. She's obviously upset him. That's not the way to deal on a business level. She has to learn to hold her emotions in. I'm going to have a talk to her.'

Tam flicked a glance at Nell, and worry churned in her stomach. 'Maybe it's better to give her some space. I've been worried about her since we arrived. Even though this is what she wants, I think she's a bit fragile.'

'Do you think so? I haven't got that impression at all.'

'Pip's always been a master at covering up her feelings and pretending she's okay. I know coming back here was hard for her. She's carrying a lot of guilt about not coming up to visit her aunt before she died. Remember how much she changed when she was living up here? It was the first time in her life she'd felt loved. And she was confident enough to tell us how she felt about it when she came down to uni. And now Aunty Vi has gone, and she's alone again.'

'She's got us. And she seems content to me.' Nell frowned as Tam crossed over to the sink.

'Yes, she has. But we also have our own families, and we're all Pip has.' Tam picked up the dishcloth and started wiping down the benchtops. 'I just remember what happens when she has a setback. In the past few weeks, she's broken up with Darren, lost the job that she put her heart and soul into, come back to an island where her aunt isn't anymore, and now the only positive— her dream of this resort—is being threatened. I'm sorry I asked Rafe over for dinner. I'll go and find her and see if she's okay.'

Nell shook her head. 'No, I'll go. You pair will end up fighting.'

'True. And that's the last thing she needs. Tell her to come in and have dinner. It's almost ready. The rice will be about another five minutes.' Tam stood at the window staring out over the small garden.

Chapter 19

Rafe

I sat on the balcony overlooking the sea and nursed my second whisky. The first one had gone down fast, and the mellow burn had gone a small way to easing my anger and frustration. I focused on breathing in and out as the sun sank behind the hills of the mainland.

The colours in the sky behind the sinking orange orb made my fingers tingle as words filled my thoughts. Vermillion, indigo, gold and pale apricot vied for supremacy as the sun slipped below the hills. Gradually, my body relaxed, and the sound of the gentle wind sighing in the rainforest below helped me calm.

No matter how much I tried to justify why I must have the whole island, I knew I was being unreasonable. My portion was less than half of the whole island, and if I was honest, I had always known the situation would change when Ma Carmichael passed away.

When I'd asked her real name when we'd first met on the wharf that had been at their end of the bay before the cyclone, she'd laughed. Ma had been a big woman, larger than life, and it was hard to imagine her outgoing personality being confined in an aged care facility.

'It's Violet, but don't you dare call me that. I've been Ma to everyone who matters to me for many years.'

I'd been honoured to join that group of people she considered friends, and if I didn't go over to her house with the whisky bottle late in the afternoon, I'd see her making her way slowly up the track to my new house on sunset. Apart from the staff at the general provisions store on Hamilton Island, Ma

Carmichael was the only other person I had communicated with for the first two months I lived on the island until she left to live on the mainland.

I'll never forget that day. I went down to the wharf to say goodbye, and the look in Ma's eyes broke my heart. She knew she'd never be coming back to the island, and I'd gripped her hand as I helped her onto the launch. It made me think more about my situation, and I vowed that I could be as strong as Ma had been. But I'd backslid and wallowed in my misery.

Jenny emailed me constantly, and I would occasionally reply, but the conversations with Ma had kept me sane. She asked no questions, but I had found myself telling my story. She wasn't one to comment or show sympathy, but one night, she'd looked at me over her whisky tumbler.

'A story shared is a way to start healing, but I think you have a way to go yet.'

That's all she'd said, and I appreciated her respecting my privacy, although a person would have had to be blind not to see how depressed I was.

I wouldn't even admit it to myself.

The problem was now that every time I looked at Pippa, I could see in her eyes that same love for the island, and I didn't want to see that same sadness that I had witnessed in Ma's eyes if I blocked her development.

I had no doubt I could take legal action and block it for years. In the end, it would go ahead, but it would stuff up her plans in the interim.

You'd think that on an island miles from civilisation, I could be satisfied with whatever happened. What was a few people wandering around looking at birds and climbing rocks?

I picked up the bottle and went to pour a third glass, but I hesitated.

Ah, what the hell. I only half filled the glass and lifted it to the sky.

'For you, Ma Carmichael. I can only hope you're not looking down and seeing me stuff things up.'

I was ashamed of myself. I'd gone hard on Pippa this afternoon. I'd hoped that she had come to the island on a whim and that she wouldn't stay, but too late, I was coming to realise that I had gone in too hard.

Way too hard.

At least I hadn't let slip that Ma had spent a lot of time talking about her great-niece and how proud she was of her. She'd told me of the years that Pippa had lived on the island and how those years had turned her around, and she'd developed confidence as she'd completed high school.

'She had a lonely childhood,' Ma had said. 'My sister's daughter—Pippa's mother—was a strange woman.'

But she hadn't ever said what was strange about her. Apparently, there'd been a tragedy that had resulted in Pippa living with Ma, but she'd never given any details, despite my curiosity.

Real lives were always fodder for an author. Even one who was having trouble writing these days, but curiosity had tugged at me.

All I knew was that Ma was the only family that Pippa had, and she'd worried about how she'd cope when she was left alone.

'When she came to me, she was damaged, and I'd hate to see her go back to that. She didn't utter one word for the first six weeks after I took her in.'

I looked up at the sky and held the glass aloft again. 'I don't think you have anything to worry about, Ma. She's a confident woman now, and she knows what she wants.'

Putting the glass on the small table beside my chair, I leaned back and enjoyed the darkness. I always felt cocooned once the sun had gone. In the tropics the dark was instant; occasionally I longed for the softness of an English twilight.

Pippa Carmichael and I were going to have to come to a compromise. I knew I was going to have to give a little. I wasn't going to leave, and I knew now that Pippa and her friends had the same intention. Their friendship seemed tight, and I wondered why they had come with her. Surely, the three women didn't think they were going to singlehandedly develop a resort from that old house and overgrown block of ground.

'Sexist, Jack.' The voice from my past drilled into my thoughts, disturbing the peace of my thoughts flitting around in the growing dark. 'Sexist, selfish and totally self-absorbed,' she'd said.

I'd glanced at Rebecca, not realising it was the last fight we'd ever have. To me, this one was no different from the many arguments that had been a feature of our five-year marriage. One of the biggest ones was her insistence on calling me by my pen name.

Rebecca hadn't stopped despite the disinterested gaze I threw her way. 'You know, I think I preferred it when you were toddling off to work at that shitty little accountant's office in the village.'

I hadn't been able to help myself. 'And you preferred living in that dark little cottage?'

She'd stared at me and then turned to look at the Thames. When my second book had taken off, we'd moved to London to a luxury apartment at Dockside.

'No, you know I love living here, but really, Jack? What's the point in living in the city when you sit hunched up at that computer all day?'

'Perhaps to make the money that you enjoy spending?' I hadn't been able to help myself, and her glare had been icy.

'We are expected at Mummy and Daddy's this weekend. There is a house party, and everyone who is everyone will be there.'

'So, we are everyone too?' I'd raised my eyebrows at that

PENTECOST ISLAND 1-3

ludicrous description. 'I have a deadline, even if they are expecting Jack Smith to be there.'

'Jesus, Jack. Surely you can take two days off.'

That particular weekend, I had a deadline for galley proofs. The proofs of *The Legacy*, my last successful novel. I'd stood and crossed to the window and put my arms around her. 'I'm sorry, sweetheart. You go, and I'll try to come up on Sunday.'

'No, you choose. Your book or me! I told Mummy we would be there tonight. Both of us.'

'I'll get the train on Sunday.' I'd leaned across and brushed my lips across her cheek, but Rebecca had turned her head away.

'Don't bother,' she'd snapped. Half an hour later, when she slammed the door on her way out, it was the last time I saw my wife.

The residual bitterness had drilled a huge hole in my self-confidence, and my ability to write, and it had been lucky that the movie deals had come through in the months following that weekend. I had a guaranteed income and moved as far away as I could.

I'd had an accountant friend who had emigrated and lived in Cairns, and he invited me over to visit.

Since Jenny had come over to see where the next book was at, I knew I had to lift myself out of this bitter self-pity and start writing again. I had wasted enough of my life.

But before then, I had to find Pippa Carmichael and tell her I was willing to compromise.

Tomorrow was a new day.

Compromise was something I was not good at. If I had been, I would still be married and living in the UK.

As the night settled around me, I drew a deep breath, determined to keep the usual darkness from my soul. I stood and made my way inside. I would find something to eat, and then I would find some new words from within.

150

I glanced at the clock in the living room on my way to the kitchen. There was a frozen quiche in the deep freezer, and I allowed myself a regretful grin. If I'd taken more care tonight, I could have been over at my neighbours' house where a tantalising smell had drifted from the kitchen.

As I opened the freezer, a loud knocking stopped me in my tracks. Not one person had knocked at the front door of this house since I'd moved in over two years ago. Ma had wandered over and settled herself on the balcony when she had visited, waiting until I came out with two glasses.

Tam and Nell stood on my doorstep and I frowned, automatically looking past them for Pippa.

They were alone.

Before I could ask them why they were at my house at nine-thirty at night, Nell grabbed my arm.

'We need your help, Rafe. Please.'

Concern surged through me when I saw the worry on Nell's face and Tam's rigid stance. 'Where's Pippa?' I asked.

'We don't know. We can't find her.'

'Find her? What do you mean?' My frown deepened as I looked from one to the other. Tam ran a shaking hand through her untidy curls.

'She didn't come in for dinner, and now we don't know where she is.'

Nell interrupted. 'I went outside to get her, and we had words. I marched inside, and Tam and I ate dinner without her. Pippa was in one of her moods. When it got late, we went outside and called her, but we couldn't find her. She's nowhere in the house, or in the garden or down at the beach. We've been looking for more than an hour now.'

'Pippa has had some issues lately, and we're a bit worried about her. She was in a bit of a state when Nell spoke to her.' Tam held my gaze steadily.

'What are you saying?' A cold pit of dread opened in my stomach. If she was in a state, I had contributed to it.

'Pippa's mother committed suicide when Pippa was twelve, and when she's down, she often wonders if she's inherited her mother's instability.' Tam's eyes were bleak. 'We've always supported her and brought her up when things got her down, but she's never taken off before. I'm worried. This move to the island has been a big thing for her. For all of us.'

'Shit.' The cold in my stomach spread to my limbs. 'Where have you looked? What do you need me to do? Where can I search?'

Chapter 20

Rafe

Two hours later, I'd twice walked the track where I'd passed Pippa on my morning walks. I walked from the bottom to the middle of the hill, calling her name until I was hoarse. Tam and Nell were looking along the foreshore in our bay—funny how suddenly I'd accepted their right to be here and now thought of it as *our* bay—and now they'd gone back to the house to see if Pippa had come home while they'd been out searching. Both times, when I reached the halfway point on the hill where we'd had a conversation, I'd been tempted to climb higher. It was hard to pinpoint why, but I had a feeling I should keep going. The second time, I stopped at the false crest of the hill halfway up and looked ahead. The moon had risen, and the wind had dropped. The side of the island and the mountain ahead were bathed in bright light.

I cocked my head to the side and listened; for an instant, I thought I'd heard a cry. As I stood waiting for the sound again, a bird dipped below the side of the hill and let out a mournful cry.

False alarm.

I knew the island well. I'd taken many walks in the two years that I'd lived here, and I wondered if maybe she'd gone to Red Wave Wall, where the rock climbers went. The cold in the pit of my stomach spread again as I thought of the high wall that rose over the sea.

I turned and pulled out my phone. I had exchanged numbers with Tam before I set off, and I pressed the speed dial I'd set.

'Any luck?' I asked as soon as she answered.

'No, not a sign of her. You?'

PENTECOST ISLAND 1-3

'No, nothing, but I've decided to go up to Red Wave Wall.' My breath hitched; I'd continued striding up the hill as I'd called without making a conscious decision to go up.

'Be careful. From memory, the path out there is a bit dicey, and it won't be easy in the dark.' What she didn't voice was what we were both thinking: the sheer cliff with the huge drop down to the water.

'I will. I've been there a few times, so I know it well. I'll call you if I—'

Tam cut me off, and I could hear the tears in her voice. 'Thank you. We'll wait for your call. Just go. We'll keep looking in the rainforest.'

For a while, the only sound was my heavy breathing and the blood pulsing in my ears. Occasionally, there was a rustle in the undergrowth on the side of the path and the flapping of wings at the edge of the cliff. The higher I got, the narrower the path got, and I was grateful for the bright moonlight. I paused to catch my breath and looked to the east. A bright swathe of moonlight illuminated the sea, and it glowed silver all the way to the horizon.

It was a beautiful sight, and I wished I'd taken more time to appreciate the beauty of this island. I reached the fork in the track and closed my eyes as I decided whether to go to Red Wave Wall or the peak of the mountain.

I let instinct guide me and took the left fork to Red Wave Wall, the escarpment that was a popular rock-climbing destination. The occasional climbers hadn't bothered me as they didn't come over to my side of the island. Sometimes, I'd seen boats moored over there, but no one had come to my bay. The track petered out, and I hugged the cliff wall. No sound disturbed my concentration as I negotiated the narrowest part of the way to the top.

I realised that I'd been quiet, too, and I hadn't called out for the past couple of hundred metres.

'Pippa! Pippa! Can you hear me?'

A flock of parrots rose, squawking from a tree about fifty metres ahead of me, and I jumped. At the same time, loud footsteps thudded on the top of the escarpment above me, and I looked up as a shower of rocks and stones tumbled down to the track ahead.

'Pippa?' I called loudly. 'Is that you? Are you all right?'

The only answer was a long, drawn-out bleating from above.

I knew there were wild goats on the island, but I'd only encountered them once before. That time, they'd taken off when I'd walked towards them, and I hadn't been too concerned, despite Ma's warning that the males could be dangerous if they felt their herd was under threat.

I swallowed as I looked at the huge drop on my left. I certainly didn't want to meet an angry goat on this track. Lowering my head so I could watch where I was placing my feet, I picked up my pace and expelled a relieved breath when I reached the top of the wall. The eastern side of the crest was clear and there was no sign of anyone there—Pippa or goats. I turned and as I made my way into the rainforest that covered the western half of the peak, I thought I heard something.

I paused and waited. 'Pippa!' I called again.

'Hello?' The voice was soft and tentative.

'Pippa?' I took off into the forest, no longer worried about encountering a goat.

'I'm here.'

I stopped and spun around. This time, her voice was behind me. In my hurry to set off, I stupidly didn't think of bringing a torch. I dug into my pocket, pulled out my phone, and turned the flashlight on. I swung it in a wide arc from the cliff face to the forest, but there was no one there.

'Where are you?'

'I'm here. Above you.'

I looked up as I realised that her voice was coming from the tree. I shone the light up into the thick foliage. 'I can't see you.'

'I can see you down there. I'm higher.'

I stepped back and, craned my head, and lifted the phone, but the light didn't light up more than the first five metres of the trunk and branches.

'Have I got the right tree?'

'Yes. I climbed higher because the branches were thicker up here, and I felt safer.'

Sweet relief flooded through me. 'Stay there. Don't move.'

'And where do you think I'm going to go?' Her voice was dry.

'Are you hurt?'

'Only my pride.'

'Just wait.' I hit speed dial, and Tam answered immediately.

'Rafe?' Hesitancy laced her voice, and I rushed to reassure her.

'All's well. I've found her. Pippa's fine.'

'Where are you? We'll come.'

'No, stay there. We're up at Red Wave Wall. I'll bring her back down. See you in a while.'' I disconnected and stood at the base of the tree.

'Are you going to come down?' I didn't dare ask why she was up a tree on the highest point of the island in the middle of the night.

'I would if I could. I'm stuck.'

'Are you all right though?' Even though I was a wordsmith, I didn't know how to put it into words, how to ask her if she was *really* okay. I needed that reassurance from her.

'Yes, I'm fine. I just can't get down.'

'Ah, may I ask what you were doing up there in the first place?'

'I was running away from the biggest, meanest goat I have ever seen.'

'A goat?'

'Yes, a goat. He put his head down and went for me. His horns were huge, and I had visions of ending up over the cliff if he caught me.'

You weren't the only one who was thinking that I thought, but I didn't say anything.

'Why can't you get down?' I peered up, but I still couldn't see how high she was.

'I didn't look when I was climbing up, but now there's a huge gap down to the next branch, and I'm not game to go down in case I slip.'

I moved closer to the tree and looked up, but I still couldn't see her. 'How far up do you think you are?'

'About eight metres, I'd say.'

'Bloody hell, that is high. What do you want me to do? It's a bit far to go and get a ladder.'

This time, her voice held a note of fear. 'No! Don't go. Stay there, please.'

'I won't leave you.'

'I thought I was going to have to stay here until daybreak. I was scared I'd nod off and fall, but if you stay there and talk to me, it'll help me stay awake.'

'And I'm probably the last person you really want to talk to, so I'll make the most of it.'

'Probably,' she said, and her voice didn't sound too shaky.

I reached up and grabbed the branch that was just below my shoulder height and swung myself up. 'I'm coming up.'

'Be careful.'

'I'll have you know I'm a very experienced tree climber.'

'Oh? Why's that? I can't imagine you being an outdoors person.'

'I'm deeply hurt,' I said. 'You've seen me out walking, how many times?'

'Three.' The reply came quickly. 'But that's not an outdoorsy thing.'

'I grew up in the country, and I even had my own treehouse.'

'Lucky you.'

Too late, I remembered her sad childhood and I cursed myself silently. 'Did you ever read the *Magic Faraway Tree*?' I looked up as I reached for the third branch and caught a glimpse of a red sneaker through the leaves.

'Yes, I did. And it's funny that you mention it because I was thinking about it while I was trying to figure out how to fill in the hours. I loved that story. I have a copy back at the house.'

As I hauled myself up to the next branch, there was a gap in the foliage, and I could see two red sneakers now dangling on either side of a thick branch about two metres above me. If I could get up there, I could help Pip back down.

'I can see you.' One hand slipped as I looked up, and I reached for the trunk with the other. My fingers touched something cold and smooth, and I pulled my hand back. 'Holy mother of God, there's a fucking snake here.'

'What colour is it? Pippa's voice was calm.

'Jesus, I don't know.' I peered down to where it had slithered past my hand. 'Green, I think.'

'Yeah, same one I saw on the way up. It's only a tree snake. Harmless. It won't bite you.'

My hands were shaking now, and I found it difficult to get a grip.

A grip on the branch and on my equilibrium.

'I'd rather face a goat than a snake. I hate them. I'm a Pom, remember.'

'Don't be a sook. I told you it's harmless.'

I swallowed and reached for the next branch, and pulled myself up. This time, the branch below was wide enough to put my feet on. 'I'm not a sook. I'm coming to rescue you.'

The chuckle from above encouraged me. I looked up, and this time, my gaze encountered a pair of green eyes staring down at me.

'Hello,' I said.

'If you were not going to be my rescuer, I probably wouldn't talk to you.' She was straddling a solid branch, leaning against a part of the trunk that had a wide curved section recessed into the timber. I felt reassured. She looked quite safe there.

'I don't blame you. I'm actually quite pleased that we've met tonight.'

'Oh? That surprises me.'

'Can you move your legs a bit closer to the trunk? I'll come up to your branch.'

I waited as she lifted her legs and tucked them against her chest. I paused when I heard Pippa drag in a deep, shuddering breath.

'I don't feel as safe with my legs up.'

I tried to inject a soothing tone into my voice. 'You look very safe where you are. You're in a bit of an alcove.'

Reaching up, I swung myself up to the branch that she was on. As I did, I made the mistake of looking down. The moonlight illuminated the ground below, and my stomach lurched. I froze.

Bloody hell. Had I climbed up that far? No wonder Pippa didn't want to risk climbing down.

'How the blazes did you get this high?'

She must have seen the expression on my face as I hung on for grim death.

'It's okay. Hang on tight, and crawl over here. The branch is wide enough, and there's room for two against the trunk.'

I took a deep breath and held her gaze in the filtered

PENTECOST ISLAND 1-3

moonlight as I inched along the branch towards her.

Chapter 21

Pippa

The last thing I'd expected when I'd strode up towards Red Wave Wall as the sun set was to spend the night stuck in a tree with my nemesis. After Rafe had crawled along the branch, we sat shoulder to shoulder with our legs just touching. Although, to be honest, since he'd climbed up to rescue me, being rude and ungrateful was out of the question. Anyway, I'd walked off my temper—and my hurt with Nell—as I'd climbed the hill.

Nell's words had been totally out of character. They had been blunt, and I'd shut down and walked away.

'It's time to grow up, Pip, and think of others,' she'd thrown at me as I'd walked towards the path. The truth often hurts the most, though, doesn't it?

The spectacular sunset over the mainland had soothed my soul, and I'd sent a quick thank you up to Aunty Vi. As serenity took over and I eased my walking pace, I thought about what I'd do. No matter what happened with Rafe Rendell, I intended to stay on the island. Surely, we could come to some sort of agreement. Once I got council approval, there was no legal reason why I couldn't go ahead with my plan. In fact, the response from the tourism body has been really positive. I'd decided to meet with him again and try to come to a compromise. Without any emotion involved.

I shifted awkwardly as I sat next to him. There had been an uncomfortable silence since he'd moved across next to me.

'Careful,' he said. 'I wanted to—'

'Wait. Before you say anything about getting down from here, I want to apologise to you for the way I spoke to you in the garden. I was rude and out of line.'

He turned his head and looked at me. I couldn't see his eyes because the light was behind him, but his words were sincere. 'You beat me to it. I wasn't going to talk about getting you out of this tree. I was going to apologise to you. I was sitting on my balcony watching the sunset, and I came to the same conclusion. The way I spoke to you was unforgivable, especially the bit about dealing with a woman. I'm very sorry.'

'Good.' I put my head down as he continued to stare at me. 'I'll accept your apology if you accept mine, and we can try to work together.'

His voice was quiet. 'I accept that you have a right to build your resort. I won't do anything to block it.'

'Really? You mean that? As I looked down, the huge drop to the ground made me shiver.

'It's okay. Please don't be scared. I won't let you fall.' Rafe reached down and took my hand in his and looked down at my fingers. 'And yes, I mean it.'

'We've still got to get down,' I said shakily.

'Let's talk and take your mind off it. When it's light, it will seem a lot easier.'

'You think so?' I stared down at my hand in his. 'Okay, talk to me.'

'You've been working hard on your project already, and I know it means a lot to you. I couldn't believe what you've done to the house and garden in what . . . less than a week?' His fingers were smooth against mine as I nodded, and a wave of embarrassment rose in my chest. My fingers were dirt-stained and rough from working outside.

I swallowed as heat rushed to my cheeks. 'Yes. And it does mean a lot to me. It's where I want to stay. Tam and Nell are here to get me started, and another friend is coming over tomorrow. I have a feeling she'll stay for a while too. Resort or not, it is where I am going to spend the rest of my life.' I lifted my head. 'For the past little while, I've not been happy, but I know now that I've come home. This is the place where I want to be.'

'We're a fine pair.' He let go of my hand, and my fingers were cool. 'I guess I could say the same. I've been finding my way since I came to the island, and it's taken a while to decide where I want to be, but I don't want to go back to what was my home.'

'In England? I asked.

He nodded.

'Why did you come here? Why did you buy half of the island?'

'Do you believe in serendipity, Pippa?'

'In what context? Finding something without looking?'

'Yes, some would say it's good luck when you unintentionally stumble across something good, but I think it goes deeper than that. I was meant to meet Ma on the mainland. She was over there for the first time in a long time, she told me. She was looking at the aged care home.'

'Where did you meet her?"

'Would you believe in a bottle shop in the whisky section?'

A grin tugged at my lips. 'I would. Aunty Vi was an expert. It was her Scottish heritage.'

'She gave me some advice, and we got talking. Before I knew it, we were in the local hotel. The deal was sealed that night.'

'She would have still been here when your house was built?' I asked.

'Yes, for a few months. We spent many nights talking. She was a good woman.'

'She was. She certainly made a difference to my life.'

Rafe turned to look at me. 'I believe I was meant to meet her, and I believe I was meant to live on the island. That's why my reaction to your resort was over the top. But I've had time to think about it. So long as I can retain my privacy, I think we can work

PENTECOST ISLAND 1-3

together.'

'Your privacy?' A rogue grin pulled at my lips. 'I was thinking of having meet-the-author drinks and afternoon teas where you could talk about your books. You know? Make it a feature of the resort.'

He stiffened beside me, and his voice was horrified. 'What!'

I chuckled. 'I'm sorry. I couldn't help it. Of course, I wouldn't do that. We won't bother you.'

'Witch,' he said, but his voice was warm. 'Not a kind way to treat your rescuer.'

'I haven't seen any rescuing happening yet.' I nudged him.

'Yes, it is rather problematic. I'm not terribly keen to go down past that snake.'

'And I'm not *terribly keen* to climb down in the dark.' I parroted his words and accent.

'Are you trying to be smart?' he said.

'Not at all. What if that big buck goat is still down there?'

'There were goats above the track as I got to the top of the hill.'

'That settles it. I'm not going down there in the dark.' I folded my arms.

'So you propose that we stay in the tree all night?'

I nodded. 'I'd already decided that before you arrived. Like I said before, I was scared of going to sleep. I put in a big day, and I'm tired. I was worried I'd fall.'

'I'll ring Tam and tell her that we are going to stay up on the hill for the night. There's no need to worry her and tell her that we're stuck up a tree.'

'Did Tam come and ask you to look for me? I thought they might be worried when I didn't front.'

'Tam and Nell both came knocking on my door.'

'Oh shit. I suppose they thought the worst.'

'They were very worried. They'd been looking everywhere for you.'

'My phone is back at the house.'

Rafe leaned back, pulled his phone from his pocket and pressed a button. 'Tam? We've decided it's a bit dark to come down safely—he shot me a look, and I smiled back—' so we'll see you in the morning.'

I nudged him again. 'Tell Tam I said to say sorry to Nell for me. And I'm sorry for taking off and worrying them.'

He did as I asked and then disconnected.

'What did Tam say?' I asked.

'You really want to hear?' He put the phone back in his shirt pocket. 'She said you're going to be very, very sorry. I wouldn't rush back.'

'I guess I'm in trouble then.'

'I guess you are.' Then, a serious note. 'You're very lucky to have good friends who care about you.'

'Yep. We're tight.' I ventured a question. 'Tell me if I'm out of line, but what about you? Don't you get lonely here by yourself?'

'I enjoy my own company.' His words were clipped.

'Fair enough.'

There was silence for a while, and then Rafe broke it. 'I was married for five years. When that ended, I decided that I'd be happier alone.'

'Well, you are certainly alone here. A bit drastic, maybe, to move to a deserted island to find solitude.'

'Perhaps.' Silence again. 'I thought Rebecca was the love of my life. I'd known her since school, and I adored her. All I wanted was to make her happy. But I wasn't good enough for her. She resented me spending so much of my time writing.'

'Didn't she know that before she married you?'

'No. I was an accountant when we were married. My first

PENTECOST ISLAND 1-3

book was accepted a couple of years after that.'

'But wasn't she happy for you?' This time, I couldn't hold my curiosity in.

'Not really. It only took me a couple of years of marriage to realise that my feelings weren't really reciprocated as I thought. I came from a wealthy background, and I was on a good salary when we were married. And then when the first book deal came through, so did the money . . .' His bitterness was obvious.

'I thought that was your wife that night last week when you were in the restaurant. She didn't look very happy.'

'That was Jenny, my publisher's wife. And no, she wasn't happy. You see, the problem is—and I haven't told anyone else this—that the dream of being here and writing didn't eventuate. I've spent a lot of time feeling sorry for myself. Jenny was here to chase my next book up.'

'And?'

'I received an email, and in a very short time, I decided to take myself off, find somewhere new to live, and devote myself to my writing. And it's strange, but these last few days, I've had some success.

'Email? What sort of email would make you do that?'

'My marriage was ended by a single email. Rebecca had gone to her parents for the weekend. I was supposed to go on the Sunday, but she emailed me before I left to tell me not to bother as the marriage was over. I haven't seen her since that afternoon she left. The settlement and divorce were all done without meeting again.'

'Sorry, but you're probably better off without someone who could do that.' He looked sad, and I felt sorry for him. Rafe was talking to me to stop me from being scared, and he'd opened up to me. Now, it was my turn.

'You want to hear something to top your email story?'

'Can you?'

166

'I can. I wish *my* partner had broken it off by email. Then I would have been spared the indignity of seeing his floozy in my bathroom in a pink G string.'

He snorted, and I wasn't sure if it was a laugh he was trying to cover up or if I'd shocked his very proper English sensibilities.

'Sorry,' he murmured. 'And yes, that would have been most upsetting, I imagine. Why was she in your bathroom? Sorry, that might be a bit personal. I'll take that back.'

'Not at all. I was in the bath, and he thought I was at work, so he brought her home for a romp in our bed.' I yawned. 'Anyway, it was all for the best. I saw for myself what Tam and Nell had been trying to tell me for months.' I covered my mouth as I fought another yawn. 'And look where we ended up. A happy outcome all around.'

'If you'd like to put your head on my shoulder, I'll make sure you don't slip if you'd like to have some sleep. It will make the time go faster.'

Reluctance fought my tiredness. 'That's very kind, but . . .' God, I was starting to get an English accent. I must be tired.

'No buts.' Rafe lifted his arm, and I paused. Then, I moved closer and rested my head on his shoulder. His white shirt smelled fresh, like linen, and I could feel the warmth of his skin through the fabric.

'Promise you won't let me fall,' I murmured.

'I promise.'

***

Rafe

I kept my promise that night and was surprised when Pippa slept against me until the first rays of sunlight broke through the leaves of the tree where we'd spent the night. The climb down had been much easier than we'd anticipated, and she'd appeared slightly sheepish.

We'd not encountered a snake or a goat on our journey

PENTECOST ISLAND 1-3

home.

I will be forever grateful that I discovered her in the tree that night, but that story will come later. Something had shifted between us, and even though we had only had a week's acquaintance—most of it acrimonious—we forged a solid friendship during those few hours in the branches of that tree.

I walked her back to the house, where Tam and Nell were waiting on the front porch. Emotion clogged my throat as Pippa left my side and ran into their open arms.

'I know what you would have thought, you pair of dills. I promised you that I would never give you any cause for worry. I was just upset, and I didn't realise how late it was.'

Tam went to say something and shook her head. I was surprised to see tears in her eyes. Nell spoke for her. 'Don't you ever, ever worry us like that again, young lady.'

'Yes, mother hen.' Pippa chuckled. 'Everything is good now.'

Tam and Nell's eyes widened when she came back to me and linked her arm through mine. 'This good man found me and looked after me until it was light enough to . . . um . . . walk back down from Red Wave Wall. Thank you, Rafe.' She reached up and brushed her lips across my cheek, and something shifted irrevocably inside me. I've always scoffed at love at first sight stories or those who said they knew when they had met their soul mate. Maybe it was on fifth sight, but I knew that Pippa Carmichael was a woman I wanted to get to know a lot better.

'My pleasure. It's time I was heading home.'

'Can we at least give you breakfast? Tam scrambles a mean egg.' Pippa's fingers rested on my arm, and my nerve endings fired.

I was torn. I didn't want to leave, but I was keen to go back to my house and sit at the computer. As Pippa had rested against me last night, and I'd felt her breath puff on my neck, I had been filled with inspiration. I had plotted most of a story as the night had passed. I wanted to get it down before it left me. 'I'll come over later today and have a coffee with you. Would that be suitable?'

As I turned to go, Pippa gasped.

'Oh my God. No!'

I turned with a frown, but she wasn't looking at me. Her mouth was open, and she was pointing at a small yacht sailing into the bay. The bright pink headsail was full of the south-easterly wind, and the boat was coming in fast. As we watched, the motor kicked in, and the pink sail dropped into the sail bag. A woman stood at the helm and waved madly as she came closer to the wharf.

'It's Evie,' Tam cried.

'Is it okay if she goes onto your wharf?' Nell asked me.

'Of course.' I saw the look that Nell and Tam exchanged.

I turned to Pippa. Her brow was wrinkled in a frown, and her hands were on her hips. 'What's the matter?'

'A bloody pink sail,' she said dejectedly.

'It's all right,' Tam said. 'It's down now. I'm sure she's got a white one.'

'All right. I guess I can live with that. See you later, Rafe.'

'You will.' I nodded and stood there bemused as the trio made their way down the path and towards my wharf.

Finally, I made my way back to the hill and ignored the call for both coffee and a shower. I sat at my desk, and the words flowed from my fingers.

Chapter 22

A month later

Pippa

Evie had kept the pink sail in the sail bag and had moved into the house with us. Her yacht, *Eros*, was moored around at Back Bay because our shared jetty wasn't big enough for three boats. She'd jumped at the opportunity of working with us, and the past month had flown by in a flurry of positives. One more added to the payroll, but it was worth it.

I was on top of the world and often found myself smiling for no real reason. It was the happiest I had been in a long time, and every day affirmed that my decision to come to Pentecost Island had been the right one.

With the backing of the tourism board, the development approval had flown through the local council. Our furniture had come across from the mainland on the barge, and we'd hired a boat to bring it over from Hamo. The floors had been stripped and sanded, and the inside of the house had been painted throughout.

It was amazing how much work five people could achieve in a day.

Yes, five people.

Rafe was a constant and *welcome* visitor. That is, on the day or two or three a week, he took off from his writing. But if he didn't come over for the day, he would come over for dinner.

I feared it was Tam's cooking that brought him over.

I'd seen the looks that Tam sent our way when we were head-to-head talking, but Rafe was simply telling me of the progress he was making with his book.

One evening about a week ago, Tam had called me into the kitchen while she was cooking dinner. Nell was immersed in adding expenses to the accounts spreadsheet—the bills were beginning to come in—at the desk that we'd set up in the alcove off the dining room. It would eventually be the reception area, and we were planning to build a wall to close it off from the back of the house. We needed a carpenter and were thinking of advertising to see if we could entice someone to come to the island for a few months. Many of the building jobs were too big for us to take on; we simply didn't have the expertise, and we had to build to cyclone specifications. Evie was out on the track checking the solar lights that she'd installed that afternoon.

'What's up?' I said as I lifted the lid of the pot that was bubbling on the stove. 'Yum, spaghetti bolognaise. Are we having garlic bread, too? I'm starving.'

Tam leaned back against the sink and regarded me steadily. 'I just wanted to check you're going okay, Pip.'

I turned and widened my eyes. 'Okay? I've never been better. Why?'

'It wouldn't have anything to do with our sexy Englishman, would it? You've been different since that night you spent up on the mountain with him.'

Up the tree, I thought, but I didn't say anything.

Rafe and I had never shared our secret about spending the night in the tree. Not for any particular reason, and we hadn't talked about not mentioning it. I think it was because it had been such a special night for both of us.

For me, at least, it had been a turning point in my life.

I shook my head. 'Rafe and I are simply good friends.'

'I don't want to see you hurt again, Pip. And I don't want it to get to a situation where it might be difficult to be on the island with him. I mean, if you did get together and then break up.'

I was hurt, but then I realised that Tam was only concerned

about me. 'My track record of breakups is only because I was shit at picking a decent guy.'

'I won't disagree with that,' she said.

I turned the tables on her. 'You think Rafe is from the same mould as Darren and the other jerks I hooked up with?'

'Hell, no. He's a gentleman.'

'So, what's the problem?'

Her expression was mutinous. 'We're just keeping an eye out for you.'

I walked over and held my arms open. 'Come here.'

Tam came over, and I hugged her.

'We just don't want to see you hurt again, Pip. Nell and I have seen you hurt too many times before.'

'I appreciate it. And you will never know how much I value your friendship and advice. Plus the fact that you both gave up your lives to take on this project with me. But I've healed since we've been here. I can't explain it. Maybe it's because it's where I grew up. And Aunty Vi made me see that I could be loved. Maybe it's simply because I'm back in the islands where I love to be. Maybe it's because I'm doing something with meaning. And that I love doing it. But honestly, Tam, I'm happy.'

'And Rafe?'

'Yeah, I think he's cute. Well, okay, he's as sexy as hell. That voice and those eyes, but I'm not going to rush into anything. Without breaching his confidence, he's been hurt, too, and he's healing. He's also focused on writing his next book, so whatever ideas you've got, we are friends. Good friends, close friends, and that's the way it will stay for the time being.'

Tam smiled at me before she picked up the spoon from the sink. 'For the time being?'

'Yes,' I said. 'For the time being. I've got a resort to open.'

##

Rafe was walking beside me as we made our way to the bay, and Tam raised her eyebrows with a secret smile as he took my arm to help me over one of the fallen tree trunks that was still across the path.

I turned and pulled a face at her. 'Behave,' I mouthed silently. It was like being a teenager again, and I loved getting to know him more each day.

Today was a red-letter day. The material for the huts had been delivered, and the workmen had arrived to build the timber floors. The hut frames were modular, and we were going to erect them ourselves. We'd planned a sunset drink on the beach to celebrate.

'Are you sure we can do it?' Nell asked for at least the tenth time as we stood at the edge of the sand and watched the joists get nailed onto the frame of the first hut. 'Don't we need a carpenter?'

'Of course, we can do it,' Evie said in her husky voice. She'd fitted into our household as I'd known she would, and her plans for the gardens and the tracks to the various bays and Red Wave Wall—yes, Rafe had given us permission to cross his land— were well underway. I reached over and squeezed his hand.

His face lit up in that beautiful smile of his, and my stomach took a tumble.

'What was that for?'

'Just a thank you.'

'No need. I'm happy to be here. You—all of you, I mean'—he glanced at Tam— 'have made my life on the island a joy.'

Tam pretended to gag, but there was a grin on her face as she went over to stand beside Nell and Evie to watch the two workmen.

'Just ignore her,' I said. The noise of the hammering was overpowering, and I gestured to the bay. We walked down to the edge of the water together.

'What's wrong with Tam? Does it bother her that I spend so much time over here? Maybe you'd better come over and visit me more often, Pip?' Rafe's eyes held mine and my stomach did that tumble again. I had trouble reading him. He was the consummate gentleman. Always polite to each of us, but sometimes there was something in the way he looked at me. Even if there was something there, like I told Tam, I wasn't ready for it. I wanted to find myself and see my plans come to fruition before I made any moves in that direction.

'Is that an invitation? For some reason, my voice was husky like Evie's, and I cleared my throat. Okay, so even if I wasn't ready for those moves, I could still flirt.

'It is.'

I didn't object when Rafe slung his arm around my shoulder as we looked over the water. Spring was not far off, and the water was a deep translucent blue. White sails dotted the passage, and a tourist launch full of backpackers hooted its horn as it motored past our bay.

'It's so peaceful here,' I whispered half to myself.

'It is.' We stood in a companionable silence, watching the water until Evie called out.

'Come and see, guys.'

We walked back to the others to see the first floor had been laid. I had designed it with Evie's help so that the hut was a hexagonal shape, with a small porch overlooking the bay.

Rafe left me at the path. He brushed a kiss across my cheek, obviously not concerned by the look of delight on Tam's face. 'Would you like to come over when you finish work for the day? I've got a bottle of white chilling in the wine fridge,' he whispered.

I smiled and pretended to misunderstand. 'All of us?' I asked cheekily.

'No, Pippa. Just you.'

'I'm sorry. Tonight, we've planned a drink to celebrate what we've achieved so far. A girls' night.'

His face fell, and he straightened up. 'Very well. It's past time I was back at work anyway.'

I grabbed his arm and moved closer to him. 'But if that invitation stands, I'd love to take it up tomorrow night.'

His smile was wide. 'Oh yes, it will stand for as long as you want it to. I can wait.'

I could hear him whistling as he headed back to his house on the hill.

Epilogue

Pippa

A bottle of bubbles didn't last long between four when there was a celebration underway. The floors of the first four huts had been laid today, and now we were ready to put up the modular buildings. The frames were stacked, waiting for us to begin work tomorrow.

I lifted my glass in a toast. 'To Ma Carmichael's Place.'

'To Ma's,' my three friends chimed in.

We clinked glasses and sipped at our champagne.

We were sitting on the sand, looking across the bay to the peak that marked the centre of the island. Evie and Nell had gone for a quick swim while they'd waited for Tam and me to come down with the bubbles and the glasses. The sun was warm as spring approached, and we all wore our straw hats.

'I think, ladies, when we get the interiors of the huts done, we might set an opening date and work towards that. What do you think of that?'

'Super,' Nell said.

Tam giggled. 'You're getting an English accent too. Or the lingo, at least.'

Nell nudged her, and Tam's glass tipped a little.

'Hey, watch it, I'll spill my bubbles!'

Evie laughed with them. 'It's just like being back at uni, being here on the island with you lot. No cares, no worries, no pressure.'

I rolled my eyes. 'No, just a resort under development, a huge landscaping project'—I nodded at Evie—'and a huge accounting task underway, thanks to Nell, and an outdoor restaurant and menus to be planned.' I raised my glass. 'Thank you, all.'

'That's right.' Tam nodded. 'Just like Evie said. No cares, no worries, no pressure.'

'And let's keep it that way. I want to propose another toast.' I lifted my glass. 'To friendship, girls. To the unbreakable bond that has seen us stay together through the ups and downs of life. And boy, there's been some of them over the past ten years.'

'To friendship,' they chorused.

As the sun slipped slowly towards the sea, we sat there in silence. Four women who cared for and looked out for each other. When the bubbles were finished, we put our glasses down and looped our arms around each other's shoulders. The sky faded from that deep indigo blue into an array of pinks shot with gold, and the only sound was the small waves breaking on the shingly sand.

I smiled as a light came on up the hill, and Rafe's silhouette appeared in the window as he looked down to the bay.

Our bay.

He couldn't see us, but I could see him. I was beside Tam, and I felt her tense as she leaned forward.

'Pip, what's that?'

I pulled my gaze away from Rafe's house and looked in the direction she was pointing. 'What?'

'There's something in the water. Look just out at the point. Something black.'

'A shark?' Nell shuddered. 'We were just swimming out there before you came down.'

'No.' Tam jumped to her feet, and we watched her run down to the water.

I stood and held out my hand to pull Nell up.

'I think it's a person,' Tam called back to us. 'I'm going to go out to the point.'

It was too dark to see clearly, and I couldn't imagine that Tam was right. There were no boats in sight and no lights unless there was a boat around the point in Back Bay. Even so, it was too late at night for someone to be in the water. I wouldn't even swim in the daytime; I was worried about the shark attacks a couple of years ago and was very wary.

When the business could afford it, I intended to put a pool adjacent to the outdoor restaurant.

And a jacuzzi and a day spa. My thoughts went into planning mode as we followed Tam out onto the rocky point. It was too dark to see, but the closer we got to the water, the more I could hear splashing in the water.

'Could be dolphins,' I said.

Tam yelled as we were almost to her. 'It's a person, and I think they're in trouble.' As we took off towards her, she threw her hat to the ground, pulled her dress over her head and stepped into the water. Before we could reach her, she was swimming out into the bay.

'Tam, don't be stupid,' I yelled.

I looked around quickly. We were at the opposite end of the bay to the jetty, and by the time I could run over and start the launch, she could be back in.

But nevertheless, I remained poised to run as Nell picked up Tam's dress and hat.

I stared at the water, and it was only a minute or two later that the splashing reached us, followed by Tam's voice. She sounded out of breath.

'I've got them. I'll swim to the beach. It'll be easier than getting out on the rocks.'

I half-held my breath as we raced around to the beach and waited for Tam to appear. By the time we got there, I was breathless, and Nell was close to tears.

'Oh, Pip, is she going to make it?' she cried.

Gradually, we could make out a disturbance in the water, and I prayed under my breath that she would get in safely.

Suddenly, there was a huge splash, and Tam appeared in front of us. She was dragging a person by the armpits, and we all hurried into the water to help her.

It was a woman. She was wearing a long white dress that clung to her legs, impeding her progress. We each put our hands beneath her and carried her to the shore.

'Are you okay, Tam?' I glanced over at my brave friend. I was in awe of her bravery. There was no way I could have done that.

'I'm fine. I think she is, too. She was swimming by herself, but I think she passed out when I reached her.'

We lay the woman on her side in the recovery position, and I was relieved when she coughed and groaned. It was almost too dark to see.

'Evie, Nell, run up to the house and get a blanket and some water,' I said as I bent down with Tam.

The woman was breathing on her own, and as I watched, her eyes flickered open.

'Thank you,' she whispered.

'Are you all right? Can you breathe, okay? Are you hurt anywhere?' Tam fired questions at her, and the woman nodded.

'I'm okay. Thank you.' Her voice was stronger, and she tried to sit up. 'Please help me sit up, it'll be easier to catch my breath.'

Her voice had a slight accent that I couldn't place, and her dark hair was plastered to her skull in wet ringlets. Her eyes were dark and wide.

Tam and I supported her as she sat up on the sand.

'What's your name?' I asked.

'Eliza.' Her voice was faint.

'How did you get in the water?' Tam asked.

PENTECOST ISLAND 1-3

She looked at us both blankly. 'I don't know.'

ELIZA

PENTECOST ISLAND 2

PENTECOST ISLAND 1-3

Prologue

Pippa -Pentecost Island

A bottle of bubbles didn't last long between four when there was a celebration underway. The floors of the first four huts had been laid today, and now we were ready to put up the modular buildings. The frames were stacked waiting for us to begin work tomorrow.

I lifted my glass in a toast. 'To Ma Carmichael's Place.'

'To Ma's,' my three friends chimed in.

We clinked glasses and sipped at our champagne.

We were sitting on the sand looking across the bay to the peak that marked the centre of the island. Evie and Nell had gone for a quick swim while they'd waited for Tam and I to come down with the bubbles and the glasses. The sun was warm as spring approached and we all wore our straw hats.

'I think, ladies, when we get the interiors of the huts done, we might set an opening date and work towards that. What do you think of that?'

'Super,' Nell said.

Tam giggled. 'You're getting an English accent too. Or the lingo, at least.'

Nell nudged her and Tam's glass tipped a little.

'Hey, watch it, I'll spill my bubbles!'

Evie laughed with them. 'It's just like being back at uni, being here on the island with you lot. No cares, no worries, no pressure.'

I rolled my eyes. 'No, just a resort under development, a huge landscaping project'—I nodded at Evie— 'and a huge accounting task underway, thanks to Nell, and an outdoor restaurant and menus to be planned.' I raised my glass. 'Thank you, all.'

'That's right.' Tam nodded. 'Just like Evie said. No cares, no worries, no pressure.'

'And let's keep it that way. I want to propose another toast.' I lifted my glass. 'To friendship, girls. To the unbreakable bond that has seen us stay together through the ups and downs of life. And boy, there's been some of them over the past ten years.'

'To friendship,' they chorused.

As the sun slipped slowly towards the sea, we sat there in silence. Four women who cared for and looked out for each other. When the bubbles were finished, we put our glasses down and looped our arms around each other's shoulders. The sky faded from that deep indigo blue into an array of pinks shot with gold, and the only sound was the small waves breaking on the shingly sand.

I smiled as a light came on up the hill and Rafe's silhouette appeared at the window as he looked down to the bay.

Our bay.

He wouldn't be able to see us, but I could see him. I was beside Tam and I felt her tense as she leaned forward.

'Pip, what's that?'

I pulled my gaze away from Rafe's house and looked in the direction she was pointing. 'What?'

'There's something in the water. Look just out at the point. Something black.'

'A shark?' Nell shuddered. 'We were just swimming out there before you came down.'

'No.' Tam jumped to her feet and we watched as she ran down to the water.

I stood and held out my hand to pull Nell up.

'I think it's a person,' Tam called back to us. 'I'm going to go out to the point.'

It was too dark to see clearly, and I couldn't imagine that Tam was right. There were no boats in sight and no lights unless there was a boat around the point in Back Bay. Even so it was too late at night for someone to be in the water. I wouldn't even swim in the daytime; I was worried about the shark attacks a couple of years ago and was very wary.

When the business could afford it, I intended to put a pool in, adjacent to the outdoor restaurant.

And a jacuzzi, and a day spa. My thoughts went into planning mode as we followed Tam out onto the rocky point. It was too dark to see, but the closer we got to the water, the more I could hear splashing in the water.

'Could be dolphins,' I said.

Tam yelled as we were almost to her. 'It's a person, and I think they're in trouble.' As we took off towards her, she threw her hat to the ground, pulled her dress over her head and stepped into the water. Before we could reach her, she was swimming out into the bay.

'Tam, don't be stupid,' I yelled.

I looked around quickly. We were at the opposite end of the bay to the jetty, and by the time I could run over and start the launch, she could be back in.

But nevertheless, I remained poised to run as Nell picked up Tam's dress and hat.

I stared at the water and it was only a minute or two later that the splashing reached us followed by Tam's voice. She sounded out of breath.

'I've got them. I'll swim into the beach. It'll be easier than getting out on the rocks.'

I half held my breath as we raced around to the beach and waited for Tam to appear. By the time we got there I was breathless, and Nell was close to tears.

'Oh, Pip, is she going to make it?' she cried.

Gradually, we could make out a disturbance in the water and I prayed under my breath that she would get in safely.

Suddenly there was a huge splash, and Tam appeared in front of us. She was dragging a person by the armpits and we all hurried into the water to help her.

It was a woman. She was wearing a long white dress and it clung to her legs, impeding her progress. We each put our hands beneath her and carried her into the shore.

'Are you okay, Tam?' I glanced over at my brave friend. I was in awe of her bravery. There was no way I could have done that.

'I'm fine. I think she is too. She was swimming by herself, but I think she passed out when I reached her.

We lay the woman on her side in the recovery position, and I was relieved when she coughed and groaned. It was almost too dark to see.

'Evie, Nell, run up to the house and get a blanket and some water,' I said as I bent down with Tam.

The woman was breathing on her own, and as I watched her eyes flickered open.

'Thank you,' she whispered.

'Are you all right? Can you breathe okay? Are you hurt anywhere?' Tam fired questions at her, and the woman nodded.

'I'm okay. Thank you.' Her voice was stronger, and she tried to sit up. 'Please help me sit up, it'll be easier to catch my breath.'

Her voice had a slight accent that I couldn't place, and her dark hair was plastered to her skull in wet ringlets. Her eyes were dark and wide.

Tam and I supported her as she sat up on the sand.

'What's your name?' I asked.

'Eliza.' Her voice was faint.

'How did you get in the water?' Tam asked.

She looked us both blankly. 'I don't know.'

Chapter 1

Marissa: Florence, Italy 2018

'Marissa Meynell! You have not changed one bit!'

Marissa looked up at her best friend with a grin and carefully stroked the last layer of pale pink nail polish onto her fingernails. The huge diamond on her left hand glinted as she moved her hand. She screwed the cap onto the tiny bottle and placed it on the table near the large metal door. 'What do you mean, I haven't changed?'

Sienna stood there, hands on hips and tapping her foot on the marble floor, her elegant brows drawn together in a frown. 'I mean it's your wedding day, we're about to be picked up'—she reached down and smoothed an invisible crease from the pretty mauve silk sheath dress that Rosco had insisted on paying for—'and you only started getting ready fifteen minutes ago and now you're painting your nails!'

'But I do look okay, don't I?' For a minute a niggle of worry flared in Marissa's stomach. The contrast with her best friend's appearance had always been obvious. Sienna had even managed to look elegant and well-groomed as she'd scooted down the hockey field at their boarding school in Kent where they'd become best friends fifteen years ago.

Marissa always managed to look crumpled and untidy. Her idea of comfort was a pair of jeans and a T-shirt and her long, curly hair pulled back in a braid. A hasty dab of lip gloss on her way out the door was her usual method of wearing makeup. She'd gone blonde when she was eighteen thinking it would help her look more elegant, but it was just a pain getting the regrowth done. But she persevered; they said blondes had more fun, and she was proving them right.

Her complete opposite, Sienna always looked perfect no matter what time of day it was. Her glossy auburn hair fell in a perfect bob that brushed her long graceful neck, and her makeup was always meticulously applied. She'd started getting ready for the wedding about two hours ago, while Marissa had roamed around the apartment wondering if she was doing the right thing.

'You look gorgeous.' Sienna reached out and tucked a stray blonde curl behind Marissa's ear. 'As you always do. If I could look like you do without the effort I have to put in, I would be one very happy woman.'

Marissa reached up and touched the blonde curls that she had tried to smooth into a semblance of order. 'The girls at uni always called me Barbie because of my thick blonde hair.' She chuckled as she looked down at the high-necked wedding dress. 'But I certainly missed out in the Barbie boob department,' she said putting on an American accent. She was a natural mimic and going to school with girls from all over the world had given her a repertoire of accents.

Sienna smiled back at her. 'You look stunning, so stop worrying. I'd much rather be a blue-eyed blonde with your olive skin than red-haired and green-eyed and a lily-white complexion.'

Their conversation was interrupted by a loud jingling and Marissa's mouth dropped open.

Bella? Are you all right?' Sienna held her hand out. 'Come on, your carriage awaits.'

Marissa nodded as she put one hand to her lips and took Sienna's outstretched hand with the other.

'Oh, my goodness. Look at that. Surely that can't be for us, Sienna. Can it? I really hope it's not.'

'I don't see any other brides here waiting for transport.' Sienna Marino squeezed Marissa's fingers and pulled a face. 'Sorry, but your Rosco swore me to secrecy.'

Marissa shook her head and leaned back against the heavy

metal door in the carriageway beneath the apartment where the girls had been staying for the past week. The horse and carriage came to a stop beside them.

'Careful.' Sienna tugged Marissa's fingers and pulled her away from the door. 'You will mark your wedding dress.' As well as having spent a week in a fifteenth-century palace that was now a modern apartment, Sienna's lilting accent was another reminder to Marissa that they were in Italy and that her best friend from Switzerland was about to be her bridesmaid.

At *her* wedding. To a man she had met six weeks ago. But, oh what a wonderful man. Not only did Rosco Bertolini have movie star looks— "George Clooney" was often whispered around them as they'd walked the streets of Florence over the past month—and a movie star name, but he was also kind and generous and as madly in love with her as she was with him.

It was like a dream . . . or a fairy tale. Six weeks ago, Marissa had been a chippie on a work crew in east London, saving for her dream holiday to Italy.

Today she was marrying the man of her dreams; the man she had fallen in love with the moment she had seen him sitting by the river Arno watching the wooden tourist boats go by. She'd never believed in love at first sight, but her attention had been caught by the billowing white shirt he wore, and the jet-black hair that gleamed in the late afternoon sun.

She'd nudged Sienna. 'Why is it that Italian men are so much better looking than men at home?' Look at that gorgeous specimen,' she whispered as she kept her eyes on him as they had drifted past in the flat-bottomed *barchetti*. It might have been the Tuscan rosé she was sipping that gave Marissa a confidence that was out of character, but she had lifted her glass in a salute to the guy as they had floated past.

When he had been waiting at the wharf when they disembarked, she had been embarrassed and surprised, but . . .

flattered. Rosco stood there holding out two glasses of champagne.

'Welcome to Florence.' His voice had matched the rest of him. 'May I take you both for dinner?' His eyes had held Marissa's and heat had rushed to her face. He was even better looking close up, but a little older than she'd first thought.

She had looked at Sienna and her friend had shrugged.

'Why not?' They'd exchanged a glance; their budget was tight, so the offer of dinner was one to jump at.

That first night Rosco had taken them to a cute little restaurant in an alleyway near the Uffizi Gallery, and Marissa had not been able to take her eyes from his gorgeous face as he'd treated them to a magnificent dinner. His deep melodious voice had kept her hanging off his every word all night as she'd watched his full lips smile back at her. His eyes were dark and held hers in their depths as they'd eaten their way through five courses—*primo, secondo,* pasta and pizza, a main course and then *tiramisu* to die for—as well as drinking a considerable quantity of fine Italian wine, and then *limoncello.*

'Come on.' Sienna's voice intruded on her thoughts. 'If you're sure you're going to do this, it's time.'

With a gentle sigh Marissa looked down at the beautiful white silk dress that caressed her legs in the slight breeze that was blowing in from the *Via dei Serragli.* She felt like pinching herself. The fabric had come from an exclusive fashion house in Florence where Rosco had insisted on paying for her wedding dress.

Not only had he paid for it, but he had chosen the design, as well as the gorgeous soft handmade leather shoes she wore. She had protested and he had waved a dismissive hand. 'It is for my beautiful wife-to-be, and *cara mia,* we will only have one wedding, so I want you to be perfect. Wait until you see the beautiful silk nightgown I have bought for our wedding night. It will match your gorgeous blue eyes.'

The usual dry retort that the old Marissa would have made,

disappeared along with many of her London habits as she had fallen under Rosco's spell more and more every day.

For a moment, she had considered protesting; it would have been nice if she'd had some say in the wedding, her clothes, and the organisation of the day, but Rosco had planned everything, and she didn't want to take away from his excitement. It was enough for her that he wanted to marry her.

'Marissa. It's not too late.' Sienna's fingers squeezed hers.

'Too late for what?'

'To change your mind and come back to London with me and think about this a bit longer. I will be there for a few months until I go home.'

'Why would I change my mind?' She stared at Sienna. 'I love Rosco.'

'I know. And he loves you. But perhaps there is no need to marry quite so quickly. You could take more time to get to know each other more.'

'No one has ever loved me like he does.' Marissa shook her head. 'I have never been so sure of anything in my life.'

The second night Sienna had met up with some Italian friends and Rosco had taken Marissa to dinner—alone—and . . .

'Come on then. If you are sure, you don't want to be late.' Sienna tugged at her hand again.

'No, I don't.' They were expected at the *Palazza Vecchio* at noon.

'We will have a civil wedding, my darling. I know you are not Roman Catholic yet, so I have booked the *Sala Rossa*. We can look at your conversion before we have children,' Rosco had said.

Marissa had opened her mouth to protest at that statement; her family had been Church of England since the Reformation, and she had no intention of embracing a new religion, but Rosco had pulled her into his arms and silenced her with a kiss.

'I cannot wait until you see the palace on our wedding day,' he said, his lips warm and soft against hers. 'The opulent furnishings and beautiful frescoes, and the masterpieces that line the walls make it a place of beauty that will give us a wonderful start to our life together.'

If she'd looked more closely then, perhaps she would have seen the unusual intensity and determination in his eyes. But today on her wedding day, excitement and anticipation tingled from her fingertips to every nerve ending in her body.

'Marissa!'

She turned from her introspection as Sienna tugged again. 'The *fiaccheraio* is waiting for us.'

'The what?'

A tall man with silver hair held his hand out to her.

'The carriage driver,' Sienna said with a giggle. 'I look forward to your grasp of the language improving very quickly when you are married to an Italian.'

'I'm not happy about the carriage at all,' Marissa whispered. 'I saw the demonstration in the square the other day, where they were drawing attention to the heat and the conditions that these poor horses have to work in. I would prefer to get a taxi. If I'd known that Rosco was going to organise this, I would have put my foot down.'

'No, no, no.' The carriage driver shook his head emphatically and pointed to his chest. 'Me, I follow the rules. I love my horse and I would not put him in any way of the harm.'

Marissa reluctantly let the man assist her into the carriage, and when she was settled on the burgundy velvet seat, Sienna followed and passed her one of the red rose bouquets that had been waiting in the foyer when they had come down from the apartment.

The ride to the *palazza* through cool and narrow side streets shaded by medieval buildings eased some of the guilt caused by riding in the horse drawn carriage. Tourists waved to them and called out as the horse clopped his way along the cobblestones.

But if she'd had her way, she still wouldn't have condoned it.

'Get the glum look from your face. We are almost there, and the photographers will be waiting.' Sienna squeezed her hand again. 'You're sure you're not getting cold feet, are you?'

Was that a glimmer of hope in Sienna's voice?

'No, of course not.' Joy filled Marissa's chest and she buried her face in the sweet-smelling roses. 'I am excited and honoured to be marrying the man I love.'

'Do you mind that your family could not make it?'

'No. We'll see them soon.' The guilt rushed back, and heat crept up Marissa's neck. Although she had told Sienna her family couldn't attend, they were unaware that she was marrying Rosco today. Sienna was the only one who knew.

Mother would be ecstatic that she was marrying into the Italian aristocracy, not to mention wealth. Marissa knew she was a disappointment to her parents with the life she led, and the profession she had chosen. She had never felt loved by them since she was a child. Her two sisters seemed to be what her parents had wanted in children, but Marissa—the third daughter—was very different to her siblings.

'A what?' Her mother's voice echoed in her thoughts.

'A chippy.' Marissa had stood in front of her mother in the hall of their thirteenth century manor, hands on hips, staring down at her work boots. Boots and socks that certainly looked out of place on the huge black and white chequered tiles of this elegant, but tired manor house.

'You are turning away a position in your father's company to be a common labourer? A position in the family company that has been an institution in this family for over two hundred years?' Mother's voice had been shrill.

'I am an artisan, Mother, not a labourer. Our first job is restoring the timberwork on a shopfront in the Royal Arcade off

Old Bond Street.' Marissa had quickly regretted trying to upset her mother by referring to her job as a chippy. 'A craftsperson. That should appeal to your sensibilities.'

One last sniff and Mother had disappeared up the stairs.

Nevertheless, Marissa had suggested to Rosco that they invite her parents to Florence for the wedding, but he had talked her out of it, and she hadn't pushed it.

'Let's surprise them with a visit. We can get your new wardrobe in Paris, and I'm sure your mother will be delighted to see you in designer labels, from what you have told me about her.'

Perhaps Mother might be delighted, but Marissa was tempted to say she was happy with her current wardrobe. But spoiling her seemed to give Rosco pleasure too, and he assured her over and over that he could afford it.

'We will visit your Meynell Manor in Derbyshire on our honeymoon, and I will meet your family. I am nervous that they will not like me. I do not want them to change your mind before you become my wife.' Rosco's voice had been uncertain as he held her.

Marissa had hugged him. 'I will not change my mind.'

It was only a small white lie she had told Sienna.

A lie that would come back to haunt her.

Six months later, Marissa was to wonder what had happened to her in those six delirious weeks. Forty-two whirlwind days that had eventuated in her marrying a man twenty years older than her.

Chapter 2

Pippa: Pentecost Island, Winter 2020

Evie and Nell didn't take long to come back from the house with a bottle of water, a blanket and a thick towel. Tam and I were sitting beside the dark-haired woman on the sand. It wasn't too cool in the late winter evening, but she was shivering as though it was the middle of winter.

'Thanks.' Tam removed her arm from the woman's shoulder and took the towel that Nell held out as Evie popped the top off the water bottle.

'A drink of water first, and then we'll get that wet dress off you,' Evie said calmly.

How the hell the woman called Eliza had managed to swim in that long dress and not drown was beyond me. It was easy to see that she wore a pair of black swimmers beneath the white dress that was clinging to her wet legs.

She said she couldn't remember how she came to be in the water, but she couldn't have come far. She had to have come off a boat because the closest island was Little Lindeman Island to the south and that was over two kilometres away. Too far to swim to our island.

As Tam helped peel off the wet dress with Nell's help, I gestured for Evie to walk along the beach with me.

'Can you jump in your tender and go for a bit of a scoot around to Back Bay. She has to have come off a boat.'

'Maybe she fell overboard and hit her head?' Evie said quietly with a glance back up the beach. 'Seems strange that she can't remember how she got in the water. Have you checked her eyes?'

'Not yet,' I said. 'Keeping her warm was our first priority. I think she's in shock.'

'If she'd hit her head, she would've gone under and not appeared at the front of our bay.' Evie's voice was still quiet. 'Someone must be out there looking for her. I'll go out now and look for a boat.'

I nodded and went back to the group on the beach as Evie headed towards the wharf at the base of the hill beneath Rafe's house.

I tapped my finger on my lips as I stared up at his house on the hill; the lights glowed softly as the dark surrounded us on the beach. I wondered for a moment if I should go up and tell him what had happened, and then realised there was nothing he could do.

Besides, he'd be working. Rafe was editing his new book and had it almost ready to send back to his publisher in London.

'Pip?' Tam's voice drew me over. 'Eliza is feeling a little better now. I think we should go up to the house.'

'Thank you for the water. My legs have stopped shaking now. I should be able to stand up.' This time there was no accent to her words.

Tam and Nell took an arm each and helped Eliza to her feet. I stood in front of them in case she fainted or anything.

'Do you remember your last name,' I asked quietly as she stood gripping the girls' hands.

She nodded. 'Pengelly. I am Eliza Pengelly.'

'Your address?'

This time a frown and her words were hesitant. 'Um. I don't have a current one. I used to live in Brisbane. At the Gap. But I don't live there anymore.'

'So where do you live now?'

'I'm on a holiday. A working holiday' Her voice was soft

and there was just enough light for me to see her close her eyes. 'I remember now. I was on my kayak.'

Tam and I exchanged a glance.

On a kayak? In a long white dress with no lifejacket? It didn't ring true for me.

'You weren't wearing a life jacket then?' Tam asked, echoing my thoughts

She shook her head. 'No, but I had been. I'd been out fishing in my kayak and when I caught enough, I went back to the island. Um, Dylan was going to get the fire going and cook them and he asked me to go to the other end of the beach to collect some firewood. That's why I was wearing a dress. I was only paddling to the end of the beach.'

'Which island?' Nell asked quietly. She had more patience than Tam and I did with the changing answers.

Eliza frowned and let go of Tam's hand and pressed her fingers to her forehead. Her short dark curls were plastered to her forehead. 'Little something I think Dylan said.'

'Little Lindeman?' I asked.

She nodded and dropped her hand. 'Yes, that was it. I've been there a few days. I joined a group.'

'A group?' Tam took her arm again.

'Dylan, Alex and Marissa. There were more, but they left when the boat came.' Her voice was getting stronger now and again there was that twang of an accent.

Maybe Kiwi, I thought.

'Oh my God, they'll think I drowned.' Confusion crossed her face as she put her hand to her head again.

'Did they see you get in the kayak? Do you know any of their mobile numbers?' I peppered her with questions. 'We could call and say you've turned up here,' I said.

Nell flicked me a glance and shook her head. 'I think before we do any of that we need to get Eliza up to the house, and into a hot shower.'

'Yes. we do. Come on. We'll help you along.' Tam's voice was brisk as she led the dark-haired woman up the beach.

I followed, a frown on my face, still wondering how and why she ended up on our island.

Something didn't feel right for me.

Chapter 3

Marissa

'Dubrovnik? I thought we were flying to Paris, and then England?' Marissa frowned as she looked down at the boarding pass that Rosco handed her at Roma International Airport the afternoon after their wedding. 'To see my family?'

They had taken the train from Florence in a first-class carriage mid-morning, and a hire car had been waiting to whisk them straight to the airport.

Rosco moved his head lower and his breath whispered along her neck. 'We are, my love, but first we are going to have a week alone on my yacht. Just you and me.'

'*Your* yacht?' Marissa widened her eyes.

My God, who is this man?

'Yes, my other beautiful lady. My *Lady Calypso*. I wanted to have some time alone with you in a beautiful place before we head to that cold and rainy island you used to call home.'

'Perhaps you could have told me your plans.' Marissa stiffened and moved away from his hold, but Rosco's fingers tightened on her arm.

'It was going to be a surprise, *cara mia*.' His face fell and Marissa reached up to brush her lips across her husband's cheek. 'It is going to be a honeymoon that any woman would want.'

'I'm sorry for snapping, darling. It sounds wonderful but perhaps next time you could tell me if there is a change of plans?'

His lips tightened. 'We are going to the Adriatic Sea and I am showing you my favourite place in the whole world. I have never taken a woman there before. Do you know how special that is?'

Even though his words made her feel a little uncomfortable,

Marissa smiled as she wondered how many women he *had* taken to other places. She was being silly. At forty-two and an eligible bachelor, she had to accept that of course there had been women in Rosco's life before he had fallen in love with her. *She* was the inexperienced one.

Inexperienced with men, love and this whole relationship thing.

Gosh, no. This *marriage* thing. A cold feeling shimmied down her back, and she bit down the anxiety that tugged at her.

'Where is this place?' Her voice was calm, and she was pleased it didn't reflect that nerves were taking hold.

'It is an easy sail off the coast of Dubrovnik. The island of Mljet.' The word rolled off Rosco's tongue and his sexy accent sent a luscious shiver down her spine. 'Legend has it that Mljet is the island of Ogygia where the nymph, Calypso, kept the Greek hero, Odysseus, captive for seven years. The ancient name for the island is Melitta, which comes from the Greek *melitte nesos*.'

'What does that mean?'

Even though they were in full view of the other passengers waiting to board, Rosco's lips settled on her neck. 'It means honey island. Perhaps you will want to keep me captive there like Odysseus' nymph did.'

'Did he escape?' she whispered back as his lips crept up her neck.

'He did. Even though she promised him immortality if he stayed with her.'

Marissa swayed as her legs trembled when her husband of twenty-four hours nipped the lobe of her ear. Pulling back, she shook her head as a blush warmed her cheeks. 'Please wait until we get to our room.'

##

The island of Mljet was everything that Rosco had

promised . . . and more. Marissa sighed as he dropped the main sail of *Lady Calypso* and it came down quickly into the sail bag. Everything happened quickly on this boat, and she had hidden her trepidation every time the boat had leaned over as they had sailed up the coast from Dubrovnik. Her experience on the sea was non-existent.

Although in one way she was pleased to learn that there were no other crew on Rosco's boat, she had learned how to help and what ropes to hold over the past day. Rosco said the sea had been smooth as they had sailed across a wide expanse of water with no land in sight.

'You look worried.'

She jumped as he came up behind her, his white-soled shoes making no noise on the timber deck.

'I'm still not used to being on board a boat that tips over with every wave and puff of wind.' The wind had picked up and was blowing quite strongly as they got closer to the rocky foreshore of the island. 'I'm embarrassed to admit it, but the only other time I've been on a boat was on the ferry from Calais to Dover on a school excursion.'

Rosco raised his eyebrows, but his smile was encouraging, even though his words came as a surprise. 'You will soon get used to living on the sea. If the wind stays like this, we will have some excellent sailing days.'

'How long did you say we would be on the boat?'

'I was thinking a week, but I have had an excellent idea. If the wind stays up like this, we could sail around Italy to the *Cote d'Azur* and fly to Paris from Nice.'

'How long would that take?' Marissa frowned, not sure how she felt about spending more than a few days living on this yacht.

'Don't you want to have a long honeymoon with me?' Rosco pulled her closer. She shivered as his hand ran down her back and lingered at the top of her shorts. 'When we travel—and we will travel most of the year, *Lady Calypso*—or my motor cruiser, *Nymph*—will take us where we want to go. And quickly.'

'Oh. Your motor cruiser?'

'Smile, my darling.' Rosco tapped a finger on her cheek as he let her go. 'Once we motor into the bay and drop the anchor it will be calm. I don't want a wife who is afraid.'

Marissa responded with a smile, despite her stomach feeling as though her lunch may not stay there. 'I'm fine.' She spread her arms wide. 'And look how beautiful it is here.' She watched as Rosco went back to the helm, and a ripple of pleasure and anticipation of the nights ahead filled her with excitement.

Her wedding night had surpassed all expectations. Rosco had insisted on waiting until they were married, and he had been a gentle and considerate lover; even listening to his deep voice now brought a shiver to her skin. Seven days alone in a boat would be wonderful, but no more than that this trip. He had promised when they didn't invite her parents to the wedding, that they would go to England and tell them in person. It didn't matter if she didn't get home to see her family for at least another two weeks. She wasn't due home from her Italian holiday until then, so they wouldn't worry. She would give them a call later—just to touch base—not to tell them she was married and on her honeymoon.

'Shit.' For the first time, reality tugged at Marissa, and a strange feeling settled in her stomach. With those words at the ceremony, her life had changed and irrevocably set her on a new path.

It didn't matter what her family thought. And it didn't matter that she wouldn't go back to her job in London—she'd hated the city anyway—she had made a commitment.

A lifelong commitment. Her fingers fluttered with nerves and she swallowed.

But Rosco turned to her, and her doubts dissolved instantly

PENTECOST ISLAND 1-3

as his lips tilted in a smile. He lifted his fingers and blew her a kiss before he took the helm.

Marissa kept her eyes on him as he steered the boat through a narrow channel into a protected cove. Thick luxuriant pine woods tumbled down to the shoreline, and the pungent smell of cypress carried across on the breeze. She breathed a sigh of relief once the anchor was over and the boat stopped rocking.

'Don't worry, I have set the anchor firmly and we have forty metres of chain holding us steady.'

Her grin was cheeky. 'That means nothing to me.'

'What it means is we won't be going anywhere.'

'Will we be eating on the boat? Or is there a restaurant that we can go to?'

Rosco's laugh blew away on the stiff wind as he stood up from the anchor bay. 'If you would like to walk four miles there is a delightful little restaurant in a small village over the cliffs. We will go there one night, but tonight I have other plans.'

'Other plans? She swallowed and her legs trembled as his smile widened.

'I think we shall strip off and cool down with a swim, and then I will lie on the deck while you cook my dinner.'

'Oh, will you?' Marissa swallowed nervously again. She hadn't told Rosco that cooking was something she had little experience with. Let alone cooking in the tiny little galley that held a small gas stove and a tiny sink.

She hadn't thought about food when he had stocked the boat assuming that they would eat out every night.

'Um, I'll just go down and get my bikini on.'

He shook his head and his smile was almost predatory. 'You won't need your bikini.' He held her gaze as he undid the tie on his white shorts and dropped them to the deck.

Oh my God.

He was naked.

And beautiful.

Marissa's husband walked over and lifted her T-shirt over her head, and within seconds her state of dress matched his.

His lips ran down her neck and desire flared as one hand cupped her breast. 'Perhaps we will swim later, my dear.'

Chapter 4

Pippa

I went back to collect the empty wine bottle and glasses from the beach while Nell sorted towels for Eliza in the bathroom and hovered outside as she took a shower. Tam got a meal underway, and soon the usual aromatic smells were coming from the kitchen she had now made her own.

I was sad that the arrival of this mystery woman had interrupted our celebration, but at the same time, I was pleased that she had swum to our bay instead of meeting an untimely end somewhere out in those waters.

As I bent down to pick up the glasses, the sound of a motor reached me. I straightened and put my hand to my eyes and squinted in the darkness. A small light shone across the water near the end of the wharf as Evie motored towards it. There was something behind her rubber tender, but I couldn't make out what it was.

I hurried along the beach and ran up the three stairs to the wharf.

'Pippa?' Rafe's voice called from above me. I paused and waited until he came down the steps on the hill and jumped down onto the wharf beside me.

'Hello.' His arms went around me, and his warm lips took mine before I could say a word. I hugged him back and then pulled away when Evie's tender bumped the end of the wharf.

'Is everything okay?' he asked. 'I saw you all on the beach and the tender go out before.'

'We've had a bit of drama tonight,' I said tugging at his hand as I moved to the end of the wharf.

Evie was still in the tender and I could see a light shape

was floating beside the rubber boat.

'Drama?' he asked.

'Yes, a woman was in trouble swimming around the point and we got her onto the shore. Evie went out looking for a boat. Tam and Nell are up at the house with her.'

'Is she all right?' His hand still held mine.

'Seems to be, but we were worried that someone was out there looking for her. She said she was on a kayak. It's too far for anyone to swim from any of the islands.'

'Found it,' Evie called up from the tender. 'This was floating around the point. She must have got caught in the rough waves at the front of Back Bay.

Back Bay was notorious for irregular tidal eddies in contrary wind and tide conditions. For the unwary sailor, it was easy for a yacht to get into trouble, let alone a kayak. Experienced sailors knew to stay to the starboard side when coming out into the channel, and not risk the conditions when the channel opening met swirling eddies.

I frowned. 'She reckons she was over on Little Lindeman.'

'Has to be hers,' Evie said. 'I couldn't see any mast lights out there. And I found this in the cavity.' As she climbed out of the tender, she held up a waterproof bag.

Rafe dropped my hand and moved over to where Evie now stood. 'Do you want me to bring that kayak up onto the wharf?'

I nodded. 'Good idea. The wind seems to be picking up, and the last thing we want is for it to float out to the channel and create a hazard for any boats out there tonight.'

Evie handed me the waterproof bag and went to help Rafe. They each lifted an end of the kayak and soon it was on the wharf.

It was almost pitch dark and Evie reached into the tender for a flashlight. She switched it on, and I could see the contents of the clear bag I was holding.

'There's a couple of envelopes in here,' I said.

PENTECOST ISLAND 1-3

'Should we look or give it to her?' Evie asked.

'Let me think about it while you two bring the kayak over to the beach. We'll put it under the trees behind the huts.'

I followed Evie and Rafe as they carried the old kayak off the wharf and along our beach. I wasn't sure what to do.

My good old "spidey" sense had kicked in, and I had a bad feeling about our visitor. Well, not bad, I suppose. Just a feeling things weren't as they seemed. I don't mean that we were all going to be murdered in our beds by some madwoman, but I just found it hard to believe that she would conveniently get into trouble in the water right where the four of us happened to be sitting on a beach, and close enough to rescue her easily. But I couldn't think of any logical explanation for it, other than what she'd said. I'd be grilling her later tonight.

'I can hear your brain whirring away,' Rafe said when they put the kayak down and joined me where I waited at the track.

I chuckled. 'I've been spending too much time with you, Mr Author. My imagination is in overdrive.'

'Not spending enough time with me, to my mind,' he said as he caught my hand.

A rush of pleasure ran through me. I don't think I've ever been happier than I've been since Tam and Nell and I came to Pentecost Island.

Our new resort—*Ma Carmichael's Place*— was taking shape, Evie had joined us, and the gardens were already looking better. The first huts were about to go up and our plans to open for business in three months were on track.

I found myself waking up with a smile most days, and the happiness stayed with me all day. There'd been no dark moments for weeks, and I was sure that the sadness that had been a part of me for so much of my life had gone. Since Aunty Vi had left me her island—well, half of it, Rafe owned the other half—I had begun to heal and look at the world in a very different way.

And I was lucky enough to have the best girlfriends as part of my life—and part of my business project.

And then there was Rafe.

I was trying to go slow. We'd had a rocky start, but he was now a very big part of my happiness. If I was honest, I would say he was more than a big part. I knew if he moved away from our island, I would be devastated.

He wanted to move faster, but with my past track record, I needed to take it slowly, and God love him, he said he would agree to any terms I offered.

'What do you think about the bag?' Evie asked. 'Is it breaching her privacy if we open it?'

'Well, we really don't know that the kayak is Eliza's, do we? She said she was in a kayak, so I guess we could look in to see if it's hers. There are clues in those envelopes.' I turned to Rafe. 'Do you think that's a fair call?'

'I do. You've rescued a woman from drowning and salvaged an unattended kayak. If there is a connection you'll hopefully find out, and it might shed light on how she got to the island.'

'Evie, can you shine the light here please,' I asked as I held the sealed bag up.

She obliged and Rafe stood close to me as I unclipped the Ziplock waterproof bag and tipped the two envelopes into my hand.

I handed the thicker one to Rafe to hold and I lifted the flap on the thinner envelope and turned it over. A small black booklet fell into my hand. Before I opened it, I shook the envelope but there was nothing else inside.

'It looks like a passport,' Evie commented.

I opened the booklet, and sure enough it was a New Zealand-issued passport. Rafe's breath brushed my cheek as he leaned forward.

PENTECOST ISLAND 1-3

'What name is in it?'

I turned to the second page and a photo of the woman Tam had rescued stared back at me. She was a very pretty woman, her blue eyes fringed by thick dark lashes—the sort of lashes I had attempted to achieve with all sorts of mascara when I was working—and her cheeks glowing a healthy pink. I scanned the printed details.

'Yep. What she said. Eliza Pengelly and her address says Krage Place, at the Gap in Brisbane.'

'She's thinner in that photograph,' Evie commented. 'Not that she's big now, but she was very thin then. What date is the passport?'

I looked at the bottom line. 'It's a newish one. Valid until 2029.'

Rafe held the other envelope out. 'I think you need to look in here. By the feel of it, I can guess what's in there.'

I looked up at him curiously and his expression was hard to read as I held his gaze. I took the envelope from him and slid my finger beneath the flap.

My mouth dropped open as I peered in. 'Holy fuck.'

'Money?' he asked.

'*And* jewellery.' I nodded and Evie peered over my shoulder.

'Wow. A shitload of money,' she said.

'And what looks like a diamond ring.' I bit my bottom lip and looked back at Rafe. 'There must be a few thousand dollars in there. All in one hundred-dollar notes. Why would someone be in a kayak with a passport and carrying so much money and diamonds?'

'And wearing a dress out kayaking?' Evie added. 'It's bizarre.'

'What do you think we should do?' I put the passport back into its envelope and then slid both envelopes back into the

Ziplock bag. 'Should we tell her we found her kayak? And the envelopes? Or should we find out more about her before we do?'

'You think they might not be hers?' Rafe asked.

'I guess they are. It's her photo, and a passport is an authentic form of identification, isn't it?' I shrugged. 'I guess we go back to the house, see how she is and tell her we found the kayak.'

Evie stared down at the envelopes. 'If she thinks the kayak is lost, she'll be pretty damned upset. Losing all that money and passport.'

'The whole situation has me intrigued. Is it all right if I come with you?' Rafe put his arm around me. I leaned into the hard angles of his body, the feel of his skin and the smell of his woody aftershave were becoming very familiar to me, and I liked that.

'Of course. I think you should join us for dinner. Tam was making a huge pot of curry when we left.' I narrowed my eyes. 'You can be the observer and tell us what you think of our mermaid.'

By the time we'd walked up to the house, Evie's comment turned into an accurate prediction. A loud shrill voice and tears met us as we reached the verandah.

Nell's always calm voice was audible between the sobs. 'It's okay. Look you're alive and anything lost can be replaced.'

The voice was even more shrill. 'But it is my passport. How can I get that replaced? I have no other ID.'

My eyes narrowed again as we walked inside; Rafe and Evie were close behind me as I held the two Ziplock bags out of sight behind my back.

I guess I wasn't feeling terribly sympathetic, and I tried to figure out why. I watched our mystery woman drop her head into her hands and sob some more. Maybe because it was my island, and I only wanted people I invited here for the moment. It would

PENTECOST ISLAND 1-3

soon be overrun with guests when we opened the resort. I didn't want a stunning looking intruder changing the dynamics of our group.

Eliza's dark hair had dried, and some colour had come back into her cheeks. She was certainly the woman whose photo was in the passport behind my back.

'Pip?' Rafe's soft voice held surprise and he nudged me. I looked back at him and he gestured to the two bags.

Guilt flooded through me. I was being a suspicious bitch. The poor woman had almost drowned and I was being precious. After all, we could have been dealing with a body on the beach instead of a crying woman.

I walked over and crouched down beside the lounge where Nell was trying to soothe her.

'Eliza?' I said. 'It's okay. Evie found your kayak.'

She looked up and when she saw Rafe behind me, the colour leached from her face. Her eyes were wide as she stared up at him.

He smiled. 'Hello, I'm Rafe. I live across the bay.' As usual his words were cultured and polite, and his posh accent made me smile.

Eliza leaned back and an expression akin to relief crossed her face. 'You found it? You found my kayak?'

'Evie did.' It was about time I was a bit more welcoming. 'I'm Pippa, this is Evie, and you've met Rafe.'

'And we've already introduced ourselves.' Tam had been watching from the kitchen doorway.

'Where is my kayak now?' Eliza jumped to her feet. 'Is it damaged? Is it okay?'

'It's fine.' I held out the two bags. 'We wanted to check it was yours and we found these in the front well.'

Eliza's hand went to her chest and she closed her eyes. 'Thank God.'

212

For a minute I thought she was going to faint, and I reached out, but she leaned across and took the bags from me.

'Thank you. Thank you so much.' She glanced down at the envelope with the money and a tinge of colour stained her cheeks. 'I always keep my money and valuables and my passport with me. I've met a few undesirables while I've been backpacking around the islands.'

'Don't thank me. Evie was the one who found the kayak.'

'Thank you, Evie, and thank you all. I am a very lucky person to have been rescued here.' She glanced across at Evie. 'You didn't find my pack with my clothes in the back hatch?'

Evie shook her head. 'I didn't look there. It was getting dark and the wind was coming up, so I just hooked it up to the tender and brought it in.'

'Your kayak is down on the beach.'

She stood. 'I'll go and look now.'

Rafe stepped forward. 'I'll go. You stay here. Tell me exactly what I'm looking for.'

'Just a small pack jammed into the back well behind the seat. My tent is on top and my shoes should be underneath. I travel lightly.'

'Okay, be back in a tick,' he said.

I didn't like the way Eliza looked at him.

I moved away and nodded to Tam. 'Dinner ready to go?'

##

The conversation around the dinner table was interesting to say the least. If it hadn't been for all of us hearing what Eliza had said on the beach about going fishing and paddling to get firewood, I would probably have doubted what I'd heard.

Rafe had brought her bag up and she'd changed into a pair

of khaki shorts and a black T-shirt. Nell had taken her to one of the spare rooms at the back that we'd been painting and preparing for staff when we hired.

'Do you have a phone to call your friends?' I asked as Tam served out the boiled rice. 'They must be worried.'

She shook her head. 'I don't, but they're not really my friends. Just other travellers who were on the island when I arrived there. I don't know if any of them have a phone.'

I stared at her. 'We'll take the boat over as soon as it's light and drop you back there.'

She shook her head. 'There's no need for that.'

'You said they'd be worried,' I said.

'No. In these groups, people come and go. They won't worry.'

'I thought you said you'd caught fish and you were getting firewood.'

'Did I?' Her wide forehead scrunched up in a frown. 'I don't remember that I was going to do that.'

'That's what you said.' I glanced at Nell as her knee touched mine beneath the table and she shook her head slightly.

'Tell us about your travels,' Nell said with a smile. 'I think you are brave to be paddling around the islands in an ocean kayak.' She chuckled. 'Living on an island is as brave as I get.'

Eliza took the plate of curry and rice that Tam held out before she answered. 'You live on the island?'

Nell nodded. 'It's Pippa's island, and this is her house.'

Rafe cleared his throat. 'Ahem.'

'Oh, and Rafe owns half the island. Sorry, Rafe.' Nell flicked him an apologetic smile.

'A fabulous place to live. I love these islands. I've been thinking of settling here.'

'You're from Brisbane?' I asked.

Eliza nodded. 'Recently. I grew up in New Zealand. I've

always loved the water. My dad was a fisherman and we lived close to the water just like this.'

'I thought I detected a Kiwi accent. My boss at the Gold Coast was from Auckland.'

'You haven't always lived here?'

'No, Tam and Nell and I have been here about eight weeks. Evie joined us a couple of weeks later. We're developing a resort.' I couldn't help the pride in my voice. Now that we knew a little bit more about her, I was relaxing.

'That must be exciting.'

Tam laughed. 'I don't know that exciting is the word I'd use this week. I wouldn't care if I never held a paint brush again.'

'But you must admit it was worth it. The place is looking great.' I took the plate that Tam held out. 'And I love you for your painting skills as much as your cooking.'

'It smells delicious, thank you.' Eliza reached for the jug and poured water into her glass. 'So you're renovating the house as a guesthouse yourselves? What about you, Rafe? Where do you fit in?'

'I'm just a neighbour,' he said but he held my gaze. 'I was here first, but we have come to an arrangement.'

'We have.' I held his gaze steadily and a flutter of anticipation tugged low in my belly. An arrangement where the terms were yet to be defined, but I was very happy with the pace we were working at.

'Pippa's a slave driver, but we love her,' Evie said. 'Best boss ever. I've been doing the gardens and planning the walking tracks and helping out with the painting.'

I pulled a face at her. 'Remember, I'm a friend before I'm a boss. We're all in this together.'

'What about you, Nell?' Eliza's expression was full of interest, and having an outsider look so impressed, reminded me of how much we'd achieved in such a short time. I was really lucky to have such good friends who had as much determination as I did to make this project succeed.

'I keep Pip on the straight and narrow looking after the finances.' Nell was calm and quiet as always.

'And she paints too.' Tam laughed. 'We all paint except for Pippa. We banned her because she made such a mess.'

'Hey, be careful how you talk about the boss,' I joked.

'So, you really are doing it all yourselves?' Eliza asked.

'As much as we can. We will hire when we need to. We had contractors over from the mainland yesterday to pour the slabs for the huts.'

'You girls are incredible.' Eliza looked around the table at each of us, and for the first time, I let go of the suspicion that I had held. 'And when you open for business, you'll need more staff?' Her voice held a hopeful note as she looked at me.

'And before.' I put my fork down and tipped my head to the side. 'Why do you ask?'

'I'd be interested in applying if you were hiring.'

'What's your background? Qualifications?'

'I don't have any formal qualifications, but I can turn my hand to most things. My father taught me everything I needed to know. As well as our fishing business, we had a market garden and a small vineyard on Waiheke Island. I can fix a motor, use a hammer, dig a garden, make wine, catch fish, and'—she was really beautiful when she smiled—'I wield a mean paintbrush.'

I nodded slowly. 'What are your plans? I mean, I—we—don't want someone who's not committed to our project. Someone who might up and leave if the going got tough.' I looked around the table. 'I trust these three girls with my life.'

'I have no plans,' she said simply.

'Let us think about it. We'll talk in the morning.'

Chapter 5

Marissa: Croatia

The first week on *Lady Calypso* was idyllic. It had taken Marissa a while to work up the courage to tell Rosco that she had no idea how to cook the fish he'd caught the second morning on board. The first night they'd sailed across to the island, they'd dined on the fresh crusty loaf and olives that Rosco had picked up at the marina where his boat was berthed when he wasn't on it.

Marissa had looked over at the heavily wooded shore. 'Is there a town? Or just that village you mentioned?' All she could see was hills covered with tall pine trees, and the occasional rocky outcrop. As she stared at the forest, she noticed there was a track through the trees.

'Only the village, but we won't leave the boat yet. I don't want to share my new wife.' Rosco pulled her close and nuzzled his lips into her neck.

'But where will we eat? And shop?

'I have enough provisions on board for you to cook. And I will catch more fish for us.'

'Cook?' Marissa shook her head slowly. 'I don't cook.'

Rosco pulled his head back and stared at her.

'Every woman cooks.'

'I beg your pardon?' Marissa took a step back.

'I said women cook. As my wife, you will cook my meals.'

Marissa folded her arms as her temper pinged. 'I'm very sorry, Rosco. I don't agree with your attitude. It is a bit old fashioned. Perhaps we should have discussed this more.'

Instead of falling in lust, she thought.

'Oh *cara mia,* already you give me grounds for divorce.' His mouth was set in a straight line. 'You cannot cook the fish that I caught for us?'

PENTECOST ISLAND 1-3

'Oh . . . oh . . .' Her mouth had dropped open and heat rushed to her face until she saw his dancing eyes. 'Oh, you are teasing me!'

'Come here.' His bare skin had pressed against hers—Marissa still couldn't get used to her husband wandering about the boat naked—most of the time she insisted on leaving her bikini on.

'There is no one here to see you,' he said, but she shook her head.

'I don't feel comfortable . . . yet.' It was taking her a while to adjust to being married and in one person's exclusive company, but she had no regrets. She just had to make some adjustments.

'I will take you down to the galley and I will teach you how to cook fish. It will be my pleasure.'

She closed her eyes and his lips pressed butterfly kisses along her jaw. 'There's only one thing I will insist on,' she murmured.

His lips paused on their journey to her mouth and his voice was stern. 'Insist on? You will never insist on anything.'

She opened her eyes and his dark eyes were intent on hers.

'Oh yes, I will,' she said. 'I insist that you put clothes on if we are working in the galley. I would hate to see'—her eyes dropped, and she summoned a sultry smile— 'any part of you damaged in the galley.'

He pulled her close again and his breath tickled her ear. 'As you are concerned about my safety, and your future pleasure, I will abide by your rule.' He lowered his voice. 'For this one time, you can tell me what to do.'

A niggle of uneasiness settled in her chest.

##

The next morning Marissa lay on their soft bed staring up

at the open hatch in their cabin. Rosco was on the deck already, but she hadn't heard any noise apart from a splash and then his feet on the steps as he'd climbed onboard a few minutes later.

Maybe he was swimming off a hangover, she thought. She hoped so.

He deserved one after last night.

All was quiet now as the boat rocked gently in the slight breeze that blew down through the thickly forested slope.

Marissa rolled over and buried her face in the pillow. How many people had their first fight within five days of being married?

It had all started last night when they were sitting on the deck having a drink before dinner. She'd been nervous about preparing the fish—even with his help—and as the sun slipped behind the wooded forest Rosco turned to her.

'What are you going to prepare with the fish I will cook with you?'

'Um? With the fish?'

He shook his head slowly. 'Yes. A salad? Perhaps some *patatas*?'

'Ah . . . *patatas*?' Marissa said. 'I thought we were going to prepare the meal together.'

'This one time I will cook the fish up here. I think it's time for you to begin to prepare the rest of the meal. And to learn.' He drained his wine glass and refilled it, and his eyes narrowed before she looked away.

'Okay.' She put her wine glass on the table in front of the deck sofa that they were curled up on. As she stood Rosco ran his hand lightly down her leg. 'You are a very beautiful woman, Marissa I am very fortunate to have you as my wife.'

'And I you, my love.'

His dark eyes sent a delicious shiver down her spine and she felt like pinching herself. How could it be that two months ago she and Sienna had been planning their holiday to Italy, and now

PENTECOST ISLAND 1-3

here she was, married to a gorgeous Italian and on a beautiful yacht on the Adriatic Sea. Marissa leaned down and brushed a kiss on Rosco's cheek.

'Let's see if you say that after you have your dinner,' she said with a laugh.

His brow wrinkled in a frown as he stared up at her. 'What do you mean?'

'You'll see,' she said.

Well, Rosco had seen, and he wasn't impressed, but she was less than impressed with his over-the-top reaction.

She done her best with what was in the galley. It was hard enough figuring out how to light the stupid gas thing to boil the potatoes—it was very different to what she had in her flat back in London—and then find a suitable saucepan, and figure out how to get water out of the complicated tap thing over the sink. Marissa was determined not to ask for help.

But when she had succeeded—and managed to throw together a salad and mash the potatoes—she took great care in arranging the food on the plates, before placing them on the dining table adjacent to the galley. She stood back and smiled as she put a sprig of some green stuff on the potatoes before she lit a candle.

'Rosco, dinner is ready,' she called up to the deck. A minute later he came down the stairs carrying a fry pan. His expression was hard to read as he lifted the fish fillets onto the plates next to the piles of mash.

He sat at the table and had not spoken as they dined on the simple meal. The salad could probably have done with some sort of dressing, but she hadn't been able to find anything in the cupboard. But it wasn't too bad; the fish was divine, and the rest was . . . well, it was edible.

And Marissa cleared her entire plate. After a while, the silence broken only by the clatter of cutlery on the fine china plates became uncomfortable. She put her fork on her plate and looked at

Rosco. He was staring at his plate; he had eaten his fish, but the salad and mash was still there. She had to break this awful silence.

'Thank you for cooking the fish. It was delicious. What was that herb you sprinkled on it?'

He didn't answer. His expression was tight as he stood and pushed the plate away without a word. Marissa's stomach dropped when he turned his back without answering.

There was no way she was going to beg for attention or conversation.

Her husband disappeared up the stairs; his bare feet making no sound on the smooth timber adding to the uncomfortable silence. She sipped her wine and sat there waiting for him to come back down. After fifteen minutes, an empty glass of wine and a stomach roiling with nerves, she stood and cleared the table, rinsed the dishes and went up to the deck. On the way she topped up her glass of wine for some Dutch courage.

Sod him. She would ignore him until he apologised for his childish behaviour.

Rosco was sitting on the front of the boat with his legs hanging over the side and as he turned, she got a whiff of sweet cigar smoke.

'I didn't know you smoked,' she said as she settled on the deck cushion to his left. He turned around and his face was cold.

'Did you need to know that? Would you have agreed to be my wife, if you had known?'

'Of course I would.'

Marissa would have liked to have said 'Perhaps not,' but his mood was too strange for her to be honest. The Rosco who was sitting next to her was not the kind gentle man she'd promised to love honour and—*oh, shit*—obey.

He drew in deeply and a moment later she held her breath as she was engulfed in a cloud of smoke.

Marissa hated smoking; watching her grandfather suffer for

months before lung cancer had taken him had been one of the hardest times of her life. She had only been ten, and Gramps had insisted on spending his last days at Meynell Manor. When she was home from boarding school she had sat by his side and helped him with his crosswords. It had turned her off smoking—and crosswords—for life.

Rosco turned his back to her again and she put her glass on the deck and damn, never one for conflict, she couldn't help herself. She tentatively touched his shoulder. His skin was warm and damp beneath her fingers, but he shrugged away from her touch.

Marissa swallowed. 'Is there something wrong?' she said quietly.

'That English stodge that you put on my plate was *pasto disgustoso*,' he said.

'I don't know what your words mean, but I guess from your tone that it was unacceptable.' She tried to lighten the mood with a chuckle and then swallowed it back. 'Did you need to know that I couldn't cook before you asked me to marry you?' she asked parroting his words of a few moments ago.

Rosco reached for her and took her wrist between fingers that pressed tightly against her skin. 'I would assume that any woman who agreed to marry a man would be able to cook.'

Marissa's jaw dropped and she tipped her head to the side wondering if he was joking. How could a man say that—or even think that—in the twenty-first century?

She tried to brush it off as a joke. 'I warned you. I told you that you would think differently after dinner, Rosco darling. I was very spoiled to grow up in a home where we had a cook, and—'

'Non mi stai ascoltando.'

'What does that mean?'

'It means you are not listening to me. Well, you will learn.'

'I beg your pardon?'

'You will learn to cook. I will not be served food like you serve me before.' Rosco's accent thickened along with his temper, and he waved the cigar around. Marissa leaned back before it could touch her face.

She pulled her arm from his grip unable to believe that the man speaking to her was the same gentle man she spent the last few weeks with. In those weeks there had never been a cross word or an expression or tone like she was seeing and hearing now. His behaviour was unacceptable. She clenched her hands by her side as her temper began to boil.

Perhaps he has had too much to drink.

She glanced at the small tumbler that was next to him. Some sort of spirit over ice filled the glass.

Fine, if he wanted to sit up here by himself and sulk over some potato mash, he was welcome to his own company.

'I'm tired. I'm going to bed.' Marissa went to stand but he held her wrist. This time it hurt.

'You will go to bed when I am ready for you to leave me.'

She tried to pull her arm back, but Rosco was holding on too tightly for her to free her arm from his grip.

'Let go of me. Now.' Her teeth were clenched, and her words were terse as disbelief flooded through her.

He did as she requested, and his eyes glittered dangerously in the moonlight.

'You have obviously had too much to drink, Rosco. I will leave you to it. I am tired and I am going to bed. Now.' Her words were clipped as she turned and strode along the deck to the stairwell.

Mocking words followed her down to the cabin. 'Ah, the poor little rich girl is worn out from trying to cook a decent meal for her poor husband.' The sound of a bottle clinking against his glass followed Rosco's slurred words.

For a while she considered locking the cabin door and

make him sleep on the deck, but with the mood he was in she was afraid of what he'd do.

Afraid? She bit her lip as she began to wonder who she had married.

Just before dawn as the sky lightened through the hatch above, she was aware of Rosco putting his arm around her waist. She squeezed her eyes shut and fell into a deep sleep.

When she opened them again, sunlight was streaming into the cabin, but she was alone.

Marissa closed her eyes again as she lay there. She couldn't believe or understand the change in Rosco. The first rosy flush of married life wasn't supposed to wear off for at least six months. She had heard her mother tell both of her sisters that when they had come home whining about their husbands.

She had been married six days and they had fought over bloody mashed potatoes. Thinking about her family sent a fresh surge of guilt through Marissa. She still hadn't contacted them. Maybe they weren't close anymore, and she was a grown woman with her own life but no matter how distant their relationship was they were still her parents and she should tell them she was married.

Every time she had gone to phone home, Rosco had distracted her. Climbing out of bed, she pulled a robe over her satin pyjamas and dug into her handbag for her phone. The screen stayed black when she held the power button in.

Damn, the battery was flat, and she didn't have a charger with her; she and Sienna had shared one as they'd travelled.

Marissa put the phone on the shelf beside the bed and frowned as she heard voices from above.

Who could it be?

When she had stormed off to bed last night, *Lady Calypso* had been the only boat in the bay.

Now there was a strange voice coming from above as

Rosco spoke to someone. Slipping out of her PJs and robe, she headed for the tiny bathroom. Once she was dressed in her bikini and sarong and had pulled her hair up with a clip, she made her way up to the top deck wondering what sort of reception she was going to get, and angry with herself that she had let Rosco speak to her like that.

And angry that she was worried about it.

'Is Celeste still asleep?' The unfamiliar voice reached her as she stood at the doorway. Rosco's back was to her and all she heard was a chuckle and a murmured reply that was too quiet to hear.

Celeste? Who the hell was Celeste?

She stepped out on to the deck and glanced across to the bay. A long white sloop that had obviously seen better days was moored quite close to them. Her gaze moved back to the deck where an olive-skinned man with dark hair stood facing her. His gaze fixed on her and she tightened the knot of her sarong more firmly as his eyes raked her from head to toe.

His smile was lazy as he nodded to Rosco and her husband turned to her with a wide smile. Relief filled her as he opened his arms wide.

'My darling, you are finally awake. Come and meet my good friend.'

She walked slowly across the deck to join them and leaned into Rosco as his hands held her waist.

Gently.

She looked up at him, and an unspoken apology crossed his expression before he leaned down and brushed his lips across hers. He whispered against her lips. 'I'm sorry. So very sorry.'

She pressed her mouth against his briefly in acknowledgement, but her smile was tight when she pulled back. It was going to take more than a whispered apology to appease her. Rosco's arm went around her shoulder.

PENTECOST ISLAND 1-3

'Marissa, this is my dear sailing friend, Ren. Ren, this is my lovely wife. Marissa has brought my dreams to life. We are on our honeymoon.'

Ren's glance was inscrutable as he reached over and took her hand. As he bent over, she noticed his hair was tied back with a leather tie. He brushed his lips across her fingers. *'Enchanté'*

Heat filled her face as he continued to hold her hand. Finally, he let go but his eyes stayed on her.

'It is a pleasure to meet you too, Ren.' She gestured to the sloop and for the first time saw that two other boats were anchored on the other side of the bay. Their idyllic private location had gotten busy overnight. 'Which is your boat?'

'Which do you think would be mine?' His voice held a delightful French lilt that sent a shiver down her spine.

Gawd, what on earth am I thinking? She'd always been a sucker for a French accent, but she was a married woman now, and it wasn't right to let another man's sexy voice give her the shivers.

Although he *was* a very good-looking man. He was a lot fitter and more muscled than Rosco, and when she looked closely, it was clear he was closer to her age than her husband's. Her glance swivelled to the three boats, and then back to him.

'The first one,' she said. *'Sea Dreaming.'*

'Not only beautiful, but very clever too, Rosco. You speak French?'

This time she didn't shiver, as she sensed a slightly patronising tone in his words. 'A little. Only schoolgirl French.' She wasn't sure she liked him.

'Marissa and I were considering going out for dinner in the village tonight.' Rosco said. 'We would be delighted if you would join us.'

Marisa raised her eyebrows and stared, but Rosco ignored her.

We were? Unless she'd been asleep when he'd mentioned

it, he was telling porkies.

What happened to 'I don't want to share my new wife with anyone'?

Ren demurred. 'Thank you, but I watch my euros when I am at sea.'

'I insist. You will be my guest. I must owe you ten dinners by now, my friend.'

Marissa didn't miss the significant look that they exchanged. 'I'm going for a swim,' she said. 'It was good to meet you, Ren. Perhaps I will see you at dinner. It would be a pleasure to have you join us.'

'If you are sure?'

She nodded. 'Of course.'

In one lithe movement Ren was over the deck and into the small rowboat that was tied up on the side of *Lady Calypso.*

Rosco looped his arm around her shoulder as they stood and watched the small boat as he rowed across the water.

Marissa was determined not to be the one to break the silence. She was still feeling fragile and hurt from last night. She stood still as Ren pulled up next to the sloop and climbed on board.

Rosco's breath warmed her cheek and he moved his hands ever so gently on the bare skin above her sarong. She relaxed as his lips settled in the curve of her neck. 'Forgive me?'

Her vision blurred as her eyes filled with tears and hovered on her lashes, threatening to fall. She bit her lip, still not wanting to speak.

'It was the *Sljiovica*, the plum brandy. It always makes me angry. I am so, so sorry.' His voice was deep and shook a little.

Her hands crept up around his neck and she rested her head on his shoulder. 'You frightened me.'

'Never again, I promise. I am so sorry, my darling girl.'

Chapter 6

Pippa: Pentecost Island

Rafe left after we had eaten Tam's amazing white chocolate and ginger cheesecake. I offered to walk him as far as the beach, and Eliza's gaze settled on us as we stood at the door together, and he said goodnight to everyone.

'Thank you for dinner, Tam,' he said politely. 'Night, Nell, goodnight Evie.' He turned to Eliza. 'It was a pleasure to meet you, Eliza, and I'm pleased that if you had to be rescued, it was on our island.'

He was such a nice guy—an absolute gentleman—and as much as I tried not to I couldn't help comparing him with Darren and the other guys I thought I'd fallen for in my past.

Rafe was different and the feelings I held for him already frightened me. What if he decided he didn't like me anymore? I honestly think it would have been enough to have me scurrying for the mainland. The resort and Aunty Vi's house were running a bit of a second now to how I felt about him. That night I had first seen him at Hamilton Island had been a life changer, although it had taken a rescue from a tree for me to realise how quickly I had fallen for him.

We were both quiet as we left the house and walked along the path to the beach. The wind had dropped, and the clouds had cleared; the rising moon promised a spectacular night as soon as it cleared the hill to the east. I let out a soft sigh. This island was one of the most beautiful places on earth. Happiness trickled through me and I embraced it; it wasn't a feeling I was terribly familiar with, but one that seemed to be overtaking me more and more since I had come to my island.

Rafe held my hand and I let my fingers lace through his. They were warm and held mine gently; it was typical of the man he was—gentle and patient—and that sort of guy was totally out of the realm of my experience.

I looked down at the ground as we strolled along.

Why me? Why had he picked me? I'd never had much self-confidence, and I knew I had to work to get over it, and to trust my feelings, and to trust Rafe.

We reached the beach just as the moon cleared the hill. A shaft of golden moonlight lit up the bay and the slight ripples on the water headed out into the passage in a circular pattern. The soft whoosh of the small waves pushing onto the beach was the only sound.

It was so beautiful I held my breath as we stood and watched the moonlight spread across the bay.

Two hands touched my shoulders and pulled me back gently. The way Rafe put his arms around me and tucked me back against his chest was like every move he made—slow and considered.

His lips ran slowly down my cheek and lingered at the edge of my mouth until I turned to meet him.

We stood bathed in moonlight as our lips met, and goose bumps ran down my neck and arms. No other man had ever made me feel like this. It wasn't the sexual attraction—although that was there in bucketloads—it was knowing that Rafe cared about me. About Pippa Carmichael the person.

As damaged as I was.

Our breathing quickened as his lips and tongue explored mine, and I responded.

I was lost as his hands lowered to hold me closer and I was left in no doubt about the strength of his desire.

'Will you come home with me tonight, Pip?'

As much as I was tempted, I shook my head.

'When?' he said softly. 'I don't know I can wait much longer. I dream about you in my bed every night.'

'Soon,' I whispered. I wasn't brave enough to tell him that I was scared if we slept together it would all come to an end. Like most good things in my life always had.

'You're hesitant, aren't you?' he said voicing the thoughts I had never told him. He was getting to know me very well.

'A little,' I admitted. 'I would like to come home with you'—I lifted my head and held his dark gaze— 'and I will soon, but tonight isn't the right time. Not with our mermaid spending the night over at my house. It wouldn't be the right thing to do. Leaving her there with the other girls, I mean.'

Rafe rested his forehead against mine. 'You are a good person, Pippa.'

'I'm not really.' I relaxed into his hold. 'But it's okay if you think that.'

'Oh, I do and a lot more than that. You know that we are going to be together, don't you? There will only be one problem that I can see.'

I moved back a little with a frown. 'A problem?'

'When the time comes would you be happy to leave your place and move into mine? I know how special it is to you and I—'

'Whoa. You're moving too fast. There's a lot you need to know about me before we think about that.' I put my fingers to his lips. 'It's only a house, Rafe. But if it does ever come to that, I can't see there will be a problem. You have a very suitable house.' I smiled.

'It's not your opinion of the house that matters to me.'

'I know. I was teasing. I think you are a very suitable man too.'

'That's what I was hoping for.' His arms tightened around me and I felt cocooned, and safe as his lips rested against mine.

'I was hoping we could spend tonight together as I have to

ANNIE SEATON

go away.' His words vibrated against my mouth. I stiffened in his hold and moved back from him as my newfound serenity fled.

'Away? Where to?'

Not that it was my business.

'Come back here.' He pulled me close again. 'You have to trust me, Pip. I have to go back to London. Just for a short visit.'

Rafe had told me all about his divorce, but now my doubts crept back in.

'I have to see Bryant—my publisher.'

Sweet relief filled me. It was nothing to do with his ex.

'Because it's been a while between books, and because I'm not prepared to do a world tour, he wants me to do a digital marketing campaign. I have to go over there and record some interviews and some promo clips for the new book. I tried to talk him into doing it over Skype, but he said the quality wasn't good enough. He's accepted that I won't do a personal tour, so I gave in on the digital stuff, even though it means a long flight over and back.'

'I'll miss you,' I said.

He held my gaze. 'I'd love you to come with me, but I didn't ask you because I know that you are so close to opening and you've got a lot of work ahead.'

'Once we get up and running, I'll go anywhere with you, Rafe.'

'That makes me one very happy man. I won't be gone long this time, and I want to be back here for your opening. I wouldn't miss that for the world. In fact, I told Bryant unless he could get this stuff organised in the next two weeks, I wouldn't come.'

'It's not far off.' Thinking about the resort put Eliza back into my thoughts. 'Come and sit for a while. I want to get your take on our mermaid.'

We settled on a wide fallen log that had come down in the recent cyclone.

'She was a very lucky woman that you were on the beach this afternoon,' Rafe said as he put his arm around my shoulders, and I leaned back against him

'She was.' I nodded slowly.

'What are you worried about?' he asked.

'I don't know. I've just got a sense that she's not telling us everything. She changed her story about the fishing and the firewood when she was pressed. And all that money and that ring seems a bit suss.'

'Does she have to tell us all about herself?'

I stared out over the water. 'She was more than happy to give us all the details of her childhood in New Zealand.'

'She doesn't know any of us. And she doesn't know us well enough to trust us.' He nudged me with his shoulder. 'And look who's talking, anyway.'

'True.'

'She said she could turn her hand to most things. Why don't you give her a trial run? You were going to advertise anyway, weren't you?'

I nodded. 'I was.'

'And forgive me if I'm overstepping the mark here, but I'm getting the impression that this is a business that seems to be hiring women?'

'I guess it is. It wasn't intentional, but it's turned out that way. 'I turned around and grinned at him. 'Why? Did you want a job?'

His chuckle was deep. 'The only thing I want at the moment is being denied to me. But I can wait. I hear the boss at Ma Carmichael's is one tough lady.'

'I'm determined to make this work, Rafe. It means so much that Aunty Vi left it to me.'

'And I have no doubt that you will. I'm looking forward to seeing it up and running and you having some free time.'

'Okay. It's time I headed back.' His rough whiskers grazed my fingers as I reached up and took his face between my hands. 'Thank you for being patient with me.'

'Sweetheart, I will wait as long as it takes.'

'Just don't go meeting anyone else in London and deciding to stay there.'

'There's no chance of that.'

The moon disappeared as he lowered his head to mine.

Chapter 7

Marissa

Ren picked us up in his boat and he rowed us around the southern point of the secluded bay where we were now anchored with several other boats. Three more boats had come in since the morning, and there had been many hand waves and greetings called out as they motored past us.

Rosco hadn't seemed to mind the end of our isolation, and our private honeymoon. We had spent most of the day sunbathing on the deck and jumping into the crystal-clear water when we needed to cool down. He had been very affectionate all day and we had gone down to the cabin for a rest after lunch, and he had proceeded to show me how sorry he was.

My confidence had been damaged by his drunken behaviour and although I assured him—several times—that all was forgiven, a part of me stayed wary.

I didn't mention anything about cooking or learning to cook in case his bad temper resurfaced. I dressed in a brightly coloured dress—one I had bought on the Isle of Capri at the beginning of the holiday with Sienna. As I dressed, I remembered the flat battery in my phone.

'Rosco,' I called up the stairs. 'Do you have a phone charger that will suit my phone. My battery is flat, and I must call my family.

'No point here, *cara.* There is no service,' he called from the deck.

'Oh, okay.' I put my phone back on the cupboard, but a niggle of worry stayed with me. Even Sienna didn't know where I was. When we'd said goodbye to her in Florence, I'd thought I was heading for the airport and France.

This was a very big step I'd taken. Away from all that was familiar and away from my family and friends.

As we rowed into the next bay, Rosco and Ren chatted in the front of the boat. I leaned back trailing my hand in the warm water, lost in my thoughts. If it hadn't been for that incident last night, I would have been in a world of happiness, but Rosco's ugly behaviour had taken away from the beauty around us.

We soon entered the small bay through a narrow entrance that was surrounded by steep rocky hills. I thought Rosco had said it was a long walk to the village. Along the foreshore were some old buildings where fishing boats were moored at a stone wharf. It was warm, protected from the wind and the water was so clear I could see the sandy bottom.

Ren tied the boat to the end of the wharf and stood next to Rosco and they both held a hand out to help me up from the rowboat. As we walked along the stone wall leading to a couple of *tavernas* fronting the small harbour, a cheery voice called out from one of the doorways ahead.

'Rosco!'

My husband hurried along the wall and spoke to the burly man who had hailed him for a couple of minutes before Ren and I caught up to him.

'You are happy to be married, Marissa?' Ren's voice was quiet, and I thought what a strange question to ask a woman on her honeymoon.

'I am,' I said firmly and hurried over to where Rosco was waiting.

'Mauro,' Rosco said as he held his hand out to me. 'This is my beautiful wife, Marissa.'

The older man took my hand and pumped it in a tight handshake. 'Ah, a beautiful wife. What an occasion. Come to my *taverna* and we will celebrate. My brother will bring out the new *Sljiovica*. We shall toast your marriage and wish you many children.'

Sljiovica! I certainly hoped not.

Rosco looked sheepish and caught my eye and sent me a reassuring smile. 'I think we will begin with a beer and then have some of that excellent wine from your vineyard, Mauro,' he said. 'The dozen bottles I took back to Florence after our last visit were very popular with my friends.'

Mauro ushered us inside and I was seated between Ren and Rosco. Ren's behaviour seemed distant now, but I didn't care. I was going to enjoy this experience.

Mauro brought a procession of relatives from the back of the taverna, and we met his mother who was the cook, as well as being the local cheesemaker and baker. His grandmother—an elderly woman with several teeth missing and dressed in a black dress—apparently looked after the gardens that supplied the produce. She hurried back outside after a brief greeting, and then we met Mauro's son who supplied the fish to the kitchen.

Once the introductions had been made, Mauro placed three carafes on the table: red wine, white wine and water.

'*Gemist* or *bevanda?*' he asked me as he picked up the glass that was in front of my setting.

I looked to Rosco for help, but he was chatting.

Ren leaned forward. 'Do you prefer to drink white or red wine, Marissa?' He glanced up at Mauro and lowered his voice. 'What the Croatians do to perfectly good wine is sacrilege to a Frenchman. The two words mean white wine with water, or red wine with water.'

'Which is white?' I asked.

'*Gemist*,' he replied.

I turned to Mauro. 'Then I will have *gemist*, please.'

Mauro nodded and hurried away and when he returned, he opened a bottle of sparkling water and added some to my glass before topping it up with white wine.

Rosco gestured to my glass. 'Forget the beer, my friend, I will have the white as well.'

There were no menus to choose from, but we dined on freshly caught scarfish and anchovies. By the end of the meal not only was I an expert on the varieties of fish, his mother had also given me the recipe for the baked fish meal we had eaten.

As she listed the ingredients in halting English, Rosco caught my eye and nodded with a wide smile.

I guess that was considered to be my first cooking lesson.

It was very late when we headed back to the wharf, with Mauro eliciting a promise from Rosco that we would return tomorrow night. It had been a pleasant evening, marred only for me when I heard Mauro mention the name Celeste to Ren when his mother was talking to me. I had strained to hear the conversation, but they had moved away. Rosco rowed the boat back as he had drunk very little with the meal and I had been pleased when he had declined the plum brandy.

We said goodnight to Ren, and Rosco waited until he got back to his boat safely, before he came down to join me in the cabin.

He nuzzled his lips into my neck and cupped my breast with a gentle hand. 'Did you enjoy your evening, my dear?'

I nodded as I leaned against him. He ran his fingers through my hair; I had just removed the clip that had held my blonde hair away from my face.

My confidence had returned, and I looked up at him as his lips descended towards mine. 'Rosco? Who is Celeste?'

He stopped and stared at me. 'Who has been talking to you of Celeste?'

'No one spoke to me, but I have heard her name mentioned a few times.'

His fingers tightened in my hair and I flinched as my hair

PENTECOST ISLAND 1-3

was pulled.

'Ouch. That hurt.'

'I'm sorry. My ring caught on your hair.' His voice was hard.

My eyes stung with tears as my head throbbed where he had tugged at my hair.

'So who is Celeste?' I persisted when Rosco removed his hand. He still held my arm with his other hand, and I looked down. I actually had a bruise where he had held me too tightly last night, but I hadn't worried as my skin was so fair, I bruised easily.

'She is dead. She is a woman that Ren used to travel with.'

'Oh. I'm sorry to hear of his tragedy.'

'Yes, it was very sad, so please don't mention her name in front of him.

He was lying. I had heard Ren's words yesterday.

I lay beside Rosco that night, until I heard his breathing change telling me he was asleep, and then I crept quietly out of the cabin and went and sat on the deck looking at the stars until I became sleepy.

In the end I didn't have to watch what I said around Ren, as his boat was gone the next morning. Rosco was extremely attentive over breakfast, and I was pleased when he discussed our plans with me.

'We will sail back to Dubrovnik in three days and then we will fly straight to London. Is that suitable to you?'

I nodded, very relieved to hear that our sojourn on this tiny boat would not be for much longer. If I was truthful with myself, I was finding it boring, even though it was supposed to be our honeymoon.

'As soon as we are in phone service again, I'll charge my phone and call my parents to let them know we are coming.'

'Shall we just surprise them? That would be more fun,' he

said.

I shook my head. 'You don't know my parents. A surprise visit would send my mother into a spin.'

'A spin? I do not know what that means.'

'It means she will like to get organised. Super organised. She'll pull out all stops and you'll have to endure a six-course meal in the formal dining room, she'll invite her friends who she considers to be landed gentry, and we'll be put on show.'

'I do not like the sound of that visit. What do you feel about it?' he asked.

'I will hate every minute of it.'

His hands linked behind my back. 'Perhaps I have a better idea.'

Chapter 8

Pippa: Pentecost Island

Rafe flew to Brisbane out of Hamilton Island airport on the first leg of his trip to London, a week after Eliza arrived. It had been an interesting week; he'd been busy finalising his book, and I'd not spent a lot of time with him. I'd put Eliza on the payroll; her skills, and her work ethic had blown me away. She took on every small job I gave her with enthusiasm, finished it quickly and cleaned up after she'd finished.

In fact, I'd been pleasantly surprised when I'd gone into the tool shed a couple of days ago; it was organised and tidy and Eliza had used the labelling thing I'd bought—and never used—to give each tool a home. She seemed to have recovered from her mishap; she didn't talk about it—it was as though she wanted to forget about her near drowning. The other girls must have picked up on that as her arrival on our island hadn't been mentioned again. Her kayak was now underneath the house and she'd settled into a room at the back. Out of the four spare bedrooms she'd opted for the smallest.

Rafe must have been reading my thoughts as we sat together in the departure lounge. 'How's the work progressed this week?'

I know I looked smug. 'Would you believe we're ahead of schedule? We should be ready to open the bar to day visitors when you come back.'

'Maybe I should stay away from you more often? Like I have this week?' He put on a sad face.

'No, it's not you distracting me when you come over; it's Eliza being there. She's been a huge help.'

'It's turned out okay then?'

'It has. She's got a very logical mind. With her help, we got the frame of the first hut up in a couple of hours.' I chuckled. 'Tam and I were trying to read the instructions, but Eliza and Nell had the timber sorted while we arguing about where to start.' I reached over and slipped my arm through his; I found it hard not to touch Rafe when we were together. His fingers closed over mine and I smiled.

'You won't do anything silly over there, will you?' It was the most diplomatic way I could ask him what he would be doing without being too intrusive.

His fingers caressed mine. 'What silly things do you think I could get up to?'

'Um, you might decide you like the cool climate again?' Spring had hit with a vengeance and the humidity on Pentecost Island had skyrocketed.

He dropped a kiss on the top of my head. 'What about you? You might decide the heat is too much for you here while I'm gone. You might leave.'

I shook my head. 'No chance of that.'

'Ditto,' he said with a grin and my heart gave a little flip.

'I'm really going to miss you, you know,' I said playing with his fingers.

'You'll keep busy, you have good friends to keep you company and I'll be back before you know it. But you know what, Pippa? You have no idea how happy it makes me to know you'll miss me.'

I held his gaze and spoke softly. 'I can't imagine you not being there. You've been here since we landed on your island and disturbed your peace and quiet.'

'The best day of my life . . . so far,' he said as he leaned forward and brushed a kiss across my lips.

Rafe's flight was called, and when we stood up, he pulled me close. 'You be careful while I'm gone. Don't go climbing any trees or rescuing any mermaids.' His smile set my heart beating faster.

'You keep safe and hurry back to me,' I said.

'I will.' One last kiss, and he was out through the gate heading for the jet that would take him to Brisbane to pick up his international flight. He turned at the bottom of the steps and waved before he headed up into the jet.

I stood there in a daydream until the plane had taken off over the Coral Sea and then I made my way back to the marina, where Evie was waiting.

As much as Eliza was working out, I was still curious about her story, so Evie and I had planned to go to Lindeman and Little Lindeman Islands on the way back to our island, just to make sure no one was looking for her. I'd asked Jiminy, my school friend on Hamilton Island, if he'd heard anything about a missing kayaker when I'd seen him at the marina, but he'd heard nothing, and if there was anything to hear, Jiminy would know; he always had his ear to the ground.

'Done all Tam's shopping?' I called to Evie as I hurried towards her boat. I was pleased to see her waiting for me; the marina was adjacent to the airport, so it hadn't taken me long to get back.

'Yep, and I've stowed it below decks already. It took a bit of searching to find those Moroccan spices she was after, but I got them.'

'Great. You want a hand to cast off?'

She nodded and I untied the ropes and jumped aboard her small yacht. As we motored out of the marina, we passed a large white sloop.

'Hasn't she got beautiful lines?' Evie commented as the guy standing at the front waved to her.

I laughed. 'Who? The boat or did you mean to say he? He's seriously cute.'

'Ha ha. I meant the boat, even though she's had a long life, she is still a beautiful boat. Although he *was* a nice guy. A French dude. I gave him one of the flyers that Nell made up for our bar opening, and he said he might call into Pentecost on his way south.'

'And you're really hoping he does.'

Evie shrugged. 'A bit old for my tastes. Heading for forty, I'd say. His name's Phillipe, but he did have an accent to die for.'

'An old salt.' I checked out the boat as we pulled away. 'Looks like his boat's done some time at sea.'

'Yeah, he's travelling around the world. Said he's done the Mediterranean, the Adriatic, and has come down through Indonesia. Plans on spending some time in the Whitsundays. I told him to keep an eye out for our opening.'

'Maybe we'll see him out at the island. I can't believe how close the bar opening is.'

'Will Rafe be back in time?' Evie shot me a curious glance.

'Should be.'

'Which reminds me,' Evie said. 'How are you going to get the word out to the sailing community about the bar being open?'

I grinned. 'My speciality. I've put together a marketing campaign and it's almost ready to send out. I'm just waiting for Tam to finalise the menu for the bar food, and then we'll set a date.'

After the slabs had been poured for the huts, the concreters had come back and done the floor for the outdoor bar. The roof was up, and the outdoor furniture was stored at the back of the house. We were going to build a small shed at the side of the area to store the furniture in bad weather. I was looking at brochures to order a bar to go along the back wall, and the suppliers had assured me it would be ready in two weeks once I placed the order.

I was pretty proud of what we'd achieved in such a short time, and the Whitsunday tourism staff had said that there was a lot of local interest in our project.

I just hoped we hadn't made it too big to start with, and that we wouldn't fail.

'Stop chewing your fingernails, Pip. It will be fine. You are such a worrier.' Evie turned the boat out of the channel.

I removed my hand from my mouth. The three girls all knew me so well. 'I know. Can't help it. Are you still right to call into Lindeman?'

Evie nodded. 'Sure. You won't relax until you find out more about Eliza, will you?'

'I just want to check that no-one's worried about her. She doesn't seem to be.'

Evie regarded me for a long time before she spoke. 'So why are you?'

I shrugged. 'Aunty Vi taught me to always trust my "spidey" sense and every time I think about how Eliza arrived it kicks in.'

Evie shook her head and increased the speed of the boat and we passed Catseye Beach on the northern side of the island. Her long dark hair flew wildly as we headed out into open water.

'If Eliza's not worried, why should we be? She's fitted in really well with us all so far.'

'Just humour me, Evie. Once I satisfy myself that there's no one looking for her, I'll let it go.'

##

We had no luck at Lindeman Island. The resort had closed about eight years ago, and I'd heard it had been sold to a Chinese consortium, but no development had taken place yet. It was sad to motor past and see the buildings standing faded and forlorn, with broken windows facing the sea. The pool was empty, and a couple of pool lounges were jammed up against the building. Plastic chairs littered the shore and I could even see a mattress lying in the long grass near the beach. I guess the last cyclone had finished off

ANNIE SEATON

the resort. There were no kayaks or boats pulled up in the bay, so it looked like there was no-one on the island.

Evie swung the boat around, and we headed for Little Lindeman Island which was only a short distance from Pentecost. There were a few small islands to the west and the east, but Eliza had specifically said it was Little Lindeman where she'd been camping. It was a part of the national park, and there were sandy beaches on two sides of the island.

'There.' Evie pointed to the northern end of the wide expanse of sand. 'Look, there's a few kayaks like the one Eliza was in pulled up almost into the bush.'

'Let's go and have a chat.'

Evie set the anchor and we both climbed into the tender and headed for the shore. A man and a woman walked down to the water and helped pull us past the coral heads once the water was shallow.

'Hi there.' The guy had an American accent and his smile was wide. 'You looking to camp here tonight?"

I shook my head. 'No. We're just after some information.'

He looked at the woman and she frowned. 'What sort of information?'

'We wondered if you were missing any of your group?' Evie said pointing to the half a dozen kayaks lined up along the shore.

'Why?'

'We heard that a kayaker had gone missing from one of the islands and we thought we'd keep an eye out on our way home.' I crossed my fingers behind my back.

They both shook their heads.

'We haven't heard anything, but we only arrived here a couple of days ago,' the guy said. He pointed to the kayaks at the other end of the beach. That group has been here for a while, you could ask Johnny.'

I held out my hand. 'I'm Pippa, and this is Evie. We're over on Pentecost Island.'

The guy took my hand and shook it vigorously. They were a fit-looking couple in their fifties or so. 'I'm Jim and this is Margie. We've been kayaking around these beautiful Aussie islands for a few weeks now.'

Margie shook my hand and then Evie's. 'Pentecost Island? You live there? It's a magnificent geological formation. We plan on visiting in a week or two. After this weather passes.' She gestured to the clouds that were moving quickly up high. 'Some wind on the way, so we'll bunker in here until it calms again. I hope no one has gone missing.'

I grinned at Evie. 'If you do head our way, our bar and food will be up and running in a couple of weeks, I hope. We have a top chef on staff and you're more than welcome to camp over at Back Bay.'

'Sounds like a plan.' Jim nodded. 'Look, there's Johnny now.'

'Thanks. We'll head over and ask. Good to meet you both. I hope we see you over at our eco-resort. It's called Ma Carmichaels.'

'We'll call in for sure. Good to meet you gals,' Jim said.

We walked along the beach to where a young guy was pulling a kayak down towards the water.

'Johnny?' I called out.

He turned and waved. 'That's me. Hi there.'

Evie murmured quietly. 'Not bad. Not bad at all.'

I nudged her. 'You are a shocker.'

Although she was right, he was tanned and muscular.

'Hi, I'm Pippa and this is Evie.'

He waved again, less formal than the older American Jim. 'Come to stay for a while?' He smiled at Evie and I rolled my eyes.

'No, were looking for someone we know who we thought might have called in here.' I changed my story slightly.

'Yeah, there's been a few of us come and go here. Who're you looking for?'

'Eliza. A friend of ours from Brisbane.'

He stared at me for a moment and then shook his head. 'Sorry. No Eliza here since we arrived. There's been a few kayakers come and go, but we've met them all.'

'How long have you been here?'

'We've been here a couple of weeks.' He frowned. 'Actually, no. It's closer to three weeks. It's a great place to snorkel and the campsite back in the scrub's a beauty.'

'What about guys called Dylan and Alex? I think he was a friend she was travelling with.'

He rubbed his chin and nodded. 'Yeah, a guy called Dylan stayed here for a few nights. He left about ten days ago.'

Jackpot. It was ten days since Eliza had arrived on our island.

'And Eliza wasn't with him?' I persisted.

He shook his head. 'No. He was by himself. He wasn't kayaking; he moored his catamaran in the bay.'

'Okay, thanks. Looks like we've missed her. Thanks for the info,' I said. 'If you head back our way'—I pointed north— 'we've got a small resort opening up over on Pentecost Island. Call in and have a drink if you come our way.'

'Sounds like a plan. We'll be heading back to Hamo in a few days.'

I didn't care if we were open or not. I'd give them a drink. I was more interested to present Eliza with the group from Little Lindeman Island who apparently didn't know her from a bar of soap.

Chapter 9

Marissa: Croatia

The second week of our marriage passed without incident, and I began to enjoy myself again.

Well, apart from one incident.

I woke early one morning to hear Rosco's voice and I sat up in bed and poked my head through the hatch. He was on the forward deck and my eyes narrowed as I saw his phone pressed to his ear.

His back was to me, so I couldn't hear what he was saying, and he couldn't see me. I stared as he continued to talk, his gestures signalling his displeasure with something or someone. I was learning very quickly that things had to go the way my husband wanted, or he got in a mood.

Before he turned, I lowered myself back down and stretched out on the bed. Rosco had told me there was no phone service and I hadn't been able to call home. Although in one way it didn't matter now as he had talked me into surprising my parents with our visit. Perhaps his phone was on a local service, but it still surprised me that he hadn't offered it to me to use.

By the time he came back down to our cabin, I had dozed back off. I decided to keep the peace and not mention the phone. It didn't really matter. Once we got back to Italy, I'd buy a charger and some more credit for my phone. I was keen to talk to Sienna, as she was due to leave Italy late next week. I was also due back home so I would have to talk to my parents or turn up there by then.

##

A week later I was relieved when we left the boat and headed to the airport. My relief made me feel guilty because it was our honeymoon, but I put it down to being out of my comfort zone.

We landed in Florence, and when Rosco slipped into the gents, I headed to the newsagent and bought a phone charger.

Just that simple purchase brought my confidence back. I slipped it safely into my handbag.

Rosco smiled at me and held out his hand as we headed for the baggage carousel. I knew I looked good. We'd spent a lot of time sunbathing, and my skin was tanned, and my hair even blonder than usual. I'd managed to do the roots at the tiny sink in the boat when he was intent on his fishing one afternoon. I took his hand and squeezed it; it was good to be back where we'd met and married.

Rosco put his arm around me as we waited for a taxi. 'I can't wait to show you my villa,' he whispered.

'And I can't wait to see it,' I said.

The trip from the airport out into the countryside took an hour, and I widened my eyes when I saw the amount of money that my husband slipped the taxi driver after he had unpacked the suitcases. Rosco had ordered new luggage and new clothes for me, and they had been delivered to the hotel in Dubrovnik before we caught our flight. For a moment I felt strange, almost wishing I had my old backpack filled with familiar things.

An attractive woman—about my age—dressed in black and white opened the door and greeted us in English.

'Welcome home,' she said. The smile she gave to Rosco was wide, but it disappeared when she turned to me and nodded. '*Signora.*'

'Davina, this is my wife. Marissa, Davina will help you with anything that you need,' he said.

I wondered if she could cook.

'Hello, it is good to meet you.' I held out my hand, but she merely gave me another nod and turned away to Rosco.

'Lucia will have your meal ready at eight. She has gone

PENTECOST ISLAND 1-3

down to the village to get some fresh herbs.'

Relief was sweet. Whoever Lucia was, she was obviously cooking, and I didn't have to worry.

I followed Rosco up a wide marble staircase trying not to show how impressed I was with the villa. He flung open the door to a large room with French doors that opened onto a small balcony overlooking the winding driveway that we had driven up.

The late afternoon sunbathed the tall pencil pines in a golden glow, and the pink brick of the outbuildings below us deepened in the fading light.

'It's breathtaking,' I said staring out over the vista, trying to accept that this was now my home. A peculiar feeling ran up my back and I shivered.

'Are you cold?' he said putting his arms around me. 'It is very different to being on my boat, isn't it?'

I smiled and nodded. 'It is, but it is very beautiful.'

'So are you, my darling. You are going to make my villa complete. I have been waiting a long time to find the right woman. You are perfect. Your blonde hair, your olive skin, your eyes'—his gaze ran down my body, and it felt as though I was being inspected rather than loved— 'you are exactly what I wanted.'

I suppressed the shiver this time. His words were strange and made me uncomfortable. It was as though I was a possession, not a wife.

Rosco dropped a kiss on my cheek. 'I have some work to do. I will call you when it is time to come down for dinner. I would like you to dress up please.'

I nodded slowly. 'I'll unpack. Will I get my bags from the foyer?''

'No, Willem will bring them up. I will ask him to get them now.'

'Willem? Just how many staff do you have?'

'Enough for my—our—needs,' he said with a brisk nod. 'I

will see you at dinner.'

As promised, Willem—a young man who looked as though he was still in his teens—tapped on the door shortly after Rosco went downstairs.

He barely looked at me as I opened the door and he carried in the suitcases and placed them beside the wardrobe that lined the wall adjacent to the double window. He left without a word.

I glanced down at the bags, and picking up my handbag I opened the French door and stepped out onto the balcony. A small wrought iron table and two chairs sat in the corner, touched by the last fingers of sunlight.

I dug in my bag for my phone. As soon as it was charged, I was going to call Sienna to see if we could catch up before she flew home. The compartment where I usually put it was empty and I dug deeper into the bag as I searched for it.

But my fingers came out empty each time. I upended the bag onto the table and frowned as the usual assortment that always filled my bag spilled on to the table, but there was no phone. I closed my eyes as I concentrated trying to remember where I had last seen it.

When I had discovered the battery was flat when we were on the boat, I'd put my phone on the cupboard in the cabin. I couldn't recall if I moved it into my bag after that or not.

But I had packed my own bag when we'd left the boat, and there hadn't been anything left in the cabin.

I went back into the bedroom and tipped the contents of my two suitcases onto the huge bed. I sifted through all the clothes, and dug into each compartment, but my phone wasn't there.

Okay, if I couldn't find it to charge, I'd have to use the phone downstairs. Thank goodness, I knew Sienna's number; I was hopeless with phone numbers but hers was an easy one to remember.

Gawd, if I'd lost my phone all my contacts would be gone.

PENTECOST ISLAND 1-3

I opened the door and stepped out into the tiled corridor and headed for the staircase. The house was quiet and when I reached the bottom of the stairs, I paused unsure of where to go.

I tipped my head to the side; I could hear Rosco's voice coming from a room at the back of the villa.

I'd taken my shoes off upstairs and my bare feet made no sound as I walked on the cold tiles.

His voice got louder as I approached and for a moment, I assumed he was on the phone, until I heard a female voice raised in anger. I walked slowly along the corridor, but I couldn't understand any of it as they spoke in rapid Italian.

But I did know that each speaker was angry.

I reached an open doorway and paused. Rosco was sitting at a desk and Davina was leaning over him, her pointed finger almost touching his face as she spat words at him. His face was flushed, and anger flashed from his eyes. I went to move back but he looked across at me, and his expression darkened further as he switched to English.

'I told you to stay upstairs until it was time for dinner.'

Anger rose up in my chest, and I strode into the room. 'I needed to speak to you. It's obviously a bad time. I'll wait in the hall until you have finished here.'

'No. Go back upstairs. I'll come up.'

I shook my head. 'No, I'll wait here. I wish to use the telephone.'

His mouth set in a straight line and he flicked a dismissive hand at Davina. *'Ne parleremo più tardi.'*

I looked around as I stepped into the room. Davina raised her eyebrows at me as she pushed past.

'I would like to use the telephone to call Sienna. My phone is missing. Have you seen it?'

'You are accusing me of taking it?'

I frowned. 'No, why would I think that?' Suspicion trickled through me.

Surely not?

'I don't know why you would think that. You have been difficult and irrational ever since we stepped onto the boat.'

My mouth dropped open and I took a step back. 'What?'

'Come upstairs. We will continue this conversation in private.' Rosco stood and came around the desk and took my arm quite roughly. This time I wasn't going to be manhandled, and I pulled away. As I strode ahead of him, and down the corridor towards the staircase, Davina walked past us looking quite smug.

By the time I reached the top of the stairs, he'd caught up to me.

'Marissa. Wait. I am sorry for snapping.' His hand touched my arm gently, but I shook it off. An apology wasn't going to cut it this time.

Walking into the bedroom, I turned to face him.

'Don't you ever speak to me like that again, or I'll be out of here like a shot.'

His face darkened as he looked past me. 'What is that?'

'What?' I turned.

'The clothes that I bought for you. You treat them like rubbish?'

'No, I haven't hung them up yet. I was looking for my phone. I would like to ring Sienna before she leaves Italy.'

'Why?'

My eyes widened as he approached me.

PENTECOST ISLAND 1-3

Chapter 10

Pippa: Pentecost Island

The opening date for the first stage of our eco-resort was six days away.

Six days! I smiled as I thought about it; that meant it was only five days until Rafe was due back on the island. I had missed him so much, and we had been so busy, but the time had flown. My life had changed so much over the past few months; I was happy and content and looking forward to the future. I think it was the first time for many years I had looked ahead rather than getting bogged down in my problems.

I jumped when Tam called out to me.

'Pip, stop mooning about and come and help me stow all these boxes.'

We'd been over to the mainland and picked up a huge supply of grog from the discount store at Airlie Beach. As I helped her move the boxes so they were evenly balanced on each side of the boat, Tam giggled.

'Whatever you do, don't sink the boat on the way back. You'll poison the ocean with the amount of spirits we've got on board.'

'As long as we get enough customers to buy it, I'll be happy.' I said as I steered us across the passage between Hamo and our island.

'Trust me, I have no doubt they'll come,' Tam said. 'Kylie over at the tourism place said the word is out already.'

'Good.' I folded my arms. 'Because that order nearly broke us.'

Even Nell who was in charge of the accounts had protested at the amount of grog that Tam had ordered.

'Trust me, Pip,' Tam said with a smile. 'Really, I've sussed out the online community and the talk around the marinas, and a bar like this where they can anchor and come and socialise with other sailors is exactly what's needed. On the mainland, they have marina fees, and if they moor out at the front of the town and pull up on shore in their tenders, they're only allowed to leave the tender there for a certain time. Our bar is not only going to offer whatever they want to drink—and excellent bar food—it's going to give them freedom to come and go as they please.'

'I hope you're right.'

'You watch, we'll have return business, and the word will spread.' Tam nodded as we stowed the last box below. 'Like I said, trust me.'

'Okay. I will.'

'Good.' She nudged me as we walked across the deck. 'Do you know how good it is to see you happy, Pip?'

I couldn't help my smile. 'Do you know how good it feels to be happy?' I replied.

'How long are you going to keep Rafe dangling? You haven't spent a night over there yet, have you?'

I pursed my lips at her in a mock stern look. 'That's my business.'

Tam shook her head with a laugh. 'Is this the same woman who came crying to Nell and me with the pink G-string story when Darren did the dirty?'

'Okay, fair enough. You two are my besties and no, I haven't slept with him. I want to be completely sure I'm not in lust.' I gave her a rueful grin. 'Like I was every other time I got let down.'

'He's a pretty decent guy, Pip. You know what an excellent judge of character I am.'

I started the engine and Tam lifted the fenders as we backed out of the berth. She joined me at the helm when we were underway, and I picked up our conversation. 'I do, and you are.' I glanced sideways at her. 'We've been so busy this past ten days; we haven't had a chance to talk. So, speaking of your excellent character judgement, tell me what you think of Eliza.'

Tam leaned back on the padded seat behind her. 'She's an incredible worker.'

'Yep, I know that.'

'She's very . . . I'm not sure if the right word is shy . . . or private.'

'Do you trust her?' I asked as I swung the helm and headed towards our island.

'In what way? I don't think she's going to murder us in our beds or run off with the silver.'

I giggled. 'We don't have any silver. Do you think she's telling the truth?' I hadn't shared what I'd found out with Nell and Tam yet.

'No. There's something that doesn't ring true for me. She's full of stories about her childhood, but when I ask about recent years, she clams right up. And her accent changes, depending what she's talking about.'

'She wasn't over on Little Lindeman before you rescued her. Evie and I went over there, and no one knew her.'

'That doesn't surprise me.' Tam's expression was serious. 'But you know? Does it really matter? She's doing a damn fine job with us, and she's good company when we're working. When she lets go, she's got the best sense of humour.'

'You've nailed it there. "When she lets go." It's as though she's playing a role to me.'

Tam nodded. 'Yeah. Maybe she'll chill a bit the longer she stays, and you know, as long as she does the right thing by us, is it really our business?'

I shook my head. 'No, it's not. I'll let it go. She can stay as long as she wants. We've certainly got ahead of schedule with her working here. Speaking of which, have you thought any more about hiring staff? We'll need help in the bar once we open.'

'When it gets busy, you mean?'

'No, from the get-go. We've all got other jobs to do. We can't do our usual stuff and man it from lunchtime until closing.'

'I was going to leave it for a couple of weeks and just see how busy we were, but I guess you're right.'

'I think you should be there as the owner of the resort to make it personal and welcoming, but you'll also need someone.'

'I have to be there anyway under the Liquor Act. Nell has already read me the riot act on that. Several times.' I rolled my eyes. '"An individual licensee or approved manager must be present or reasonably available during ordinary trading hours."'

'I think seeing we're on an island you'll be reasonably available, but you do need a bar person.'

'Is this leading to something?' I asked suspiciously.

Tam had the grace to look embarrassed. 'One of my workmates at my old restaurant in Brisbane emailed me. She heard what we were doing up here and said if anything came up to let her know. She'd be perfect and she'd fit in with the rest of us.'

'Did I ever meet her?'

'Maybe. She was in the bar there. Long black hair past her waist, and she mixed the best cocktails ever.'

'I think I did. Maybe when I first moved to the Gold Coast. Was her name Cherry?'

Tam nodded. 'That's her. Cherry Chilcott.'

'So, is she available?'

'Between jobs, she told me.'

'Okay, tell her if she's interested to come up and we'll interview her. At least we know she's got her RSA.'

'*We'll* interview?' Tam said as I turned the boat into our bay. 'You're the boss.'

'Yep. And you're the hospitality person. You can pick your

staff.'

Tam grinned. 'Thanks, boss.'

Chapter 11

Marissa: Tuscany

'Marissa! Where the hell have you been?' Sienna's voice screeched though the landline. Rosco was standing beside me in the study, so I was very conscious of what I said.

'On my honeymoon, you goose.'

'I've tried to call and call, and your phone kept going to voicemail. I was so worried I rang your parents.'

I swallowed. 'You rang my parents?' I half-turned my back so Rosco would get the hint and give me some privacy, but he crossed to his desk and sat down. I extended the cord on the phone—I couldn't believe the villa didn't have a cordless phone—and sat in a chair near the window. It had a high back and gave me a bit of privacy.

It bothered me that I felt the need for that. We'd been married three weeks now, and I was losing my confidence more each day. Up in the bedroom earlier when Rosco had snapped at me for emptying my suitcase on the bed, I had been taken aback, but he had got over it as quickly as his angry mood had come on. He had seen my uncertainty—at this stage it wasn't fear—as he'd approached me, but he'd put his arms around me and rubbed my back until I relaxed in his hold.

'I am sorry, my darling. I was angry because I argued with Davina. She did not follow my instructions while we were away, and I have lost a contract. I am so sorry that I snapped at you.'

I had leaned into him and buried my face against his neck. The familiar smell of his aftershave and the warmth of his skin soothed me, but there was a part of me that couldn't let go of the fact that he was so moody and unpredictable. I was getting reluctant to show what I was thinking and say what I wanted.

PENTECOST ISLAND 1-3

'Do you forgive me?' His lips moved against my neck and his hands lifted my T-shirt, his fingers warm on my bare skin.

'Of course, I do.'

It didn't seem to matter to him that we fell onto the bed and were on top of all of the new clothes that he had seemed so worried about a few minutes earlier.

A very pleasant half hour ensued, and my confidence was restored. As we got out of the shower in the marble bathroom adjacent to our room a while later, Rosco flicked my wet hair with a finger.

'When you are dressed, come down to my study and I'll show you how to use the telephone.' He chuckled. 'You are in Italy now, my darling, and it is not as simple as you are used to.'

'Thank you,' I said as I towelled my hair dry. 'I guess I'll get used to things being different. I wonder where on earth my phone got to. I'll have a to get another one.'

My husband shook his head as he headed for the door. 'No. You don't need one.' As he'd shut the door behind him, I'd stared at it in disbelief.

I didn't need one? The first chance I got, I'd be into the village we'd driven through on the way to the villa and I'd be buying a phone. No way was he going to tell me what I could or couldn't have.

I dressed quickly and hurried down to the study before he could change his mind about me making a call. The call went through to Sienna's mobile quickly and she answered on the first ring.

Gawd, she'd rung my oldies. I swallowed again. 'Um, what did they say?'

'They weren't home. I wasn't able to talk to them.'

Thank God.

'I lost my phone. At least I remembered your number. I've lost all the others. You know I don't even know the number for the manor.'

'Marissa, you are so hopeless. There's no need to worry. When you get a new one, use the same email to set up your phone and your contacts will all be in the cloud.'

'Oh, of course they will. I'd forgotten about that.'

'So, what did your parents think of Rosco?'

'We haven't been home yet. We went cruising in the Adriatic on Rosco's sailing boat instead.'

'Nice one. I bet you've got a tan. I'm going back home with one. I ended up going down to Sorrento after your wedding. I hooked up with a group. We had such a blast.'

'Sounds like fun,' I said.

'Where are you now? Any chance of catching up before I fly out?'

'We're back at Rosco's villa. I'll talk to him and see what our plans are, and I'll get back to you. I'm sure he'd love to see you too before you go back.'

A shadow fell between me and the window. I looked up. Rosco was shaking his head. He made a cutting motion telling me to end the call.

'Sienna, I have to go. I'll call you back in a while, okay?'

'Sure. It was great to hear from you. I have really been worried.'

'Why would that be?' I glanced up at Rosco. His face was set in a frown as he stared at me.

'I'll tell you when I see you. Okay, love, *Ciao.*'

The call ended and I handed the phone back to Rosco.

'I told you, you don't need a phone,' he said with an intent stare.

'I do.' I stood my ground. No one, not even my new husband was going to tell me what I could or couldn't do.

'You do not need a phone.' He reached out, and his fingers were cruel on my arm. 'Are you listening to me?'

PENTECOST ISLAND 1-3

I pulled away from him and tried to stay calm. 'I'm sorry, Rosco, but we are going to have to disagree on this. I need a phone, to get all of my contacts and numbers back. I also need a phone to maintain some of my independence.'

The look on his face that accompanied the short huff that came from his mouth was ugly.

'And you expect me to pay your bill, so you can keep in touch with all of your past friends? Oh no, no, no. You are my wife now, Marissa, and you will do as I say.'

'I will pay for it myself, and I will pay for the calls.' I took on a deep breath as I stared at him.

A smile crossed his face, but it wasn't pleasant and did not reassure me. 'And what money are you going to use for that? You will not work while you are married to me, Marissa. It is your job to be my wife.'

I kept my voice even. 'Yes, I am happy to be your wife and not work, if that is what you want, but I will also have a phone.'

'You no longer have your own money. You are dependent on me now. But do not worry. I will provide you with the best. All I expect in return is to have a beautiful wife in my house, and a wife to travel with me.'

I stared at him for a few seconds before I turned away. 'I will leave you to your work. I am going back to my room to have a rest for a while.'

That's what I told him, but what I intended was to get my purse and go down to the village and find somewhere to buy a phone.

Today.

His smile was strange as he pulled me close and kissed the top of my head as though I was a recalcitrant child. 'I will see you at dinner. Please wear the royal blue beaded dress.'

I managed to keep my expression neutral as I looked at Rosco and nodded briefly.

But my thoughts were dark and circling around my head. *What the fuck had I done?*

Chapter 12

Pippa: Pentecost Island

Life on the island was getting frantic. With Eliza's help, the huts were almost complete, and as soon as the cladding went on, we were ready to fit them out with simple furniture and bedding.

The bar was opening in three days, and Tam was like a bear with a sore head. She was a perfectionist, and I had never seen anyone stress so much about bar food.

'All they'll want is a drink, Tam. Any extra is a bonus,' I said one afternoon as we stocked the bar with the bottles we'd bought on the mainland. Eliza was helping us carry the boxes down and she nodded.

'Pippa is right, Tam. Any food to soak up the alcohol will be welcome. You could put out potato crisps and a sailor would be happy.'

Tam shook her head with a mutinous look on her face. 'There will be no potato crisps from my kitchen. Pip, I want you to look at the menu for the bar food and approve it before I go ahead.'

'Why?' I said as I decided what colour bottles to put together on the shelf.

'Because you're the boss. Someone has to sign off on what I propose.'

'Nope.' I shook my head. 'That's your department, and I give you full responsibility. It's called trust, Tam. I don't look over Nell's shoulder at the spreadsheets and the software, and I don't tell Evie what plants to buy. So just like that, I don't pretend to know what bar food you're going to make to go with all these pretty drinks.' I put the blue bottle next to the red one and stood back and admired my handiwork. We had designed the bar with a nautical theme—duh, of course we did, we were on an island—and nets and knotted ropes were draped behind the bar. There were six high stools along the front of the wooden bar top and a scattering of tables and chairs undercover on the paved area. The bar had no walls and the view from every stool and chair out over our bay was superb and unhindered. On a nice day we'd move the tables out onto the sand.

Tam groaned. 'Are you sure?'

I walked over and put my hands on her shoulders. 'Of course, I'm sure. Um, how long have we known each other?'

'A bloody long time,' she replied with a frown.

'And in that twenty something years, you have never let me down, so why would you do it now? This bar is going to be a rip-roaring success, and the word about your food will spread from one end of the islands to the other. And wait until the restaurant gets going. Your food will bring them from further afield.'

Tam finally smiled. 'It will be good, won't it?'

'Yep. Ma Carmichael's is going to be the best place in the islands to stay and to dine.'

Eliza emptied the bottles from the last carton and sat them on the bar before she turned to us. 'Have you ever thought of having a theme here?'

'What do you mean by a theme?' I asked.

'Maybe theme isn't the right word. I've done a bit of travelling around the world, and there were many places that were booked out for months ahead. Some places specialised in weddings, and others in fishing charters.'

'We're going down the eco-resort path, but I'd love to hear about what you've seen,' I said. It was unusual for Eliza to initiate a conversation and share anything about herself and her recent life.

She pulled out a chair and turned it around and straddled it with her arms along the back.

I pulled out a chair and sat facing her. 'I like this conversation. Tam, I think you should whip up a cocktail for us

PENTECOST ISLAND 1-3

and we'll throw around some ideas. Eliza, hold those thoughts. I'll go and find Evie and Nell.'

##

Evie had just come in from the vegetable garden and headed straight down to the bar, but it took me a few minutes to entice Nell away from her desk.

'Come on, Nell. You need some down time.' She had been working on projections and spreadsheets for the past week. Like Tam as our opening approached, Nell was getting nervous. My calm was out of character and I realised what a long way I'd come.

'Thanks, Aunty Vi.' I looked up at the sky as I murmured under my breath. I could only hope she was up there looking down on us and smiling. It had taken me a long time to come to terms with death after I had lost my parents at such a young age, but again, Aunty Vi had played a big part in teaching me acceptance.

'I'm having trouble with the backup system,' Nell said as she followed me down the stairs.

'Step away from it for a while. It could be the internet connection. My phone has been dodgy all day. When Rafe called this morning, it kept dropping out.' He'd rung me twice a day for the last two weeks and I was so looking forward to his return. Being apart had made me realise it was time to take our relationship to the next level.

I was ready. I'd learned to trust again.

Nell nodded. 'It could be. I'm going to have to go to a hard disk backup as well as the cloud. Is that okay with you?'

'That's your baby, Nell. You're the boss.' I grinned. 'I've just had the same conversation with Tam. And Eliza has come up with some ideas. That's why I want us all together.'

'Okay, give me five minutes.'

##

Ten minutes later I stopped at the end of the path where Evie had created a small garden edged with logs. Already some of her tropical plants had flowered and were providing a pretty show.

Ahead of Nell and I was the most incredible palette of colours as the sun dipped towards the water. A lone sailing boat was the only thing between the shore and the magnificent sky, the headsail billowing in the afternoon wind; a backdrop of burnt orange cloud edged with silver contrasted with the white sail and the silvery-blue water the boat glided over.

'Thank you, Pip.' Nell's voice was hushed. 'Thank you for sharing your island with us.'

I linked my arm through hers as we walked across the sand to the bar. 'Thank you for being here. I think we've got a pretty tight group here now. I appreciate you all.'

'Even Eliza?' she asked quietly.

'Yes, she's a hard worker. Whatever secrets she holds are her business. And I've got to like her more each day.'

'Good. I think she is a great addition to the team. And how gorgeous, is she? She could have been a model.'

'She can turn her hand to anything, that's for sure. Plus, she's got some great ideas. That's why I want everyone down here to listen now.'

When we reached the edge of the open space of the bar, I stood back and looked at it. The girls had shelved the rest of the bottles and hung a row of champagne flutes along the two stainless steel wires that Eliza had suggested would be perfect for hanging glasses.

'I saw it up in Cairns,' she'd said the other day. 'Cheap, simple and effective.'

I picked up the wire when we were over on the mainland,

PENTECOST ISLAND 1-3

along with a list of other bits and pieces that Eliza had suggested. What she had done with some cheap fittings and the contents of our toolbox amazed me.

Yes, she was a great asset to our team, and I wanted her to stay.

Tam was shaking a silver cocktail shaker with flair and did a fancy manoeuvre before she lifted it and poured a fluffy blue concoction into the cocktail glasses lined up on the burnished timber bar top—another of Eliza's creations in the past week. That had saved me a fortune.

'That looks interesting it. What are we having?'

Tam grinned at me. 'We're starting with the PI Special.'

'Ah. Let me guess. Pentecost Island?' I reached for it to take a sip, but she grabbed the glass before my hand reached it. 'Okay, and what do you mean by starting with,' I asked.

Tam came out from behind the bar, placed the five glasses on a tray and carried them over to the table where the others were sitting. 'I'm a chef, not a bar person, so I need to practise my cocktails on some volunteers.' She passed the glasses around the table, and I sat down in one of the vacant chairs.

'Okay, first sip and an immediate ranking out of ten, please ladies,' Tam said.

We all obliged.

'Yum, what's in that?' Nell asked. 'I'll give it a ten.'

'Vodka, coconut rum, blue curacao, pineapple juice, lemon soda, and a twist of lime.'

'Wow, that's some hangover material.' Eliza took another sip and then smiled. 'But I can live with that. A ten from me too.'

Evie nodded. 'And me.'

'Pip?' Tam looked at me anxiously.

I slowly lifted the glass and took another sip as I looked at the women sitting around the table. Contentment filled me; I felt comfortable with all of them and would never stop appreciating the

ANNIE SEATON

effort they were all making to help me achieve my dream.

'Not a ten.' I shook my head and drained the glass to everyone's astonishment. 'That's an eleven from me.'

By Tam's third creation—a pink one to follow the blue and the yellow—we were all getting mellow, if not a little tipsy.

I held up my hand. 'We need to slow down and listen to Eliza's idea. Finish what you started to tell us before.'

She put her glass down and fiddled nervously with the paper straw. 'Well, I was wondering if you might have already considered this. I would suggest that the island and the house is the perfect location for an exclusive day spa.'

I tipped my head to the side as I watched her. Sometimes Eliza's speech was very formal, and sometimes her Kiwi accent was strong, and other times it seemed to be blended with something else. All part of her mystery package.

She held my gaze aware of my scrutiny. 'I was looking at the layout of the house the other afternoon and had an idea. If everyone moved into the rooms at the back, you could open up the four front rooms, and put in bigger windows opening out onto the verandah and that gorgeous view. You could have a variety of exclusive treatments, with natural products to fit in with the theme of your eco- resort.'

I nodded slowly as I considered the idea. 'We did discuss something on a smaller scale before we even moved here. It would cost a lot to make the structural changes to the house though.'

'I can do that,' Eliza said.

I raised my eyebrows. One thing she didn't lack was confidence in her work.

'And what about beauty therapists or whatever it is they're called these days?' Tam said. 'Would it be hard to get someone to come to the island? We're pretty isolated out here.'

'If you put out what you want to the universe, you will get what you want.' Eliza's voice seemed deeper and her words

PENTECOST ISLAND 1-3

surprised me. I didn't see her as a New Age type of person.

'You think it's that easy?' I tried not to be too cynical.

'Can you visualise it?' she asked. 'Close your eyes, Pippa. Imagine a room, a peaceful room with royal blue curtains blowing in the gentle breeze of the bay. Soft pipe music drifts from the room. Two women sit on the verandah with fruit juice waiting for their treatments. Calm and serenity surround them.'

Damn, I could see it. My interest flared.

'I have a friend who might be interested in working here,' Eliza added. 'She's a qualified therapist.'

'I'm loving the sound of this,' Evie said with a grin. 'Could staff book in?

'What do you think, Nell? Do you have time to do a feasibility study?' My practical side chimed in despite the two and half cocktails.

Nell's chuckle belied her always-serious expression. 'I can make time.'

'Excellent. Thank you, Eliza. It's this hive mind that's going to make our resort a success.'

Eliza beamed as she reached for her drink. 'Thank you for letting me be a part of it. The more I can help, the less of an intruder I feel.' She stared past me and her eyes narrowed.

I turned to see what she was looking at. The sailing boat I had admired when Nell and I had walked down from the house was coming into our bay. I stood and walked down to the sand and as I watched, surprise filled me. The skipper headed directly to the channel between the coral heads and within minutes was safely in our bay.

'He's done that before.' Tam came to stand beside me.

'Apparently.' I looked more closely at the boat. It was an old white sloop; she had graceful lines but had seen some wear and tear. The skipper brought her right into the sand, jumped over the front and tied the bow onto two palm trees that were near the water's edge. A tall man in white shorts and a navy-blue T-shirt strolled up the beach towards us.

I turned around. 'Evie, isn't that your French friend from Hamo the other day? You said you'd invited him, but he's arrived a bit early.'

Chair legs scraped on the pavers that we'd laid for the bar floor as Eliza stood.

'I have some emails to send to my family. Thanks for the cocktails, Tam. I'll see you all in the morning.' She turned quickly and walked past the bar, but Tam called after her.

'What about dinner?'

Eliza waved her hand and her voice was short. 'No thanks. I'm not hungry.' She was out of sight in seconds.

Evie hurried down to meet the man who was tying off his boat, and I followed.

'You've done that before,' I said. 'You knew where to find the channel, especially as it's almost dark.'

'I do.' He nodded and held out his hand. '*Bon soir.* I am Phillipe Renton. I hope it is allowable for me to moor here for tonight. And yes, I was in the Whitsundays about eight years ago, and learned about your channel that the Americans made in the Second World War. There's another one over at Happy Bay on Palm Island, but not many sailors knew about this one when I was here last time.'

My eyes widened. 'The Second World War? I didn't know about them being on the island.'

Phillipe walked up the beach behind us. 'This must be the bar that Evie told me about. And I heard that you are planning a restaurant also?' His accent was divine, and I could see Evie hanging off his every word.

'Not yet, but we will. And yes, you are more than welcome to moor here for the night. Oh, and I'm Pippa.'

'Your bay is not in the *One Hundred Magic Miles* book, so

I wasn't sure if it was acceptable to moor in the bay.'

'What book is that? I asked as we reached the bar.

'It's the bible for sailors in the Whitsundays, and it lists the anchorages and moorings for all of the bays and resorts.' He stood back to allow Evie and I to go in first.

'I think the tourism girls on the mainland told me about it. And as you are our first visitor, there will be no charge. We are not quite open for business. We're almost ready.'

'Three more days,' Tam said. 'But we have drinks in the fridge here. What would you like?'

Jiminy's best mate, Taj, who lived on Hamilton Island was an electrician, and he'd spent a day over here running the power down to the bar. We'd decided to have LED lights in the huts, but there was a charging station with six double power points on a bench at the far side of the bar.

'A cold beer would be excellent, but I insist on paying for it, and for my mooring too.'

I introduced Tam and Nell and he shook their hands in turn.

'*Enchanté.*' His voice was deep and accented, and I would swear I saw the three girls swoon. But not me; even though he was a honey, my heart was firmly in Rafe's safekeeping.

'This looks very good.' Philippe looked around. 'You've changed it a lot. The last time I was here this was an old boatshed.'

'Yes, the only things we kept were the original timber posts,' I said. 'Did you meet the owner when you were here?'

'I did. She was a delightful woman. I assume she's passed on for you to be developing a resort.'

'Yes, she was my mother's aunt. We all live up in the old house now. We're slowly doing it up.'

His gaze flicked over to the huts. Eliza and Evie had the frames finished and we were waiting for Bunnings to call to say the cladding was in. I was hoping to pick it up when Rafe flew into the mainland airport the day after tomorrow. He'd changed his flight destination especially so it would save me an extra trip over to the mainland.

'We?'

'There's five of us working here at the moment. Eliza is back at the house. Friends as well as staff. I have a good team.'

'I had heard on the sailing grapevine that there was a tribe of Amazons doing it all themselves on this island. I guess they were referring to you and your team.' He looked suitably impressed and smiled as he took the glass of beer from Tam. 'Thank you. I'll have to spread the word for you.'

'Best form of advertising,' I said. 'But leave it for a few days. The official opening is next weekend.

'Would you like another drink, Pip?' Tam asked from behind the bar.

'Just a soda, thanks.' I'd been getting tipsy on her potent cocktails and I didn't want the sailing grapevine to put about that we were a party island. 'Then I've got some work to do, but you three are on your own time now, so please keep Phillipe company.'

Tam shot me a look telling me she understood where I was coming from. Evie smiled and Nell looked impatient. I knew she'd be anxious to get back to her files. She worked way too hard.

I finished my soda and stood. 'Because you insist on paying for your mooring, I'll insist that you join us for breakfast on the house verandah in the morning. I want to hear all about this war channel dredging. I'd always assumed it was natural.'

'That would be my pleasure.' He stood when I pushed my chair in. Nell was right behind me as I headed for the beach.

'See you tomorrow,' she said with a wave.

I grinned as we walked back to the house. 'I think both Tam and Evie have fallen under the spell of our first guest.'

'Nope. Not Tam,' Nell said. 'She's just being polite.'

'Do you know what happened with Chad?' I asked curiously. 'I know it was a messy break up, and I don't think she's been out with anyone since then.'

'All I know is Chad broke her heart. I don't think she's ever got over him. Last I heard he was marrying some girl from Sydney.'

'Maybe a hot French dude is just what she needs.'

'Probably, but I think Evie's got her eye out there, don't you?'

'Seemed to have.' We climbed up the steps and went inside; the house was in darkness and there was no sign of Eliza. I flicked the lights on. 'I'm going to cook some toast and work on a flyer to take over to the mainland on Tuesday. Is the printer working?'

She nodded glumly. 'It's about the only thing that is. I'm going to try and get it all sorted tonight. Throw a couple of pieces of toast in for me too, please. I need something to soak up those cocktails and clear my head.

It might have been the residual effect of the cocktail, but a huge surge of happiness went through me. I grabbed both Nell's hands. 'This is going to be *so* good, isn't it?'

Her smile was wide. 'It already is good. I'm very happy working here. Even when I struggle with the IT.'

'And I'm happy to have such fantastic friends.'

'Don't forget that gorgeous man who's almost on his way back to you. Have you heard from him?' She laughed and said. 'Okay, silly question. Of course, you have.' After a moment her expression grew serious. 'Are you okay with this, Pip? I mean, I think Rafe is a great guy, but I—and Tam—well, we don't want to see you hurt. There's been a lot of changes for you in the past few months.'

'Oh, Nell.' I reached out and hugged her. 'You know I love you both for worrying about me. But, honestly? I don't think I've ever been this happy—or so sure of anything in my life before. Rafe is the man for me, and I know he feels the same way. I would trust him with my life.'

'That's a sweeping statement.' The cynical voice came from behind me and I turned. Eliza stood in the dark hall and had obviously been listening to our conversation without making herself known.

'It might be,' I said rather tersely. 'But it's the way I feel.'

'Just be careful.' Eliza's voice was soft and as she stepped out into the light, I could see her face was pale.

'Don't worry, I am. We are. We've all been hurt at one time or another and we know the way it can be.' I glanced at Nell. I knew she'd had a bad experience at uni and as far as I knew she'd never gone out with a guy since. 'Sounds like you're part of the club too.'

I thought of the ring that Eliza had in her safekeeping.

'The club?'

'The been-dumped club.' I said. 'A shame our visitor interrupted us, we could have had a good girls' night on the cocktails and a natter.'

'Is he still down there?' Her voice was still quiet as she went into the kitchen and filled the jug.

'Evie and Tam are keeping him entertained. He's already said he'll recommend our place.'

'Your place. I just work here.'

She was in a strange mood.

'I like to think it's a team effort,' I said as I reached for three mugs. 'You might have only been here a couple of weeks, Eliza, but I'd like you to know I do appreciate how hard you've been working. And your ideas. I hope you'll stay with us for a while before you move on.'

'I'll see. It depends on a few things.' Eliza jumped as the kettle gave its shrill whistle.

'Fair enough. Tea or coffee, Nell?' I asked.

'Coffee please. I'm going to work until late.'

I thoughtfully watched Eliza take her coffee back to her room. When I went to bed well after midnight, I noticed the light was still shining under her door.

Chapter 13

Marissa: Tuscany

Staying in Rosco's villa—I still couldn't think of it as home—before we went to visit my family, was both a good and bad thing. It gave me more of an idea of what my life was going to be like as Rosco worked in his study with Davina each day before he came up to see me in the afternoon to tell me what he would like me to wear for dinner. It also gave me a yardstick with which to compare my family home. Meynell Manor certainly didn't measure up to this luxurious villa, and I worried about Rosco's reaction when we arrived.

Every day I wondered why he had married me, and every night, my doubts fled as he told me—and showed me how much he loved me.

I'd had no contact with anyone apart from my husband, and the cow who'd worked with him since we'd arrived. I was beginning to loathe Davina. The way she looked at me made me feel uncomfortable, and a couple of times when Rosco had not been around, she had called me Celeste.

'My name is Marissa,' I informed her coldly.

'Oh. So it is,' she said with a strange smile. 'I do get you all mixed up.'

I had no idea what she meant, and I wasn't sure whether to ask Rosco or not. It really bothered me how much my confidence was disappearing. Maybe it was marriage that did that to you. All of a sudden, you were one of a pair and had to think about another person's happiness. I didn't like upsetting him.

Back in those early weeks, I didn't realise that my reaction was a form of self-protection. Sure, Rosco might have been moody, but he smothered me with love when he was out of his study. So much so that, at times, I felt like a princess.

Before I had a chance to walk to the village alone, he took me for a walk one afternoon and we'd had a drink at a small café before we'd come back to the villa for dinner. The visit to the village showed me I would be wasting my time if I thought I could get a phone there. There was nothing there apart from medieval buildings, a lace shop, a leather shop and a couple of outdoor bars.

There was a cook and a guy to look after Rosco's cellar, so I was at a loss to understand what the fuss about me not being able to cook was all about.

When we were in England, I fully intended to get a phone. I was going to go stir-crazy not talking to any of my friends. Even talking to my two bitch sisters would be better than this quiet life.

'What are you thinking about, my love?'

I jumped as Rosco sat next to me. 'Oh, nothing much,' I lied.

'I have something to tell you that I think will bring your smile back. I haven't seen it much these past two weeks.' His words held a note of criticism. 'Don't you love my home?'

'I've been adjusting,' I said slowly, then immediately worried that I had said the wrong thing.

Where had that confident, sassy person I had been six weeks ago disappeared to?

The woman who had set out on an adventure with her best friend.

'As long as you don't change your mind.'

'Change my mind?'

'About being my wife.'

I shook my head quickly, very pleased that he couldn't read my thoughts. 'Of course not. I am just getting used to living—' I bit my words off before I put my foot in it. 'Living in a beautiful villa and getting to know the countryside and the customs,' I finished off feebly.

'If you ever did change your mind, I would not allow you to leave, you know. You are my wife now. And you will be forever.'

I reached out and took his face between my hands. His skin was smooth beneath my fingers and I noticed his hair was wet. He had showered and shaved even though it was only mid-afternoon.

'Don't even think that. I love you Rosco, and you are my husband. I will adjust.'

'You shouldn't have to make an effort to adjust,' he said coldly.

'I'm trying. But you have to understand. I was someone who went to work every day, and I had to get used to this freedom in my days.'

His face split into a sudden smile, at odds with the tone of his voice a minute ago.

'What would you say if I told you I had bought tickets to fly to London tomorrow? It is past time that I met your parents.'

Sweet relief flooded through me. 'Really?' Despite my determination to be reserved, I almost squealed the words.

'Yes, really.' Rosco put his arms around me and rested his chin on the top of my head. When he held me all my doubts fled, and I knew I had to make more of an effort to be happy here.

'Tomorrow. We will leave after breakfast.' He pulled me closer and it was hard to breathe. 'But tonight, we have a guest for dinner. Please wear the beige silk dress.'

I nodded. As much as I hated him telling me what to wear nothing was going to interfere with my happiness tonight.

We were going home.

Dinner was unpleasant, and my happy mood didn't last long. As well as Ren—the yachtsman I had met on our honeymoon, who Rosco had apparently recently conducted business with—the cow, Davina, made up the numbers. She was also dressed in silk, but the yellow made her olive skin look puce.

What was happening to me? I was changing into a person I sometimes didn't like very much. I swallowed and tried to join in the conversation.

My grasp of Italian was improving, but I was grateful to Ren, who switched to English, every time Davina chattered on in staccato speed dialect.

'Are you enjoying the countryside?' he asked me. 'Or would you rather be living on Rosco's boat?'

I tipped my head to the side, conscious of Rosco's interest in my answer. Davina's eyes glittered as Ren took his attention from her.

'I enjoy both,' I said carefully.

Ren turned to my husband. 'Are you taking any trips this winter?'

'Quite possibly. What do you suggest?'

'I spent the winter in the South Pacific six years ago. It was one of the most beautiful places I have been, and I intend going back one winter. The Whitsunday Islands.'

I carefully sliced the meat on my plate before looking across the table at him. 'I was under the impression that you lived on your boat, Ren.'

He laughed and held my gaze. I looked down, again conscious of Rosco's eyes on me. He didn't look happy and a small spurt of anger played havoc with my digestion.

'I wish that I could live on the sea. I spend as much time as I can on the water, but my business takes me away.'

I nodded and focused on my food.

'One day I will retire and travel the seven seas.'

Rosco's laugh was harsh. 'I will believe that only when I see it. You love making money too much, my friend.'

I thought that was a very rude comment, and Davina chimed in, in Italian, obviously backing him up.

The atmosphere was quite tense for a while, and the only noise was the clinking of cutlery on the fine china.

Finally, when we finished our coffee, Rosco stood. 'I have some business to conduct with Ren before he leaves. Good night, my dear.'

I felt like a child banished to bed, and I protested. 'I am quite happy to wait here until you come up too.'

Davina looked gleeful, and Ren looked embarrassed as Rosco snapped at me. 'Do as I say.'

To my disgust, I did as I was told, but I was aware of sympathy—and perhaps concern—in Ren's eyes as I walked up the wide staircase.

If I'd thought dinner was unpleasant, the treatment that I received when Rosco finally came to our bed, reeking of brandy was even worse. I pretended to be asleep as he pinned me to the bed and put his face against mine. 'I saw the way you looked at my friend. And so did Davina and of course, Ren. Don't you ever embarrass me like that again, Marissa?'

I rolled away from him and sat up. 'You are drunk,' I said coldly. 'I will ignore the rubbish that you are saying.'

I cringed as he raised his hand to me. I pulled my head back as his hand slapped against my cheek. If I hadn't moved, it would have been a stinging blow, but it just glanced across my cheek.

I scurried across the bed and climbed out before he could reach me, unable to process that he had tried to hit me. 'How dare you!'

I ran across the room and pushed open the door to the en suite bathroom, as Rosco came after me. The heavy door had a lock on it, and I pushed the door shut and flicked the lock over. I turned my back and leaned against the door, my knees shaking so much I was barely able to stand. I slid down the door and sat on the cold tiles and put my hand over my eyes.

'*Bella*, I am so sorry. Please forgive me. Please come out. I should not have done that.'

I shook my head from side to side. No, he most certainly shouldn't have done that.

I sat there trying to figure out what to do until the first glimmer of dawn crept through the window.

When I unlocked the door an hour later, I pushed it open as quietly as I could. Before I could take a step, I was taken in a stronghold as Rosco pulled me to him. He put his face against mine and I was taken aback to feel his cheek damp against mine.

His voice broke and his words shook as he begged me to forgive him. 'I will not drink again. I am sorry. I was drunk and out of control. I am so, so sorry, my darling. Will you please forgive me? I will do anything. Buy you anything you want. I will take you anywhere you want to go. Just please forgive me and tell me you love me.'

I had stopped shaking finally, and the warmth of his skin against mine was soothing. I lowered my head and rested my face in the hollow of his neck as his tears continued to splash onto my skin. 'Do I have your word you will never raise your hand to me again?'

'Of course. I will swear it on our family bible.'

'And that you will never speak to me like that again? Either in private or in front of people?'

'I swear. I love you, Marissa. I could not bear to lose you.'

'And you will buy me a phone so that I can have contact

with my friends and family without having to ask your permission.' I felt him tense against me, but he nodded. 'Of course, I was going to get you one and surprise you as soon as we got to Rome.' His words vibrated against my cheek. 'I love having you as my wife, and I will do anything to keep you. Will you promise me you won't leave me?'

I nodded slowly. 'I promise.'

It was a promise that I would find very hard to keep over the following months.

Chapter 14

Pippa: Pentecost Island

I was up early the next morning knowing Tam would be in the kitchen at dawn. If our first official guest was coming for breakfast, she would be pulling out all stops.

I was right; as I walked towards the kitchen, a tempting aroma tickled my nose and my stomach gurgled in anticipation. Tam was singing quietly as she stood at the stove and I smiled. She was in the full getup; the high-collared white shirt was tucked into the black and white checked chef trousers, and her hair was pulled back under a white bandana.

'I'm impressed.' I said as I headed for the coffee machine.

'None of us had dinner last night so I thought I'd do the full works. When you pour your coffee can you help me move that long table out to the verandah, please? I'm going to set up a hot and cold buffet.'

I walked over and looked over her shoulder. She had three pots bubbling on the stove. 'Jeez, what time did you get up?'

Her grin was cheeky. 'I was too pumped after we'd had a few more drinks. I didn't.'

'Didn't go to bed? You're mad, woman.'

'Nuh. I'm excited. This is getting very real, Pip. I want it to be perfect.'

'It smells pretty damn perfect to me. We'll clean up after we eat, and you can go to bed.'

Another grin. 'I was counting on that.'

I leaned back on the bench and sipped my coffee. 'Did you get in touch with your friend who you suggested for the bar?'

'Yes, I emailed the other night, but she hasn't replied yet.

She might be away.'

'Before we have our first bookings for the huts, we're going to have to get some wait staff.' I took another sip and frowned. 'It's a hard call. We're a bit isolated, there's no boat service from Hamo to here, and we really don't want *every* staff member living on site just yet.'

'It is a bit tricky. Get Nell onto it. She thinks outside the square.' Tam leaned over and turned on the new grill we'd installed, and then opened the oven a crack and nodded. A mouth-watering aroma immediately filled the kitchen.

'Bread?' I almost moaned. 'You've cooked fresh bread too?'

'I have. Now finish that coffee and help me get set up. Phillipe said he'd come over about seven-thirty. He was going to head off today, but I think Evie talked him into staying in the bay for a few days. He was talking about going over to Indian Head to look at the summit. He's talking about climbing it.'

'That's a big climb. He'd have to start early. Seems like a nice guy.' I rinsed my mug.

'It would be a lonely life living on a boat by yourself though. I couldn't do it, could you?' Tam said.

'Never know until you try it.'

As we moved the table out to the verandah, Tam stopped in the doorway. 'I have an idea. What about Jiminy?'

'What about him?'

'Didn't he say that he was getting less work? Instead of you running over to the island and picking up guests, why don't you ask him if he would start a service? It could be lucrative for him, and you would save time and money. He could also ferry staff over for day shifts.'

I nodded. 'That's not a bad idea. I'll swing into Hamo and see him on the way to the mainland on Wednesday. You're certainly on fire this morning.'

##

By seven thirty, the buffet table was loaded with cereal and freshly baked bread. Two pitchers of milk sat side by side, with a jug of pineapple juice next to a platter of fresh fruit. Tam had even found time to pick some hibiscus flowers for decoration.

'I didn't realise you'd done so much shopping,' I said.

'I've been stocking up every time we go over to Hamo. Evie took me over the other day too.' Tam smoothed her hands down the front of her trousers. 'Here comes our guest, now. You can do the meet and greet.' She flashed me another grin. 'I'm just the kitchen staff.'

I rolled my eyes. 'Go on then. Get back to the stove, cook.'

'Chef, please. He looks like a fried egg man to me. What do you think?'

'Nuh, five bucks says poached,' I said with a laugh.

I went to the steps and waited for Phillipe to cross the lawn. Evie had worked magic with the old garden already. She had salvaged a lot of plants that had been hidden by overgrowth and had edged the gardens with more small logs she'd carted from the forest. The lawn was lush and green, and she had cleared around the large paving stones that had been there since I was a child.

'*Bonjour,* Phillipe. Welcome to Ma Carmichael's.'

He held out his hand and took mine in a half shake, half squeeze. 'Good morning, Pippa.'

I led him to the table we had set and gestured for him to take the chair that gave him a view of the bay to one side and the house on the other.

He waited for me to sit first and then looked out over the garden. 'This is delightful. Thank you for allowing me to be here.'

'Our pleasure. It's special to me knowing that you were here when my aunt was here.

His smile was gentle. 'We sat on those steps and she made me a cup of strong Australian tea. I was polite but I have never tried it since.'

I laughed. 'Aunt Vi loved her cuppa strong enough to stand a spoon in it. I'll get you a coffee.'

Before I could move, Tam appeared with the coffee pot.

'Good morning. Coffee?'

Philippe nodded. '*Merci.* There is a delectable smell coming from the kitchen.'

How would you like your eggs?' she asked.

'Scrambled, please, he said.

Tam and I exchanged an amused look as she put the pot on the table and disappeared back into the kitchen.

'Tam's been busy. I'd say we're in for a feast. Now tell me about the channel to the bay you mentioned last night.'

Phillipe leaned forward and picked up his coffee. 'In World War Two the US servicemen used to come to the islands for R and R. Your aunt told me how they discovered Pentecost Island, and they organised to have a channel blasted so they could get here quickly and easily. Apparently, her father was very welcoming, and they wanted to pay him back for his hospitality.'

'Wow, I never knew that. There is so much I don't know about the island, or her family for that matter. We lost so much history when she passed away.' I stared out over the bay imagining what it would have been like back in the war. 'Aunty Vi must have been a child then.'

'She said she was about ten at the end of the war.'

I nodded. 'That would be about right. Thank you, Phillipe, it means a lot to me to hear some island history'

Tam's head appeared around the kitchen door. 'I'm putting the eggs on now, Pip, if you'd like to call the girls.'

As I stood, the door at the end of the verandah opened with a loud creak. Phillipe looked up and his mouth dropped open. Eliza

PENTECOST ISLAND 1-3

was walking towards us, her attention on her phone. Phillipe's eyes widened, and his mouth opened.

I moved away from the table and Eliza looked up. 'I've had a reply from my—' She stopped when she noticed Phillipe sitting at the table.

I watched curiously as the colour leached from her face and she stopped. She stared at Phillipe for a moment, and her phone slipped from her hands.

She bent to pick it up. 'Oh, I'm . . . er . . . sorry. I didn't realise that we had company.' Turning swiftly, she took a step back towards the door.

'Wait.' Philippe shot to his feet. 'Please. Ma—' He shook his head and stopped talking, his eyes fixed on Eliza.

Eliza shook her head and quickly disappeared through the door.

I looked from the closed door to Phillipe. He looked like he'd seen a ghost.

Picking up the coffee pot, I topped up his cup.

He picked it up and I noticed his hand was shaking. 'What is her name? Please?'

'Eliza.'

'She is another friend of yours?'

'She is becoming one.' I was intrigued by his reaction. Eliza was very beautiful, but she downplayed it in the way she dressed and the messy way her short dark curls framed her face. 'She's only been with us for a short while.'

'How long?' His words held urgency.

'About three weeks now. Why do you ask?'

'She looks very much like someone I know. I mean, someone I knew. She died a few months ago.' His face was still pale.

'I'm sorry to hear that.'

He drained his coffee and I topped it up again.

'What is her whole name? Do you know where she is from?' He fired the questions at me.

'Eliza Pengelly. From New Zealand.'

He shook his head. 'I thought perhaps Marissa may have had a sister. They could almost be doubles, but she was English. I'm sorry, I am being very rude.'

'It's fine. They say we all have a *doppelganger* somewhere in the world. Eliza is a private person. I'm sorry to hear about your friend.' I reached over and squeezed his hand.

Eliza's fast disappearance had me curious. I had seen the look of terror on her face when she had first seen Phillipe, but she had masked it very quickly. I also remembered how she had disappeared as soon as his boat had appeared in the bay yesterday.

Curiouser and curiouser.

Nell and Evie surfaced and sat at the table beside us. Phillipe had recovered his equilibrium, but he was quiet. Evie tried to get him talking but soon gave up as he focused on eating the laden plate that Tam brought out.

By the time we had all eaten, there was still no sign of Eliza, although Phillipe kept glancing towards the closed door. Eventually he stood and I pushed my chair back.

'Thank you for breakfast,' he said. 'Please tell Tam it was most enjoyable.' He still seemed preoccupied.

'I'll walk you back to the beach. I hear you're thinking of going to Indian Head today?'

'Perhaps. Is it acceptable if I stay moored in your bay for a few days? I will pay of course. I would like to climb the summit one day.'

'Yes, we would be pleased to have you stay.' I knew I would, but I wondered about Eliza's reaction. I was going to search her out as soon as Phillipe was back on his boat. I'd accepted her secrecy since she'd arrived, but if there was something that was going to impact on our guests, I wanted to

PENTECOST ISLAND 1-3

know what it was.

The sun was high, and the day was promising to be a beauty. A few sails dotted the passage, the wind filling them as the yachts scooted along at a good speed. Philippe's boat showed its age in the daytime.

He saw me looking and gave me his first smile for a while. 'I know she looks tired, but she is a solid boat. She has taken me all around the world.'

'As long as she floats.' I cleared my throat. 'May I ask what happened to your friend?'

He stared out over the bay. 'Marissa was married to a business colleague of mine. She wasn't a very close friend. I only met her a few times, but there was something about her . . .' He swallowed. 'I caught up with them in Cairns, and we had dinner on Rosco's boat one night. I set off to the south, and he called me distraught two days later. Marissa drowned one night when they were out near Green Island.'

'Oh, I'm sorry. That is very sad. No wonder you looked so shocked when you saw someone who looked like her.'

'Yes, but now that I think about it, they are different. Your Eliza is taller and more, how do you say, slight, I think, and her hair is dark. Marissa's hair was long and blonde. She was very beautiful.' He almost seemed to be talking to himself. 'Rosco's wives were both very beautiful.'

'Both?'

'Yes, sadly his first wife was killed in a car accident.'

'Oh, such tragedy. I'm sorry you've had a sad morning.'

'Thank you for listening and thank you again for breakfast. I'm going to go and get some exercise.'

'I hope you do stay a few days. My partner will be home from Europe this week, and you will have some male company. Anyway, have a good day. Time for me to head to work. I'll see you later, Phillipe.'

He nodded, and his smile was sad.

I headed back to the house: I wanted to have a chat with Eliza.

Chapter 15

Marissa

The visit home was not what you'd call a happy event. Dad was okay about our marriage, but I could see the hurt lurking beneath his usual jovial exterior. My mother's reaction was as I'd expected; she was in awe of Rosco, his charm—he really turned it on—and his obvious wealth. He seemed to feel the need to tell them about his business, his villa, his boat—boats—yet little about himself.

I guess I was still angry with him and I had pretty much shut down. I hated being home. Being in the light and airy villa for the past couple of weeks, and before that living on the boat, made our ancestral home seem darker and dingier than it usually did.

On the second morning we were there, Rosco came to seek me out. He put his arms around me and dropped a kiss on top of my head. He seemed to have forgotten all about the recent incident, although it seemed that when he was trying to ignore his bad behaviour, he was more affectionate to me.

'I have to beg a very big favour of you, *cara mia.*'

'Yes?' I said warily as I stepped out of his arms, but he came after me and held me close again.

'I have had a call from Davina, and there is a crisis at home. One of my suppliers has breached our contract, and I need to be there to sort it out. Would you be very unhappy if we left today?'

He didn't have to be Einstein to see how unhappy I was here.

But I was torn. It would be nice to have some space. If I stayed here for a week, I could go to London and catch up with my friends.

And buy a bloody phone. I had managed to make a brief call to Sienna on the landline in the kitchen, and I knew I'd worried her as I'd fobbed her off. She had always been able to read me well.

If I was totally honest it would be nice to have some space from Rosco.

'How about you go back, and I'll follow in a few days. You're going to be busy.'

Wrong answer.

His fingers tightened on my upper arms and I tensed.

'No. You will come home with me. I have bought our tickets. We fly out of Gatwick at three o'clock this afternoon.'

I couldn't help myself. Maybe being in my home gave me courage. I shook his arms off and folded my arms. 'So, what was the point in asking me a favour? You have already decided what is happening.'

'Yes, that is correct. I am your husband.'

'So? Does that mean I have no say in any decisions we should make together?'

His dark eyes glittered with suppressed rage. Maybe knowing that my father was in the house bolstered my courage.

'I'm going to stay here. Change my ticket and I will follow you on the weekend. I haven't even seen my sisters yet.'

'We are being picked up at noon. Be ready.' He turned on his heel and left the room.

I sank onto the bed and put my face in my hands

Was I strong enough to disobey him?

To my disgust, I knew I wasn't.

##

We'd been back in Italy for three months, and Rosco's behaviour had improved. He hadn't been drinking much and had been at several meetings in the city, leaving me to explore the villa. I still didn't have my own phone, but he often gave me his—and privacy—to call my friends. I was even allowed to go down to the village by myself some days. It had been thirteen weeks since we had left my parents' home. To my surprise, my father had called the villa the week after we got home and asked to speak to me.

'Dad? What's wrong?'

'Nothing,' he replied, his voice bright. 'Can't a father ring his daughter and say hello?'

I held back my cynical reply that I couldn't ever recall him ringing me before.

'I just wanted to call and see how you had settled in Italy. It's a big step, Marissa.'

I had a feeling that Dad had overheard our argument the day we left, but he never said anything specific.

'It is.'

Rosco was hovering.

'If you ever need anything don't you hesitate to call me.'

'Thank you, Dad. That's kind of you.'

'You just remember that we love you, chicken. No matter what you might think.'

My eyes had welled up at that. I'd forgotten the nickname Dad had had for me when I was a child.

I hung up the phone and went to walk out of the study.

'What was kind?' Rosco asked.

'Dad asked if we'd like to visit soon.'

'We will try.'

But of course, we didn't.

Sometimes a niggle of doubt crept in and I wondered if Rosco could somehow hear the calls I made on his phone, but I shook that suspicion off. I was getting paranoid. Sienna and I chatted at least once a week and I had become very skilled at sounding happy and prattling on about the villa and the countryside, but never anything about my marriage.

Rosco had asked me to redecorate one of the smaller guest rooms, and I soon discovered that his interpretation of the word was very different to mine. Beautiful timber panelling covered the far wall and needed resealing.

I was in my element. I found an old pair of shorts and a stained T-shirt deep in my luggage, and I went ferreting in the barn down behind the villa and discovered some tins of varnish. I had spent two peaceful days rubbing back the timber and resealing it. The smell of the old timber soothed me, and my fingers itched to build something.

My joy was short-lived. I heard Rosco's car roar up the long drive mid-afternoon on the second day, and Davina must have told him where I was because only moments later, he was at the bottom of the ladder I was perched on.

'What the hell are you doing?' His voice was thunderous.

'I am doing what you asked me to. You said the guest bedroom needed redecorating.'

I climbed down the ladder and wiped a hand over my sweaty brow.

'You look like an *il lavoratrice.*'

'A lavatory?' I gaped at him. Something had gone astray in the translation.

'A labourer,' he said impatiently. 'I meant for you to choose the fabrics and the colours and order them online, not ruin your beautiful hands and nails scrubbing down walls.

I stared back. Hard.

'It might be that "lavatory" word, but that is my trade. I was a woods craftsman in London.'

'I don't care what you were in London, my wife will not work like a common labourer.'

I sighed and climbed down the ladder.

'Well, what can your wife do to fill in her days?'

He looked at me as though I had two heads.

'Be a wife.'

'Yes, Rosco,' I said with a bit of snark in my tone. 'I guess I can be a wife. But perhaps not to your satisfaction.' His disparagement of my profession had rankled. 'Perhaps we have different ideas of what a wife should be. Perhaps this isn't going to work.'

'What?' He screwed up his face. 'The room? I can get someone in to fix it.'

'No, our marriage. I think I need some time away.' I half turned away and I didn't see the blow coming.

The next thing I knew I was on the floor, my head hard up against the ladder and my left ear ringing like a church bell. He leaned over and grabbed my hair and pulled me up. Searing pain ripped through my scalp. He held me upright as he yelled into my face. My head was spinning but I could hear his words.

'You will not leave me. If you do, I will kill you. Is that clear? You took a holy vow, and you are my wife for the rest of your life.'

'What?' I whispered as shock flooded through me.

'If you don't believe me, think of Celeste. She, too, wanted to leave me.'

'Who is Celeste?' I whispered as I moved my tongue around my mouth. I had a feeling I had a loose tooth. My cheek was stinging and aching where I had hit the floor.

'Celeste was my wife, and she tried to leave. She met with an accident and I was heartbroken as I would be if you were to meet with an accident.'

Horror filled me as I stared at my husband, but his face disappeared as he pulled me close and my face was pressed into his linen shirt.

'My poor darling. How clumsy of you to fall off the ladder. Shall I get Davina to call the doctor?'

'No.' My voice was muffled against his shoulder as I fought tears. 'I will have a shower and lie down.'

'And you will be more careful next time.' His voice was full of sympathy. 'Although there will not be a next time, will there?'

'No, Rosco, there won't.' My voice was dull.

The diamond necklace and matching earrings that appeared on my dressing table the next week were obviously supposed to make me forget what he had done this time.

Chapter 16

Pippa: Pentecost Island

Eliza was sitting on the steps when I walked back through the gate.

'I was waiting to see what you had lined up for me today, Pippa.' Her smile was wide, but her eyes didn't quite meet mine.

I cut straight to the chase. 'What was all that about?'

'What?' she asked innocently. 'What was what about?'

'All that guff with Phillipe. You disappeared like a shot when he arrived yesterday, and you were off like a frightened rabbit when you saw him this morning.'

'I was doing the right thing. You had a guest and you surely didn't want the handy man hanging around.'

'Handy woman.' I sat on the step beside her. 'You are more than a worker, Eliza. You fit in so well with us all, I thought you would consider yourself a friend by now.'

'I'm sorry if I did the wrong thing.'

'Are you sure you don't know him? He said you reminded him of someone.'

'No, I don't know any Phillipe from France. A bit out of my league. A girl from a fishing family in little old EnZed. I've never been to France.' Her smile was rueful. 'Not the sort of circles I mix in.' She lowered her head. 'I am a bit shy too. I had a tough childhood, so I don't have a lot of confidence around people. I'll probably move on when you start getting guests here.'

'So, you're sure you don't know him? He said you looked like someone called Marissa. A sister? A cousin?'

'Nope.' She shook her head. 'I don't know anyone of that name.'

'Okay. Come on then. Let's get to work.'

'What's on the agenda for today?'

'I'd like to tell you about some ideas I've had for knocking some walls out in the house. And to see if you think it can be done.'

'Thank you,' she said quietly. 'You don't know how much it means to me, to have my opinion valued.'

'I've really taken on your idea of the spa too. I couldn't get to sleep last night thinking about it. I think it would be a fabulous drawcard. I was even thinking about building a lodge further into the bush so we could use the house for the restaurant, the spa and a sitting room for the guests. I know what it's like on a boat. If they came up for lunch or dinner, they might appreciate a space to relax in afterwards.'

'You've got some plans, that's for sure.'

'Can I just ask you one thing?' I said carefully.

Her eyes narrowed. 'Does it involve people?'

'No. It only involves you and trust.'

'Okay, ask away.'

'Will you promise me that if it does come time for you to leave you'll tell us and just won't disappear into the night the way you arrived?'

She nodded.

I held up my pinkie and crooked it. 'Promise?'

She looked at me blankly.

I chuckled. 'It's a tradition that Tam, Nell and I started at school. Make a promise, crook fingers.'

She slowly lifted her left hand, and for the first time, I noticed that her little finger was already crooked.

'It might be hard,' she said. 'But I'll do my best.'

'That's great. It's the most I can ask.' I looked at her finger as she lowered her hand. 'What did you do to your finger?'

'Jammed it in a door.' She didn't meet my eye again. 'And I was nowhere near a hospital, so the break had to heal by itself.'

PENTECOST ISLAND 1-3

##

After we'd looked at my ideas and Eliza came up with some great ideas to add to what I suggested, we went down to the huts. Each hut was small but had a sandy level verandah at the front covered with an overhang of the roof. The cladding I had ordered from the hardware store was a sandy colour and the huts with their straw-look roofs would blend into the beach.

'Have you thought about hanging some rope hammocks with coloured cushions on the verandah?'

I put my hands on my hips and regarded Eliza seriously. 'The day you decide to leave here is not going to be a good one. We might find some jobs for you out of the public view if that is what it will take to keep you here. Hammocks are a fabulous idea. See, I don't think of those things, although I do remember Nell imagining them between palm trees before we arrived. I'm into marketing; Tam is the foodie, Nell is the figures gal, and Evie is the landscaper. A side photo of the hut with a hammock looking out over the blue water of the bay would be a great shot for our brochure. I've been waiting for Rafe to come home to help me design it.'

'When does he come back?'

'Two more sleeps.' I grinned.

As we turned to head back up to the house, voices came from the bush.

Eliza froze. I glanced at her and put my hand on her arm. 'It's okay. It's only Evie and it sounds like Philippe.'

As we stood there, her hands went behind her back, and I could see them twisting nervously. She was tense and poised for flight and I wondered why she was so intimidated by strangers.

Evie's laugh preceded them as they stepped out of the rainforest.

'You didn't go climbing?' I addressed Philippe.

'No, Evie took me up as far as the beach to see Indian

Head, but I'll leave it for a couple of days. I think that wind's going to come up today. Good for sailing but not so good when you are stuck on the top of a rock.' He looked at Eliza. 'Hello. I'm Phillipe Renton. I'm sorry I was rude this morning, but for a short time I thought you were someone else. Someone I used to know back in Europe.'

Eliza nodded. 'It's fine. I was rude too. I don't cope with strangers well.' She kept her hands behind her back, until Philippe held out his hand. She took his right hand with hers and they shook briefly.

'Eliza Pengelly. And I've never been to Europe,' she said.

Phillipe stared at her and she lifted her chin and stared right back.

Chapter 17

Marissa

The next twelve months was like living in a nightmare that I couldn't wake up from. I had no direct contact with my family or Sienna, as Rosco, and I travelled around the coast of Europe in his *Lady Calypso*. I was permitted to send a postcard every few weeks, but he scrutinised my message each time.

He was so clever, making sure no one was concerned about me or my whereabouts. No one knew of my real situation. As far as they knew I was having a wonderful life with my millionaire husband.

I should have been grateful that I was seeing so much of the world, but it was very hard to focus on the beauty and scenery around me when I was so tense. Occasionally, we would have dinner with Ren, but most of the time, it was just the two of us.

At least Davina was off the scene, but Rosco spent a lot of time on the phone with her, discussing business. Would you believe I still didn't know what his actual business was? The one time I asked all I got in response was a casual hand wave.

'Don't you worry your pretty little head about that, *cara mia.*'

Occasionally, I was allowed to go into some of the small villages for shopping, but Rosco was always by my side, holding my hand, watching my every interaction and doing the talking for me.

'You must learn to speak Italian.'

I had picked up a lot of the language, but I kept that to myself.

I began to abhor his touch, even when he was telling me how much he loved me and held me gently. I found it difficult to eat and I knew I was losing weight. One thing I did do religiously, was take my contraceptive pill; if I was going to escape this monster—and yes, that is what he was—I couldn't afford to have a child with me when I finally got away.

He had now told me several times that if I left him, my life would be over; and I know he meant it literally. My days were filled with frustration and fear, and at times, I thought I was going to go crazy. But I was constantly seeking ways to get away.

I *would.*

And if I died in the attempt, it would be better than the life I was living with him

One day when we were moored off the Italian coast, I disagreed with Rosco about something minor. It was so inconsequential I can't even remember what it was now. He walked over to me with a grim smile.

'I don't like it when you are rude to me,' he said. He took my hand and slammed it in the cupboard in the galley. My little finger broke and I lived on painkillers for a week.

Of course, even though it had been deliberate, my husband was full of remorse. 'I am so sorry, Marissa, but you need to be more careful.'

'Yes, careful with who I pick to marry,' I thought cynically.

Careful about what I say. Careful about what I think. Careful about how I look at any man who may walk past or wave from another boat.

My finger hadn't healed when Ren joined us for dinner in the first little *taverna* we had visited on our honeymoon near the island of Mljet. I recalled Rosco's story of the man imprisoned on the island by the nymph and thought about how our roles had been reversed. Is that why he had chosen that destination? I wondered.

Ren was as reserved as ever with me, but this time I saw him looking at me with concern. I had come to like him very much

PENTECOST ISLAND 1-3

and I couldn't understand his friendship with Rosco. I loved listening to him talk; his views on life were very philosophical. His manner was always calm, and his voice was pleasant to listen to. Some nights, I would simply sit there and listen to the cadence of his voice, not hearing the words that he was speaking as he and Rosco spoke.

'You have lost weight, Marissa, and you are very quiet. Are you well?' he said as we waited for our meal. I had barely said a word since we had sat down.

Rosco interrupted before I could reply. 'We are hoping that a *bambino* is on the way. She has the morning sickness.'

Liar, I thought. We'd never even discussed that. *Thank God.*

'What did you do to your finger?' Ren asked looking at my bandaged pinkie.

'She jammed it in the cupboard in the galley. Silly girl.'

This time when Rosco replied for me, Ren raised his eyebrows and looked at me.

'Is it broken?'

I shrugged and an unspoken message passed between us. Luckily Mauro, the owner of the *taverna,* had come over to speak to Rosco and he didn't notice, or I would have paid for that too.

I could sense that Ren wanted to speak more to me, but Rosco didn't leave my side the whole evening.

He never did.

I felt sad as we waved Ren off early the next morning. Even though he was Rosco's friend he had always been kind to me.

'I won't see you both for a while. I am going to Australia.'

He hadn't mentioned that at dinner.

'*Bon voyage,*' I called.

He tipped his head and stood there looking at me until he was no longer in sight.

I felt bereft and turned with a sigh to go down and prepare Rosco's breakfast. I had finally learned to operate the stove in the galley and to cook.

As he sat there chewing a piece of toast, slowly and methodically—even that habit annoyed me now—Rosco slapped his hand on his thigh.

'Let's go to Australia too.'

'What?' I swallowed nervously. 'Sail *Lady Calypso* to the other side of the world?'

'No, don't be so stupid, Marissa. I will get my crew to take my motor cruiser there and when it has arrived, we will fly over.'

##

Three months later, we arrived in Australia, flying into Cairns International Airport in the southern spring, eighteen months to the day after we had married. We made our way to the marina, and sure enough Rosco's super yacht was there. I had never seen this one before—she was called *Nymph*—but I was very pleased to see the vessel had a crew. A captain, a chef, and three deckhands, one of whom doubled as a hostess who serviced the rooms.

And more than that, as I was to discover.

The crew lined up—just like on a TV show about the rich and famous—and Rosco introduced them to me. 'This is my wife Marissa. Marissa, this crew has been on *Nymph* since I purchased her. They are loyal to me.'

Was it a hidden warning? Or was I completely paranoid?

Captain Sterling was an Englishman with silver hair and a cultured voice, but his eyes were cold. Jacques, the chef, was French and had a nice smile. Dylan, Gareth and Rosa were the three deckhands. Of course, Rosa, an Italian, was very beautiful,

PENTECOST ISLAND 1-3

and I noticed the way she fluttered her eyes at Rosco as she chattered away to him. Gareth seemed shy, and Dylan was Australian, a serious young man who shook my hand warmly.

It was wonderful to have other people around. Maybe Rosco would be more like the man I had married with others onboard.

'I'm very pleased to meet you all,' I said quietly, not sure how much I was supposed to say or interact with them, but Rosco beamed.

He was in a good mood, which boded well for my peace of mind and physical well-being.

We cruised north to the tip of Australia, and the weather was so hot, I spent most of my days in the air-conditioned saloon.

Rosco had words with me one night, but he didn't touch me. He yelled so loudly I'm sure the crew would have heard his raised voice.

'You are letting yourself go, Marissa.'

I looked at him, surprised as he pointed angrily to a chip in my fingernail polish. 'I want perfection,' he screamed.

Dylan brought me a cup of tea up from the galley the next afternoon. Rosco was in the small office off the bridge on the floor above our cabin.

'I know you enjoy your cups of tea,' he said with a smile. 'Earl Grey, okay?'

'Thank you.' I took the tray from him and smiled back when I saw the two homemade biscuits on the tray. 'You are very kind.'

He looked nervous and lowered his voice. 'Madam, I hope I am not speaking out of turn . . .'

I raised my eyebrows as he glanced at the door.

'If you ever need anything, I can help.' With those enigmatic words he left, and I wondered what he meant. I wondered if Celeste had been on this boat before me, and they all knew what Rosco was like.

But I didn't trust anyone. For all I know Rosco could have put him up to it.

##

As the weeks passed, and we cruised to the Kimberley coast and back to Cairns, I learned to trust Dylan. He never spoke to me or looked at me in Rosco's presence, but we had many long conversations when Rosco was onshore conducting business in Cairns and Darwin or locked away in the office. One thing I did notice was Rosa's absence each time Rosco went ashore, or into his office, but I really didn't care. I guess I knew now I was merely an ornament for him. Hopefully, I might be replaced by the young Italian woman. That would be an easy out.

When I went up to the deck, Dylan talked to me and told me about his life travelling around the world. One day, he told me he would be leaving Nymph at the end of this voyage. He had secured another position on a boat in the Whitsunday Islands, where he had grown up; his best friend from school was looking for a second skipper.

'Jiminy emailed me; he knew I wanted to come home. And that is home for me. I've seen enough of the world.'

'I'll miss your company and our talks,' I said, keeping an eye out for the taxi that would deliver Rosco back to the boat.

Dylan's brown eyes were intense as he looked at me. I was lying on a sun lounge on the upper deck and he was polishing the rail. Like everything else Rosco owned, the boat was expected to be gleaming and spotless at all times. Woe betide anyone who let a drop of water mar the shining surfaces.

'I find it a very difficult environment to work in. It's past time for me to leave,' he said. 'I'm going to leave *Nymph* when we return from Green Island. I know he'll be angry, but I'll give up a

PENTECOST ISLAND 1-3

month's pay to get off.'

'Lucky you,' I muttered beneath my breath, but his hearing was acute.

'Forgive me if I am speaking out of turn, but why do you stay with him, Marissa? He treats you very badly.'

I shrugged. 'I have no choice.'

'You do, you know.'

I shook my head and Dylan put down the cleaning cloth and crouched beside me. 'Get off the boat at Cairns and fly back to England.'

Tears welled in my eyes. 'If only it was so easy, Dylan. You know yourself what he's like. He can't handle not being in control. I don't have any money, and I don't even have a phone.'

'Has he ever hurt you?' he asked softly.

I held up my left hand and showed him my crooked finger. 'He regrets it now as he says I am flawed. Rosa is now the one in his sights.'

'But you're his wife!'

'Trust me, I would do anything not to be. He told me if I ever leave, he will kill me. And I know he means it. His first wife died in an "accident".' My voice shook and I looked over to the terminal at the end of the wharf. Rosa and Rosco were walking on their way to the wharf where *Nymph* was moored. I could hear his laughter and her chatter from where I was sitting.

'They're on their way back.'

Dylan picked up the cloth and moved to the far end of the top deck. As he walked away, he looked at me. 'I have an idea.'

##

Two weeks later, Rosco decided we were going to go to the outer reef.

'The snorkelling is very good at Green Island. I think you

308

will enjoy it, Marissa,' he said as Gareth served our meal. 'We are leaving tomorrow.'

'Thank you, Rosco. I will enjoy that.' The correct responses came easily now. I was a fast learner. My only regret was that after we went to Green Island, Dylan—my only friend— would also leave the boat.

When Rosco disappeared into his office and I went up to the deck the next morning, Dylan sought me out, his eyes gleaming with excitement.

'I have a plan.'

I listened as he told me what he had done.

And smiled.

Everything was going to be all right. Or as right as my life could be from this point on, if I wanted to live.

Chapter 18

Pippa: Pentecost Island

The night before I went to the mainland to pick Rafe up from Airlie Beach was the longest in all the weeks we had been on the island. I was so excited, I couldn't sleep, and when I did my dreams were full of Rafe. The usual doubts flew in, and for some reason, I thought about Darren and how gullible I'd been there.

I knew it wasn't about sex for Rafe . . . because we hadn't slept together. I'd insisted on a slow and steady build to our relationship. I'd been hurt too many times before.

What if he had changed his mind about me while he was back in his familiar territory?

Why would a famous author want to hook up with a damaged PR consultant?

I got up at dawn, made myself a coffee and talked sense to myself as I sat out on the verandah. I looked across our beautiful bay, past Philippe's old boat, and up the hill to Rafe's house.

I had to learn to trust.

The girls had taught me that, and I knew I could trust each of them. True, they all had their own issues, like I did and like Rafe did, but we all cared about and looked out for each other.

Even Eliza, now.

That was life, and we had the best life on Pentecost Island.

Rafe was flying into Proserpine and catching the bus into the marina where I would be waiting for him. I'd organised for Bunnings to deliver the cladding we needed to the marina at ten o'clock, and God love Jiminy, he had offered to bring his boat to share the load.

Eliza had been online and had ordered the fittings for the interior of the huts, and I think she was as excited about the huts as

I was about Rafe coming home.

Phillipe had been helping Evie in the gardens, and everyone was keen to make the place look good for the opening and Rafe's return. Evie had ordered supplies as well. The boats were going to be laden on the way back.

It was hard to believe we had been here for almost four months, and summer and the cyclone season were ahead of us. The friendships I had now were the backbone of my life. Even Eliza had thawed more, and I had a feeling she might stay.

The progress we had made while Rafe was away was amazing, and I knew he would notice a huge difference. Eliza was chafing at the bit, keen to get the cladding on the huts and get the interiors finished.

Nell had sorted her software and backup issue and was quietly working away in the office, but we enticed her out the night before Rafe was due home to have another get-together in the bar. I was so pleased with how it had turned out. Now, we had to get the customers.

'Can we invite Phillipe?' Evie asked with a hopeful look. She had been trying hard to get his attention, but I don't think there was any interest on his part.

I shook my head. 'Let's make it a girls' night. We'll invite him tomorrow night when Rafe is home.'

Eliza sent me a grateful look. I know she still felt uncomfortable when Philippe was around, but I had seen them have a couple of brief conversations in passing.

Tam, Nell, Evie and Eliza and I had a pleasant night in the bar. Tam cracked a bottle of bubbles and we sat watching the mast lights come on as the sun set. There seemed to be a lot of yachts in the Passage and I hoped that they would come to our bar when it was open.

We talked—even Eliza. It was one of those nights where everyone opened up, and we had a few "deep and meaningfuls".

PENTECOST ISLAND 1-3

'Of course, we won't see much of Pippa for the next few days.' Tam's grin was evil. 'There's a bit of catching up to be done there.'

Even Eliza smiled. 'Let her be. It's good to see someone happy.'

Evie leaned forward. 'What about you, Eliza? Anyone special on your horizon? Anyone at home in NZ?'

She shook her head but didn't say much. 'No. How about you, Evie?'

'I've had a couple of relationships, but both guys were ready to settle down, and I was keen to keep travelling. We parted on good terms, and I'm happy with the way things are for a while.'

'What about Phillipe?' Tam said. 'I thought you were interested.'

'He's a nice guy but a bit serious for me. Intense. He's got his eye on Eliza,' Evie said as she held up her glass. 'I've seen the way he looks at you. Very interested, I'd say.'

'He needn't waste his time,' Eliza said. 'He'll move on soon. He wanders the world.'

Nell frowned. 'How do you know where he's been? I didn't think you spoke to him much.'

Eliza flushed and waved her hand. 'I'm just assuming that by looking at his boat.'

'It's got character,' I said.

'I think Pippa's the only one destined for a happy ever after,' Tam said with a sigh as she opened the second bottle of bubbles.

I put my hand up. 'No more for me. I want a clear head tomorrow.'

'Aw, come on. You're no fun anymore.' The cork flew off with a loud pop, and Tam laughed.

'If we keep doing this, we'll drink all the profits,' I replied, shaking my head. 'Won't we, Nell? All right, one more and then

312

I'm off to bed.'

##

Rafe's flight was on time and I'd worked out almost to the minute how long it would be before the bus dropped him at Coral Sea Marina. I was waiting on the wooden benches underneath the big umbrellas near the roundabout when I saw the airport transfer bus come down the hill from the main road. I usually wore shorts and a T-shirt on the boat, but today, I'd dug out one of my floral sundresses and a straw hat.

I stood up as my heart picked up its pace, and a wonderful feeling of anticipation ran through me.

My gorgeous man was first off the bus, and my eyes drank him in as he looked over and saw me waiting. His gaze held mine, and a slow smile spread across his face.

Rafe strode across and stood in front of me, his smile growing wider as he held my gaze.

'Hello there,' I said shyly.

'Hello, back. Oh, how I've missed you, Pippa.' He lifted both hands and cupped my cheeks gently, holding my gaze. He leaned forward until his lips met mine.

I lifted my arms and linked my hands behind his back, revelling in his long kiss. Finally, we were interrupted by a call.

'Hoy, mate. Do ya want your bag or not?'

Rafe chuckled and pulled away. He turned to the bus driver and waved. 'Just leave it there, please.'

'Whoa.' I fanned myself. 'I'm glad you don't go away too often.'

We walked over together to collect his suitcase, and I held onto his hand, not wanting to let him go.

'It's so good to have you back,' I said.

'It's good to be back. I told Jenny this is the last trip back there for a long time. Now that this promo model is set up, we can do the next one over the internet.'

'The next one? I'm pleased to hear that.

He nodded. 'Jack Smith signed another three-book deal with Jenny and Bryant.'

'You're going to be too busy for me, then.'

'Never,' he said, dropping another kiss on my lips. 'But you might have to spend some nights up at my place.'

'Might I?' I said as I held his gaze.

We walked towards the wharf, and he looped his arm around my shoulder, the warmth of his body pressing against mine.

'How's everything back on the island?' he asked. 'And everyone?'

'I can't wait to show you what we've done. The bar is finished, but we delayed the opening until you came home. It looks fantastic, and we've sort of already got our first guest moored in the bay. He's a Frenchman who knew Aunty Vi.'

'I can't wait to see it all.'

As we reached the wharf, Rafe paused and looked down at me.

'Have you had time to think while I've been away,' he asked quietly.

I nodded and tried to look serious. 'I have. I do have one question for you.'

Rafe's eyebrows rose, and his brow crinkled in a frown. 'Is there something wrong?'

'Maybe.' I bit my lip. 'It all depends on you.'

'What do you want to know?'

My smile was wide as I reached up and touched his face. 'Can I have a sleepover at your place tonight?

Chapter 19

Marissa: Great Barrier Reef

The voyage out to Green Island was rough, but I was almost shaking with excitement. I had to quell the anticipation that was zinging through me. I avoided any contact with Dylan as I couldn't trust myself not to smile, and I didn't want Rosco to notice anything different about my behaviour.

As Jacques served our dinner the night before we were due to arrive at the island, Rosco was particularly pleasant to me.

'Are you looking forward to snorkelling on the reef, *Bella*?'

I looked down and nodded. 'I am. It will be good to get off the boat for a while.'

'You are sick of being on our beautiful boat,' he snapped as soon as Jacques went back to the galley. 'You are ungrateful for your good fortune.'

'I'm sorry, I meant it would be good to get in the water.'

That seemed to placate him, and he narrowed his eyes as he lifted his glass. 'Your cheeks are very flushed. You are not getting the flu, I hope.'

'No, it is just warm in here.' I said.

'Perhaps we should go to bed.' His eyes gleamed. 'It will be cooler in our cabin.'

'I would like to go and look at the stars on the deck with you.' I couldn't stand the thought of him touching me.

'Jacques, we shall have our dessert on the upper deck,' he informed the chef.

It was cool and windy on the deck and as I had hoped, Rosco was soon bored with the magnificent view of the stars, and with my company.

'I am going to work in my office for a while,' he said.

He stumbled on the way back to the stairs, and I smiled. It was a rough night, just as Dylan had said it would be. The wind whistled past the boat, and the waves slapped noisily on the side as we ploughed through the swell.

I waited until Rosco had disappeared, and my hands shook as I hurried across to my usual sun lounge. I lifted the cushion and as Dylan had promised, there was a black stinger suit and inflatable PFD beneath the cushion. I carried them to the small deck at the back of the boat, sick with nerves, watching for the light that I had been told to wait for.

It was not the sea that was worrying me, it was the thought of my husband coming up and discovering me. I quickly pulled the suit on over my clothes, willing my hands and legs to stop shaking. I kept my shoes on and made my way to the ladder at the side of the deck. I slipped the flotation device over my head, then gripping the sides that were wet and gritty with salt, I climbed down to the second lowest rung of the ladder and waited.

He must have been watching. Not far from the left side of the boat, I saw a light flashing, and then the faint sound of a motor. I took a deep breath and stepped into my next life.

Chapter 20

Eliza: Pentecost Island

Knowing that Ren—or Phillipe as he seemed to be known now— was on the island stressed me out no end. I wondered whether to stay or go, but in the end, I figured he would eventually move on. As long as he knew me as Eliza, and he didn't know it was me, or what had happened, it would be fine. Rosco could never, never find out where or who I was now. If he did, well . . . I didn't want to think about it.

I also knew in the worst possible situation that Pip, Tam, Nell and Evie would support me. I would trust those girls with my life. I know Pippa had been slow to accept me, and I could understand that because I'd screwed up my story when my kayak had rolled, and I'd ended up almost drowning in front of their island. How ironic would that have been. As I'd come to, I know I'd made up names, and that Dylan, Alex and Marissa had rolled off my tongue.

Such a stupid mistake.

But Pippa had learned to trust me, and I admired her for that. She was a great boss, and I loved working here with the girls on the island. I didn't want to go.

But I couldn't risk Phillipe knowing, or anyone finding out who I was and telling Rosco I was here. I knew he would come after me.

Eliza Pengelly had come into being on a rough and windy night near Green Island when Marissa Bertolini had fallen overboard and drowned. There were only three people in the world who knew the truth and I was one of them.

I trusted the others implicitly, especially Dylan. I owed

PENTECOST ISLAND 1-3

Dylan my life. He swore that his brother, Alex, on Green Island could be trusted too.

Jumping off the ladder into the waters of the Great Barrier Reef that night had been a shock, and my head had gone under the water briefly, before the flotation device had brought me to the surface. Within a minute, a small rubber duckie had pulled up alongside me, and two strong hands had pulled me over the side.

The noise of the wind and the sea had covered the small motor, and the darkness soon swallowed the bright lights of *Nymph* as Alex took me to safety.

I spent two weeks in total seclusion in a small two-room staff apartment on Green Island. Dylan's brother worked on the reef as a diving instructor and Dylan had organised my escape with him.

I had to stay inside until the fuss died down, but I didn't mind.

Two weeks after I had "drowned" there was a tap on the door of the apartment. Alex was out on a charter and I crossed the room hesitantly to stand at the door and listen, but I didn't speak or open the door.

'Marissa, it's okay. It's me, Dylan.' I opened the door and he held his arms open for a hug, and I fell into them.

I was shaking uncontrollably as reaction set in, and it took a good half hour and three cups of tea before I could speak calmly enough to thank him for what he had done. 'I owe you and Alex so much. How will I ever thank you?'

'By keeping safe, and not letting that bastard know you are alive.'

As we sat and drank endless cups of tea, we planned my return to the mainland.

'Have you left *Nymph* now?' I asked.

He nodded. 'Yes, it wasn't pretty. Even in his supposed grief, ten days after losing his wife, Rosco was able to call me every swear word that I've ever heard. English and Italian. Rosa and Gareth quit too. He is not happy.'

I shook my head, still unable to believe the generosity of Dylan—and his brother.

'It's over to you now, Eliza,' he said.

'Eliza?' I frowned.

'We went back to Cairns, and I was able to get you these.' He handed me a packet and I tipped it up. A black passport with a silver coat of arms on the front fell into my hand.

'Open it.'

I did as he bid, and stared at my face, but my long blonde hair had gone, replaced with dark curly hair cut short. My eyes dropped to the text below.

Eliza Pengelly, current address-Brisbane, Queensland.

'A passport! How did you do that?' I whispered. 'Where did you get it?'

'I have some very clever friends. That's all you need to know. What you need to do now, is cut your hair and dye it black.'

'I've been bleaching my hair since I was eighteen, 'I said. 'That photo is close to my natural colour.'

Dylan reached into the bag that he'd put on the floor. 'Until it grows out then . . . ta da!' He held out a packet of black hair dye.

Tears choked my throat and I put my hands over my face. 'How can I ever thank you?'

He rubbed my back gently. 'By becoming Eliza and staying safe. You realise that you can't let anyone know you are alive. Not your family or your friends? Not for a very long time anyway.'

'Could I go to the police? Tell them about Rosco?'

He shook his head. 'Do you think they would believe you? Has he broken the law? We know what he is like, but he is very clever. Did anyone ever see how he treated you?

I shook my head again. 'No.'

PENTECOST ISLAND 1-3

'Once we get you across to the mainland, I'm going to take you down to the Whitsunday Islands. There are thousands of backpackers down there, and a very casual employment system. You'll be able to find somewhere to live, and somewhere to work. Get yourself settled. We'll get you a kayak and I'll teach you how to get around. It would be wise to stay off public ferries and the like for a while.' He reached into his bag and pulled out a plastic bag. 'There's some money here to start you off. It should keep you going for a few months.'

'I will pay you back every cent,' I swore fiercely as I looked at the roll of bank notes.

'There's no need. I was very well paid on *Nymph*. Your—I mean Rosco—expected quality service, and he paid double the going rate.'

'Are you sure he believes I'm dead?' Uncertainty filled me, and I began to feel sick.

Could I do this? Take on a whole new identity and a new past? And not have any contact with my family? Could I start again?

Dylan reached into his bag and pulled out a newspaper. 'I knew you'd need reassurance. This is the *Cairns Post* from last weekend.'

My photo stared back at me, the headline announcing ***Italian Millionaire's Wife Pronounced Dead.***

Oh God. My family. My friends. Sienna.

They all thought I was dead.

But most important of all, so did Rosco Bertolini.

Chapter 21

Eliza: Pentecost Island

Pippa arrived home with a boatload of supplies, accompanied by a second boat skippered by her friend, Jiminy, and with Rafe. I said hello to them briefly, but I was more interested in the supplies on the boats.

'I'll help you get unloaded, Jiminy,' Rafe said with a yawn, but Pippa shook her head.

'No, love,' she said. 'You look tired. Go up to your place and I'll come up later.'

I felt sorry for Rafe when I saw the look on his face.

'We'll be fine. There's nothing heavy, you go up with Rafe,' I offered.

Evie came through the forest and waved to me. 'I'll give you a hand, Eliza.'

Evie was pleased because she had ordered a few dozen tubes of starter shrubs for the gardens around the huts.

Jiminy's boat was unloaded first and we soon had a pile of building materials next to the huts.

'Oh. Look at these,' Evie exclaimed as she found the box of shrubs on Pippa's launch.

I walked along the wharf on the way back from unloading the boxes of squares that would clad the huts. As I looked up Phillipe walked out of the rainforest, a knapsack on his back, and a water bottle swinging from his hand.

'How was it?' Evie called out from the wharf. 'Did you get to the summit?'

'I did,' he called back. I'll just throw these on my boat, and I'll help you.'

'We're fine, almost done,' I said without looking at him.

PENTECOST ISLAND 1-3

The less time I spent in Phillipe's company the better.

He ignored my comment and soon returned and helped Jiminy unload the last boxes of cladding. I muttered under my breath as I finished off the load on Pippa's boat and Evie looked at me curiously. 'Calm down, girl. He's only trying to help.'

'I know.'

'And he's a nice guy.'

'I know that too,' I muttered again.

'So, what's your problem?' she persisted.

'I don't have one.'

Evie stood there with her hands on her hips. 'Sure looks like it to me. And Pippa won't be happy with you being rude to the guests.'

'I wasn't being rude,' I said in a low voice. 'And Pippa won't want the guests working on the island. What if he hurt himself? He wouldn't be covered by insurance.'

When we were done, Phillipe disappeared and Jiminy motored out of the bay and headed back to Hamo.

I grinned as he waved. I was feeling accepted and even starting to think like a local.

##

The next day I started work lining the exterior of the huts. It was a simple job as the cladding came in squares that I could manage. It only took me an hour to get the first hut finished. I slowly stepped backwards towards the rainforest keeping my eye on the angles and the joins to check it was all square. I nodded with satisfaction as I took the last step back and let out my breath as I walked backwards into someone.

'Oh, sorry,' I said turning around and held my breath as I looked up into an intense dark gaze. Of course, it had to be Ren.

Phillipe, I corrected myself silently.

He stared at me for a long moment, his gaze raking my face. He reached up and smoothed his finger along my eyebrow. 'Do you know you have the most unusual eyebrows?' he said softly.

'What?' I said.

'I noticed them the very first time I saw you when you came up on the deck wearing that colourful sarong.'

I took a step back as dread pooled in my stomach. 'I don't know what you're talking about.'

'I was horrified to see that Rosco had a new wife, and it didn't take me long to figure out that you knew nothing about Celeste.'

I tried to speak but the words wouldn't come as my throat closed.

'I didn't know what to do or say. I knew what Rosco could be like, but he seemed to be treating you well.' His voice surrounded me, and I felt faint.

I backed away further and my ankle twisted on a log as Ren followed me into the dimness of the rainforest. The only sound was my laboured breathing and the swish of leaves as the gentle morning breeze blew in from the bay.

'No,' I finally managed to say.

'I made sure I knew where you were sailing, and I followed you as much as I could without Rosco getting suspicious. I couldn't tell you that I knew what he could be like, in case he was different with you.' He reached for my left hand and held it up. 'But when I saw your broken finger, I knew.'

I choked on a sob. 'Please, please don't tell him where I am.' My hands were shaking, and silver lights began to prick at my vision. Just when I thought I was safe, he had to come to our island. My knees were trembling so much that I slid down onto the bed of dead leaves that littered the floor of the forest.

PENTECOST ISLAND 1-3

'Marissa . . . Eliza.' Ren crouched down beside me. 'It's all right now. Everything is going to be all right.'

I put my hands to my face as his arm went around my shoulders. As much as I was scared of what was going to happen, his touch calmed me.

'You don't know what has happened? How long have you been on this island? How did you get here?' His questions tumbled one after the other as I moved my hands and turned my face into his neck. His skin was smooth and smelled of the sea. 'When I thought you had drowned, I was sick with guilt. I blamed myself. If I had interfered and stopped Rosco—'

I lifted my head and looked at him. Calm and gentle eyes held mine. 'You won't tell him, will you?' I whispered.

'I can't tell him, *mon ange.*'

'Thank you.'

'*Non.*' He shook his head. 'I cannot tell him because Rosco is dead.'

I widened my eyes and my breath caught. 'What? How can he be dead?'

'You do not read the news here?'

'No. Are you sure?' I lifted my hands and tugged at the front of his shirt. 'Or are you tricking me? Did he send you after me?' My voice was shrill, and I started to cry in great choking sobs.

'Marissa—'

'Eliza?' Pippa and Rafe were hurrying along the path towards us. 'Are you all right? What's happened.' Pippa's voice was full of concern.

Ren stood and put his hand up. 'She is fine. Can you both wait with us while I tell her one thing, please?' He took my hands, helped me to my feet, and kept hold of me.

'Rosco's boat was hit by a container ship as it headed north of Cairns about three weeks ago. There were only two on board,

Rosco and the skipper. For some reason they did not show up on radar. The boat was destroyed.'

'Are you sure? It's not a trick?' My voice was hoarse from crying.

'No, Marissa. Both bodies were recovered.'

The last thing I saw before I fainted into Ren's arms was Pippa stepping towards me.

Chapter 22

Marissa: Pentecost Island

Ren was flying back to England with me. He had called my parents and spoken to them first, so the call from me wouldn't be too much of a shock. Hearing my dad cry on the phone, saying, 'Oh, chicken,' over and over again, brought me to tears. Even Mum had a bit of a weep. I'd been crying a lot these past few days too.

I'll never forget the call I made to Sienna that night. I cried and she screamed and sobbed over the phone.

'I'm coming home for a while in a couple of weeks,' I said. 'We'll come to see you.'

'We?'

'I have a friend who is coming with me.'

Dylan was on Hamilton Island. I called him, and he came over the next morning. Knowing that Nymph had been destroyed and Captain Sterling and Rosco hadn't survived, I shook him up. He put his arms around me and rested his forehead against mine.

'I thought I'd taught you better kayaking skills than that. You were supposed to paddle into the beach and say you'd heard that there might be some work going here. Not try and drown yourself around the point, girl!' He looked over at Pippa. 'I remember you from high school, and Jiminy is singing your praises about what you're doing over here.'

Pippa, Rafe, and the girls wanted me to go home straight away to see my family, but they already knew I was alive and safe, and I insisted on finishing the four huts, both exteriors and interiors, and then staying for the bar's opening. Ren did not leave my side for the whole two weeks as I worked. He was an excellent labourer.

The night that the bar opened the bay was full of boats. Ren had been out and put channel markers along each side of the channel and fifteen boats were tied to palm trees along the sand.

Pippa looked gorgeous as she greeted each of the guests. She was dressed in a pretty pink dress and Tam and Nell had burst out laughing when she walked into the bar before everyone arrived.

I frowned. 'What's wrong?'

Ren was beside me and looked at Pippa. 'You look very lovely. I cannot see why it is funny.'

Tam held her sides. 'Oh, Pip. You are completely in control now, aren't you? Pretty in pink of all colours!'

Rafe was beside her and Nell gave an unusual cheeky grin. 'All we want to know is if you have a pink G string too.'

Rafe and Evie looked confused, but Pippa, Nell, and Tam were almost in hysterics.

'We'll tell you the pink story after a few drinks,' Pippa said wiping the tears of laughter from her eyes. 'Now look, my mascara's run.' She took a breath and looked around at us all. 'Before everyone comes up from the boats, I want to say a few words.'

She took a deep breath. 'I want you to know how much I love you all.' She nodded at Ren too. 'Yes, Phillipe, Ren or whoever you are, you too. You've also been a fabulous help getting these huts ready these last few weeks.' She gripped Rafe's hand. 'Rafe, I want you to know how much I love you. You, my darling, are the love of my life.'

Rafe held her close and as they kissed, I wasn't ashamed to say that I blinked away tears.

Love could be real, and I had to learn to trust again. Ren was slowly helping me do that.

Pippa held her hands out, and Rafe and Ren stood back as she got Tam, Nell, Evie, and me to form a circle with her.

'You girls are the best friends a girl could ask for. You support me, you've helped me through the good and bad times, but most of all you have all worked your butts off to get Ma Carmichael's ready to open. I just want to thank you all before the party starts.' Pip turned to me. 'Eliza, one of the best things about the last few days was hearing that you and Phillipe are going to come back to the island after you go home. There will be a place here for both of you for as long as you want.'

We stepped out of Pippa's circle, and soon, the popping of champagne corks was the only sound. Ren touched my shoulder lightly and smiled down at me as he passed me a glass. A moment later, he held his glass to mine.

'To new beginnings, Eliza?'

I smiled at this gentle man. 'To new beginnings, Phillipe.'

When his lips brushed mine, I knew I was healing.

Epilogue

Nell: Hydeaway Bay-50 kilometres north of Airlie Beach

The forecast had been for a late storm, and for once, the weather bureau had been spot on. Nell O'Leary leaned forward, her attention focused on the road ahead as the clouds grew darker and the wind whipped the low-hanging branches of the trees into a frenzy. She clutched the steering wheel harder as the dirt road petered to a track.

Surely this couldn't be the right road?

The address for *ND IT Services* had read 655 Dingo Beach Road, Hydeaway Bay, and the signpost about five kilometres back had confirmed that she had taken the correct turn when she'd pulled over and checked her phone.

She was on the right road—although it was more a track—and she was determined to find the blasted place.

Frustration vied with anger, and she considered turning around, but the track was so narrow it would take about a ten-point turn to go back the way she'd come.

Besides she *had* to see this guy. She'd had no luck in Proserpine at the computer store and the technician there had sent her fifty kilometres north to Hydeaway Bay, where he had assured her there was a networking guru who would go out to Pentecost Island and solve her problem. But it was heading for five o'clock and she was worried the company would be closed when she got there. She'd tried to call, but the phone had gone to voicemail. She'd left a message, with her name and a quick outline of the problem, so at least they knew she was on her way.

Finally, a gate appeared ahead, and in the fading light, she could just read the number 655.

'Thank God,' she muttered under her breath. This was her

last chance; if this guy couldn't help her, the opening of the resort was at risk. It was too late to get someone to fly up from the city and look at the problem; their opening was less than a week away, and she just couldn't let Pippa down.

The gate was closed, and Nell pulled over to the side of the road. The track was so narrow, another car couldn't get past her anyway. She grabbed her laptop and climbed out of the car.

With a frown, she looked ahead as she swung the gate open, again doubting that she had the right place.

'I've come this far, I might as well keep going,' she muttered.

Sure enough, a timber sign on the small dwelling ahead read *ND IT Services*, and Nell puffed out a sigh of relief. It wasn't an office, but a private house. A light was shining in the front window and she set off looking nervously at the long grass that was brushing her legs below where her shorts ended.

Please, no snakes.

A flash of lightning followed immediately by a huge crack of thunder that shook the ground, had her running fast through the long grass towards the two steps at the front of the house.

Nell stepped up onto the verandah and raised her hand to knock, but the door swung open before her knuckles reached the timber.

With a gasp, she took a hurried step back, but a hand shot out to grab her arm before she could fall backwards down the steps.

'Careful, sweetheart. I don't have any public liability insurance.'

Her heart thumped hard and she stared into the eyes of the man who had once made a fool of her. It might have been a long time ago, but she had never forgotten or forgiven him.

'Nat Dwyer, what the bloody hell are you doing here?'

'I could ask you the same thing, Nellie.'

Nell

Pentecost Island 3

PENTECOST ISLAND 1-3

Chapter 1

University of Queensland, Brisbane...2010

Nell O'Leary was bored stiff.

And cranky.

She stretched out her legs, pointed her toes, and then rolled her ankles. Fiddled with her bracelet, flexed her fingers and tapped her pen on the desktop in front of her seat. Leaned back, rolled her shoulders and tried not to yawn. Looked down and admired the pretty ballet flats she'd chosen to match her dress. Hummed a song in her head and then blushed when Nat Dwyer, the student she always sat with, nudged her.

Oops, maybe it hadn't been in her head.

There was a lot of pen tapping, doodling, and staring into space by most of the students around them as Professor McMinn went on about macro and microeconomics.

The monotonous voice of the most boring lecturer in the university, Professor McMinn, droned through the speakers. It was an additional lecture that had been added to their timetable just for this week. The same night, Cat Empire, her favourite band, was playing at the university bar. Tonight's lecture was scheduled to go until nine o'clock, and knowing old, dry and dusty McMinn, it was sure to go over time. Tam and Pippa had promised to save her a seat in the bar, but she'd be lucky to find them in the crowd she knew would be there. They'd be dancing now, and where was she? Trapped in boredom city.

The lecture was compulsory—with nonattendance threatened as due cause to fail the course—and each student had to sign in when they entered the massive lecture hall.do Nell looked around and smiled before she leaned over to nudge Nat.

'Easy to see why we had to sign in. I don't think anyone would have come tonight if it hadn't been compulsory,' she whispered.

'Yeah, he's a crafty old bastard.' Nat leaned over as he replied quietly. 'Not to mention as bloody boring as bat shit.'

Nell stifled a giggle. Nat was always able to make her laugh. They'd met up at the beginning of first year and were good mates. 'And we're only halfway through.'

'Have you decided on your major for next year?' he asked, keeping his voice low. His minty breath brushed her cheek, and she gestured to the pack of mints on the desk and smiled as he handed the packet over.

'I'm changing courses,' he said as she popped a mint into her mouth.

Nell nodded and whispered back. 'Yep, me too. I'm going to switch to accountancy. This economic stuff bores me to tears. What about you?'

'I'm moving across to a computer degree. It's what I want to do. My old man told me economics was a better choice. He was way wrong.'

'Better choice for you, that's for sure. You've saved me a few times over the past two years.'

'That's only because you don't back up your work, and then you can't find where you save your files.' Nat's chuckle was low. 'You have to get better organised, Nellie girl.'

Even though they were in the second back row, Professor McMinn had eagle eyes and was glaring at them as he spoke.

'Ssh. We've been spotted.' Nat elbowed her and stopped talking.

They both sat up straight and pretended to be focused on the ins and outs of microeconomics.

One very long hour later, the professor nodded and turned off the microphone.

'Thank God for that,' Nell said as she stretched her arms above her head and rolled her neck before she stood.

'That's two hours of our lives we'll never get back,' Nat gathered up his books and pens and mints and then stood beside her. She looked up at him as he towered over her; he was a great-looking guy. His blond curls—always tangled—were well past his collar now, and his brown eyes were fringed by thick dark lashes.

'Coming to the Student Union to hear the band?' she asked. Nell was happy with the relationship she had with Nat. They had different friends but occasionally ended up at the same parties. He was smart and funny, and she knew she could trust him, but no matter how gorgeous he was, she'd never considered going out with him.

Not that he'd asked her.

Maybe because he had such a reputation as a lady-killer. As much as Nell liked to dress up and party, he was out of her league.

"Love 'em and leave 'em" was Nat's attitude. Or so it seemed to Nell.

Friends were good, and friends they'd stay.

She stared at him and wondered idly if he'd ever thought about asking her out. His gaze stayed on hers, and for the first time ever, her tummy gave a funny little flip, and her fingers tingled.

'What's wrong?' he asked with a frown.

She shook her head quickly. 'Nothing. I was waiting to hear if you were coming to hear the band.'

'Nope.' His white teeth flashed in his tanned face. 'I've got a hot date.'

'You've always got a hot date. Selina?' Nell asked. At least, she thought that was the name of his most recent lady.

'Nope,' he said as they walked out. 'A hot date with a fileserver over in the medical faculty. My mate's the computer tech over there and they can't get it to back up to tape every night.'

'Boring.' Nell rolled her eyes. 'Why don't you come over

to the bar when you're done?'

His eyes held hers for a little longer than they usually did. 'You know what, Nellie. I might just take you up on that.'

'See you there, maybe.'

'Yeah, baby, yeah,' he responded in his best Austen Powers voice.

'Oh, behave,' she came back at him with a cheeky grin.

Nat winked and took off towards the door.

Chapter 2

Pippa: 2020

'Don't stress, Nell. We'll get it sorted.' I gently placed my hands on Nell's shoulders as she sat in front of the computer in the space at the front of the house we'd turned into an office and reception area. Her shoulders were rigid, and I could feel the tension radiating through her body. 'It's not that important in the scheme of things.'

Tam and Evie had gone to bed, and I'd been heading over to Rafe's when I'd come across Nell in the office, her shoulders shaking and her face in her hands. Eliza and Phillipe flew out of Hamo airport today and headed for the UK. I'd left it later than I usually did to go across to Rafe because he'd been waiting for a video call from Jenny and Bryant, his publishers.

'It is important!' Her tone was full of worry, and I frowned as if it was out of character. Nell was usually cool and calm—the one who always told *us* to chill, and it upset me to see her stressed.

'This is going to impact on the whole business. Everyone has worked so hard. Ma Carmichael's resort is *your* baby, and your leadership has been so motivating, not to mention the great advertising campaign you've created. Tam's got the kitchen running like clockwork, and the new menus look fantastic. Evie has the gardens looking a picture, and Eliza worked her butt off to get the huts finished before they left, and I've let you—'

'Nell.' I crouched down in front of her and tried to make light of the situation. 'And you've just been sitting at your computer playing computer games while we've all worked hard, have you? Give yourself a break, chickie. You might be in the office, but I reckon you've put in more hours than the rest of us.

PENTECOST ISLAND 1-3

I've seen the light on in here in the middle of the night when I've come out for a drink. You're not kidding anyone.'

'Only when I can't sleep,' she mumbled.

'Now let's look at this logically. Tell me exactly what the problem is, and we'll come up with a solution.' I stood and crossed to the chair beside hers and sat down. 'Two heads are better than one.'

Finally, a glimmer of a smile. 'Thanks, love, but it's not that easy. I've talked to a few of my contacts down in the city and some online forums and I'm sure it's a networking problem. I'm an accountant, and I can sort out all the software stuff, but my skills don't stretch to networking.'

'You can't get anyone to log in remotely for you?'

'No, it's a physical issue, I think.' Nell shook her head. 'But the bottom line is, I've lost all the bookings we had for the first month, and all of the accounting stuff has disappeared. *And* Tam's food orders to the mainland supplier.'

'But you've backed it up, you said?'

'I did,' she said glumly. 'But I can't find that either. I think you're going to have to find someone who knows what they're doing a bit more than I do.'

I reached across and took her hands in mine. Despite the warm night, Nell's hands were icy. At school, she'd been the chubby one of us, but she'd lost weight when we were at uni and never put it back on. I think she thought the shorts and loose tees she wore hid how thin she was, but she hadn't fooled Tam and me.

'Don't you ever dare think that? I wouldn't care if we had a scrap of paper to write the bookings on, and an old-fashioned ledger book for the accounts. We're all in this together, girl.'

Nell chuckled and her eyes brightened a bit. 'Well, *I'd* care.'

'Let's make a plan then. We've got four weeks until our first guests are in the huts and a week before the bar officially opens for business full-time.'

We'd had a few casual afternoons in the bar when boats had moored off the island, and their crew had come into the beach in their tenders. The word about the bar—that Rafe had christened Gilligan's—was spreading. It had been good for Tam too, the informal start; her bar food had gone down very well. We'd decided to have an unofficial opening for those regulars who were starting to call in every few days

Eliza had been pleased they were still here for the opening before they left. Our casual sailors had all come back and the bay was full of boats. Phillipe had put channel markers along each side of the channel and fifteen boats had been tied to palm trees along the sand. Business was so good we'd all taken turns to help Tam behind the bar.

'Gotta get more help, Pippa,' she'd said as she flopped into a chair at the end of the night. 'I can't keep this up.'

Eliza and Philippe could have stayed another two weeks for the main opening, but understandably she was super keen to get back to see her family. Plus, she had a lot of financial sorting out ahead of her with her deceased husband's estate apparently in chaos.

'I need a favour, Pip.' Nell leaned back on her chair and rubbed her eyes when I went into the office later that night. 'One of my contacts in Brisbane told me that the computer store in Proserpine has a networking guru on staff. I'll get you to take me across to Hamo tomorrow and then I'll catch the ferry across to the mainland and hire a car. I need to talk to someone face to face, not online or over the phone.'

'Okay, on one condition,' I said.

'What?'

'As long as the cost of the ferry and the hire car and any other costs come out of the business. You might have to stay overnight if you miss the last ferry back.'

PENTECOST ISLAND 1-3

She looked at me over the top of her glasses, and then nodded reluctantly. 'All right. But I have a condition too.'

'Hmm?' I raised my eyebrows at her.

'If we lose any bookings or any money because of my stuff up, I'll put some of my savings into the business, and I won't take any pay until it's all sorted out.'

'No.'

She leaned back and folded her arms. 'Then I guess we're at a stalemate.'

'No.'

She stared at me and didn't look happy.

'Nell? It's not your stuff up. You've worked so hard, putting yourself in here night after night. You don't have fun like the rest of us. Yeah, we all work hard, but you've got to learn to chill a bit.'

'Are you saying that's why I'm making mistakes?' Her chin lifted.

'No, that's not what I meant at all. When Aunty Vi left me the island I came up with the idea of the resort and you and Tam came on board, and yes my vison was to make a living, and make profit, but also to have a great lifestyle here. Can you remember what you said in the bar at Surfers when I asked you what your dream job was?'

'If I could do any job we wanted, anywhere in the world, what would I choose?'

'That's the one.' I watched her expression close down even more and my worry increased. Tam, and Evie, and now Eliza, had taken to island life like I had imagined. And wanted them to. And as for me, I'd never been happier, but Rafe had a lot to do with that. But Nell? She always seemed so serious and unhappy. She was even quieter since we moved to the island at the end of autumn and lately she seemed to be spending less time with us when we went for a chat on the beach at sunset.

She worked too hard, long hours, and it was almost impossible to coax her out to the beach or the bar at night.

It was hard to reconcile this Nell with the girl Tam and I had gone to school with. When I thought about it, back in those days and in our early uni days, Nell had been the loud one, and the party animal at uni. She'd worn the shortest figure-hugging dresses and she'd always looked vital and attractive. She'd been the first to suggest a party, or going to the bar to see a band, or just hanging out with friends. As she'd got further into her studies, Nell had taken it so seriously her social life and her outgoing personality had been consumed by study and work.

'And what did you tell me your dream job was?'

'I said'—she tapped an ink-stained finger on her lip— 'somewhere warm. No winter, lots of blue skies, and near the ocean. And being in charge of a business. I think that's what I said.'

'That's it. And that's what you're doing. What we're all doing. Nell? Can I ask you something and get an honest answer?'

Her eyes were wary, but I got a nod.

'Are you happy here? Is it too quiet? Or claustrophobic being on the island? Or is the responsibility too much for you?' I hated asking that because I had no doubt in Nell's ability.

Her face reddened, and I noticed that she wasn't wearing her usual lipstick. Tam and I had often wondered when Nell had changed her style of dress and stopped wearing makeup, why she had only kept the red lipstick.

'No, Pip.' Her voice was fierce. 'I love living on Pentecost Island, and I love what I'm doing. I couldn't imagine going back to live in the city. We have a perfect life here.'

'So why are you unhappy?'

Her brows lifted in surprise 'I'm not unhappy. What makes you think that?'

I stared at her for a while. 'You don't seem to enjoy the

sorts of things we do to chill. Or enjoy being with us all. Is it because it's not just the three of us now? Is it because we have Rafe, and Evie and Eliza and Phillipe? You seem to prefer being in here by yourself.'

Nell took a deep breath. 'I do prefer to be by myself. That's just me.'

I was shocked when her eyes filled with tears. I opened my arms and I was pleased when she accepted my hug.

Her voice shook. 'I love this job with you and Tam, and the others. I know it's a dream come true for you, Pip, but it is for me too. I can do what I love and not have to deal with people all day long. Setting up the network and the systems let me be in my own company. So of course, I want to stay.'

She wriggled away from me and I stepped back holding Nell's gaze steadily. 'I don't know what happened to make you feel that way, but I know something happened at uni. You changed almost overnight.'

'I learned to be responsible.' She kept her eyes on mine but there was a tinge of bitterness in her voice. 'It's just me. Like it or leave it.' I was surprised at her sass as Nell was usually quiet.

'Okay,'—I held up a finger and wagged it at her—'enough of this "more than you can handle" crap. Do what it takes to get it sorted, and you're not paying for one cent of it, or going without your pay, girlfriend. You got that?'

'All right.' Nell lifted a shaky hand and wiped the back of her hand over her eyes. 'You're the boss.'

'Only when I need to be. The rest of the time, we're equals in Ma Carmichael's.'

We walked out of the office and Nell looked up at the big clock in the hall. 'You're late going to Rafe's place. You'd better get going or he'll be over here looking for you.'

'He will.' I put my hand on Nell's shoulder and was surprised when she tensed. 'Now you get to bed and forget about numbers and computers for one night. I'll meet you down at the jetty at seven, and we'll go to Hamo so you can get the first ferry across to the mainland.'

I was thoughtful as I made my way up the hill to Rafe's house. I was going to have a chat to Tam. We needed to get to the bottom of what was wrong with Nell.

For her sake and the sake of our venture.

Chapter 3

Nell: Hydeaway Bay-50 kilometres north of Airlie Beach

The sun shone from a cloudless sky as Nell boarded the ferry the next morning. The passage was calm, and the mid-morning service was almost empty. The trip across to Port of Airlie was fast and Nell picked up a hire car in town and was on her way towards the computer store in Proserpine by lunchtime.

'Sorry, love. We only sell computers and fix minor issues here.'

'I called yesterday. I was told you had a networking specialist here.' Nell looked around the store as if to conjure up a technician.

'Well you weren't talking to me. Probably that useless bloody apprentice I've got.' He shook his head. 'Do you know how hard it is to get a kid who wants to work and learn these days? I thought I'd hit the jackpot with the new bloke, but he changed his mind. Said it was too far from the islands, moved further north, Bloody hell, it's only half an hour.' He settled back, ready for a chat—and a whinge by the look of things. 'More competition for me.'

Nell tried not to snap back; the day started off well and was fast going downhill. 'Can you tell me where to find him please.

'Up to Hydeaway Bay. Do you know where that is?'

'No.'

'Go up the highway a bit and take the Gregory River turn off and head for Dingo Beach. It's about fifty ks north.'

'Do you have an address please?'

He scrawled on a scrap of paper and handed it over.

'Thank you.'

Before she left the small town, Nell decided to do the shopping there that Pippa and Tam had requested. There was a good kitchen store there, and by the time she had found all of the obscure things on Tam's list and picked up some art supplies for Pippa's advertising, her stomach was growling with hunger. She sat in a small bakery, and had some lunch, enjoying being away from her computer and desk for the first time in many days.

An hour later, she regretted taking the break. Five different lots of road work on the short stretch of highway, and then a wide load moving a huge piece of mining machinery up the highway added almost two hours to her trip.

By the time Nell approached Hydeaway Bay the sky had clouded over and the weather was closing in. Pippa had been right; she was going to have to find somewhere to stay after she talked to the networking guy. She sent a quick text, so Pippa knew there was no need to take the boat back to Hamo to pick her up this afternoon.

The forecast had been for a late storm, and for once, the weather bureau had been spot on. Nell leaned forward, her attention focused on the road ahead as the clouds grew darker and the wind whipped the low-hanging branches of the trees into a frenzy. She clutched the steering wheel of the unfamiliar car tightly as the dirt road petered to a track. She hated storms and wind, especially at night. Some nights when they had first arrived on the island, Tam and Pippa had sat out on the veranda watching the wild weather come in across the passage.

Nell had hated storms since her days at Queensland University. She shook her head and swallowed.

Don't go there.

She peered through the windscreen as she set the wipers to the fastest speed. The rain was getting heavier, and it was hard to see where she was going.

Surely this couldn't be the right road?

The address the guy had scrawled said *ND IT Services* 655 Dingo Beach Road, Hydeaway Bay, and when she'd pulled over and checked her phone, the signpost about five kilometres back had confirmed that she had taken the correct turn. The sat-nav system had her going in the right direction. It was the right road—although it was more a track—and Nell was determined to find the blasted place.

Frustration vied with anger, and she considered turning around, but the track was so narrow it would take a ten-point turn to go back the way she'd come.

Besides she *had* to see this guy.

As she'd left the computer store owner had assured her that he was very good and would go out to Pentecost Island to solve her problem. In fact, he told her that the guy was so good, several businesses on Hamilton used his services, so he should be able to come out to Pentecost Island without a problem. Maybe she should have gone back to the island, and just called him.

Nell shook her head as she peered ahead. This had to be sorted quickly, and she could convey that urgency much better with a personal visit than by phone or email.

But it was heading for five o'clock and now she was worried the store would be closed when she got there. She'd tried to call, but the phone had gone to voicemail. She'd left a message and a quick outline of the problem, so at least they knew she was on her way.

Finally, a gate appeared ahead, and in the fading light, she could just read the number 655.

'Thank God,' she muttered under her breath. This was her last chance; if this guy couldn't help her, the opening of the resort was at risk. It was too late to get someone to fly up from the city and look at the problem; the bar opening was less than a week away, and she just couldn't let Pippa down.

She *wouldn't* let Pippa and the team down.

The gate was closed, and Nell pulled over to the side of the road. The track was so narrow that another car couldn't get past her anyway. She climbed out of the car. She put her hand over her eyes to stop the rain from blurring her vision.

With another frown, she looked ahead as she hurried across and pushed the gate open, again doubting that she had the right place.

'I've come this far; I might as well keep going,' she muttered, closing the gate behind her.

Sure enough, a timber sign on the small dwelling ahead read *ND IT Services*, and Nell puffed out a sigh of relief.

Finally.

But then she frowned. Despite the sign, this wasn't a store or an office, but a private house, and there were no other houses within sight.

Nell swallowed and wondered if she was game to continue. The wind whistled and the tree branches creaked against each other as it picked up more speed.

I have to. I will not let the girls down.

A light was shining in the front window and she set off across the front yard looking nervously at the long grass that brushed against the bare skin below where her shorts ended.

Please, no snakes.

A flash of lightning was followed immediately by a huge crack of thunder that shook the ground. She took off from the gate and ran through the long grass and up the two steps at the front of the house.

Nell came to a stop on the veranda and raised her hand to knock, but the door swung open before her knuckles could connect with the timber.

With a gasp of disbelief and dismay, she took a hurried step back. She teetered on the edge of the veranda, but a hand shot out to grab her arm before she could fall backwards down the steps.

The last time Nell had felt this bone-chilling fear she'd been nineteen and halfway through her accountancy degree.

'Careful, sweetheart. I don't have any public liability insurance.'

Her heart thumped hard and her mouth dried as she stared into the eyes of the man she had once been close to. It might have been a long time ago, but she had never forgotten—or forgiven him.

Her voice was low and angry. 'What the bloody hell are you doing here?'

He narrowed his eyes and looked at her, and she knew the moment that recognition dawned.

'I could ask you the same thing, Nellie.' His voice was as deep and smooth as ever and Nell shook his hand from her arm as her skin crawled beneath his touch.

Chapter 4

Nell

'It's been a long time,' Nathaniel Dwyer said.

'I'm leaving.' Nell turned around to the stairs, but as she took the first step a bolt of lightning hit a large tree on the other side of the gate, followed by a deafening roar. Goose bumps rose as static ran up her arms, and the smell of something burning surrounded them as she stared at the tree, now cleaved right down the middle. Half of it had landed across the gate that she had walked through only minutes ago. It had missed the hire car by centimetres.

'Don't be silly.' Nat opened the door and gestured for her to go inside. 'I don't think you're going anywhere for a while.'

She stood there and stared at him before turning and looking at the sky. Dark, angry clouds pierced every few seconds by lightning forced her to make the decision she didn't want to, but she had no choice.

Reluctantly Nell looked at the open door and took a step inside.

'Wise choice.' He closed the door behind her and gestured for her to follow him. 'Come down to the kitchen.'

Nell took a deep breath as she followed Nat into the house. She squeezed her hands into fists and her nails cut into the skin of both palms.

He led her down a narrow hall towards the back of the house. On each side the doors were closed, and as they walked past, a loud humming noise was evident despite the rain that hammered on the tin roof. Finally, the hall opened out into a large kitchen and there was room to keep her distance.

PENTECOST ISLAND 1-3

A large old-fashioned kitchen.

The old wooden cupboards reminded her of the kitchen in her grandparents' house at Sandgate. When she was a child, they had visited there every Saturday, and her Nana had made pink lamingtons, especially for Nell.

Those visits had been a treat. She would sit at the end of the old Laminex table eating cake and drinking lemonade while Dad played cards with her Nana and Poppa. In the background was the constant noise of the Saturday horseraces on the transistor radio punctuated by Dad's and Poppa's call of 'Mugs Away' every few minutes. They had kept the visit routine going after Mum had gone.

When Nell had finished her drink and cake, she had been allowed to go underneath the old Queenslander by herself and watch the chickens hatch in the specially heated incubator under the house. Poppa had had chickens for as long as she could remember and—

'Nellie?'

She blinked and lifted her gaze from the table that had brought those memories to the surface. Nat stood there scratching his head, with a quizzical expression on his face.

'It's Nell,' she said crossing her arms.

Nat looked at her, his brow wrinkled. 'How did you know I was here at Hydeaway Bay?' he asked. 'And more to the point what are you doing here?'

Nell took a step back and put her hands behind her back, clutching at the kitchen bench behind her. If she held it tight, she could control her shaking hands.

If she'd known that she would be in a house by herself with him—with any man, but even worse with Nat Dwyer—she would not have opened the gate. By now, she would have been roaring back down the road towards the ferry, the island and her safe haven. What had she been thinking to set off on this journey?

You were thinking of Pip, and the resort, a stern voice told her.

'I didn't know it was you.' Nell was quite proud of how firm she managed to keep her voice. 'I guess you must be the local networking expert I have heard about.'

'Was that you who left the message on the phone earlier?' he said slowly. 'From some new resort over on the islands?' As he gestured to a chair, he pulled out another one and sat down. 'Please. Sit down.'

She nodded but remained standing. 'Yes, that was me.'

'So how can I help you? I thought you were working down at the Gold Coast.'

He'd kept tabs on her. Nell tried to speak but her mouth opened, and nothing came out. Her heart thudded and her mouth was as dry as a bone. She jumped when Nat stood suddenly and pushed his chair back and crossed the kitchen towards her. He walked past her, and she tried not to cringe as he reached into a cupboard and took out a glass before filling it with water at the sink. He handed it to her and held her gaze steadily, but his voice was gentle.

'Are you scared of storms, Nell?'

She nodded and he gestured to the chair again. Let him think that, it was better than him knowing that she was terrified of being in the house with him.

'Sit down, and you can tell me why you need my services.'

Keeping one eye on the door, she pulled the chair out and slid into it.

'Are you hot? Would you like me to open the door?' His voice was quiet.

Nell watched as Nat flicked the lock over and opened the back door, pushing a chair against it so the wind didn't slam it shut. She let herself really look at him now that they were inside. Nat had lost weight over the years. When they'd been at uni, she'd teased him about the amount of time he'd spent working out. Those years of happy teasing were a long time ago. He'd conned her for a long time, and eventually shown what he was really like. The long tangled blond curls were gone, along with the board shorts and surfie look. She'd grown up fast, and it looked like Nat had grown up too.

Through the screen of trees in his back yard she could see the dark sea surging onto a beach that was at the back of his house. The wind was roaring outside, but the noise of the waves crashing on the beach soothed her.

Because she knew she could get out that door if she needed to.

Nat walked around and sat in the chair opposite. 'Last time I saw you, I think you were working in the accountant's office where we set up a new fileserver. Broadbeach, wasn't it?' His tone was conversational and had lost the aggression that it had held when she had been at the front door. 'I guess you must be working up here now if you are looking for networking help. Are you still in the accounting game?

'I am, and yes I do need help.'

Thank God the words came out this time.

Even though they sounded breathless.

'I'll give you a brief rundown of what we need and then I'll be on my way.'

Nat shook his head and she tensed. 'You won't be going anywhere for at least a few hours. Probably not until the morning. This storm is going to get worse before it gets better. I've been up here a couple of years, and I've seen some doozies.' He looked up at the ceiling, and she followed where he was looking. There was a big circular water stain on the ceiling above the fan.

'I was here when Cyclone Debbie hit, but this old house is solid, and there was no major damage.' Nat chuckled, and it was like being back in the lecture theatre beside him. 'The only damage was to my mental health. I thought I was going to be stuck in this house, listening to the wind for the rest of my life. Were you up here for the cyclone? Is that why you're scared of the storm?'

She shook her head and managed to speak again. 'No. We've only been up here for a few months.'

'We?' he said with raised eyebrows. 'Husband? Kids?'

'No. Pippa and Tam and me, and some others.'

'Wow, it must be ten years since I've seen them.' Nat's eyes widened. 'Not since we were at uni. What are you all doing up here? Working?'

'Pippa has a resort on an island and I'm looking after the office. Front and back end. We have a networking problem that needs immediate attention, or we are in trouble. You were recommended.' She took a breath and relaxed a little more.

'And the last person you'd want to help you would be me, wouldn't it? Looks like you're stuck between a rock and a hard place, Nellie, because I'm the only one who can help between Mackay and Townsville.'

The Nathaniel Dwyer of old was back.

There was no way she was going to spend the night in this house with him.

Chapter 5

Nat

Nat found it hard to stop looking at Nell. She was different to when they'd been at uni together. She'd lost a lot of weight, and by the look of things, she'd changed in more ways than that.

When they'd been mates in first and second year, she'd been full of life and sass. She'd met life head-on, and she'd had the best sense of humour; it was hard to believe that this fragile-looking woman was the same Nell he'd known.

After Nat changed degrees and took up computing science, he hadn't seen her around campus much, and he'd only seen her once since uni, and he'd regretted that meeting for a long time.

The night they'd had that boring lecture with McMinn—it had been so boring he could still recall it almost ten years later—Nat had looked into her eyes and felt an absolute jolt go through him. They'd shared an Austen Powers joke, and he'd had full intentions of going down to the bar after the computer job he had to do.

By the time he got there and went looking for Nell, she'd gone. Tam and Pippa were there, and Nat had asked where she was.

'Gone home,' they'd screamed together over the music as they'd danced. The gloss left the night, and he went home.

I'll see Nell in lectures or on campus, and ask her out, he'd thought.

That had been his plan, but it had never happened. He'd got busy—between his studies, his computer jobs and the bar work he did to supplement his student allowance—there was no spare time to socialise. Nell for some reason, took to sitting in the back row of the lecture theatre by herself, and Nat took the hint. But it had hurt.

He knew he had a reputation for being a bit of a player on campus, but that had suited him. He didn't want to get tied down into any relationship. He had a career and a life ahead of him, and he was way too young to settle down.

Uni finished, and they all went their separate ways. Nat got called to a job three years after graduation, and there was Nell in the office where he was supposed to be fixing a fileserver.

He'd sauntered over to her desk and put his well-practised charm to what he had thought was good use.

'Nellie. What a great surprise!' Nat leaned on the corner of her desk and looked down at her.

Surprise filled him. Her usual smile was nowhere in sight, and the drab khaki T-shirt made her face look sallow. Her pretty hair was scraped back into a tight ponytail, and the only colour was a vivid slash of red lipstick, that somehow looked bizarre.

She looked up at him as though he had just crawled out from under a rock, but Nat ignored it, thinking she hadn't recognised him.

'Yeah, baby, yeah?' he ventured in his best Austen Powers accent. 'It's me, Nat.'

'I know perfectly well who you are.' She gestured coldly to the receptionist who was standing near the door. 'Charlotte, can you please show Mr Dwyer where the computer room is.'

She had turned her attention back to the computer and he had been dismissed. The whole time Nat spent in the back room fixing the fileserver, he stewed; her attitude had pissed him off. It made him wonder what he'd done to make Nell ignore him those last few months in lectures, but he knew he hadn't done anything to her. He'd been judged on his reputation, and that made him angry.

But to this day, he regretted the way he had spoken to her on the way out. When Nat walked through the foyer, Nell was standing at the front desk talking to the receptionist. The drab T-shirt was tucked into a pair of knee-length black shorts. On her feet were joggers and white socks. What had happened to the pretty feminine Nell? But despite her appearance, that old jolt of attraction had rocked through him.

'And don't ever speak to a client like that again, please. It was unnecessary.' Even though her words were soft, he could hear the grilling that the poor receptionist was getting. It must have been the joke the girl had told him on the way in.

Nat shook his head as he walked past and caught the eye of the receptionist. She put her head down and he could see tears glinting in her pretty eyes.

'It's okay, love,' Nat said. 'Nervous Nellie here could take some lessons in manners from you.'

He wouldn't have said any more, but Nell followed him to the door and then outside the building. Her face was white—apart from the slash of red lipstick—and she pointed at him as she spoke.

'I would appreciate you minding your business when you are in our workplace. I'll be contacting your employer and making a complaint about your attitude.'

Nat had shaken his head. 'Jesus, Nell. What's happened to you, the kind and pretty girl who used to joke with me back at uni?'

'It's all about that, isn't it?' she snarled. 'What we look like, and how attractive we might be to the male of the species.'

He took a step back with my hands up and put on his best Austen Powers voice. 'Whoa, baby. What's your point?'

Her stare was glacial, and she turned and opened the door.

'For God's sake, Nellie. I'm joking. Chill.'

'Grow up, Nat.'

The door closed in his face, and he couldn't help having the last say. 'Not so shagalicous these days, baby,' he'd called through the door.

It was a cruel barb, and Nat regretted it as soon as the words came out of his mouth, and he hoped she hadn't heard the insult. He'd thought about calling her and apologising afterwards, but she had turned into such a cold fish, he decided to let it go. She never did call his boss anyway.

Now as he looked at her sitting at his kitchen table, it was as though those years had not intervened. The same khaki shorts and T-shirt, and the same red lipstick. The same closed expression.

Nell stood and gripped the back of the chair. 'If that's the case, and there are no other local experts, I'll get someone to come up from Brisbane. I won't bother you any longer.'

Nat kept his voice calm. 'Let's go back to the beginning. Forget we know each other. You need some network help, and I can provide it. No past, no insults, no nothing. Okay?'

Her hands let go of the chair and she nodded slowly. 'Yes. I need someone to address the problem very quickly.'

'How about I make coffee and then you can tell me what the problem is.'

She took a deep breath. 'My laptop is in my car; I've written down all of the things that seem to have compromised the network. I'll go out and get it.'

'It's pouring.' Nat shook his head, determined to be a gentleman. 'You put the kettle on, and I'll go out and get it. Is your car locked?'

'No. The laptop is on the back seat in a leather case. Thank you.' A glimmer of the Nell of old came back.

He gestured to the cupboard above the sink. 'Cups and coffee are in that cupboard. Milk's in the fridge.' Nat figured if he gave her something to do, she might settle a bit more. 'I'll grab a brolly and be back in a minute.' He didn't look at her again before hurrying up the hall, but he did hear the cupboard open as he reached the front door. Nat picked up the umbrella that he'd left there earlier and ran down the steps and across the yard towards the gate.

The wind roared in from the sea, whipping the mango trees around the house into a frenzy; the rain was horizontal and stung his face. One tree had already come down near the gate, and he had to clamber over it. Waves crashed on the beach behind the house; the normally smooth water was churning like a washing machine. As he wrenched open the back door of Nell's car, a loud and ominous creak caught his attention. He swung around as a deafening crack came from around the back of the house. For a second he thought it was another lightning strike, but his mouth dropped open as a massive branch of the towering mango tree at the back of the laundry sheared off and fell onto the roof of the house.

'Shit!' He slammed the car door shut, forgetting all about the laptop in his haste to get to the house and Nell. The roof over the back of the house had collapsed and loose sheets of corrugated iron were lifting in the wind. As Nat ran across the yard, a sheet of iron sheared off with a loud screech. It blew along the side of the house, slicing open the side of the water tank before landing in the front yard. He ignored the water pouring out of the tank at the side of the house and raced up the stairs. He threw the umbrella on the porch and pushed the front door open.

'Nell,' he yelled. 'Nell, I'm coming.'

There was no answer and his blood ran cold. Only the sound of the wind and sea, and the continuing screeching of the flapping iron reached him. He raced down the hallway into a gust of cold wet wind. Above, live wires sizzled and snapped in the wind.

'Don't move,' he yelled, racing back down the hall and out to the front porch. He turned off the power before running back to the kitchen. Hopefully, the battery backup had enough juice to keep his computers going, but that was the last of Nat's worries.

His passage was blocked by the end of the huge branch that had pierced a hole in the wall at the kitchen end of the hall. Heart thudding, he climbed over the thick branch, hands slipping on the wet bark. It was almost dark now.

'Nell, can you hear me?'

Nat pushed away the foliage that blocked his view as he carefully climbed over the branch that was wedged firmly across the kitchen and end of the hall.

Bloody hell. And into the computer room.

The branch had brought down the whole ceiling; he could see the sky through the huge gaping hole.

'Nell! For God's sake, where are you?'

Visions of her trapped beneath the huge branch filled his thoughts. 'Nell! Can you hear me?'

'I'm in here.' A faint voice came from the middle of the room.

'In where? Are you hurt?' He leaned forward and caught sight of her shoes sticking out beneath the kitchen table. He grabbed both sides of the table and, with strength born of fear, lifted it above his head, moving it to the side of the room.

As his eyes adjusted to the dark, Nat could see Nell lying on the floor, her arms over her head. He reached down and gently touched her hands. 'Are you hurt?' He couldn't see any marks or blood anywhere, but that didn't mean the tree hadn't hit her when it came through the roof. 'Can you move, Nell?'

'Don't touch me.' She flinched at his touch.

He lowered his voice and spoke slowly. 'I have to get you out of here. I'm worried the rest of the roof will come down.'

'Don't touch me. I can get out myself.' As she spoke, she lowered her hands, and her eyes connected with his. Her face was pale, but he couldn't see if she'd been hurt.

'Don't move until I know you're okay. Did you hurt your back? Did the tree hit you?'

She shook her head. 'I'm all right. If you get out of my way, I'll get up.'

He held out his hand, and this time, her voice held anger.

'I told you, I'm all right. Don't touch me. Please.'

'All right, all right.' He stepped back with his hands raised. 'I'm just worried you're hurt.'

Despite Nell's assurances that she was okay, Nat could see her shaking as she rolled over and pushed herself to her feet.

She lifted her hand and gripped the side of the table. 'I heard the first crack, and I dived under the table. I thought it was a lightning strike.' She inched along the table, putting distance between them, as much as she could anyway, with the huge branch filling the kitchen.

'No.' He looked up through the gaping hole in the ceiling. The wind had eased, and the rain had stopped. 'It was the mango tree out the back.'

'I can see it was a tree. It's a bit hard to miss.' Her voice was soft, but she forced a smile. White-faced, her hands shook as she reached up to push her hair back from her face. Enough to make him worry about her. For a moment, he caught another glimpse of the softness of the Nell of old, not this new hard woman she had become.

'Nell, I'm sorry this happened, but we need to get out now. We can get to the back door easily, but I need to know that you're okay first.'

'I'm all right. I'm not hurt.'

He nodded and held his hand out to help her over the branch, but she ignored it. With a shrug, Nat walked to the small landing at the top of the back steps, and she followed him without another word. He watched to make sure she was telling the truth about being okay.

The branch had hit the side of the steps on its way down, and one of the posts halfway up had collapsed. Nat bit back a groan as the steps wobbled when he stood on the landing. There was a lot more damage to the house than he'd first thought. Not only the roof, the kitchen, the water tank, and the wiring, it looked like the structural integrity of his house had been compromised.

He couldn't bring himself to think what damage it had done to the equipment in the computer room. The room was next to the kitchen, and the roof over it had blown off. But until he got Nell out safely, Nat wasn't going to go and check it out.

'I'll go down first, and then when I get to the bottom, you come down after me. The stairs are a bit shaky.'

She nodded, and Nat took off, jumping down the last three stairs. The staircase shook beneath his weight but held firm.

'Come on. If they collapse, jump, and I'll catch you.' He held his arms out and could see the eye roll from where he stood.

It was only a matter of seconds before Nell scurried down the stairs, and they were both standing in the yard looking back at the house. The storm was moving inland quickly, and the sky had cleared. Brilliant stars began to appear in the night sky.

'What are you going to do? The house is a mess,' she asked softly. 'Do you rent? Or is it yours?'

If Nat didn't look at her, he could pretend that the concern came from the Nell he'd once known. He folded his arms and leaned back on the fence—the only part of the property that seemed to be intact. 'It was my grandparents' house. They left it to me. I moved up here just before Cyclone Debbie.' He uncrossed his arms and walked back towards the house. 'I can't believe the house survived that cyclone and that it only took a piddly storm like this to damage it.'

'I wouldn't call it a piddly storm.' Her voice was soft. 'I'm sorry your house is damaged. Do you have somewhere else to stay?'

'I haven't thought about that yet. We need to get you out of here, though. I don't know what condition the road back to town

PENTECOST ISLAND 1-3

will be in.'

'Look, I'll leave you to it. I'll drive back to Airlie Beach. I was going to anyway.'

'No, I'm not going to let you drive by yourself. The road could be blocked by more trees that have come down, and then you'll be stuck.' Nat frowned as thoughts whirled through his head. 'Come around to the front and wait near the gate; I just want to check something and get a couple of things. And please don't be tempted to drive off, because you'll leave me stranded. My car is in town getting fixed.'

He stared at her, surprised when she chuckled. 'The thought did cross my mind.'

'I thought it might have. Just give me a couple of minutes.'

Nat left Nell standing by the gate in the dark and headed for the front door.'

Chapter 6

Nell – 2010

'Nell, will you chill a bit? What in the bloody hell is wrong with you lately?' Pippa reached for the wine bottle and filled her glass to the top. They had spread a picnic rug in the park on the riverbank down the street from their flat.

'You've had enough.' Nell folded her arms and looked at Pippa with a scowl.

'Come on, you pair, stop fighting. We're supposed to be having a celebration picnic.' Tam reached for the bottle, topped her glass, and held it up to Nell.

'No, thank you.'

Tam shrugged and put it back in the chill pack before lifting her glass. 'Well, here's to another year over.'

'And one closer to making our mark in the world.' Pippa squealed and took a slurp from her overflowing glass. She glanced across at Tam when Nell lay back on the grass and put her forearm over her eyes.

Nell knew they were both looking at her, but she didn't care. She was over this partying and being stupid most of the time. For goodness sake, they were almost twenty and should be taking their university studies more seriously. The spring sunshine was warm on her skin, and she kept her eyes closed, listening to her two friends talk.

'What's your plan for the long vacation, Tam?' Pippa's voice was always loud. Her clothes were always colourful and flamboyant, and it seemed as though she tried to match them with her voice and behaviour. She wanted to be seen, and that was the last thing that Nell wanted to do.

Nell tried to quell her growing irritation. It wasn't the girls' fault that she was a stick in the mud these days. She knew she should try harder, but some days, it was hard enough to get out of bed. Her two besties were worried about her, but that was the least of her problems.

'I . . .um . . . have something to tell you,' Tam replied. 'Nell, are you awake? I want to tell you both at once.'

Nell rolled over and leaned on her elbows, resting her chin in her hands. 'Yes, I'm awake.'

'Tell us what?' Pippa said.

'I've decided to drop out.'

'What!' Nell sat up now and stared at Tam. How many times since last winter had she dreamed about doing the same thing? Leaving university, leaving Brisbane, leaving the girls behind and going somewhere new where she'd feel safe.

The problem was she didn't know where to go, nor could she afford it.

Tam cleared her throat. 'I've been offered an apprenticeship at Peppers. And they are going to pay for my course.' Her eyes lit up with excitement. 'Not at TAFE, but a private course that fast-tracks me and puts me with some of the top chefs in the country.'

'Here in Brisbane?' Nell's voice was quiet.

'No, Peppers by the Surf. Down at Surfers Paradise, and the problem is, it means letting you both down. I'm going to have to move down there and give up my room in the house.'

'How did that happen, Tam?' Nell asked quietly.

'Well, you know how I've been working as a kitchen hand at night in the city?'

Nell nodded.

'I've been doing a bit of preparation for the entrees there, and I impressed one of the chefs with something I suggested one night. He took it up and added it to the menu, and it was a hit.

Chad moved down to Peppers, and he put my name up for a traineeship. He knows that my dream is to be a chef. So, to cut to the chase, I've had two interviews, and I was offered the traineeship this morning.'

'Who's this, Chad?' Nell asked.

Tam ignored her question. 'And it's great timing because I've got two years of my degree behind me, and I'll defer, and I can go back and finish externally in a year or two if I want to.'

'Who's this guy?' Nell repeated. 'He seems to know more about you than we do. *I* didn't know you wanted to be a chef.'

'Me either. I just thought you liked to cook,' Pippa said.

'Well, I always have.' Tam said quietly. 'I just didn't share it with anyone. 'I guess I thought it didn't have the prestige of going to uni and getting a degree.'

'Oh, shit. Where are we going to get a third at this end of the uni year?' Pippa huffed.

'I know. I feel bad, but I might have someone for you. Have you seen Nat lately, Nell?' Tam asked.

Nell froze, but she kept her voice even. 'Nat who?'

'God, you know who I mean. That cutie, Nat Dwyer, the guy who goes to lectures with you.'

'No, I haven't seen him, but what about him?'

Since that night last winter before "it" happened, Nell had avoided everyone. She made sure she got to lectures late, sat in the back row of the lecture theatre near the door, and was the first to leave. A few times in the beginning, she had seen Nat turn around and look for her, but she'd pretended not to see him. It was hard enough sitting next to anyone, let alone a guy.

'I know he's looking for a room. I heard he lost his place in the residential hall.'

'I heard that, 'Pip said. 'Too many parties and he got caught with a couple of girls in his room after curfew one night. I'm sure it was innocent.'

PENTECOST ISLAND 1-3

Tam and Pippa exchanged a glance and burst out laughing, but Nell pursed her lips and looked away.

'Oh, God, we'll miss you, Tam,' Pip said. 'But thanks for suggesting Nat. Nell, can you tell him the room's available when you see him at lectures?'

'No!' Nell knew her voice was unnecessarily loud, but she stared back at them.

'Why so adamant?' Tam frowned at her. 'I thought you were mates, aren't you?'

'No, he's just someone I used to sit with in lectures. I hardly know him.'

'Used to?' Damn, she'd slipped up there, and Pippa picked straight up on it. 'Why used to?'

'We've changed majors.'

'Well, I vote we offer it to him. We can't afford to split the rent two ways, Nell. And it'll go up after the long vacation too. It always does.'

'No. I don't want to share with a guy. I don't want to have to worry about wandering out in a towel or running out to the laundry to get my knickers out of the dryer. But most of all, I don't want Nat Dwyer. He'd have a different girl in there every night. You know what he's like.'

'You're being too hard, Nell. He's no worse than any other guy on campus.'

'No. No guys. Please.' She looked past the confused looks on Tam and Pippa's faces. A CityCat was cruising silently up the river, and the ducks that had been on the edge of the grass took off with raucous honks. 'All the guys on campus are like that, so we'll have another girl, thank you. Otherwise, I go too.'

'All right,' Tam conceded, reluctance in her voice. 'You'll have to find someone then. I don't want to go through this every time I come up with a name.'

'I will.' Nell pushed herself to her feet and tucked her black

T-shirt into her khaki pants. 'I've got to be somewhere. I'll see you both later.'

She knew that Tam and Pippa stared at her as she strode off. Okay, she felt bad, but she couldn't help it. These days, she didn't care what anyone thought about her.

Even her best friends.

Chapter 7

Nell 2020

Nell sighed while she waited for Nat to come out of the house. Her hands were shaking, but the close call when that blasted tree had come through the ceiling had at least taken away the fear of being in the house with him, even though it had given her one hell of a fright.

If she'd known the business was run from a private house, she would never have come this far.

But really, she didn't have a choice; she would have come because she had to get the problem fixed. She was caught between a rock and a hard place; there was no way Nell would let Pippa down, so she had to get someone to fix the network, and Nat was the only local someone. She leaned back against the car, her thoughts in turmoil as she looked up at the sky.

It was hard to believe that there had been such a violent storm a short time ago. The wind had gone, and the sky was full of stars; even the noise of the sea had abated. As she stared out over the sea, her phone trilled in her pocket.

She glanced at the screen and answered. 'Hey, Pip.'

'Nell. Where are you? I just wanted to check you didn't get caught in that freak storm that roared over us and towards the coast.'

'I'm fine. Just a bit of wind and rain. Is everything okay out there?' She gripped the phone and frowned.

'Yeah, there was a lot of thunder and lightning, but no damage, thank goodness. Rafe heard the storm warning, and we got the outdoor furniture away in the bar just in time. A couple of trees blew down, but nothing near the house or the huts. Where are you?'

'Um, I'm just at the networking . . . um. . . place, and then heading back to Airlie Beach.'

'Okay, that's good then. The other thing I wanted to tell you was that Jiminy's coming to the island tomorrow late morning, so if the time suits you, jump on his boat. If it doesn't, ring me, and I'll come and get you whenever you're ready.'

'That should work out okay with me. I'll probably get the early ferry over. If there's anything you want, text me a list, and I'll pick it up at Hamo. What's Jiminy doing?'

'Okay, I'll ask Tam, and I'll text you. We've got another staff member arriving tomorrow. He's bringing her over.'

'Who's that?'

'Tam's friend—the one from the Gold Coast.'

The door to the house banged shut, and Nat walked across to the gate, his keys jangling in his hand.

'Okay, sounds good. I have to go. See you tomorrow.' Nell disconnected before Pip could ask any more questions.

'Thanks for waiting,' Nat said, but as he looked back at the house, his lips were set, and his brow wrinkled.

'What's wrong?' she asked. 'Apart from your caved-in roof, I mean.'

'There's a fair bit of damage inside. There's no power now, and my backup system didn't come on, so I've got no computer system going. The room copped a fair bit of rain. I've covered it up as best I could, but I don't think I'll be working from there for a while. I took some photos, and I'll have to get onto my insurance company.'

For the first time, Nell noticed he was carrying a case and a backpack slung over his shoulder.

'I brought my laptop and some clothes and stuff. Hopefully, I can help you out.'

Nell went to the driver's side to open the door, but Nat walked around beside her. She took a step back, wondering what

PENTECOST ISLAND 1-3

he wanted.

'Um, Nell? How would you feel about me driving your car?'

She shrugged. 'It's not my car. It's a hire car. I don't care. You probably know the road better.'

'And you can tell me what's wrong with your computer system as we travel. Where did you hire the car?'

'Port of Airlie, where the ferry from Hamilton Island comes in.'

'Okay. I've got a mate with a two bedroom unit at the Mantra near there. Once we get there, we can grab something to eat, and I can try to log into your network remotely and have a look around. If that suits you?'

Nell hesitated. She knew she couldn't afford to be precious, but—

He glanced across at her as he turned the car. Just like she'd thought it would, it took Nat about six goes to turn it around.

'I'm happy to look at the network together, but I'll find my accommodation and dinner.'

He shrugged. 'Suit yourself. The apartment's free.'

She didn't answer, and there was no more talk as Nat concentrated on the narrow dirt road. Night had fallen, and velvety darkness surrounded them as the headlights picked out the lonely road ahead. Eventually, they reached an intersection, and he turned right onto a bitumen road.

'Okay, we're on the main road now. We've got half an hour or so for you to tell me about the setup you have and then tell me what problems you're having.'

Nell cleared her throat, ill at ease. She didn't know the right language to use to an expert. 'Okay. I'll keep it simple. I've set up one more powerful computer in the office to run the various software packages we use rather than installing them on the individual laptops that we use in other places around the resort.'

He nodded. 'Good. What networking software are you using?'

'Um, I'm not sure what you mean.'

His voice was patient. 'Okay, are you PC-based, or is it an Apple Network?'

'PC. Windows, I mean.'

'And the proprietary software to set up your network?'

'I'm not sure.' Heat ran up Nell's neck, and she was pleased it was dark in the car. 'Maybe we're better off waiting until you can log in and look.'

'Let me explain, and you might know what I mean. The hardware that you'll be using will be on the server—that is, the backend computer you described to me—the clients, that is, your laptops, and the transmission medium and connecting devices. The software components are the operating system and protocols that make them all talk to each other.'

'Yes, I understand that, but I don't know the name of what I'm using to put it all together.'

'Okay, not a problem. I'll see when I log in. Tell me a bit about the resort and what you're using the network to do.'

Finally, a question she could answer. Nell relaxed and settled into her seat more comfortably. She hadn't realised how tense she'd been holding herself.

The wheels hummed on the bitumen, interrupted by an occasional splash as they hit puddles on the road as she outlined the accounting software, the reservations system and the ordering system on Tam's laptop in the kitchen.

'Good, sounds simple and effective.'

'There's one thing I need more than anything, Nat. That's why I came over to the mainland today.'

'What's that?' Nat changed back a gear and they slowed down. 'Meets all your needs?'

'What are you doing?' Nell shot an anxious glance across

PENTECOST ISLAND 1-3

the car. 'Where are you going?'

He looked at her briefly, his brow furrowed in a frown. 'I'm looking out for the turn-off to Cannonvale. It's hard to see in the dark between the sugar cane fields. The signpost blew down a couple of storms back, and they haven't replaced it yet. You can't see the road until you're just about at the turnoff.'

'Cannonvale?' Her voice was a squeak. 'Why are we going to Cannonvale?'

The car picked up speed again, and Nat's voice was firm yet patient. 'Because we go through Cannonvale to get to Airlie Beach and then on to Port of Airlie.' A road came up on the left, and he quickly indicated and took the turn. 'This is it now.'

'Oh, sorry, I've only been to the mainland once before. We usually only go from the island to Hamilton for anything we need. Our supplies and stuff come across on the barge, and then we pick them up. Pippa—or the resort, I suppose— has a launch that's big enough to take a fair bit onboard.' Nell tried to take a deep breath and relax, but her whole body was tight. Conversation was hard. She hadn't been this close to—or alone with— a man in ten years.

'What was the one thing you need?'

'I need this problem fixed now. Not later this week or next week. The first part of the resort is opening next week, and I must have the network up and running. I have to be able to access the bookings that I've lost.' Her voice dropped. 'And Tam's orders and the rest of the data I've backed up.'

'Okay. If you can give me half the morning tomorrow to get my insurance sorted and collect my car, I'll probably be able to come over tomorrow. Would that suit?

'Oh God, yes.' Relief zoomed in, and she leaned her head back on the headrest.

'I have to go out to Hamo. I've got a few jobs out there that I have to touch base on.' He shook his head ruefully. 'The way my computer system was looking, I think I'll be doing a lot of onsite jobs in the next little while.'

'Thank you,' she breathed out quietly.

'Nellie? I mean Nell. Can I say something to you? I'd like to clear the air before I start working with you.'

'Y … es,' she said slowly. Nerves were skittering all through her. Her stomach was churning, her fingers were aching, and it was hard to swallow. Her skin tingled as though there was an army of ants marching over it. She tried to close her eyes and visualise something pleasant. She'd learned that strategy from a YouTube clip on anxiety attacks. That's the closest she'd ever got to counselling.

Something pleasant. Take a breath, close your eyes and think of something you love to do. A place where you feel safe, calm and happy. The words ran through her head, and she let her imagination conjure up a happy picture.

Sitting on the beach at Pentecost Island, watching the sun go down with the girls. A bottle or two of bubbles, lots of laughter, lots of happiness. Except for the night Eliza had almost drowned, but that had turned out okay. Her eyes flew open as Nat spoke again, interrupting her meditation.

'I want to say sorry.'

She turned her head slowly to look at him. He was gripping the steering wheel, his attention fixed on the road ahead.

'Sorry for what?' Her words sounded husky to her ears, but over the stupid buzzing that nerves had kicked off, it was hard to tell if the huskiness was real or not. Nell cleared her throat and said it again. 'For what?'

'For that time, I came to your office on the Gold Coast and was really rude to you when I left. It bothered me for ages afterwards. I'm sorry, it was an awful thing to say, and I didn't mean it. I lashed out at you, and I had no right to. I was rude and cruel, and you didn't deserve that.' He shook his head as he stared at the road ahead.

PENTECOST ISLAND 1-3

'I did.' Heat filled Nell's face, and she looked straight ahead. 'It was eight years ago. And I goaded you into it. I was in a bad place then, and I'm sorry. I said some rude things, too.'

'Okay then. Apologies exchanged and accepted. I'm cool with that, are you?'

She nodded.

'Can I ask you one more thing? It's something else that's bothered me since we were at uni. Maybe I'll need to apologise again.'

Nell closed her eyes; she knew what was coming, but for some unknown reason, she felt safe, cocooned in the car with Nat. Safer than she had for a long time, listening to his gentle voice as the wheels humming on the bitumen soothed her, and the dark of the night closed everything else out. It was as though they were in a different world, and what had shaped her into the person she was now receded.

'What did I do to make you hate me so much, Nellie? I went down to the bar the night that *Cat Empire* was playing. The night we sat together for the last time in that lecture hall. Was it because you thought I was playing with you? Going to lead you on? Treat you like the playboy I was supposed to be? It wasn't true, you know.'

The first tear that plopped onto her hand surprised Nell. She lifted her hand and looked at the damp spot. Turning her hand around slowly, she rubbed her eyes and then took a long, shuddering breath in.

'I'm sorry that it worried you so much, Nat. It wasn't you. It wasn't about you. It never was. Something happened that night, and I've never got over it.' Her voice fell to a whisper. 'I've never told another soul what happened. I was so ashamed, and I blamed myself. I've never even told the girls. I thought if I didn't tell anyone, I could forget it, and it wouldn't be real.'

'The girls? You mean Pippa and Tam? You lived with

them, didn't you?'

'Yes, I did. What happened was all my fault. I'm sorry that you thought you'd done something. For months afterwards, I didn't give anyone else a thought. It was all me and it was all my fault. I brought it on myself. The way I'd dressed, and the confidence I had. I thought I was invincible, and the world was at my feet.'

'You were a hell of a lot of fun to sit with in lectures. I used to look forward to those subjects.'

'Thank you. After that night, I lost a lot of trust and all my self-confidence. That's why I sat by myself in lectures and spent the rest of the time in the apartment I shared with Pippa. Tam moved out, and it was just the two of us. I didn't want anyone else there, so I scrounged and paid two shares of the rent. I told Pippa I was studying, but most of the time I sat in my room or slept.'

'Depression?' Nat's tone was kind. 'I'm no stranger to that. My sister had a breakdown in her teens.'

'In hindsight, yes. I was young and stupid. And like I said I thought I was invincible.'

'Will you tell me what happened? Maybe it would help to talk about it?'

Nell felt as though she was in a dream state. Was she really sitting in a car with Nat Dwyer? Was she really about to tell him what had happened to her?

PENTECOST ISLAND 1-3

Chapter 8

Nell 2010

The students from the lecture hall jostled at the entrance and Nell soon lost sight of Nat in the crowd. For a moment she stood looking at the spot where she'd last seen him.

It would be great if Nat came down to the bar. A happy, warm feeling settled in Nell's chest, and she headed outside into the colder night. The way he'd looked at her was different tonight; it was as though he noticed her for the first time.

Winter was around the corner and she pulled her bright red cardigan around her shoulders. Her dress was short, and her legs were bare; she hadn't thought about how cool it would be tonight when she'd got dressed for lectures on the warm autumn morning.

Before she'd left the apartment, she'd slipped on a dress and shoes that would do for both the lecture and dancing in the bar afterwards. She was really looking forward to having a few drinks and letting her hair down with the girls. Uni was great and having Tam and Pippa on the same campus meant good times most nights of the week. They'd been friends since primary school; she and Tam had been over the moon when Pippa moved back to Brisbane to go to the same uni. They were all doing different courses and they'd found a cheap house to share over at Bardon. The ferry terminal at Milton wasn't too much of a walk from the house.

There was always something on at the uni bar, but *Cat Empire* was going to be awesome tonight. She just hoped they had come on late as most bands seemed to. What rotten luck that it was tonight of all nights when they'd had to go to that boring lecture.

A southerly change had come roaring in while they'd been in the lecture, and now the wind was whistling through the tall gums along the riverfront. At least it would be warm down in the student union . . . once she was inside. And a few wines would soon warm her up; she just hoped that Tam and Pippa hadn't got too much of a head start.

Nell shivered and paused outside the building. Most of the students were heading towards the car park, but she'd caught the CityCat to uni this morning, so she was going to have to walk down to the bar. She stood there, tapped her fingers on the side of her thigh, and looked around, deciding which was the best way to go.

Two choices.

The long way along the path that wound through the campus, and led to the front of the bar, or the shortcut that she took up from the ferry terminal at the river every morning. There was a path halfway along that shortcut that led down to the bar. There'd been rumours of a couple of assaults there over the past year, but she put it down to the usual gossip that circulated. It was always someone who told someone who told someone else.

Nell hesitated as she looked at the path. It would be dark, but it would be so much quicker. The campus was big, and the shortcut would save her at least fifteen minutes in the cold wind, and that was fifteen minutes extra she could listen to the band. And fifteen minutes sooner that she could start partying. She stood there for a moment, considering her options, and as she waited, the faint sound of the band drifted across from the other side of the campus, enticing her. A shiver ran up Nell's back as the wind whistled through the gap in the buildings, and that decided her.

With a confident nod, she held her book and bag close to her chest and took off towards the path that was almost hidden between the trees.

Nell was focused on meeting Tam and Pippa, and she didn't notice the figure standing in the shadows at the side of the building.

She only had fifty metres before she reached the student union building when it happened.

"It"—the event that would change her confidence and define her new personality overnight. In the months and the years that followed, she always remembered that night as the catalyst for changing the Nell of "before" into the Nell of "after".

As she hurried past the Law building and into the narrow corridor leading to the bar, a rustle in the shrubs behind her sent her heart rate up a notch. She glanced behind her, and a fleeting shadow brushed against the side of the building near the steps leading into the foyer.

It was just the wind moving the trees, she told herself.

But her heart was in her throat, and when she heard footsteps behind her, Nell knew she was in trouble. She took a deep breath and started to run, but before she could get away, a firm hand gripped her arm. She didn't even have time to pull out the pepper spray she always carried.

Before she knew it, she was on her knees and was being dragged into the shrubbery at the side of the building.

He didn't say one word to her the whole time.

Her assailant's other hand moved to her face and covered her mouth and nose. She tried to scream, but the hand pressed hard against her lips. An overpowering smell of dirt and car oil made her gag.

'Please, don't hurt me,' she tried to whimper, but no sound came out. Something cold and sharp touched her neck, and stars dotted her vision.

It was only a few minutes later, but it seemed like a long time had passed before he left her huddled in the wet leaves of the garden next to that building. A couple of guys had walked down the dark path, talking and laughing, and her assailant had put his hand over her mouth again so she couldn't call out. She'd lain there with her eyes closed, trying not to make a sound as the knife pressed against her neck.

He must have been worried that they would come back because he'd shoved her away and taken off. Her handbag was gone, and a thin trickle of blood was running down her neck where the knife had nicked her skin when she'd tried to move. Before the men had walked past, he'd pushed her dress up above her waist, and her knickers had twisted.

Nell knew it could have been a lot worse if he hadn't left her, but her hands and legs were shaking so much she couldn't move. He had intended to assault her sexually; he'd pressed against her just before the two guys had almost come upon them.

Her heart pounded in time with the deep throb of the music from the bar close by.

Footsteps crunched on the path nearby, and she froze.

What if he came back?

Maybe he'd opened her purse and seen how little was in there. Maybe he'd decided to finish what—

It started to rain as she pushed herself to her feet, one of those heavy tropical Brisbane showers that could soak you in two minutes and then stop as suddenly as it began. She rearranged her knickers so they weren't cutting into her, pulled her dress down and smoothed her shaking hands over it. Hurrying out to the main path, she joined the throng of students who were drinking on the ground-level covered veranda.

Pushing herself into the middle of the crowd, she let the sweaty bodies press against her until she felt warm again.

##

'What did you do to your neck, Nell?' Pippa had spotted her when she and Tam had come out of the bar between songs. 'It's bleeding.' Pippa reached down into her bra and pulled a tissue out. 'It's clean.'

'I . . . I . . . ran into a tree when it was raining. I fell over.'

PENTECOST ISLAND 1-3

Shame filled Nell, and she swore that no one, not even her best friends, would ever know what had happened. She swallowed and forced her voice to stop shaking. 'Would you believe I've lost my bag? Can you please give me your key, Pip? I'm going home. I'm soaked.'

'Aw, come on, Nell. The band's fantastic. You've been waiting for them for ages. Come and dance.' Pippa tried to pull her into the bar, but Nell stood firm.

'No. I want to go home. I don't feel well.'

'Okay, party pooper.' Pippa dug into her jeans pocket and produced her key to the small flat they shared over in Milton.

'Can you lend me five bucks for the bus? I lost my purse too.'

Tamsin narrowed her eyes and zoomed in close to her face. Both girls had obviously had a few beers and it was dark outside. 'You okay, love?'

'I'm fine. It was a shit lecture. I got wet. I fell over. I lost my bag. Are you satisfied? I'm not in the mood to party. I just want to go home to bed.' Her teeth were chattering from cold and shock

Tamsin nodded and Pippa shrugged as she handed over a handful of gold coins.

The band started up again, and the two girls squealed as they ran back into the bar. 'We'll see you at home.'

By the time Tamsin and Pippa arrived home after midnight, with much noise and hilarity, Nell was in bed in her room pretending to be asleep. She'd stood under the shower for half an hour until she stopped shaking, and then collapsed into bed.

***

Nat pulled the car over as soon as they reached town. 'God, Nell. You never told anyone? You didn't report it?'

'No. I was too ashamed. And it didn't matter. Because he assaulted another girl in the same spot a few days later, and she screamed blue murder, and he was caught.'

'I remember that.' He looked at her and his face was shadowed inside the car. 'He was charged with a few counts of sexual assault and went to jail.'

'He did. I followed the case, day by day, and I thought that I'd start to feel better when it was all over. He got a long time, because the last charge was attempted murder too.' She sniffed. 'But I didn't. It set me back even further, thinking that he could have raped and killed me that night. I lost my confidence. In everything. I didn't want it to happen again. The sensible part of me tells me it was a random attack, and I was lucky he was interrupted, and he didn't—' she drew in a long shuddering breath. 'I stopped wearing dresses and anything colourful. I just wanted to blend in and be a nobody.'

'Oh, Nellie, you could never be a nobody.'

'Thank you, Nat. But it's what I wanted to be. The last few months on the island have given me a lot more confidence. I'm gradually getting more confident when there are men around, but it's taken me a long time. Pippa has a partner, Rafe, and we've had another man, a French sailor helping out on the island for a few weeks.'

'Bloody ten years of your life, Nell. Did you ever go to counselling to try and work through it?

She shook her head. 'No, because I was too ashamed. Like I said I didn't tell anyone. I could have gone to the police when he was arrested. He might have got an even longer sentence, but I just couldn't.' Tears began to run down her face again and her throat clogged. 'I don't know why I told you, Nat. You'll think even less of me now.'

'Never, Nell. Please don't think that.' Nat hesitated and then lifted one hand from the steering wheel, reached over, and squeezed her hand briefly. 'I feel very honoured that you trusted me enough to tell me about that night.' He turned his attention to her for a fleeting second and she held his gaze.

Even though it was dim in the car, she could see the determination in his eyes.

'And I'm going to do whatever I can to help you heal.' He squeezed her hand again. 'Friends?'

She nodded. 'Yes, Nat. Friends.'

Chapter 9

Nell

'Are you sure you want to get your own room?' Nat said as they turned at the roundabout into the Port of Airlie. 'My mate's is a freebie.'

'Yes,' Nell said softly. 'I'd be more comfortable. Please don't take it personally, it's just me. And besides, I don't have to pay for it. Pippa said all the costs of this trip can come out of the company.'

'Not a problem,' Nat said kindly. 'Just offering.'

He'd called his mate before they pulled back onto the road at Cannonvale and got the code to collect the security card to get into the unit. Nell had composed herself as Nat approached the turn to park in the private and gated car park beneath the multi-story building.

'Wait.' She swallowed and held her hand up. 'If you don't mind a short walk, drive over and park it over in the rental car park and I'll do the paperwork in the morning before I catch the ferry back. It will be . . .um . . . easier.'

'Good idea. I wasn't sure if I remembered the code for the car park anyway. I forgot to ask Brent for it.'

'You've stayed here before?' she asked.

'Yeah, Brent and his family live over on Hamo and he keeps this unit for when they come to the mainland. He's one of my clients. He's got a couple of businesses over there. And a house and the kids go to school on the island.'

'I heard you do some work at Hamilton. It's a fair way for you to go from your place.'

Nat nodded as he parked the car. 'I stay on Hamo

PENTECOST ISLAND 1-3

sometimes because I have a dozen or so clients over there now. It's the biggest part of my business, that's why I wasn't keen on taking the job down in Proserpine. I think he wanted a cut of the business. And yes, it's a pain getting down from Hydeaway Bay and catching the ferry across as often as I have to. Brent offered me this unit at a good rate, but I said no, because I know he and his family use it pretty often.'

'You haven't thought about living over on the islands?'

He smiled ruefully. 'That would be ideal, but the rent over there is too high. Maybe when I build my business up a bit more, I might be able to consider it.' He opened the back door of the hire car and took the two laptops and his backpack out while Nell retrieved her overnight bag from the boot. After clicking the remote he handed the keys over.

'Thanks. I'll go to reception and book a room for the night.'

Nat walked towards reception with her. 'I'll wait until you know you can get a room for sure, and then I thought we might grab something to eat and we can work over dinner. How do you feel about that?'

Nell stepped through the door into the foyer when he held it open. 'Thank you. Yes, that sounds good.'

##

It didn't take long to organise a one-bedroom unit and as luck would have it, it was on the same floor in the north wing along the corridor from the one that Nat stayed in. They caught the lift up together.

'I've booked a table in the fish and chip place for seven-thirty. Does that give you enough time?

Nell glanced at her watch. 'Yes, thank you. I'll see you down there.' As he walked away, she put the key card over the security sensor. When it clicked open, she called him. 'Nat?'

384

'Yes.' He paused a short way along the corridor.

'Thank you.' She stepped into the apartment and closed the door before he could reply. The first thing that caught her eye was the glittering lights of the marina below. Walking slowly through the apartment, Nell put her bag on the king size bed before she pushed open the doors and stepped onto the small balcony. The air was fresh and held a hint of a tropical spice from the trees that formed a privacy screen between her balcony and the next. She slipped her shoes off and wandered into the kitchen and opened the fridge. There were a couple of small bottles of bubbles in there and she took one out and reached for a glass before she headed back out onto the veranda. She pulled a second chair out and put her feet up before she popped the top of the bottle. The bubbles fizzed over the side of her glass.

She yawned; it had been a big day and it seemed like more than one day had passed since Pippa had dropped her off at Hamo this morning to catch the ferry.

Things hadn't turned out too badly after all.

Apart from the storm, and the damage it had done to Nat's house. He was a kind and gentle guy—just like he had been at uni—and she was feeling more at ease in male company than she had for a very long time. Sometimes, she had to force herself to relax when Rafe and Phillipe joined them in the bar at the island.

Talking to Nat had been cathartic and an unfamiliar lightness relaxed her. She sat on the balcony for half an hour watching the people walk along the edge of the water and listening to the happy voices that drifted up. Someone turned some music on below, and she jumped up realising how much time had passed; she had to get tidy and meet Nat at the restaurant.

Nell unpacked the small overnight bag and pulled a face when she pulled out the spare pair of khaki pants and a clean T-shirt. Maybe it was time to break her habits.

She knew when Nat looked at her that it wasn't what she

wore that made the person she was. Clothes weren't important; it was what was within and she knew he would have treated her exactly the same polite way if she'd been wearing a dress. The hang up was all hers.

Nell was thoughtful as she jumped in and took a quick shower in the luxurious bathroom. Tam and Pippa had been on her back for ages, and on very rare occasions they had got her into a dress. After dressing in her clean clothes, she quickly dried her hair and reached for her red lipstick. Hesitating she stared at herself in the mirror and held the lipstick up.

After "it" had happened, she had used the red lipstick as a deliberate reminder about how she looked and the image that she presented in the world. After a few years it just became habit. Slowly, Nell put the red lipstick back into her toiletries bag without opening the case.

A relaxed face stared back at her as she pinched her cheeks and pulled her hair back into a scrunchie. Her cheeks were pink with a healthy glow. Her eyes were bright, and she felt light, and confident that Nat was going to be able to solve her network problem, and she wouldn't have to worry any more about putting the resort opening in jeopardy.

Nat sounded as though he knew what he was talking about, although that shouldn't be a surprise. Even before he'd finished his degree, he'd been a whiz at that stuff, and now he had ten years in business under his belt. She wondered if he could fix the problem remotely, but she doubted it.

No, I'm getting ahead of myself.

She'd wait until he had a look downstairs after they'd eaten. With a rare smile, Nell picked up her laptop, closed the unit door behind her and headed down to the concourse where the fish and chip restaurant overlooked the marina.

##

Nat hadn't come down to the restaurant yet, and Nell waited at the counter until the waitress was free to take her over to a table overlooking the water. She unpacked her laptop and turned it on, taking the opportunity to use the local Wi-Fi to check her email. When she'd cleared her email, she decided to see if she could log onto the resort network remotely before Nat arrived.

Nell bit her lip and waited for the usual disconnect thirty seconds after her password was accepted.

She waited, and counted and sure enough, she was disconnected before she reached thirty. With a sigh, she closed the lid and had reached for her water glass as Nat walked across to the table. His hair was damp, and he'd changed his clothes.

'Sorry I had a few calls to make. I was trying to sort out the insurance on my house and my computers,' he said as she sat across from her.

'What will you do? You won't be able to live in the house, will you? The kitchen is demolished, and half the roof came down.'

'Yeah, that's right.' Nat ran his hand through his damp hair. 'I'll talk to my mate and maybe stay down here for a few days, but I'll see how we go trying to log into your network before I make any calls or decisions. I've got a couple of jobs out on Hamilton Island so if I need to come out and look at your physical setup, I'll fit that in in the next day or so.'

Nat caught the attention of the waitress as she walked past the table. Nell was sipping on a glass of water. He gestured to the drink's menu. 'Would you like a drink before we eat?'

Her lips tilted in a smile. 'I'll admit to a quick drink on the balcony before I got changed.' She thought for a moment and then nodded. 'Why not? After the day we've had, I think we deserve one tonight.' She knew her smile was tentative, but she got a wide grin back from Nat.

'I think we do too. Wine?' He raised his eyebrows as he

held up the menu.

She nodded. 'Yes, you choose.'

Nell watched as Nat quickly perused the wines on offer. His hair shone from the soft light above them, and a slight frown wrinkled his brow as he concentrated. His face was as familiar to her now as it had been ten years ago. Finally, he chose, and the waitress nodded.

'I won't be long. Perhaps you'd like to look at the food menu while you wait. We're going to get busy in the next little while. If you get your order in before that big table, your meals will come out a lot quicker.'

Nat looked up and held Nell's gaze. 'How does that sound to you? If we eat first, we can focus on your laptop after?'

She quickly agreed. 'Sounds good to me. I'm a bit hungry. It's been a long time since lunch at Proserpine.'

Nat grinned back and her tummy did a funny little jump as she noticed the familiar dimple in his left cheek.

'I was going to offer you a biscuit with the cuppa we were going to have,' he said.

'Before the roof blew into your kitchen,' she said with a laugh before she killed the smile. 'Sorry, that was really rude. It's not a laughing matter.'

Nat flicked a dismissive wave. 'Might as well look on the bright side.'

Their eyes met and held, and Nell started to hum the tune from the Monty Python movie they'd both loved.

Nat chuckled loudly, and a few heads turned to look at them. 'How many times did you sing that to me in lectures when we got bored shitless?'

'Lots. Mainly in McMinn's. Remember him?'

'How could I forget? Hours and hours of my life—our lives—never to be gotten back.' He held her gaze a little bit longer until Nell dropped her eyes. She felt uncomfortable and kept her head down as she twisted her hands in her lap.

Why on earth did I let my guard down and hum that silly song? He must think I'm an idiot, she thought.

'But he chuckled,' a little voice inside told her. 'Nat's a good guy. One of the really good ones and you are being way too hard on him.'

Heat suffused her face, and she pulled her laptop over to try to focus on what they were there for.

What she was here for. No other reason.

'I managed to log in, but the connection dropped out like it usually does,' Nell said firmly. 'It wasn't the Wi-Fi here because I cleared my email first.'

'Boot it up then, and I'll take a quick look while we wait for the waitress to come back. But have a look at the menu first.'

'I know what I want. Fish and chips will be fine for me,' she said as the laptop started up with a whir. 'This is how I get into the network when I'm off-site.' She half-turned the laptop so Nat could see it and craned her neck so she could point to the screen and see what she was doing.

'It's hard to see the screen with the laptop at that angle. Do you mind if I come around to your side of the table and have a look?' Nat asked.

'No, of course not.' She knew her voice was a little hesitant, but she appreciated his consideration and moved her chair further to the left. Nat stood and brought his chair around next to hers, and she moved away a little bit further.

Calm down. He's a good guy. Nell repeated that over and over as Nat's knee brushed against her bare leg. It was all she could do not to get up and run.

But she soon found she needn't have worried as Nat was totally focused on the screen in front of them. After a few minutes, he seemed to forget that she was even sitting next to him. Nell leaned back in her chair and let her gaze run over him as he clicked

PENTECOST ISLAND 1-3

keys and looked at her screen. A waft of something fresh and citrusy drifted over to her. His chinos and shirt were perfectly pressed, and she wondered if he'd ironed them before he'd come down.

Nell looked down at her wrinkled shirt and shorts and knew she needed to make more of an effort from now on. Nothing to do with Nat, but it was time to stop this silly obsession with drab clothes and bland colours. Spilling her story to him had been a wake-up call, and she felt like she'd woken from a long sleep. From now on things would be different; it was time to get herself out of the introverted state she'd been in for way too long.

Nell nodded as she made her decision, but embarrassment flooded through her. She lifted her head and was surprised to find Nat looking at her intently.

Chapter 10

'Was I talking to myself?' Nell asked.

'Um. No? Were you?' He frowned. 'But I think I've found your problem.'

'Already?'

'Well, one of the problems anyway. Some of the codes in the back end need work. But it looks like the main problem is your physical set-up. I'll have to come out to your resort.' Nat closed the laptop and Nell relaxed as he moved his chair around to his side of the table. 'I thought I'd have to look at your set-up. This was a long shot at trying something to trick it into letting me stay logged in,' he said as he reached for the carafe of water on the table.

'I thought you might.' Nell bit her lip as she thought of the bar opening that was getting closer by the day. 'I hate to ask you this after all that's happened to your house, but do you think there's any chance you could come out tomorrow?'

'Maybe. I'll have to make some calls. How do you get there? Do you have a boat service to the island for your guests?'

Nell shook her head. 'We're not open yet, but I know Pippa is looking into that. One of her friends has a charter business that takes passengers to the outlying islands. Apparently, there used to be more resorts on other islands, but there's not many left now. I have to meet Jiminy at the marina at noon.'

'Jiminy?' Nat's eyes lit up. 'That's an unusual name. It has to be my mate from Hamo.'

'You know him?'

'Yeah, he's a little bit older than me. I spent a lot of time up

PENTECOST ISLAND 1-3

at my grandparents' place in my teens.' He chuckled. 'Mum was working full-time, and she didn't trust me at home alone. I was a bit of a wild one in those days, so I got packed off to the islands to be babysat. It was great. I had more freedom with my grandparents than I'd ever had. But I stayed out of trouble up here. There was so much to do.'

'Did you live in the house at Dingo Beach with them?'

'I did. I met Jiminy when I was learning to sail. He lived at Dingo in those days, too, and he had an old sailing boat that I helped him do up. We'd sail and camp on the islands. I know Pentecost. We used to go rock climbing there.'

'Sounds like you had a great time.'

'I did. It was really hard to go back to the city at the end of the school holidays. Then I didn't come up much when I started uni, and then both my grandparents passed before I finished my degree.' He looked at her with a sad smile. 'As you know, I spent some time down at the Goldie, but it was way too hectic for me. I packed up and started my own business up here when I inherited the house.'

'And it's going okay?'

'I'm slowly building it up. I've picked up quite a bit of business on Hamo, and the word is spreading.' He shook his head. 'The damage from that storm is going to set me back a bit though.'

'Well, I appreciate your expertise. And I'm pleased you can come out to have a look. I'm at my wit's end. I really need it fixed. I don't want to let Pippa down.'

'Okay, I don't think there will be too much of a problem. If you can give me a couple of hours in the morning to sort out my house and my insurance and get some stuff happening there, I'll grab the eleven o'clock ferry with you and come out.'

'Do you have any idea how long it will take to fix?'

'I won't know until I look at your network. It could be a couple of hours, or it could mean reloading all of your network software, looking at your Wi-Fi and then it could take another couple of days.'

'Oh.' Disappointment shot through Nell.

'If it does take longer, is there anywhere there I can stay overnight on the island?'

'I'm sure we can find room for you. We've got another new staff member coming out with Jiminy tomorrow, but there's a stack of rooms spare in the house. We're still modifying it, but the staff are going to live at the back when the guests arrive.'

'How many staff are there?' Nat paused and looked up at the waitress as she came back to take their order. 'Two of the house fish and chips, and some bread please. Is that okay, Nell?'

'That's fine. Well, it started with Pippa and Tamsin—Tam is a chef now—and me, of course. We have Evie who looks after the landscaping, and Eliza who is doing the smaller carpentry work when we don't have builders in. She's gone back to Europe for a while but she's hoping to get back before we open.'

Nat raised his eyebrows. 'All women?'

'Well, there's Eliza's . . . friend . . . Phillipe. I think he's coming back, and Pippa was talking about employing him to run the guests over from Hamo and the mainland. He's a very experienced sailor. Oh, and Rafe lives on the island, but he has his own place. He's Pippa's partner.'

'Partner in business or partner in life?'

'In life.' Nell knew she sounded wistful. Would she ever get over this stupid fear of the opposite sex and find a life partner? 'Rafe is Jack Smith, the author. He was living on the island when we arrived.'

'Wow, *the* Jack Smith, the English author?'

'That's him.'

'Sounds like you have an interesting community over there.'

***

Nell's face softened as she looked back at him. He reached across the table and took her hand in his. For a moment his fingers held hers lightly, until she tensed and pulled away from him.

'I'm sorry,' he said. 'I just wanted to say thank you for choosing me for the job. I appreciate the work. And I'm looking forward to seeing what's been done over there.'

'As far as I know you're the only network specialist in the area,' she said.

For a moment Nell's grin was almost cheeky and it reminded Nat of the vibrant woman he had known at university. Seeing how that guy who had assaulted her had taken the life and joy from her personality was hard. If only he'd walked down to the bar with her that night, her life would have been very different.

Nat held her gaze for a while and then he grinned back. 'No, there's a couple up at Bowen and a few in Townsville. But you've picked the best one, Nellie.'

'Such confidence,' she said. 'You haven't changed a bit, Nathaniel Dwyer.'

Nat considered reaching out and taking her hand again, but he hesitated. 'Nell? Can I talk to you some more about what you told me in the car?'

She bit her lip as she stared back at him and nodded slowly. 'What do you want to talk about?' Her tone was defensive, and he was sorry that he'd said anything.

'If there's any way I can help you overcome this. . . this shyness . . . I'd love to help you work through it. You said you didn't go to counselling. How did you cope?'

'I changed my life. I didn't go anywhere except to lectures and I didn't go to any at night. I skipped the night lectures. I took a couple of lessons in self-defence but when the guy asked me why I had decided to do it, I stopped going. I didn't want to talk to anyone. I guess I was so embarrassed about what had happened, I didn't want anyone to know. I blamed myself, and I always felt guilty. I hid behind a confident and mean personality, for quite a while. And that's what you saw that day you came to my office.'

'I can still see the real Nell, you know.'

Her eyes filled with tears as she looked back at him. 'Sometimes I can still feel the old me in there, and then the doubts creep in again.'

Nat put his hands on the side of the chair and gripped it. All he wanted to do was reach out to her.

'I'm a classic case,' she said, bitterness lacing her voice. 'And since all this "me too movement" stuff has been on the news, it's brought it back even more. I did lots of reading back then and I knew the stuff I was doing was a reaction —and still is ten years later.'

'Would it help you to talk about it? You said you never told anyone?'

She nodded. 'Not one person. Not even Pippa and Tam. Oh, don't get me wrong, they knew something was wrong, and they tried, but I didn't spill a word. And you know the best thing?'

Nat swallowed as the first tear spilled onto her cheek. 'What was that?' he asked softly.

'Despite me turning into an utter non-communicative bitch who wouldn't go out with them, they stayed friends with me. Even after Tam moved to the Gold Coast when Pippa and I were at uni, she would ring me two or three times a week, just to talk.'

'I remember what great friends you were.'

'And we still are. They stayed with me through thick and thin, even though they didn't know what was wrong.'

'I'm sure you were a good friend back to them too. It's in your nature, Nell.'

She dug out a tissue and wiped her eyes. 'Sorry. Yes, we've all had our ups and downs, and we were both there for Pippa when she went through a hard time. I guess what I learned from it is that others can carry stuff inside and put on a brave face to the world.

PENTECOST ISLAND 1-3

Pip was a master at that and then she'd crash and burn. But she's okay now. Her aunt leaving her the island has been amazing for her. For all of us actually. We have a pretty good life.'

'I'm looking forward to seeing it.' Nat said as he wondered whether to let go or push it as Nell had opened up to him.

'Did I ever tell you my Mum was a psychologist?'

Nell shook her head.

'She still has her practice in Brisbane. When I was a kid, I couldn't get away with much. Mum always seemed to know when I'd done the wrong thing. She used to tell me it was written all over my face.' He clenched his fist beside his thighs. 'But Nell, she taught me a lot, and one of the big lessons was about facing your fears. I guess I'd be right in saying that you've never done that?'

'You'd be right.' Her voice was soft. 'I've avoided men, and over the years I've adapted the way I do things to stay safe, rather than facing my fears. Or talking about them.'

'Would you let me help you? I mean, I really appreciate that you trusted me enough to tell me what happened back then.'

She took a deep breath and her shoulders relaxed. Slowly, tentatively her hand reached across the table. Nat lifted his hands onto the table and waited patiently, as Nell's hand crept onto his.

'Would you really do that?' she whispered.

'Yes. Don't you think it's time you re-joined the world?'

She cast her eyes down, and he was worried he'd gone too far. The last thing he wanted to do was push Nell away. Finally, Nell looked up at him and her eyes were bright with hope.

'It's way past time.'

Her hand was still in his when the waitress brought their meals to the table.

Chapter 11

Nell woke the next morning to the sound of a trolley being dragged along the path beneath the apartments. At the same time, a boat motor started up, and a couple of seagulls swooped past the bedroom window, their squawks raucous. She lay on her back and put a hand over her eyes. It was a change to wake up to all this noise; she had become used to living over on Pentecost Island, where the only noise in the morning was usually Tam banging about in the kitchen or Evie heading out to the garden. Occasionally, Evie started the mower early, but she soon learned that Nell liked to sleep in after working late into the night.

Talking to Nat last night had made her think of the friendships she had. Pippa and Tamsin were always there for her, even when she refused to ask for help. The opportunity that Pippa had given them to be a part of her venture on Pentecost Island was one Nell would always be grateful for.

But she couldn't hide there forever. Maybe a couple of years until Pip got the place up and running, and then it would be time to go back to the real world and build up a career.

It would be hard to leave. Nell loved living on the island, but she realised she was cocooned in a false sense of safety. Once the guests started to arrive, she was going to have to get used to having other people around, and it was time for her to change her behaviour.

Warmth settled in her chest as she thought back to last night and Nat's offer to help her adjust. Spilling her story to him seemed to have shifted something inside her and she felt lighter today than she had for a long time.

It was time to make changes in her life. In fact, it was way

PENTECOST ISLAND 1-3

past time to pull up her big girl panties. She rolled her eyes at the analogy— maybe not a good one – but it was time to put things into perspective and learn to cope with being a little bit more normal. She wondered if Nat realised what a huge thing it had been for her to put her hand in his last night.

But once it was there, she had been able to leave it there. It had felt good.

And right.

It wasn't as though Nat was the sort of person who would take advantage of her. She knew that, so there had been no fear.

Despite his reputation on campus at university as a "love 'em and leave 'em" ladies' man, he had always been polite and a perfect gentleman to her.

Today, when they met, she was going to try to be a tiny bit normal again. Maybe put her hand on his again. Maybe touch his shoulder, or maybe greet him like normal people greeted each other instead of crawling back into her shell. That imaginary shell that had kept her safe for a long time. No one was going to hurt her in broad daylight, least of all a man she had known and trusted before that awful night.

Her breath hitched in her throat as she thought of the effort it would be to do that.

One day at a time, Nell. One day at a time.

She jumped out of bed with new energy in her step and made herself a cup of coffee before wandering out onto the veranda to watch the marina wake up for the day.

The early ferry's horn blared as it came into the marina, and the passengers disembarked. A group of people chattering in a dozen different languages walked along below the apartments, looking tanned and happy and carefree. They'd obviously been out on the islands relaxing and having a good time.

That's how Nell wanted to be—well, maybe not the tan, she didn't have the skin for that—but to have that lightness and happiness that exuded from those people walking past.

There was no reason why she couldn't do it. But could she really accept Nat's offer to help her?

What would that sort of help look like? What would she have to do?

With a frown she looked across the park that was to the town side of the apartments, as she pondered his offer. She'd leave it for later; there was a beautiful morning out there to enjoy.

Two rows of brightly coloured tents lined the foreshore. She'd heard there were markets on at Airlie Beach a couple of times a week. Quickly finishing her coffee, she headed for the shower.

Fifteen minutes later, Nell was wandering through the markets, looking at the stalls. The tents edged the sand, and the gentle whoosh of the small waves was overlaid by the happy chatter of the early crowd. A stall filled with exotic vegetables and herbs beckoned—Tam would love it—and by the time Nell had completed her purchase, she was carrying three large bags.

The next stall sold handmade baskets and she quickly added a basket to her purchases, transferring the produce into the woven basket.

'Planning on lots of cooking, love?' the man asked, and she smiled back.

'Not me.'

Stalls loaded with hats, sunglasses, and an array of clothes lined the foreshore. Nell was tempted by the fragrant aroma coming from the food stalls and wandered over. She bought an egg and bacon roll at one and stood there watching a sand artist create a dragon in the sand.

Her problems with the network, and her worry about the changes she was going to try to make in her life dissolved in the early morning warmth. She chuckled as the artist lit a small fire in a round metal receptacle and put it inside the dragon's mouth.

When she'd finished her breakfast roll, she pulled out her phone and glanced at the time. She had an hour before she was due to meet Nat at the ferry terminal. Two unread messages sat in her inbox, and she realised they must have come in last night when they were at dinner and she had turned her phone to silent.

One from Pippa: **Forgot to tell you. The new girl is Gina. She will meet you at Hamo at noon at Jiminy's boat.**

Nell quickly texted back. **Okay. All good. See you this afternoon.**

The other text was from Tam, and Nell smiled

If you get to the markets on your way back, I would love a new dress. Something stunning to wear to our opening. You should get one too Nell.

Her fingers flew over the keys. **OK, on it. What colour?**

Yellow, with a smiley face and a love heart, was the instant reply.

Nell put her basket over her arm and hurried across to the dress stall she had noticed on the way in.

There was a huge selection of styles and colours filling the tent; her attention settled on a bright red and yellow dress that she knew Tam would love. A sweetheart neckline and cinched in at the waist, it was the epitome of the vintage fifties style that Tam loved and carried off so well. Nell pointed to it, and the woman behind the table lifted it down.

Nell looked at the label and the price and nodded to the woman. It was Tam's size and she pulled out her purse. 'I'll take it, please.'

'I think it will be a little bit big for you, love,' the woman said. 'It's a fourteen, and you look like an eight to me. Do you want to try it on?'

'Oh no, it's not for me. It's for a friend. It's her size.'

ANNIE SEATON

'Can I tempt you with something for you?' The woman was obviously a good salesperson. She pointed to a short floral dress hanging on the back wall. 'With your fair skin and your pretty hair, that dark green would look fabulous.'

Nell took a step back and looked at the dress hanging up. 'I don't wear dresses often,' she said hesitantly. 'And especially not that short.'

The last time she'd worn a dress was when Pippa and Tam had made her dress up on Hamo on their way to the island for the first time, and the barman in the Italian restaurant had tried to flirt with her. That had sent her spiralling down for days, but she'd never told them that. Pippa hadn't noticed because she had only had eyes for Rafe that night—it was the first time she had seen him— and Tam had been too busy checking out the menu. It wasn't their fault, and she knew they had only been teasing that night. Tam and Pippa would never do anything to hurt her deliberately.

'What do you think, love?' The woman's voice interrupted her musing, and Nell jumped.

'Come on, there's a change area over here at the back of my tent.'

Nell put the basket down on the grass, took the dress that the woman held out, and slipped behind the makeshift change room. She stepped out of her shorts and T-shirt and slipped the silky dress over her head. The fabric was cool and silky against her skin, cooler than shorts and a cotton T-shirt that had hugged her limbs in the early morning tropical heat.

'Got it on yet?'

Nell stepped slowly out from behind the curtain, and the woman put her hands on her hips and nodded. 'I'm not just saying it because I want a sale. That dress was made for you. It's stunning.'

Nell chuckled. 'You're a very good saleswoman. But I do

love it. It feels great.'

'And, sweetie, it looks fabulous. It's only twenty bucks and I've got it in other colours too.

Something shifted inside Nell and she looked around the tent at the different coloured dresses blowing in the light breeze.

'Yes,' she said slowly. 'I'll take this green one and the red one, the blue one, and what do you think about the white one?'

'Hon, with your colour, I'd avoid the white; how about the black? A girl can always do with a little black dress.'

'You're right, and I know exactly the occasion for it.'

The woman was full of questions, and Nell told her about the resort and the opening that was coming up.

'Sounds great. I'll have to get my hubby to bring me out there. We live on our boat. It sounds right up our alley.' She tapped her finger on her chin as she looked down at Nell's joggers. 'You know, I've got a lovely pair of sandals that will match that green dress.'

By the time Nell had paid for the dresses and three pairs of sandals and had been talked into keeping the dress and sandals on, the market was getting crowded. She glanced at her watch and gasped, hurrying along the path that led back to the apartments. The black and brown wooden necklace that the woman had placed around her neck as a thank you for her large purchase moved against her bare skin as she almost ran back to the building. Her shorts, T-shirt, and joggers were in a bag on top of the new clothes and the veggies. By the time she stepped into the lift, Nell's hand was chafed from holding the handle of the now heavy basket. She hurried into the apartment, used the bathroom and glanced in the mirror as she washed her face and hands. A stranger with flushed cheeks, and wearing a green dress looked back at her.

Hmm. Different. But okay.

There was no time to change, so she grabbed her laptop and bag, juggling them with the basket that now seemed heavier than ever. She left the security card on the kitchen counter, did a final check that she hadn't left anything and pulled the door shut behind her. Luckily, it was only a hundred meters across to the ferry terminal, and she made it with minutes to spare.

Chapter 12

'It's important that you understand what actions she's taken to protect herself and understand how she feels about that. You will have to be very careful, love. You're not a professional.'

'No, but I am a friend. But, thanks, Mum. I knew you'd be able to give me some advice.' Nat tucked his phone between his shoulder and his ear. He pulled his wallet out to pay for his ticket to Hamilton Island while keeping an eye out for Nell at the entrance to the terminal. It was close to ten-thirty, and the building was milling with tourists, backpackers and workers heading to the island for the midday shifts.

'I know you'll go carefully, darling, but you said it's been ten years. If it's taken her so long to talk about it to anyone, as she told you, there will be long-term effects, and you'll have to go very gently if you're to help her. Tell her to make an appointment if you think she'd come and see me. Some professional help wouldn't hurt. Have I met her? Was she ever a girlfriend?'

'No, Mum. Just a uni friend.' Nat chuckled. 'Did you forget I've moved? I'm back up in the islands.' Nat shook his head as he smiled to himself. His mother was very good at what she did, but she could be vague at times.

'Sorry, and yes, of course, I do know you moved. It just slipped my mind for a moment. I hate you being so far away, I'll have to come and visit. Well, if your friend is ever down this way, I'm here, or I can give you the name of a good psychologist in Mackay.'

'Okay, if that's needed. I'll call.'

'And like I suggested, the most effective treatment, if there are any risk avoidance behaviours, is probably systematic desensitisation. I'll email you some links.'

'Thank, Mum. I've got to go. Love you.'

'Love you too, Nat. You're a good boy.'

Nat chuckled. 'I'm almost thirty-one, Mum.'

'You're still my boy, and you always will be. Check your email.'

'Yes, Mum.' Nat disconnected the call and slipped the phone into his shirt pocket before he paid for his ferry ticket. There was still fifteen minutes before he was due to meet Nell; he checked around, but there was still no sign of her. He found two vacant seats together, put the carton of networking equipment on the floor, sat down and opened his laptop. He smiled as Outlook dinged with an email from his mother. Vague but reliable.

There were confirmation emails from the insurance assessor and one from the car service place with a quote for fixing his car.

Nat groaned. Maybe he'd be better off buying another car. He sent a quick email back, asking them to wait a couple of days, and he'd been in touch.

The calls Nat had made this morning had achieved what he'd been after. He'd organised for an insurance assessor to come out to the house on Friday and transferred a couple of his non-urgent jobs at Hamo to later in the week. He was free now to give Nell two or three days on their island if the problem was what he thought it was going to be.

First up this morning, he'd called his mate, Brian, at the computer store at Cannonvale.

'I need some gear, mate, and I don't have transport.' Nat listed what he needed. 'I'm over at Port of Airlie and heading out to Hamo. Sorry for the short notice. Add twenty bucks to my bill and put it in a taxi for me.'

'No prob. I'm on it now. I've got all that in stock. Is that all you need?'

Nat frowned. 'I'm not sure what the Wi-Fi is like out there, so throw in some ethernet cable and connectors, too. Thanks, Brian. Appreciate it.'

Brian had put the equipment Nat had ordered in a taxi and sent it to reception at the apartment, and now Nat was pretty much prepared for any problem he might encounter in Nell's network.

He clicked on his mother's email; in the subject line, he read Physiological and Psychological Desensitisation. He was pleased to see the article was written in layman's terms rather than the scientific language Mum mostly talked in, and he focused on the content for five minutes before thoughtfully closing the laptop.

Without knowing what he was doing or what it was called, he had actually carried out what the article was talking about with Nell last night when he'd touched her hand.

And she'd responded.

Who needed a psychology degree? Most of it was common sense. Nat grinned wryly; there was no way he'd ever say that in front of his mother.

He glanced at his watch and stood, picking up the box and his bag before he made his way over to the entrance to the ferry terminal to see if Nell was on her way across. He hadn't known whether to buy a ticket for her; she might have a season ticket with the ferry line. If she was much later, they'd miss the ferry and be late for Jiminy.

A woman in a green dress juggling a basket passed him at the door. He went to step outside and look across to the apartments to see if there was any sign of Nell when a familiar voice called him.

'Nat!' Nell's voice held amusement. 'I'm here.'

He stopped and turned slowly, and his heart lifted a couple of beats as he looked down at Nell's smiling face.

Nell in a green dress. He had walked straight past her.

Nat stumbled over his words, feeling like a gawky adolescent. 'Oh, um. Sorry, Nell. I . . . didn't see you. I was looking for someone in shorts.'

Not a gorgeous woman in a short dress displaying legs that went forever. Jesus. How could a change of clothes make someone look so different?

Drop dead gorgeous. She took his breath away.

He dropped the carton to the floor and sat his laptop on top of it. 'Here, let me take some of that off you. Have you got a ticket yet? I didn't know whether to get you one or not.'

'No. I haven't. If you can keep an eye on my stuff, I'll go and get one now.'

'Sure.' He held his hand out for her basket, and she put her laptop and bag on top of him.

'I won't be long,' Nell said.

Nat tried not to look after her as Nell hurried across to the counter, but he couldn't help himself. He was finding it hard to reconcile this woman with the one he'd had dinner with last night. Not only was she dressed differently, but her hair was different too. Last night, she'd worn it scraped back. Today, her hair was loose, falling around her face in soft waves.

Bloody hell. His heart was still pounding. Nat had spent a lot of time with women over the past ten years; he enjoyed their company, and he had several close female friends. He'd even had a couple of relationships that had fizzled out when he hadn't been prepared to commit on a more permanent basis, but he had remained friends with Josie and Ellen.

'It's okay, I'm not heartbroken,' Ellen had said on their last date. 'You'll meet the right partner one day, Nathaniel. And when you fall, you'll fall big time.'

He hadn't fallen as Ellen had predicted. And never in all that time had one woman brought him to this state. He shook his head, trying to figure out what it was that had reduced him to a quivering mess. His heart was still thudding, he was hot, and his legs felt shaky.

What the hell was wrong with him? Maybe he had food poisoning?

He took a deep shuddering breath and straightened when Nell walked back over to him, holding her ticket in her hand.

It was just because she looked so different; that's all it was. Nothing more than that; he'd got a surprise when he'd seen her. That's all.

But as he watched her walk over, his breath caught, and a warm feeling settled low in his belly.

And it had nothing to do with the fish he'd eaten last night or the one wine he'd had with dinner.

He was in trouble here.

And in trouble with a woman who was just learning to trust him.

A woman he couldn't afford to hurt.

***

Nell was standing beside Nat on the back deck of the island ferry. A stiff breeze blew from the southeast, and small waves with white foam curling on their tops dotted the Passage across to Hamilton Island as they left the bay. She had decided to stand out on the back deck rather than sitting with most of the passengers in the enclosed air-conditioned cabin; the diesel fumes seemed to filter into the sealed doors. They passed half a dozen yachts with their sales billowing, taking advantage of the strong breeze. A red thundercat roared past, and Nell caught a glimpse of excited faces as the boat sped past. One day when she was comfortable in her own skin again, she'd love to do that. Take a day off with Tam and Pippa and have some fun instead of working twenty-four-seven.

Guilt trickled through her. How could she think that when she lived on one of the islands? She was so lucky—they were all lucky—that Pippa had asked them to join her up here. She could still be working in an office at the Gold Coast.

Nat had seemed preoccupied, and she had stayed quiet for the first part of the trip. After all, it was business, and he wouldn't expect conversation. After a while, the silence became a bit uncomfortable and she decided to chat to him.

'It's good outside. Fresh air,' she said leaning over to Nat so he could hear her words over the roar of the diesel motors. 'That smell makes me feel ill sometimes, especially when it's a bit bumpy like today. I'd much rather be out here. Are you happy to be outside too?'

'Yeah. There's a much nicer view out here,' Nat said. 'I can't believe that passengers sit in there watching the scenery on the television when they could be out here seeing the real thing.'

'It's bit windy out here though,' Nell said, but Nat shook his head and pointed to his ear.

'I can't hear you,' he yelled.

'It's a bit windy out here, I said,' she yelled back, leaning over closer to him. As she moved, Nat had the same idea, and their cheeks brushed against each other.

Nell froze as the warmth of his skin burned against her face. She jumped back, her blush heating her face even more.

Her face burned with embarrassment when the wind caught her dress and lifted it, showing off her black lacy knickers. If there was one thing she had indulged in over the past few years, it was pretty underwear beneath the plain shorts and tees. No one ever saw it and it made her feel a little bit pretty beneath the drab shorts and tees. Nell grabbed at the hem and pressed the fabric against her thighs as she walked across to the railing and leaned against it.

Used to her usual shorts, she'd forgotten what the wind could do to a dress. But to Nat's credit he looked away, but Nell could see the sides of his lips tilting up as he tried not to smile.

She pulled a face at him and pointed to the door and called out. 'Maybe we should go inside? That wind is getting stronger.'

PENTECOST ISLAND 1-3

'If you want to.' This time his grin was wide. 'Like I said I'm quite enjoying the view out here.'

Her face stayed hot as he grinned at her, and finally she smiled back.

'How about a cold drink or a coffee inside?' Nat walked across to the edge of the deck and stood beside her again.

Nell nodded and pressed her hands to her thighs as they made their way inside. They'd stowed their laptops, her basket and Nat's carton of networking equipment in the luggage bay behind the seats. She glanced over as they went into the cabin to make sure everything was still there.

All good. The basket of vegetables was still on top where she'd left it.

They sat quietly as they drank the coffee that Nat had collected at the bar. The only sound was the low hum of the motors and the quiet conversations of the other passengers.

Nell looked through the salt-stained windows, lost in her own thoughts as they ploughed through the waves on the way to Hamilton Island. It was strange; she was feeling so different today. She'd woken up in a calm and relaxed mood—for a change—and then the saleswoman at the markets had made her feel good when she'd told her how lovely the dress looked.

She allowed herself a sideways glance at Nat, but he was staring ahead, a frown wrinkling his brow.

She hadn't missed his reaction when he'd spotted her in the terminal, and as much as she hated to admit it, she had taken some feminine pleasure from the admiration that had been in his eyes. Maybe that was one step towards healing; she hadn't felt that way for a long time.

But it was probably because it was Nat. She trusted him.

She doubted she would have felt like that if it had been another man.

The trip was quick and within an hour the ferry turned into

the quiet waters at the marina at Hamilton Island.

'Right to go?' There was an intense look on his face as he held out his hand to help her up from the low seat. Nell hesitated and reached out and when she took his hand, his smile was sweet. She had forgotten what a good looking guy he was.

His fingers were firm and cool, and he kept hold of her hand as she stood beside him. A sudden lightness filled her as the tension left her body.

'Nell?'

'Yes?'

'I'd like to take some time with you after I have a look at the network. It's not the right time to talk now, we'll be meeting Jiminy and your new staff member soon. Can we set aside some time tonight to have a talk? I think . . . I'd like to think . . . I can maybe help you. If that's okay with you, that is.'

Nell looked down at their fingers and exhaled quietly. She nodded as she looked back up and saw the worry in his eyes. 'Yes, Nat. We can talk. God knows, I've avoided asking for help for a long time.'

He squeezed her hand. 'As long as you know you can trust me. I'd never do anything to hurry you, or make you feel uncomfortable.'

'I know that.'

He dropped her hand and nodded. 'Come on then. We'll get our stuff and go find Jiminy.'

'Better not be late. It's good of him to take us over and save Pippa a trip.'

Chapter 13

'Hey, Jim Boy!' Nat picked up his pace for the last few metres of the wharf. Nell strode along beside him. Jiminy's launch was in the same place as last time and he was at the front of the boat talking to someone on the wharf.

He looked up and waved back. 'Hey, Nat! What are you doing here? I thought you were a landlubber these days.' Nat reached the boat and Jiminy leaned over and shook his free hand 'Hi, Nell. How did you get hooked up with my old mate here? You watch him.'

'I knew Nat in Brisbane.' She flicked a glance at Nat. 'A lifetime ago. He's coming out with us to do some computer work at the resort.'

'Great. We can catch up on the way out. Have you met Gina yet?' Jiminy addressed his question to Nell. She shook her head and turned to the woman who was standing a little way away from the bow.

Nell put down her basket and held out her hand as she looked up at one of the tallest women she had ever seen. 'Hi, Gina. I'm Nell. I work out at Pentecost too, and this is Nat.'

'Gina Gagne. So please call me GG.' Her hand was taken and pumped vigorously. Gina—call me GG— was as strong as she was tall, but it was the unusual accent that surprised Nell the most.

'*Bonjour*. I am so excited about coming to your island. Tam has told me all about it, and it sounds amazing.' She turned to Nat and held out her hand, her smile widened. Her other hand went to her hip and she struck a "come hither" pose.

Nell smiled, and tried to push back the little niggle of something that lodged in her chest. Not jealousy.

No.

'*Bonjour*. My, my, aren't you a fine specimen? I'm very pleased to hear you are another worker on the island. For a moment there, I thought you were a couple.' She wiggled her eyebrows and Nell smothered a giggle.

Nat's face coloured as his hand was gripped and pumped by this larger-than-life woman. Tam was going to love her style; her shorts set was vintage, and her hair was wound into a fifties beehive style on top of her head. Gina's expression was bright and full of interest.

What a fantastic asset she would be to their team. Nell could already see her behind the bar talking to customers in that husky voice.

'Um,' Nat said. 'Well, Nell and I—'

Nell surprised herself as she slid her arm through Nat's interrupting him. 'Nat and I are very good friends. I'm so happy he's coming out to the island too. It's good to meet you, Gina. Tell me where are you from? I can't place that accent?'

'Come on board, guys, and we'll get going.' Jiminy interrupted before Gina answered.

Nat looked down at her arm through his, and Nell slowly pulled it away.

How did I do that? she wondered. *More to the point why did I do that?*

Nat met her gaze and she shrugged and smiled.

Gina followed Nat and Nell onto Jiminy's boat. A strong white-musk perfume wafted across to them and Nell smothered her smile when Nat frowned and turned away wrinkling his nose.

'Sorry,' he mouthed when he realised she'd seen him pull a face. He headed over to the helm to Jiminy, as if to escape the women—or one woman, Nell thought. It was the first time she'd ever seen Nat intimidated by a member of the opposite sex.

She followed Gina to the front of the boat, and they settled

PENTECOST ISLAND 1-3

themselves in the shade underneath the canvas cover as Nat stood beside Jiminy at the helm.

'So where are you from?' Nell repeated.

'I might look and sound French, but I'm from the good ole US of A,' Gina said as she lifted the straw hat she'd been holding and fanned herself. 'South Louisiana, so I'm used to this damn hot moisture.'

'Tam said you're going to be helping out in the bar.' Nell leaned back against the soft burgundy cushions as Jiminy fired up the engines. She looked across and her face heated when she encountered Nat's steady gaze on her.

'That I am, sweetie, and when it gets busy, I'll do some shifts in the kitchen too. I'm so looking forward to seeing your little ole island. I've heard good things about it.'

'You have? We haven't even officially opened yet.'

'No, I know, but there's a buzz about the resort and bar around the islands. You've had a few drop-ins and they're spreading the word fast. Mighty fast. I was talking to different groups in the bar at the Reef Resort and they said it's a must visit.'

'Pippa will be pleased to hear that,' Nell said quietly. She was a little bit in awe of this woman.

'So, tell me all about you, darlin'. Where do you fit in?'

'I look after the business side of things.' Nell reached down and held her dress flat as the boat backed out of the berth.

'And Mr Gorgeous over there? How long has he been on the scene? I saw the way he looked at you, sweetie, so don't worry, I won't muscle in.'

Nell opened her mouth to deny what Gina had incorrectly assumed, but for some reason she hesitated. She waved a hand. 'Oh, Nat and I go back a long way. We were at uni together.'

'Well, you hang onto him, precious. He's a keeper, I can see his aura. Gorgeous gold. Once I get settled, I'll get my cards out and we'll have a reading.'

His aura?

'A reading,' Nell repeated in a weak voice. Who the heck was this woman? Nell began to doubt her first impression. She wasn't too sure how Gina was going to fit in on the island after all. Pippa's reaction was going to be very interesting.

'Yeah, look we could have a quick one now.' Gina delved into her hot pink handbag. 'How long does it take to get to this island?'

'Oh, not long. We won't have time,' Nell said hastily. She pointed as Jiminy took the boat around the eastern shore of Hamilton Island. 'Look, see that peak sticking out of the water over there. That's our island.'

'Well, how damn spectacular is that! I sure am looking forward to living on an island. Have you been away long?'

'No. Only one day. What about you? When did you arrive?' Nell asked.

'A couple of weeks ago, but I haven't been out there yet. I've been really hoping to get a job out there. It was all organised by phone. Tam knows I'm a good worker, but your boss wanted to talk to my bosses down at Surfers Paradise. It's a while since I worked with Tam. I couldn't believe it when she left the restaurant to go and work in a shopping centre. A jewellery store of all things! She should have been wearing jewels, not selling them. There was something strange back then. She decided to pack up and leave at the end of a shift. Didn't even say goodbye. Next I hear she has moved up here! Did you know her before you came to the island? She was one of the best chefs I've ever worked with, and believe me, *bébé*, I've worked with a few.'

Nell was tired of listening to Gina talk. She obviously didn't expect an answer to the questions she was firing as she spoke, because she barely drew breath before she started again.

'Yep, I've worked bars from New York to Paris, and now I can add Pentecost Island to my list. I didn't know what you had there, so I've bought a whole case of all my cocktail mixing gear. Jiminy nearly died when the boxes arrived at the wharf. Between you and me, sweet pea, I didn't think he was too fussed on taking me out there. Until you turned up, I thought he was going to change his mind, but he's good looking too, just like your man. I wonder if he's married. I checked his hand. Not a ring to be seen.'

Sweet pea! Nell had never been called sweet pea in her life.

She nodded, bemused by this Amazon chatterbox, and unable to get a word in. Relief filled her ten minutes later when Jiminy turned the launch into their bay. How were they going to put up with this constant talk? She was pleased she would be able to disappear into the office.

The translucent blue-green of their bay shone ahead and Nell let out a sigh of satisfaction. Glancing over at Nat she saw the amazed expression on his face. Everyone looked the same when they first came to the island; the vista was beautiful.

It was so good to be home. A lot had happened since she'd left. It seemed as though she'd been gone a week, not only early yesterday.

Pippa and Tam were standing on the wharf, and Nell caught Nat's eye and they shared a smile as Gina called a booming hello across the water.

Life at Pentecost Island was getting interesting.

Chapter 14

Pippa

'Holy hell, Tam, is that your friend?' I stared at the woman who stepped off Jiminy's boat.

Tam didn't hear me; she'd passed me and was hurrying along to the end of the jetty.

'GG,' she squealed. 'You're here!'

The reunion of my friend and her former co-worker reminded me of that scene from *Mamma Mia* where Meryl Steep caught up with her girl band friends. It was almost as cheesy. There was lots of yelling and dancing around, and hugs shared.

Gina Gagne was certainly a striking-looking woman. I shrugged as I walked along to the boat. Her references had been really good, and Tam had said she was an excellent worker. As long as she worked hard and fitted in with the rest of us, she'd do.

If she didn't, she would go. I was quite pleased with myself. I was starting to get a bit more business sense—mind you, it was Rafe who had all the good ideas—and I'd hired her on a two week trial.

Nell came off the boat carrying a basket full of produce and shopping bags. I was pleased to see that she looked less tense. My mouth dropped open as I noticed the guy standing behind her.

He looked like Nathaniel Dwyer, her friend from uni. I knew Nell had had a thing for him back then, but she hadn't mentioned Nat for a long time. Tam noticed him the same time I did, and her greeting confirmed what I'd thought.

'Hey, Nat Dwyer. What are you doing out here?'

I reached the boat as Nell answered. 'Would you believe Nat was the networking guy who was recommended to me? I

PENTECOST ISLAND 1-3

didn't know until I turned up on his door—at his business.'

There was a flurry of greetings and introductions, including a loud one from our newest staff member as she grabbed my hand.

'*Bonjour*, Pippa, thank you so much for giving me a chance. I promise you; I won't disappoint. I say *laissez les bons temps rouler.*'

I raised my eyebrows and switched my gaze to Tam who grinned back at me. I still had enough high school French to understand Gina.

Let the good times roll? As long as you're a good worker, I thought. I wasn't worried about good times yet.

'Yes,' I said rather tersely. 'We hope our guests certainly do have a good time out here. But we're all going to be busy before then.'

'I've gotta head, Pip. Another job on,' Jiminy called out when the various bags and boxes were offloaded. 'Sarah and I will be here for the bar opening next week. Do you want me to bring some passengers out?'

'Great. I'll look forward to seeing you both. Thanks for bringing my cargo over. I'll let you know about bringing guests out. That could be handy, thanks.'

The water swirled behind the boat as he started the motor and the launch cruised out of the bay.

Nat was loaded up with a couple of bags and a box, and I held my hand out. 'Hi Nat. It's good to see you. Let me carry one of the bags for you.'

'Thanks Pippa. You're looking good. The owner of a tropical island, I hear.'

'A long way from our uni days, isn't it?' I replied. 'So you're working up here now?'

'Yep. Business is building. I do a fair bit of work on Hamo and I'd heard about your resort. I didn't have a clue it was you guys until Nell came knocking on my door the other night.'

418

'Pip?' Nell tugged at my arm as I reached over and took one of Nat's bags. 'Nat might have to stay a night or two to get the network running properly. I said we'd be able to find a bed for him. That's okay, isn't it?'

'Sure. One thing we've got Nat is plenty of room. It might be a bit basic, but we've got lots of spare rooms in the house and the outbuildings. Come on, we'll show you around.'

'Thanks. I'm keen to get started.'

I wondered what was going on between Nat and Nell. She walked close to him and their heads were together as they walked across the beach.

Tam had taken the basket from Nell, and was walking ahead of them, chattering away to Gina, who was carrying a large box as well as a suitcase. She'd left another one on the jetty and I heard Nat offer to come back for it.

I walked across the sand behind them all and wondered how the dynamics were going to work.

We were growing fast. When Eliza and Phillipe returned— I'd an email overnight to say that they had sorted things much more quickly than they had expected to and would be back in time for the opening. I still hadn't replied to Eliza's email and would reply tonight when I got Nell to check the bookings. I hadn't been able to access anything since she'd left. I was pleased that Nat was here on site to get it fixed.

Eliza was bringing a friend back with them, and she asked if she could book one of the huts.

'No matter if she can't,' Eliza had written, 'she can stay over at Hamilton Island. I want you to meet Sienna. She's a qualified beautician and therapist and can give you some advice about starting up a spa when you're ready. I hope I'm not being too forward, but I know you'd talked about it. If not, she wants to come for a holiday anyway, so all's good.'

I had a lot to organise before our launch next week. For a

moment, I felt a bit overwhelmed and a flutter of panic stirred in my chest. I hurried to catch up to the others as we approached the house and I couldn't help my smile when Rafe stepped off the veranda to meet us.

***

Nell

Being back on the island and having Nat here where she lived and worked was strange for Nell, but he was keen to start work. His manner seemed a little distant now that they were on the island, and as they walked from the boat to the house his conversation had been all business.

'That's the bar over there, and that's the first of the huts.' Nell gestured down the path that led to that part of the resort. Evie's plants were blooming, and the path was edged with colour. A delectable aroma drifted from the house; Tam had obviously prepared a special lunch.

But Nat didn't appear to notice any of it. He was talking Wi Fi, and protocols and asking questions. Nat, the friend, has disappeared and been taken over by the networking guru Nell had gone looking for.

Well, I'd found one so I shouldn't be feeling this disappointment, she thought as Nat stopped and gestured to the house.

'The line of sight to the bar and the huts seems to be uncompromised in any way.'

Nell knew she was a bit snippy when she replied. 'That's worked out very well then because we didn't know to consider anything like that. We're certainly not experts as you'll soon discover, but we all do our best.'

'Oh, I wasn't being critical. Please don't think that.'

'That's fine then. I'll show you where the office is and leave you to it.'

'I'll need you there with me, Nell. If that's all right?' Nat frowned.

Rafe was waiting on the veranda and Nell stopped beside him. 'Nat, this is Rafe. He lives over on the other side of the hill.'

They shook hands, but Nat didn't stay to talk as she walked into the house. He was two steps behind her, and she hadn't expected him to follow right away. She wanted to get out of this stupid dress, put on her usual clothes and pull her hair back.

Nell turned around to apologise to Rafe, but Pippa had already reached him, and he had his arms around her.

'Hi, my lovely. I missed you,' he said.

Nell ignored it and opened the office door and stepped inside.

'Make yourself at home. I'm going to get changed and freshen up. I'll be back in ten minutes. If you want to log in, the admin name and password is taped to the top of the desk.

'Okay, I'll unpack my gear and get started.' Nat's voice was brisk and businesslike, and Nell felt as though they had gone back a few steps.

Where was the kind man who had listened to her last night?

Her thoughts must have been obvious because he put the box on the chair and came straight over to the door where Nell was standing. 'What's going on? Have I upset you somehow, Nell?

She shook her head. 'No. Why would you think that?'

'You're very businesslike all of a sudden.'

Ha, that was the pot calling the kettle black.

'Well, you're on the clock now, Nat. So, it's all business,' Nell said briskly.

'Fair enough, but the clock will go off at five o'clock and then we'll have that talk I mentioned. Are you still okay with that?'

She shrugged and stepped away. 'If you want.'

Before Nell could get away, Tam appeared in the hall. 'Hey guys, lunch is ready. I've set the big table on the side veranda. Come and eat while it's hot.'

PENTECOST ISLAND 1-3

'I'm fine, thanks. I'm here to work, not to socialise.' Nat's tone was polite.

A shimmer of guilt ran through Nell. She knew she was the cause of that.

'Don't be silly, Nat.' Pippa had appeared in time to hear his refusal. 'I insist. Rafe's looking forward to having a chat to you. I think he gets a bit overwhelmed with all the women here sometimes.'

'I certainly do.'

God, everyone was trying to cram into the office. Nell fought the eyeroll that threatened when Gina's husky voice added to the conversation.

'Yeah. Come on, Nat. I want to talk to you too.'

Chapter 15

Lunch was more a social occasion, rather than staff having a meal break together.

Because that's what we all are, thought Nell. It was strange having so many people here with them.

All staff. Well, apart from Rafe, who was Pippa's partner.

The staff now comprised a chef, an accountant, a gardener, a wait person, a computer contractor and a boss who did the PR. Evie was still outside; apparently, she was too busy to come in and join them.

Lucky her, thought Nell.

Nell sat there quietly pushing her curried chicken from one side of her plate to the other. In the end she picked up a pappadam and nibbled on that. Her appetite had gone.

'Aw, Nell, what happened to your pretty dress?' Gina had asked when they came out to the veranda. Nell saw Pippa and Tam exchange a glance, but she smiled amicably. 'I'm back at work now so I'm in uniform.'

The conversation was lively, and Gina's effervescent personality had the rest of them—most—in fits of snorting laughter as she recounted stories of some of her more "interesting" experiences around the world. Nell was horrified by some of her stories.

Gina had certainly had an "out there" career and she wasn't backward in talking about it. Nell sat there and thought she must be a prude.

Or maybe I'm just plain boring these days. Maybe she'd led a sheltered life, but the more she heard of Gina's exploits, the less comfortable she felt. Even Rafe and Nat were looking a bit discomforted as she kept talking.

'One night when I was working in New York, we had this cross-eyed customer, I mean, I knew he was cross-eyed, but—'

To Nell's surprise, Nat pushed his plate away and put up his hand. 'I'm sorry to be rude, everyone, but I have a lot of work to do. Thanks for asking me to lunch, Pippa. And Tam it was a great curry.' He turned to Nell. 'Will you come and help me log in and get started, please, Nell.'

Relief shot through Nell and she nodded. Nat held her chair steady when she stood. 'Thank you,' she said quietly.

It seemed to be the catalyst for everyone else to leave.

'I'll have to make a move too.' Rafe stood and nodded to Tam. 'Thanks for a great meal. I've got a book waiting for me at home.'

Gina chimed in. 'Oh, *daahling* Rafe. Do you like to read? I've always got my li'l ole nose stuck in a book.'

If you ever stopped talking long enough to do that, Nell thought uncharitably.

'Maybe I could come over and borrow one. I'd love to hear what you like to read,' Gina persisted. 'A man who wants to get home to read. How wonderful!'

Pippa stood and she didn't look at all impressed. 'You'll find a considerable amount of reading material in the living room, Gina. Come with me and I'll show you your room in the *staff* quarters.'

It was the first time Nell had heard Pippa talk about the house in that way, and she got the distinct impression that Gina was about to learn her place in the scheme of things. A shame that things were going to change, but she guessed it would be inevitable when the resort was open, and they had more staff here.

All the more reason to get the network up and running.

'Come on, Nat, I'll get you started.' She froze when his

warm hand settled gently against her back.

Her indrawn breath must have made Nat realise what he had done, and he quickly moved back, dropping his hand. No one else noticed as there was a lot of movement and talk around the table as Tam and Pippa cleared the plates.

Nell slipped quietly inside and headed for the office, not surprised to hear Nat walking close behind her through the living room.

She could hear the amusement in his voice as he pointed to the bookshelves. 'Pippa was right, you've got a lot of books here.' He crossed the room and stood there looking at the titles. 'A great collection and some classics there too.'

'Most of them belonged to Pip's aunt. The one who left her the house. We found them packed carefully in crates in the back shed. Do you like to read?'

'I do. When I have time. Does that surprise you?'

'No? Why should it?'

'I guess because we don't know each other very well. I'd like to remedy that though, Nell. I missed you at uni after we changed courses.'

'We'll see what happens.' She felt self-conscious when Nat said things like that. When they'd been off the island, it had been easier for some reason. Now she was back in familiar territory, she was extra sensitive. 'At the moment though, our priority is getting this system up and running.'

'It is, come on. Are you happy to sit with me for the first little while in case I have questions?'

Nell nodded. 'I might as well, there's nothing else I can do until you get it up and running.'

The desk holding the main computer wasn't very big and their chairs were close together. Once Nat managed to log in and keep the network up, he reached over and pointed to different things on the screen with each question.

PENTECOST ISLAND 1-3

'Is this the icon you use to see if the clients are attached to the network?'

Each time he did, his arm would brush against hers and his thigh pressed against her leg.

She nodded. 'Yes.'

'There's the first part of the problem,' he said.

Nell leaned forward, keen to see what he was looking at but reluctant to move any closer.

'Would it be easier for you if I stood?' he asked kindly.

She shook her head. 'No, that's silly, Stay there. I'm fine.' But her breathing was a bit ragged. It was hard to focus on the screen and listen to Nat's deep voice as his finger traced the network setup on the large screen in front of them.

It took a while, but Nell admitted to herself, that she enjoyed sitting close to him.

'So that's what we have to do, to get this end sorted. It won't be too hard, but it will take the rest of this afternoon, and a chunk of tomorrow.'

'If you're happy to come in here with me after dinner tonight, I usually work in here until very late.'

'Uh uh. Not tonight. We have a date, remember.'

'A date? I don't recall that.' She moved away slightly.

What was he playing at?

'Not a date then. A talk. You agreed to set some time aside so we could talk.'

'I'm sorry, with all the fuss and bother here at lunch, I forgot all about that.'

'So, are we on then? I'd like to maybe go for a walk. Somewhere we can talk without interruption. I don't want you to feel uncomfortable, Nell. The reason for this is to make things easier for you. I've got some ideas.'

'It's okay. We agreed.' She tipped her head to the side and shifted her gaze to him, aware that he'd been looking at her for a

minute or more. 'I agreed.'
'Excellent.'

Chapter 16

Nell led the way down to the place on the beach where the girls usually watched the sunset and celebrated another day. The same spot where Tam had rescued Eliza when she had arrived on their island.

They were earlier than usual, and although the sun was low in the sky—it was an hour until sunset—and they had no bottle of bubbles or glasses with them.

Pippa and Tam had been curious when Nell had asked them to come down to the beach with her.

'Too early for bubbles? Tam asked.

'Yes, I just want to talk to you both. It won't take long,' Nell replied. She didn't want Gina listening to their conversation. Evie was mowing down around the huts, and Nat was immersed in wires, cables, routers and other bits and pieces that Nell hadn't heard of before.

And Gina—well, who knew what she was doing—she had made herself right at home in a very short time. Nell had already noticed Pippa looking at her with concern in her expression a couple of times.

But before they sorted the Gina situation, Nell wanted to get something off her chest. Now that she had told Nat what had happened at university, she knew that she owed it to the girls to tell them. Maybe that would help her on her journey of healing; maybe she should've done it a long time ago.

There were lots of maybes.

Nell headed over to the flat rock on the north side of the beach.

'Okay, Nell, spill.' Pippa sat on the rock beside her. It was still warm from the sun and Tam sighed as she leaned back.

'Oh, that feels so good. I could go to sleep here.'

'Don't do that. I want to talk to you both.' Nell sat straight as nerves played around in her stomach.

'What's up? I'm worried you're going to tell us one of two things,' Pippa said. 'Had you already decided you want to leave or has Gina brought you to that point in one afternoon? If so, I fully understand, But Nellie, you're not going anywhere.'

Nell couldn't help but laugh. 'No, silly it's neither of those, although Gina is a bit of a unit.'

Pippa and Nell looked at Tam. She raised her hands. 'Trust me, gals. GG'll be fine. She's a good worker and she's always been a bit over the top. She's been much worse today because would you believe she doesn't have a lot of confidence?'

Pippa and Nell both shook their heads and spoke together. 'No.'

'Okay, maybe she's changed a little bit since I knew her, but trust me, she's still a great bar person. The customers loved her down at Surfers.'

Pippa looked thoughtful as she stared out over the water. 'She's got almost two weeks to prove herself, including the bar opening, and that worries me a little bit. While Nat's here, we'll go down to the bar tonight, and Rafe can come over, and we'll see how she goes. I'll ask her to tone her performance down a bit. I don't think our sailing clientele will appreciate the over the top act. But nothing personal, please, Tam. If she doesn't work out, she'll go after the two weeks. Do you think she'll be okay for the opening?'

'Maybe,' Tam said slowly. 'I would have said certainly before today, but I guess I'm a bit worried too, to be honest.'

Pippa rolled her eyes. 'Okay, tonight will be her main trial. I told her to go down and we'd all come down about seven.

PENTECOST ISLAND 1-3

Anyway, we didn't come down here to talk about Gina, or GG or whatever her name is. If she's not the problem, what's up, Nell?'

'I need to tell you both something.'

Tam narrowed her eyes. 'Does it have to do with Nat?'

'Not completely, but sort of,' Nell said. 'Nat and I had a bit of a heart-to-heart last night, and it's really helped me and made me realise that I haven't been honest with you. You're my best friend and because I've told Nat something, I need to tell you. You've been really patient with me. I should have told you a long time ago.'

'Told us what?' Pip said. 'Is there something wrong with you?'

Nell chuckled, but it was from nerves more than mirth. 'No more than usual, but I'm hoping that I'm going to get a bit better over the next few months. Things are going to change. Hopefully.'

Tam reached over and took her hand. 'You're talking in circles, love. What's going on?'

'What's going to change?' Pippa asked with a frown.

'Me. I'm going to try to be more confident and outgoing,' Nell said.

'I thought you looked a little bit more out there than usual when you got off the boat before,' Pippa said. As usual, she was the one to cut straight to the chase. 'What's caused all this? Nat?'

'In one way,' Nell said.

'You looked gorgeous in the green dress,' Tam said squeezing Nell's fingers. Tam had always been the intuitive one, and she obviously knew this was a hard conversation for Nell to have. 'I haven't had a chance to say thank you for my dress yet. It's absolutely gorgeous. You know me well, sweetie.'

'I had fun at the markets. Would you believe I bought myself more than one dress?'

'Really? No more Nell of the shorts and tees? No way.' Pippa grinned.

ANNIE SEATON

'Yep, *and* three pairs of sandals.'

'Has this sudden interest in how you're looking got anything to do with a certain good-looking networking guy?' Tam let go of her hand and looked at her intently.

'Not really, but sort of. In a way, I guess.' Nell stumbled over the words. 'I mean it's not that I'm attracted to Nat—'

Tam raised her eyebrows.

'No, it's not that, at all, Tam. No matter how many faces you pull at me. It's all about me.'

'Oh, for God's; sake, Nellie, stop beating about the bush and tell us. I've got things to do.' Exasperation vied with impatience in Pippa's voice. 'So instead of not really, in a way, you guess, does that mean you're about to run away with Nat? And leave us in the lurch?'

Laughter bubbled up from Nells' chest and it felt good. 'I love you pair, you do know that?'

'Well, tell us!'

Nell looked down at her hands. She wasn't sure how Pippa and Tam would react. Or if the truth be known, she knew them both well enough to have a fair idea. And that's why she was nervous.

'About me having the confidence to dress like a woman again. To have the confidence to be a woman again and not simply remind myself to be careful with a slash of red lipstick. I've wanted to tell you for a long time. But the more time that passed the harder it was. Maybe I should've told you back then, but I felt so bad about it I couldn't.'

'Back when?' Pippa narrowed her eyes. 'Back at university?'

Nell nodded. 'The night we were supposed to see *Cat Empire*. Actually, the night that you girls did see them.'

'I remember that night,' Tam said. 'We had a fair bit to drink and you decided to go home.'

PENTECOST ISLAND 1-3

'I didn't even see the band. I didn't even have a drink.'

'I remember that,' Pippa said. 'I thought it was funny because I knew you were so keen to see them. What happened?'

Nell took a deep breath. 'I decided to walk down from the lecture hall, and I was really excited because Nat said that he was going to come down after he finished a job for a mate. Back in those days, we were good friends, and that was the first night that I knew that I was interested in him, and he seemed different.'

'So, what happened? Did he put the hard word on you?' Pippa said. 'If he let you down, it was because he was a bit of a player back in those days.'

'No! It had nothing to do with Nat. Just let me get to it, will you? I never even saw him again after that lecture. Because . . . because when I was walking back—' Nell's voice broke; even after ten years the memory was enough to make ice run through her veins. She shivered and rubbed her arms.

Tam moved closer and put her arm around Nell's shoulder. 'It's okay, love. Keep going.'

'I took the river path. I was so close to the bar I could see the lights and I could hear the music.'

'What happened?' Pippa's eyes were wide.

'I was assaulted.' Relief flooded through Nell as she finally said the words. They sounded clinical and were detached from the fear that had wracked her body that night. The fear that he was going to hurt her, the fear that her life was in danger.

Her tone was bland. She might as well have said "I went shopping" or "I had dinner."

'Bloody hell.' Tam pulled her into a tight hug, and for a moment, Nell let her face drop into her friend's shoulder, and she shut her eyes.

'Why didn't you tell us, Nell? What aren't you telling us?'

'What sort of assaulted?' Pippa almost growled. 'How bad was it? Did he—'

Nell lifted her head and held Pippa's gaze. 'No. But that was his intent. Someone came along and he put his hand over my mouth. He had a knife. He put it against my throat, and he nicked the skin. I bled.'

Pippa's eyes flashed with anger. 'Why didn't you tell us? Why? I can't understand it. Did you go to the police? Did you tell anybody?'

'No. I went home and got in the shower and scrubbed myself red raw. I felt guilty. I thought it was my fault.'

'Are you serious? I can't believe that you didn't trust us, Nell. I know it hurts, but for fuck's sake, we were supposed to be good friends.' Pippa's glare was unforgiving, and anger rippled through Nell.

Tam dropped her face into her hands. 'And in the middle of all this I dropped the bombshell that I was moving out.'

'Is that why you didn't want anyone to move into the apartment? You were scared?' Pippa's face was set.

'I've been scared for a long time.'

'And that's why you wore those ridiculous shorts and T-shirts. That's why you weren't ever interested in guys.' Pippa sat there with her arms folded. 'What's the story with the red lipstick?'

'It sounds stupid now, but that was a daily reminder for me. Not to look attractive, not to look as though I was trying to attract a man.'

'You're right. It was stupid.' Pippa shook her head. 'It just looked stupid.'

'Thanks, Pippa.' Nell was feeling stronger. Now that she had finally told them, it was as though the strength that had surfaced when she told Nat began to grow a little more.

'Well, I'm sorry that it happened but I can't for the life of me understand why you didn't trust us enough to talk to us about it. We could have helped you and taken you to see the right people.' Pippa sat rigidly and stared at Nell.

Nell stared back. Pippa's cheeks were flushed, and her eyes were full of something. Anger? Disappointment? It was hard to tell. 'I blamed myself. I told you I didn't want *anyone* to know.'

'How could you possibly blame yourself? God, how stupid could you be?'

Nell's mouth dropped open. This was not how she had expected the conversation to go. 'Stupid? You're calling me stupid? Thanks for the support, Pippa. I've been calling myself stupid for the past ten years.'

'Pippa, calm down.' Tam's tone held a warning.

'No, I won't. We have a really strong friendship. Or I thought we did. I mean, look how you girls supported me when I was going through all my shit and you really helped me, and I thought we were tight. But then something happens to Nell here, and she shuts herself down and then turns into a person we didn't even like very much sometimes.'

Tam interrupted. 'Hey, speak for yourself, Pippa, and don't be so bloody unsympathetic.'

'No, Tam, you listen too. It really pisses me off that there was no trust there. I don't know if I even know you, Nell.'

Shock filled Nell. 'Hey, I'm the one it happened to. I'm the one who had my life screwed up.'

'And hey, we were friends and we could've been there for you to help you. You should've gone to the police. You should've told somebody instead of having a shower and trying to pretend it didn't happen and look at what it's done to you. You've lost ten freaking years of your life now. I can't believe it. You don't think it was a stupid reaction?'

'No, I don't. Not now.' Nell's words cut the air like a knife. 'I'm sorry I told you. But I've finally admitted to myself it's time for a change. Nat's going to help me.'

'Ah, we couldn't help you, but cute little Nattie can.'

'For God's sake, Pippa. Will you listen to yourself? Stop

ANNIE SEATON

being such a bitch.' Tam jumped off the rock and stood in front of Pippa.

'Well, she couldn't trust us. How many times over those years have we asked her if something was wrong?'

'Don't talk as though I'm not here! I didn't want to talk about it, and it was my business.' Nell stood up next to Tam, and it was as though they were a united front against Pippa's anger.

'You really think so?'

'Pip, let it go. You are being a total bitch.'

'Well, I'm finding a lot out today. I've had enough and for the record, Tam, I don't like your friend GG at all.' Pippa pushed herself up and headed up the beach.

Nell's eyes filled with tears as she watched Pippa walk away. When she got to the path Nell was pleased when Pippa turned towards Rafe's house.

'Are you okay, sweetie?' Tam put her arm around Nell's shoulder.

'Yeah, I'm fine. I just thought seeing I'd told Nat that it was time I told you and Pippa.'

'At least she can vent to Rafe,' Tam said. 'He's so sensible and calm, he'll calm her down a bit.'

Nell lifted a shaking hand to her mouth. 'I can't believe her reaction. It was as though something happened to her, not me.'

'She'll come around, Nell. You know what she can be like. She still carries a lot of baggage that she keeps hidden.'

'I guess I do know that, but we haven't seen that side of Pippa since we've been here.'

'I can sort of see where she's coming from, but I don't blame you in any way. I wish you told us at the time, but I can truly understand why you didn't. It's one of the worst things that can happen to a woman and I don't know how I would've reacted. But hey, the bottom line is you're here. And hopefully after all this time you can start to put it behind you. You've expressed that you want to do that, and you will. We're safe here on the island. Pippa will get over her little dummy spit, and you're just going to get better.' Tam kept hold of Nell's hand as they walked back up to the house. 'You feeling okay now?'

'I am.'

Tam glanced at her with a smile. 'You know you looked gorgeous in that dress, don't you? You should have seen the way Nat was looking at you.'

'No.' Nell shook her head and chuckled. 'He looked the same way at Gina—sorry, *GG*—when he saw her the first time.'

Tam's laugh rang out. 'I doubt that very much. It would have been more that he couldn't believe what he was seeing. God, Nellie. I think I've made a big mistake there.'

'I have a feeling you have too. Time will tell,' Nell said with a giggle.

Chapter 17

Pippa

The darkness was deepening as the sun disappeared behind the mountains on the mainland; the rising moon bathed the calm waters of the passage in a cold silver. I tore along the track and up the hill to Rafe's house as fast as I could. My eyes stung, and my throat ached as I fought back tears. All I wanted was Rafe's arms around me, to lose myself in his embrace and feel needed . . . and loved.

There! I'd finally admitted it to myself. Even though he hadn't put it into words, I knew Rafe loved me.

I trembled as a shiver ran down my back when I pushed open the front door. There was no knocking anymore; this was more home to me than Aunty Vi's. What is it they say? Home is where the heart is. Well, my heart was certainly here.

The house was in darkness, but the glow of the lamp on Rafe's desk in his study shone through into the large living room. He was still working, and I hesitated before I stepped into his inner sanctum. Biting my lip, I brushed my hand across my eyes to wipe away the couple of tears that had leaked out despite my best efforts.

Taking a deep breath, I walked over to the desk, and my man reached for my hand without taking his eyes from the screen.

'Just give me about half a minute, love. I've only got one page left to check.' His other finger ran down the large screen and his lips moved as he read the words silently.

I stood with my hand in his and stared through the huge window in front of Rafe's desk. In the far distance, the mountains were bathed in a soft mauve that transformed into a deep purple

PENTECOST ISLAND 1-3

and then deepened to black as I waited.

Calm stole through me, and my breathing evened out, and then the first wave of guilt trickled in. I closed my eyes and focused on breathing evenly, even as panic threatened to overtake me.

What had I done? How much had I hurt Nell?

Tam was right. I had been an utter bitch, but I hadn't been able to help myself.

I jumped as Rafe tugged at my hand, and I was soon sitting on his lap secure in the warmth of his arms.

'Tell me what's wrong,' he said smoothing my hair back from my brow.

'I just needed a hug.'

'I saw you running up the path. You looked like you had the hounds of hell after you. What's happened? I can feel the tension in your body.' His hand reached up and kneaded the muscles at the base of my neck.

'Thank you. That feels good.' I sat straight and rubbed my forehead with one hand. 'I did something awful.'

'I can't believe that.' Rafe pressed his lips to my cheek. 'Do you want to talk about it?'

'I don't know. I don't want you to know what I'm really like.'

His chuckle was low and husky. 'Sweetheart, I think I know what you're like.'

'I don't want you to think less of me. To stop liking me.' A tear plopped onto my hand.

'If you don't know by now that I more than "like" you, you're not very good at reading me. I've never put it into words, because I didn't want to scare you away. What we've got together is much more than "like".'

Rafe lifted his hand and used his thumb to gently wipe away the next tear. 'Pippa, I love you. Maybe it's not the best time to be telling you, when you're upset about something, but I don't want you to have any doubts about that. Nothing you could do, or anything you tell me will change that. You are in my soul. And sweetheart, I am not letting go of you; I just hope you recognise what we share.'

My breath hitched as he held my gaze and I was lost in his brilliant blue eyes. I swallowed, determined to let those words out. 'I love you too, Rafe.'

His lips slid slowly down my cheek to my mouth and I closed my eyes, lost in his kiss.

When he finally pulled back, Rafe rested his forehead against mine. 'Well, now that we've got that out of the way, tell me what's upset you so much. But not here at my desk.'

I climbed off his lap and he stood.

'It's a beautiful night. I'll pour us a drink and we'll go and sit outside.'

I followed him to the kitchen and looked around. It was spotless and there was no sign that he had been in the kitchen since he'd come home. I'd tidied the breakfast dishes away before I'd left this morning.

'Have you eaten since lunch?' I said. 'Or even had a coffee? Or a glass of water?'

As Rafe looked at me blankly, his stomach gave a large gurgle.

'I guess that's a no?' I said.

'I wanted to get the book finished.' His smile was wide. 'I'll email the manuscript to Jenny tonight. And besides after that huge lunch, I wasn't hungry.' His eyes widened and he stared at me. 'I know what's wrong! That new woman's upset you! I knew it wouldn't take long. She's a bit of a dill. What's she done?'

I pointed to the fridge. 'You get us a drink, and I'll get some cheese and crackers and then I'll tell you what *I* did. And no, it wasn't Gina or GG, or whatever she calls herself.' I was trying to

PENTECOST ISLAND 1-3

focus on the mundane—the drinks, the cheese and crackers; the words of love that we had exchanged so unexpectedly had filled me with a warm glow, but I needed to tell Rafe what I'd done before I basked in that feeling.

First, I needed to figure out how to make things better with Nell. How to make her understand why I reacted like that. My stomach clenched as I remembered my cruel words

Soon we were sitting out on the terrace. Small creatures scurried around in the gardens that spilled down the hill—Evie had been doing work for Rafe in her spare time—and the occasional bird called to its mate from the beach below.

Rafe half-filled my wine glass before doing the same to his, and I pushed the plate of cheese across to him.

He chose a sliver of brie and placed it on the cracker before he leaned back in his chair. 'Are you feeling a bit calmer now? Ready to talk?' His eyes were shadowed from the candles I had lit on the table.

'I was horrible to Nell. I really upset her, and I think I've done our friendship some awful damage.'

'Tell me what happened.' His voice was low and soothing. 'And I doubt it. You three are rock solid. I've seen the way you watch out for each other.'

'And I've broken that trust.' I ran my fingers slowly around the top of the glass. 'Nell wanted to see Tam and I. To talk to us. We went down to the beach, and she told us something that had happened to her a long time ago. I won't tell you what it was, because it's not my story to tell, but it explained a lot about the way that Nell is.'

Rafe nodded. 'Nell isn't comfortable around men. I noticed that early on and I've gradually gained her trust, I think.'

'You have. She thinks the world of you.'

'So, what happened then?'

'I was awful to her. I yelled at her, and I made it all about me. I took it personally; the fact that she hadn't told us when it happened.'

'Why do you think you did that?'

'Because she was just one more person who didn't need me. Another one in the long line of people who thought I didn't matter enough.'

'Whoa, slow down there. Nell and Tam love you like a sister. Your friendship is pretty special. You each know what the other is thinking, and like I said, you look out for each other. I doubt very much that you've destroyed that with one argument.'

'It wasn't an argument. It was all me. Nell didn't flare up.'

'Fill me in on this "long line of people" who don't need you.'

I picked up my glass and sipped so I didn't have to answer straightaway. 'I guess I was exaggerating. It's only two people. Mainly.'

'Two?'

'You know all about Aunty Vi and how she left me the island.'

'I do,' he said with a chuckle. 'You were the woman who arrived out of the blue. The one I didn't want interfering with my solitude.'

'Until I got stuck up in a tree and you saved me.' I reached for his hand and kept hold of it. 'I haven't told you anything much about my parents, have I?'

'I just know they both passed away and you don't have any siblings.'

'That's right. How my mother died has caused me a lot of grief over the years. You need to know this Rafe, if you want to stay with me. My mental health has always been fragile. The psychologists have always told me it was because of what happened, and not because I've inherited my mother's instability.'

Rafe squeezed my fingers but didn't say anything.

I stared out over the dark sea. It was still hard to talk about, no matter how many therapy sessions I'd sat through over the years. 'I've never shared this with anyone except Nell and Tamsin, and of course Aunty Vi knew. My parents adored each other, to the exclusion of all else, even me. I do think my Dad loved me though. I can remember him holding me, and I can remember his rough cheeks and his special smell. I don't ever remember feeling loved like that by my mother. The counsellor Aunty Vi sent me to when I was in my teens told me I craved love and didn't want to risk losing it. He was talking about Mum, but I know the pattern continued with some of the relationships I've had. I never chose well; it wasn't ever about picking the right person. It was all about wanting someone to love me. To need me' I turned to look at Rafe and his eyes were fixed on me.

'But when I fell for you, it was so different. I fought what I was feeling. I've never fought going into a relationship before. I've always chosen what I wanted to do and been in control. With you, it was totally different; it wasn't me choosing someone I thought I wanted to love or be with. Or someone I wanted to love me. I didn't think I even liked you, but I still remember that first incredible moment when I saw you in that restaurant. I fell in love before I even knew you.'

'And I, with you,' he said softly.

'Sorry, I'm getting off the track here.'

'I like this track,' Rafe said softly, running his thumb over the back of my hand. I'm listening, sweetheart. Go on.'

'I was almost eleven when Dad was killed in a work accident.' I pushed back that ever-present grief and held Rafe's gaze steadily. 'My mum couldn't live without him and she took her own life the same year. That's how I ended up living with Aunty Vi, and that's how I ended up in therapy. And that's why I've always had a thing about being needed by somebody, although I've made some pretty awful choices over the years.' Her voice trembled. 'Nell and Tam have been my rocks, and that's why I was so awful to Nell. My reaction was over the top, but I couldn't help myself. She suffered something dreadful, and all I could do when she finally told us both, was abuse her for not telling us. I am a selfish bitch.'

Rafe let go of my hand and stood. He moved across to my chair and his hands pulled me up into his embrace.

I buried my face in his soft shirt. 'Thank you. I love you so much, Rafe. It's such a relief to be able to say those words and not be judged.'

'We were meant to be together, Pippa. I was destined to come here to this island, and I was here waiting for you to arrive. I think Vi had a hand in it from up there too, don't you?'

'Maybe. I do know she loved me, even though she could be a tough old stick.'

He chuckled. 'That she was. Now, you know there's two things you have to do.'

I pulled away and nodded. 'I know. I have to go and find Nell and tell her how sorry I am.'

'You do.'

'What's the second?' I frowned.

The moon had risen high while we had been talking, and Rafe led me over to a patch of bright moonlight at the edge of the terrace. For the rest of my life, I would remember this moment in the soft white light with the strong spicy smell coming from the tropical creeper that grew along the low trellis.

'I want you to wait here while I get something. Promise me you won't move.'

'I promise.' Curiosity filled me as Rafe hurried back inside.

He was soon back, and he took my hands again. 'I've waited for the right time to ask you, and this is it. I know you're unsettled because of what happened with Nell, so we don't have to tell anyone until you're ready.'

'Ask me?' A strange and unfamiliar feeling ran through my limbs and I trembled. 'Ask me what? And tell anyone what?'

'Patience, sweetheart.' For a long moment, he held my eyes with his, and all the love that I knew he had for me shone brighter than the moonlight pouring down on us.

My mouth dropped open when Rafe dropped to one knee.

'Phillipa Carmichael, will you do me the honour of pledging your life to mine? Will you share your life and your love with me . . . as my wife?' Rafe reached into his shirt pocket and pulled out a small velvet case. 'Not only do I love you, I *need* you in my life to make me whole.

He opened the case, and moonlight hit the ring nestled in the white satin casing. Shards of blue and pink light came from a large white moonstone, that was nested in a circle of diamonds.

'I will,' I said simply, never surer of anything before in my life. I held my hand out and Rafe stood and slipped the ring onto my finger.

He pulled me close against his warm body, and the moon shone down on us as I lifted my lips to meet those of the man I loved with my heart and soul.

Chapter 18

Nell

Tam was banging about in the kitchen when Nell went looking for her.

'I don't know if we're going to be down at the bar tonight. Pippa hasn't come back yet, has she?'

Tam shook her head. 'No, not since she went up to Rafe's, but Gina's down there setting up all her cocktail shakers and things ready for the night. She's raided my fridge and taken most of the cream I had, and all my pineapple. I'll get sorted here and have a quick shower and grab Evie. I'll meet you down there.'

'Don't rush. I'll be a while yet. Nat and I are going for a bit of a walk.'

Tam looked at her curiously. 'And you're okay with that?'

'I am. I trust Nat. He wants to help me.' Nell gave a shrug. 'At least I can give it a go.'

'As long as you're comfortable with him.'

'I am. We won't be long, just a bit of a stroll and a chat. We'll come back to the bar. Do you think Pippa will come back?'

'Of course she will. She'll be over to say sorry to you and—'

'You think?'

'I know. She'll be back because it was her idea to give GG a trial run tonight. She said she'd told her to be at the bar at seven. GG was pretty pumped when she left here.'

Nell wrinkled her nose. 'Pumped about serving drinks to just us?'

'And Nat. And Rafe. I think she might be a bit of a good-time girl. I do remember her down at the coast a few times. I'd

PENTECOST ISLAND 1-3

forgotten about those nights until I saw her in action. But like I told Pip, she was a good worker and a great person behind the bar. The customers loved her.'

'I wonder if that's the sort of clientele we'll have here though. She didn't shut up once in Jiminy's boat today. She wanted to read my cards!'

'Yeah, she tried that with me too, but I said a polite thank you, but no.'

Nell giggled. 'Might be an interesting night tonight. If Pip's over her dummy spit.'

'She'll be feeling bad, I can guarantee that. You're okay now?'

'Yeah, I've spent the afternoon with Nat, doing what I love best.'

'Oh yeah?' Tam wiggled her eyebrows. 'And what would that be.'

Nell pursed her lips. 'Playing with spreadsheets on the network. Nat's got into the cloud and got all my data back. The accommodation bookings and all your menus and orders.'

'Oh, I love him already.'

'There are still some problems, though. It won't stay connected, and he's working on fixing that. He thinks it might take a couple of days.'

'And how do you feel about that?'

'I'm fine. I enjoy his company, and he's taught me a lot about our setup already. By the time he goes back, I should be right, but he's offered to do a fairly reasonable deal, where he can log in remotely if I have any problems. I need to talk to Pippa about contracting him. Once we grow, we're going to have to expand the network.'

'He lives over on the mainland?'

'Yeah, that's another story. In that storm last night, there was a lot of damage to his house. A tree came down and I ended up under the kitchen table.'

'Jeez, you've had a big couple of days, girl. You really are okay?'

Nell nodded firmly. 'I am.' And she meant it. She was feeling good, even after Pippa's rant. Telling Nat and then telling the girls about the event in her past had lightened the load, and she was finally starting to believe that she could return to some sort of normality. Slowly, but surely.

Her face split into a wide smile. 'I'm happier than I have been for a long time. I feel like I've got myself back if that makes sense.'

'It's good to have you back. Can I ask you one favour though?'

Nell frowned and looked at her friend.

What sort of favour?'

'I'm going to need a whole heap of cleaning rags?'

'And?'

'A good start would be those awful T-shirts and shorts of yours. And when you go for your walk and come down to the bar, wear one of your new dresses. Start like you plan to continue.'

'Yes, Mum.'

***

Nell slipped into her room and crossed to the small space where she hung her clothes. The house—especially the rooms that the girls had taken for their own—still needed a lot of work. The hanging space was simply a small alcove with a rusted curtain rod jammed diagonally in the corner between two walls. Not that Nell had a lot of clothes to hang. Apart from the new dresses, there were only three others that she'd brought with her when they'd moved to the island. On the other hangers were six khaki T-shirts neatly pressed.

She stood there for a moment before she reached for a short floral dress that she'd fallen in love with at a store in Brisbane

PENTECOST ISLAND 1-3

years ago and, of course, had never worn. She kicked off her shorts and her T-shirt and pulled it over her head. The tag caught on her ponytail and her hair fell around her face. She grabbed her hairbrush and pulled it through the tangles, and then fluffed it up a bit.

The new Nell. Taking notice of her appearance. She wasn't making the effort for Nat; it was to look presentable in the bar later. She opened her small makeup bag, dug around and pulled out a pale pink lip gloss and smudged her lips. It had been in there so long, it was a wonder it wasn't hard.

A nervous frisson ran through her nerve endings as she slipped on a pair of sandals. They could just go down to the beach, and sit on a rock, and then once they were done talking, they could go over to the bar and see what was happening there.

She composed herself and headed back to the office.

Nat looked up. For a moment, his eyes widened as his gaze ran over her, and then his expression cleared.

Oh God, why did I get changed?

'Ready to go for a walk?' he asked.

'Yes, and then we're going over to the bar for a couple of hours. GG's trial run.'

'Okay, wait on the veranda for me. I'll just change my T-shirt and have a wash. I've spent the last half hour on the floor sorting out some cables.'

'Thank you, Nat. I really appreciate what you're doing for us.'

And me, she added quietly to herself.

Nell waited on the veranda. She looked up at Rafe's house on the hill above the bay, but strangely it was in darkness apart from the moonlight shining on the windows that faced the sea.

Maybe Rafe and Pippa were in the bar already?

Nat was as fast as he said he'd be and was back with her after only a few minutes.

'I'm sorry,' Nell said. 'We haven't sorted a room for you yet, have we?'

'No matter. I can bunk down on the sofa in the office, if that's okay. '

'No, we'll get a room for you. Eliza's room is made up.'

'Eliza?' he asked. 'I haven't met her yet.'

'Eliza and Phillipe—her friend—have gone to Europe to sort out some stuff, but they'll be back soon. Eliza is a carpenter; she does a lot of the building work here. I think Pippa has some work in mind for Phillipe too—if he comes back with her.'

'You certainly are an interesting group,' Nat commented as they went down the steps. 'Lots of skills between you all. And the place looks great. How long did you say until you open?'

Nell gestured to the path that led to the beach. 'Come this way. I've only got sandals on. The bar opens Saturday week, and the accommodation is booked for the first few huts the week after that. The bar will have some restaurant service to start with tapas and that sort of thing, but once Eliza's back, she's going to oversee the major renovation on the house. The front living room is going to be a restaurant that leads out to the veranda, and the kitchen will be converted to a commercial standard.'

'Wow. It is going to be a big concern. It sounds great. It's all Pippa's idea?'

'Yes, it's her baby. Financially, it's hers, but we've all been involved in the planning, and yes, it's coming together well.'

'You're going to need a lot more staff.' Nat stood back as the path ended. Nell bent down and slipped her sandals off and left them on a log at the end of the path.

'We are, and I think that's one thing we've been a bit slack on. We've been so busy getting everything done, I think we should have spent more time thinking about hiring staff with suitable skills, and staff who will really fit in with our vision.'

Nat chuckled as they walked along the beach towards the

rocks at the northern end. There was just enough moonlight to see where they were going. 'Are you thinking of GG when you refer to fit in?'

Nell sighed. 'Yes, I wonder, but maybe we're judging too quickly. We really need to get our vision statement into a staff manual and be explicit with our expectations.'

Nat stopped and turned to face her. He pointed to her hand. 'May I?'

Nell nodded and Nat's fingers were warm against hers, as he took her hand in his. 'Pippa is really lucky to have you on board. You've had enough business experience to know what needs to be done.'

'Yes, between the three of us, we've covered most bases, I think. We've been lucky with Evie and Eliza. Evie was a uni friend, and Eliza literally washed up in the bay.'

'Really? I'd love to hear that story, but Nell?' His fingers squeezed hers and she looked down at their joined hands. Funnily enough, it didn't bother her; in fact, it was rather pleasant having Nat hold her hand. She looked up at him and stepped back a fraction as his eyes were intent on hers.

His face was all angles and shadows, and her heartbeat picked up as a small trickle of memory ran into her consciousness. She must have tensed because Nat let go of her hand.

'Yes?' she said.

'We're here to talk about you tonight. Come and sit over on that flat rock with me.' His voice was calm.

Nell smiled. 'That's our thinking and drinking rock. There's been a lot of decisions made there.'

'Well, it sounds like a good place to talk. Good vibes.'

Nell climbed up onto the rock. Even though the sun had been gone an hour, it was still warm against her bare legs. The sounds she loved and that were becoming very familiar to her filled the air, the swish of the tiny waves on the shingly sand, the mournful calls of the curlews and the chirping of cicadas in the bush up the hill.

'It's heaven, isn't it,' she said softly as Nat sat beside her.

'Paradise. I don't think I'll ever go back to the city, much to my mother's disappointment.'

'Did you get the insurance sorted on your house this morning?'

'I did, but I'm going to have to find somewhere else to live and maybe an office space to set up my equipment. I was thinking about Hamo, but I imagine the rent there would be beyond me. Anyway, Nell, we're here to talk about you.'

She nodded without speaking.

'I didn't breach your confidentiality—you don't know how much I appreciated that you trusted me enough to tell me what happened at uni—but I spoke to my mother and I've done some reading.'

'Your mother?' Nell didn't know how she felt about that. All of a sudden it seemed a lot of people were knowing what happened. Nat, the girls, his mother—

''It's okay. I told her it was someone I knew but I didn't say where from or how long ago. My mother is a psychologist, and very highly regarded in her field.' He lowered his voice a little. 'She has had a lot of sexual assault clients.'

'Oh.' Nell bit her lip. It was the first time Nat had used those words with relation to "it", and she felt unsettled.

'It's okay, Nell. She sent me a couple of articles and a couple of websites. I'm sure you've read them all, and you know what they say. The thing is reading them, and knowing what to do to get yourself better, is much easier than putting that stuff into practice.'

'What stuff?' she said suspiciously, moving a fraction further away from Nat.

'Have you read about physiological and psychological

PENTECOST ISLAND 1-3

desensitisation?'

'No.' Nell stared at him. 'I didn't read anything. Then or now. I didn't talk to anyone; I didn't see anyone, and I didn't go Googling anything. I knew how I felt. I didn't need anyone to tell me that.' Belligerence had crept into her tone.

Nat was quiet for a moment, and then his voice was gentle as he replied. 'I'm certainly no expert, but I did a lot of reading about it from the stuff Mum sent to me. You've taken the first massive step by talking about it. Now it's time to put some new habits in place.'

'What sort of habits? What's this desensitisation stuff.'

'Jeez, Nell. I'm going to sound like a psychologist here. Just bear with me. Please? Trust me?'

She nodded.

'It's about confronting your fears. Facing those things and doing the things that you haven't done over the past ten years because you were scared of what would happen, or because you were scared it would bring the fear of that night back.'

'I get that.'

'So, tell me the sorts of things you did to stay safe, and kept you feeling okay about yourself.'

Bitterness surfaced and Nell took a deep breath. 'I haven't felt okay about myself since then.' She stared past Nat over to the water. A boat was slowly making its way down the passage and music drifted across the water. 'To keep myself safe, I wore clothes that would let me blend into the background. I didn't interact with men unless it was necessary in the workplace. I didn't go out after dark.'

'You've come a long way in the last few days. Since you told me what happened. Look at yourself now, Nell.'

'And Tam and Pippa too. I told them this afternoon.'

'Excellent. But look at yourself tonight.'

'How do you mean?'

'By letting it out, you've changed some things already.' Nat gestured to the sky. 'It's dark, and you're out. I'm a man, and you're out here with me. And you're not wearing clothes that would make you blend into the background as you said. You're wearing a colourful dress. In my mother's words, you have already engaged in some psychological desensitisation. And it's been your choice. How are you feeling tonight? Are you scared?'

'Of course not. I trust you.'

She could just see the narrowing of his eyes in the faint moonlight. 'That's interesting, because you don't really know me. It's been at least eight years since we last met.'

'But I knew you then, and I guess I'm taking you on trust now.'

'Okay, that's fair enough. What we need to teach you to do is to take people—particularly men—on some level of trust when you first meet them.'

'How is that going to happen?'

'I'm not saying that you can go out and put yourself in dangerous situations. I mean, any woman should be careful about that.'

Nell nodded slowly. Nat was making sense. To overcome her fear, she had to listen to him. 'Yes, I put myself in a foolish situation when I chose to walk through the bush that night.'

'Yes, in an ideal world you could do that, and it's sad that you couldn't. But it comes down to common sense. But we'll talk about that more later. I'm only going to be here for another day or two and I'd like to get to work.'

'Work? What do you mean?'

'I want to help you with the physical desensitisation, Nell.'

Nell ignored the panic that began to rise in her throat. 'Like what?'

'First up, will you read the articles? I want you to understand that the sorts of things I'm going to suggest are based on scientific study.'

Suspicion flared. Was this the Nat of old, just looking for a woman? Was she being completely gullible here? 'What sorts of things?

'A personal question. Have you had any partners since it happened?'

Nell shook her head and her cheeks heated as he continued.

'So, no sexual partners? No sex life?'

'No.' She cleared her throat. 'So, what I'm understanding here . . . that this is all about having sex with you—otherwise couched in the fancy term of "physical desensitisation" and I'll magically be cured.' She swung her legs off the rock and tensed as Nat reached for her arm. 'No, thank you.' Anger flared through her, but no fear. Just anger and a crushing disappointment.

'Stop, Nell. Of course not. That's not what I was talking about at all.' She turned to look at him and he ran his hand through his hair. 'I didn't express that well.'

'What did you mean then?'

'Small steps. Like tonight, you're out in the dark with me. You've let me hold your hand. I meant things like that. God, I'm sorry. I didn't mean it to sound like that at all. You make me sound like an absolute sleaze.' His laugh was bitter. 'I guess I had that reputation back at uni, but there is a story behind that.'

She folded her arms.

'It's things like being comfortable when you stand near someone. Being able to be touched. Platonically! Not flinching if I took your elbow to guide you. Understanding that a simple touch is not physical assault. Look, I'm sorry. I totally stuffed that up. That's why I am a computer bod, and not a psychologist. I'll give you the articles to read before I go. I'm really sorry you thought I was putting the hard word on you.'

He jumped off the rock and stood next to her. Nell reached out and put her hand on his arm and Nat looked down at it before he lifted his gaze to meet hers.

'No, Nat. *I'm* sorry. You've given me absolutely no reason to think that and I shouldn't have reacted so badly.' Surprise flooded though Nell as her fingers tingled to life. Alive from the feel of his skin beneath them. The surprise deepened when she realised that she liked touching Nat, and that if she was honest, she was attracted to him.

Just like she had been all those years ago.

Chapter 19

'Nell!' They turned as one when Pippa called from the path. Nell hadn't heard them approaching; she was too immersed in her thoughts and the revelation that had just hit her.

'Excuse me a moment,' she said quietly to Nat. 'I'll just talk to Pippa for a minute if you want to go with Rafe. We have some unfinished business.'

Pippa stepped onto the sand and Rafe waited on the path. Nat did as Nell asked and she stood and waited at the rock for Pippa to come over. The two guys walked up towards the bar together and Nell squared her shoulders as Pippa walked across to her.

'Nellie? I'm so, so sorry.' Pippa held her arms open, but Nell stood there with her arms folded.

Seems like everyone was sorry about things they'd said tonight. Nell surprised herself again. For the first time in a long time, she was strong inside. She'd had the courage to stand up to Nat when she misunderstood his intentions, and now she fronted up to Pippa.

'It's going to take more than a sorry.'

'I know. I was way, way out of line.'

'You were.'

'I can explain, I just want you to accept my apology. I was a cow to you. You dumped something pretty bad on us and I didn't think of you at all. It was all about me and my 'woe is me' Nobody loves Pippa.'

'It was.' Nell's arms were still folded. A glimmer of sympathy rose in her chest, but she was not going to give in easily. 'Did Rafe make you see sense?'

'No. I knew how awful I'd been before I even got there.' Pippa's mouth lifted in a small smile. 'But yeah, Rafe told me I had to come and apologise before I did anything else.'

Nell nodded.

'He also told me how stupid I was to compromise the friendship we have. He told me how special it is. I know that, Nell. And I know I put it at risk by only thinking about me.'

'You did.'

'So?' Pippa's voice shook.

'So, come here, you big galoot, and give me a hug. I know you didn't mean it.' Nell held her arms out and Pippa hugged her back. 'You were just being you.'

'Well, I'm going to think more about being me and what that is, before I do something like that again. Seriously, Nell, I am so sorry I went for you.'

'I know you are. And I know you didn't mean it. And you know what? I should have told you both at the time. That was the second mistake I made.'

'What was the first?'

'Taking that shortcut along the river. I thought I was invincible. It was a good wakeup call in life.'

'Friends?' Pippa rested her head on Nell's shoulder and her voice was muffled.

'You think you were going to get rid of me that easily? No way, girlfriend. You're stuck with me as a friend, until we're old and grey-haired and on our walking frames.'

'Good.' Pippa stepped away and wiped her eyes.

'There's no need to cry.'

'They're happy tears. Come on, we'll go and see what GG's got to offer.' Pippa put one hand on her hip and Nell linked arms with her. 'I don't know how she's going to fit in.'

'It's going to be interesting.' The smile stayed on Nell's face as they walked to the bar. It had been a good night so far.

PENTECOST ISLAND 1-3

***

Pippa

The night in the bar was more than interesting. Tam met them halfway along the beach before they got to the bar. The music coming from the sound system was loud.

'Pleased to see you pair haven't killed each other,' she said drily.

'Of course, we haven't. A minor tiff,' Pippa said. 'First one we've had for ages. All good, and all happy here.' Now that she'd apologised to Nell—and Nell was cool with her— she was floating on air again. She reached into her pocket and rubbed her fingers over the ring that Rafe had brought home from England.

'Excellent.' Tam said. 'So, you're in a good mood, boss?'

'Boss? Pippa screwed her face up. 'What's this "boss" shit?'

'I think you're going to need it.'

'Need what?'

'A good mood. I'd hate for you to get stuck into me next.' Tam turned and led the way to the bar. 'It's my fault.'

'What's your fault?'

'You'll see.'

The lights of the bar were all on as they stepped from the bush into the cleared area. Strange music was blaring over the sound system. Evie was standing at the bar holding a drink, her eyes wide when she saw the three of them walk in. Nat and Rafe were sitting at a table, each holding a tall coloured cocktail decorated with pineapple leaves.

Pippa looked around. 'Where's Gina?'

'Um, she just went for a break. I suggested it might be an idea if she got some fresh air,' Tam said with a strange look on her face.

'Fresh air?'

Tam nodded. 'I'm sorry, Pip. I think I've stuffed up with

this one.'

'Gina? It wasn't just on your recommendation. Her references were excellent.'

'Hmm,' Nell intervened. 'You know how sometimes people give a good reference to get rid of someone they don't want?'

'Okay, what's she done? And can you please turn that music down. Or better still, turn it off.'

As Tam headed to the sound system they'd installed behind the bar, Pippa walked over to the table where Rafe and Nat were sitting looking bemused. As well as the two coloured cocktails, there was a box of cards there. She picked the box up and read the label.

'*Tarot d'Amour?* What are these for?' The label on the box was graphic to say the least. She narrowed her eyes and peered close. The blonde model on the cover of the box was wearing very little and looked very much like GG.

It was GG!

Rafe chuckled. 'Apparently they're guaranteed to improve anyone's sex life.'

Nat grinned and didn't say anything, and Pippa put the box down when she heard Tam's laughing snort behind her. Before she could turn around, two firm hands grabbed her shoulders as a musky perfume surrounded her.

'Come see, boss *bebe*. I'm goin' to show you how good I am, me.'

Pippa turned around and looked up at GG. Her cheeks were flushed, and her lips were lifted in a crazy grin.

'I beg your pardon?'

'Come with me, *bebe* and I'll mis . . . mix you three ladies, a cocktail to knock your li'l ole socks off. And then we're goin' to play some fun games.'

Evie put a hand over her mouth and giggled, and Tam

snorted again as Gina sashayed over to the bar. Pippa followed her.

'You do know tonight was a trial run to see if you were suitable.' Her mouth dropped open when she saw what GG was wearing. The shortest skirt that Pippa had ever seen, and unbelievably, a red suspender belt and black fishnet stockings.

'*Le fe cho,*' Gina said as she picked up a handful of ice, ran it over her flushed cheeks and then dropped it down the front of her lowcut black top with a smile in Rafe's direction.

'What?' Pippa's blood began to boil. She turned around to Evie, Tam and Nell who were all smiling. Rafe quickly dropped the grin when he saw the expression on Pippa's face. 'Is she drunk?' she hissed. 'What is '*le fe cho*? A cocktail?'

Gina rolled her eyes and almost purred. 'No, *bebe.* It means it's hot in here, and I'm hoping it might get a little hotter when we get to the cards.'

Tam snorted again. 'Sorry, Pip,' she muttered.

Pippa narrowed her eyes as Gina tried to reach for a glass and missed it. 'Are you drunk?'

'Oh, maybe just a little one or two while I was waiting for you to come.'

Pippa looked at her. 'I'll have champagne, please.'

'Oh, no *dahlin.* You ain't havin that bubble stuff. Three more cocktails coming up.'

'No. That's enough.' Pippa's voice was like steel. 'Come back to the house with me please, Gina. We are going to have a little chat.'

Chapter 20

Nell

By the time Pippa came back to the bar—alone—they'd cleaned up the bar. Two broken glasses, and a smear of cream and chopped pineapple over most of the counter.

Tam's mood moved between the giggles and worrying. 'We've left this too late. There's no way we'll be able to find someone suitable for the bar before the big opening next Saturday night.'

Nell nodded. 'After that experience, Pippa will be way more careful. No more relying on word of mouth or references. Interviews from now on.'

'Was Gina like that when you worked with her?'

'She was a good worker, but yeah, I suppose she was a bit out there.' Tam picked up the pineapple pieces and put them in the bin beneath the bar. 'What a waste. But she was nowhere near like that. And you know what?' She tipped her head to the side. I don't ever remember the Cajun accent or the French words.'

'Just goes to show. Take references with a grain of salt,' Nell said.

'As long as Pippa's not too upset. We're going to have to work mighty hard to get someone before next weekend.'

As always when Nat came anywhere near Nell, she sensed him before she turned.

'Ah, ladies?' he said with a grin.

'Don't you start on me, Nat. I've got to face the music when Pippa gets back,' Tam said putting the last of the mess in the bin.

'Here she is now,' he said catching Nell's eye. A quiver

tugged at her lower belly, and she dropped her eyes, pretending to focus on the cleaning cloth.

Nat cleared his throat. 'Nell?'

She looked up and held his gaze. 'Yep. What's up?'

'I've got an idea to run past you. Solves a couple of problems, but I want to run it by you before I talk to Pippa. Come outside with me for a sec?'

Evie had gone to her room, using the excuse of an early night, and Rafe was sitting at the table flicking through Gina's tarot cards. Every so often, he would chuckle and shake his head.

Nell pointed to the door on the beach side and Nat followed her out. They hadn't gone far when he touched her elbow and she looked down at his hand, quite happy for him to touch her.

No tensing and no flight or fight response. She smiled. 'What's up?'

'Well, I want to check with you before I suggest this to Pippa.' Nat's eyes held Nell's and a shimmery feeling ran all the way down to her toes.

'What would that be?' Her tone was maybe a little bit shorter than usual because she was trying to ignore the way her nerves were going haywire.

'I need a place to live for a while, and you gals need someone to man the bar. I've got my bar tickets and a heap of experience in bar work. Do you think it would be over the top to run that by Pippa?'

Nell tapped her top lip with her index finger, thinking what it would mean if Nat was on site.

Only if we had more computer problems, nothing else, she tried to tell myself. If Nat was here, the network would run like clockwork. Someone they knew and they all liked would be in the bar, and they already had a spare room where Nat could bunk down.

Nell growled silently at the little voice in her head to shut up. *And Nat would be here all the time.*

But her mouth ran away with her thoughts before she could put a stop to it. 'And you'd be here to help me desensitise.'

'It sounds like a win-win situation to me,' he said.

Nell nodded and went to the doorway. 'Pip. You got a minute?'

Despite the fiasco with Gina, Pippa was still smiling; Nell had never seen her look so happy. If she believed in auras, she would have said Pippa's was shining tonight.

'How did that go?' Nell asked hesitantly.

'What? With GG?' Pippa shook her head and chuckled. 'We've come to a mutual agreement, and I've already called Jiminy. He'll be here at 7.30 in the morning. She said she didn't like the bar and wasn't happy about staying so I didn't have to sack her, before she even started.'

'Phew. Pip? Nat's got an idea.'

She tipped her head to the side and levelled her intense gaze at him. Pip could be scary at times, but the soft smile on her lips dispelled that tonight. 'Yep?'

'Fire away, Nat,' Nell said.

Once Nat had outlined what he'd suggested to her, Pippa smiled. 'That's a fantastic idea. Are you sure it won't take away from your work?'

Nat's smile was wide. 'You would be doing me a huge favour. Only thing I'd have to ask for is a room with a bit of space to put a couple of computers. Even down the back of one the garden sheds would do. I had a bit of a look at them before. There's power down there.'

'If there's one thing, we've got plenty of,' Pippa said. 'It's room. It sounds like a great solution to me. What do you think, Nell?' Her glance was wary.

'Perfect,' Nell said.

Pippa held out her hand and shook Nat's firmly 'We have a

deal. Only one thing I want to ask you.'

Nat shot a worried glance at Nell. 'Yes?'

'Could you start now? Rafe and I have some news to tell you all.'

Chapter 21

Nell

That night in the bar celebrating Rafe and Pippa's engagement was one of the happiest nights of Nell's life. Rafe had stood and told them that Pippa had accepted his proposal. And Tam and Nell had swooped on her screaming with happiness.

'Gina's snoring in the back room,' Evie told us with a grin.

'As long as she doesn't miss her boat tomorrow,' Pippa added. 'I'm afraid I don't want to see her again.'

Nat was kept busy behind the bar and there were a few empty bottles of bubbles by the end of the night. Rafe had insisted on top shelf, and said he would pick up the tab.

'It's not every night a man gets engaged,' he said with his arms around Pippa.

As for Pippa, she was absolutely glowing.

Nell kept looking at her and was ashamed to admit that her friend's happiness made her the tiniest bit jealous.

She shook herself. No, Pippa deserved every minute of it. 'So, when's the wedding?' she asked with a smile. 'I know this really good island to come to for your honeymoon'.

'Ha ha,' Pippa said 'And don't worry, it won't be for a while. But one thing, if it's okay with you girls.' She looked from Tam to Nell to Evie. 'I'm going to move up to Rafe's house.'

'Of course, it's okay,' they all rushed to say.

'It leaves a big room for Nat to move into, with all his computers. I'll take you over to the mainland in a day or so, Nat, and you can get what you need.'

'Thank you, Pippa', Nat said.

Eventually the party broke up, and Rafe and Pippa headed

back up the hill. Evie went to bed with a yawn, and Tam carried the leftovers back to the kitchen in the house.

Nell sat at the bar while Nat rinsed the glasses and wiped down the countertop. When he'd finished, he came around the bar and sat beside her.

'How about a night cap?'

'I think that's a good idea. I'm too pumped to get to sleep. What a day it's been.' Despite her words, a yawn blurred them.

'What would you like?' Nat asked.

Nell was aware of him looking at her and looked down at her hands, ignoring that warm rush that she'd had on and off all day. 'Would I sound silly if I just asked for some warm milk in the microwave? That'll help me sleep.'

'Whatever works.'

Five minutes later, she'd finished her warm milk, and Nat switched the light off in the bar.

They walked along the path, close to each other but not touching, with an awkward silence between them.

They had almost reached the house when Nell stopped. 'Nat?'

'What's wrong?'

'Nothing. I just wanted . . . I just wanted to ask you something. Two things actually.'

His eyes shone in the moonlight, but his brow was wrinkled. 'Yes?'

'Would you, would you hold my hand again? Just practice, you know.'

He reached for her hand and as his fingers curled around hers the strangest feeling of all being right with the world overcame Nell.

'What was the second thing?' he asked softly.

'Um. Now that you're going to be here for a while would you make up a schedule?'

'A schedule for what?'

'For me. For that desensitisation stuff.' She knew she was speaking too quickly but was embarrassed to ask. 'I'll leave it to you. You know. First week, hold my hand, second week, maybe try to put your arm around me to see how I cope. You know stuff like that.'

It sounded so stupid when she put it into words, but Nat nodded, and his expression was serious.

'I'm sure I could manage that. Do you want me to send you those articles I read?'

Nell shook her head. 'No. I'll leave it all in your hands.'

'Okay. I'll work something out. Do we need a contract or anything?'

'Oh, heck no. It'll just be something on the side while you're here working the bar and looking after the network. And um, living here until your house is fixed.'

'Good, not a problem,' he said briskly. His words were what she wanted to hear, but Nat had a strange, distant look in his eyes, and for a minute, Nell thought she'd said the wrong thing. But her hand stayed in his as they walked towards the house, and into the office.

'Are you happy to sleep on the sofa bed in here tonight until we get organised?'

'That's fine. Anyway, I'm tired. I'll see you tomorrow.'

She looked at Nat and, for a moment, was tempted to stand on her toes and brush a kiss across his cheek, but common sense chimed in.

Nell knew she was a job to him, and the last thing he would want was an old friend mooning over him.

'You know where the bathroom and everything is? I'll put a towel out for you.'

'Thank you.'

The silence was long, and she shuffled backwards towards

the door. 'Okay, night, Nat. And thank you for everything.'

'Good night, Nell. I'll see you in the morning.'

***

Nat Dwyer lay on the sofa bed for a long time before sleep claimed him.

Was agreeing to help Nell a good move or not?

He was damned if he did and damned if he didn't. All he'd wanted to do was take her in his arms tonight and hold her and keep her safe from her fears.

Over ten years ago, he'd fallen for this gentle woman, and it had broken his heart when she had wiped him. He'd got over his broken heart that day in the office where she'd worked, where she had spoken to him so rudely.

Now he knew why she had done that, it made it a little easier to bear, but it had brought all of his feelings for her screaming back. Nat knew he had no chance with Nell. She'd always thought of him as a womaniser, and she had no reason to change her mind. He was big enough to help her through this and help let her learn to trust again.

Could he go softy, softly, and show her that he wasn't that man she'd thought he was?

Nat rolled over and punched his pillow.

Maybe if he gave it his best shot.

And he was going to.

Chapter 22

Nell

The week before the bar opening flew by. Tam was cranky as she immersed herself in menus and orders, and Nell soon learned to keep out of her way. Evie was out in the garden from daylight until dark, mowing, and putting the finishing touches on the gardens around the huts.

Pippa seemed to be everywhere, supervising, barking orders, and worrying about what could go wrong.

But she always had a smile on her face.

Nat was busy setting up his own network; Pippa had taken him over to the mainland and he'd brought most of his gear back. Since then he'd spent a lot of time in the front room, setting it up.

When he wasn't there, he was down in the bar, reorganising it to suit him.

'What's got you looking so unhappy?' Pippa pulled Nell up two days before the opening. She was sitting on the front veranda looking across the water. The smell of freshly mown grass drifted across from the side of the house, and the smell of something delectable baking came from the kitchen.

Nell lifted her head. 'Me? I'm okay.'

'No, you're not, Nell. I know you too well. Spit it out. What's on your mind? Is it Nat? You two have been mooning about looking at each other all week. Every time he looks the other way, you're looking at him, and he's the same with you.'

'No. No way.' Nell frowned.

Pippa huffed. 'Trust me, Nellie. He's got it bad for you, and at a guess, I'd say you wouldn't be unhappy about that. Tam agrees with me.'

PENTECOST ISLAND 1-3

'Don't be silly. I'm just bored. You need to find me a job to do. Since Nat's got the network running smoothly, everything is up to date, and it only takes me a couple of hours in the morning to get the accounts done and check the online bookings.'

'Okay. I've got a job for you.'

Nell glanced across at Pippa, because there was something in her tone, but her expression was innocent.

'What sort of job?'

'I think you need to go down and help Nat in the bar. He's going to be run off his feet on Saturday night. I've had so many more people say they're coming over; the bay's going to be full of boats.'

'You mean get ready for the night, or help him in there?'

'Both. You can clear glasses and that sort of thing, can't you?'

'I guess so.'

'Go down to the bar now. Nat's down there. I was just talking to him. He seemed a bit stressed.' Pippa looked at her from beneath her lashes.

'What about?'

Pippa shrugged. 'I don't know. You're mates with him. Maybe you could ask if everything's okay? We can't afford to lose him now. We'd really be up shit creek if we did. Can I leave it to you to sort out?'

'Okay. I'll go down there now.'

Nell didn't see Pippa's devious smile as she headed into her room to comb her hair and put some lip gloss on.

A groan escaped Nell's lips as she walked towards the bar. Nat was stocking the two big fridges at the back with beer. Jiminy had delivered another load of food and drink this morning.

The weather was warming up quickly and Nat had taken his shirt off. She watched the play of muscles across his tanned back as he lifted each carton across from the counter to the fridge. A warm feeling gripped her lower belly, and a shiver ran down her back, and it had nothing to do with being scared. Her lips parted and she took her pleasure watching him.

She stood there for a full five minutes and jumped when Nat called over his shoulder. 'Are you going to just stand there gawking, or are you going to give me a hand?'

'Sorry. I was daydreaming.'

The look he gave her was interesting.

Nell hurried over. 'How can I help?'

'If you hold the door open for me, it would make a difference. Just until I get these bigger cartons to the top shelf.' Nell did as he asked, and he'd soon loaded the shelves.

'I've just got to get rid of these boxes and I'm done. If you want to go. Thanks for your help.'

Nell shook her head. 'No. I'll keep you company for a while. I was . . . I was . . . um. . . wondering if you'd thought any more about my program.'

'Which program? The accounting package, you mean.' Nat lifted his arm and wiped the perspiration from his brow with his forearm and Nell's breath caught in her throat, as the combined smell of sweat and man hit her.

'Um, no. My program. You know, touching me and everything.' Her face heated as she realised what she'd said.

Touching me!

Nat took a step closer to her and his eyes narrowed. 'I have. Do you want to practise now? Maybe I should surprise you, so you don't know what's coming and see how you handle that.' His eyes were dark and intent on hers. 'What would you think about that? DO you think you could cope with some surprises?'

Nell lifted her chin. 'I think I could cope.'

Nat came closer and she leaned back against the wall, not knowing what to expect. What was his second move going to be?

PENTECOST ISLAND 1-3

Touch her elbow? Put his arms around her.

Oh, she wished, how she wished.

Nell looked up and he held her gaze as he lifted one arm above her shoulder, and then put his hand on the wall to her left. Slowly he lifted his other arm, and she waited for his touch, but he put it on the wall on the other side of her head, effectively trapping her.

'Are you okay?' His face was only a few centimetres from hers, and her breathing quickened.

She nodded mutely.

'You seem to have been going okay this week, so I thought I might skip a few steps. Sort of like shock therapy.'

Nell held his eyes and nodded. Nat was so close to her now his breath was warming her lips. She didn't move a muscle as his head lowered and his lips slid over hers. Shock, but no fear rocketed though her. She didn't move as his lips played over hers. Eventually she lifted her hand and placed it against his bare chest, but his lips stayed where they were.

'Are you coping?' he murmured against her mouth.

'I am. Very well,' she replied, surprised by the desperate need that was rising in her. The need for him to stay there. A need she had never felt before. Nell squeezed her eyes shut, willing him to stay.

'Still okay?' His mouth was firm on hers now, almost demanding, and Nell opened her lips to give him access. Her legs were shaking so much, she could barely stand, and she grabbed onto his waist with her other hand. His bare skin was sleek and smooth beneath her touch and she was gratified by his small intake of breath.

Maybe it was more than helping her for Nat?

Maybe she could dream?

For the first time in a long time, Nell stopped thinking things through and surrendered to her feelings.

Need pulsed through her in time with the beat of her heart. Like a flower unfurling its petals to the warm sun, Nell felt herself opening to him. No fear, no worry and no self-consciousness.

Nat moved away and loss hit her like a physical jolt. Reaching out again, she opened her eyes. His were guarded as he looked at her. Leaving her hand on his chest, she looked him square in the face.

'Thank you.'

'For?' His voice shook a little and hope unfurled in her chest.

'For showing me how I feel.'

'How do you feel?' Nat lowered his arms and put his hands on her shoulders. His touch was gentle, and she kept her eyes on his face as she leaned into him. A slow smile lifted his lips.

'I feel . . . I feel happy that I *know* how I feel now. I'm happy that I can admit it. And not be embarrassed, and not be scared.'

His voice was low, and his lips hovered over hers. 'Tell me, Nell. What were you scared of?'

'I was scared that I wanted you, and you didn't want me.'

The groan that came from Nat as he wrapped his arms around her told her everything she wanted to know.

'Pippa came to see me,' he said. 'She gave me some hope. That's why I tried the shock therapy.'

'I like the shock therapy.' Nell knew her smile was shy. 'It worked.'

Nat's head lowered to hers, and Nell put her arms around him. Her fingers played over his skin; she couldn't stop touching him.

'I'm very happy it did. Do you know how long I've been waiting to kiss you?' he asked.

'How long?' she whispered against his mouth.

'About eleven years. We've got a lot of catching up to do.'

PENTECOST ISLAND 1-3

Nat's head lowered to hers as he proceeded to catch up, until a voice interrupted them.

'About time,' Pippa said, but she was smiling. 'Sorry to disturb you guys, but we came down for a drink. We have some new arrivals.'

Nell lifted her head and peered around Nat's shoulder and let out a squeal. Eliza and Phillipe were standing next to Pippa.

She looked back to Nat shyly, still not able to believe that he had kissed her. That he cared about her. And being in his arms had felt right.

Perfect.

'It looks like we're all here for the opening. Come and meet Eliza and Phillipe,' she said, but her smile was for Nat.

He threaded his fingers through hers and held Nell close as they walked across to the others.

'Looks like you've been busy while we've been gone,' Eliza said.

Nell nodded. 'We all have.'

Nat slipped his shirt on as the introductions were made. In her fluster, Nell hadn't noticed the other woman who was standing near Eliza.

'Nell, this is my friend, Sienna. She's come to stay for a while,' Eliza said. 'And we've got news. Fabulous news that's going to make a huge difference to Ma Carmichael's.'

Phillipe nodded. 'It is the best news we could bring back with us.'

'Don't keep us in suspense.' Pippa was almost jumping out of her skin. 'Spill. What news?'

Eliza shook her head. 'Wait until Tam and Evie join us. And Rafe. It's time for a big celebration.'

Also available in print

Pentecost Island
Books 4-6
Tamsin
Evie
Cherry

Pentecost Island
Books 7-10
Odessa
Sienna
Tess
Isla

OTHER BOOKS from ANNIE

Daughters of the Darling
From Across the Sea
Over the River (2024)
Porter Sisters Series
Kakadu Sunset
Daintree
Diamond Sky
Hidden Valley
Larapinta
Kakadu Dawn

Pentecost Island Series
Pippa
Eliza
Nell
Tamsin
Evie
Cherry
Odessa
Sienna
Tess
Isla

The Augathella Girls Series
Outback Roads
Outback Sky
Outback Escape
Outback Wind
Outback Dawn
Outback Moonlight
Outback Dust
Outback Hope

Augathella Short and Sweet Series

An Augathella Surprise
An Augathella Baby
An Augathella Spring
An Augathella Christmas
An Augathella Wedding
An Augathella Easter
An Augathella Masquerade Ball

Sunshine Coast Series
Waiting for Ana
The Trouble with Jack
Healing His Heart
Sunshine Coast Boxed Set

The Richards Brothers Series
The Trouble with Paradise
Marry in Haste
Outback Sunrise
Richards Brothers Boxed Set

Bondi Beach Love Series
Beach House
Beach Music
Beach Walk
Beach Dreams
The House on the Hill

Second Chance Bay Series
Her Outback Playboy
Her Outback Protector
Her Outback Haven
Her Outback Paradise
The McDougalls of Second Chance Bay Boxed Set

PENTECOST ISLAND 1-3

Love Across Time Series
Come Back to Me
Follow Me
Finding Home
The Threads that Bind
Love Across Time 1-4 Boxed Set

Bindarra Creek
Worth the Wait
Full Circle
Secrets of River Cottage
A Clever Christmas
A Place to Belong

Others
Whitsunday Dawn
Undara
Osprey Reef
East of Alice
Four Seasons Short and Sweet
Follow the Sun
Ten Days in Paradise
Deadly Secrets
Adventures in Time
Silver Valley Witch
The Emerald Necklace
A Clever Christmas
Christmas with the Boss
Her Christmas Star

About the Author

Annie lives in Australia, on the beautiful north coast of New South Wales. She sits in her writing chair and looks out over the tranquil Pacific Ocean.

She writes contemporary romance and loves telling stories that always have a happily ever after. She lives with her very own hero of many years and they share their home with Barney, the ragdoll puss, who hides when the four grandchildren come to visit.

Stay up to date with her latest releases at her website: http://www.annieseaton.net

Awards

2023: Winner of the long contemporary RUBY award for Larapinta

Finalist for the NZ KORU Award 2018 and 2020.

Winner ...Best Established Author of the Year 2017 AUSROM

Longlisted for the Sisters in Crime Davitt Awards 2016, 2017, 2018, 2019

Best Established Author, Ausrom Readers' Choice 2017

Finalist in Book of the Year, Long Romance, RWA Ruby Awards 2016 Kakadu Sunset

Winner, Best Established Author of the Year 2015

Printed in Dunstable, United Kingdom